Battle History
of the United States
Marine Corps, 1775–1945

ALSO BY GEORGE B. CLARK
AND FROM MCFARLAND

*The Fourth Marine Brigade in World War I:
Battalion Histories Based on Official Documents* (2015)

*The United States Military in Latin America:
A History of Interventions through 1934* (2014)

*The American Expeditionary Force in World War I:
A Statistical History, 1917–1919* (2013)

United States Marine Corps Medal of Honor Recipients
(2005; paperback 2010)

*United States Marine Corps Generals
of World War II* (2008)

*Decorated Marines of the Fourth Brigade
in World War I* (2007)

The Second Infantry Division in World War I (2007)

*The Six Marine Divisions in the Pacific:
Every Campaign of World War II* (2006)

Hiram Iddings Bearss, U.S. Marine Corps (2005)

Battle History of the United States Marine Corps, 1775–1945

GEORGE B. CLARK

McFarland & Company, Inc., Publishers
Jefferson, North Carolina

The present work is a reprint of the illustrated case bound edition of Battle History of the United States Marine Corps, 1775–1945, *first published in 2010 by McFarland.*

LIBRARY OF CONGRESS CATALOGUING-IN-PUBLICATION DATA

Clark, George B., 1926–
Battle history of the United States Marine Corps, 1775–1945 / George B. Clark
    p.   cm.
Includes bibliographical references and index.

ISBN 978-1-4766-7981-5
paperback : 50# alkaline paper ∞

1. United States. Marine Corps—History.
2. Battles—History. I. Title.
VE23.C4929   2020   359.9'60973—dc22   2010022735

British Library cataloguing data are available

© 2010 George B. Clark. All rights reserved

No part of this book may be reproduced or transmitted in any form or by any means, electronic or mechanical, including photocopying or recording, or by any information storage and retrieval system, without permission in writing from the publisher.

Front cover: Iwo Jima Memorial, Arlington Cemetery
© 2020 Getty Images; American flag © 2020 Shutterstock

Printed in the United States of America

*McFarland & Company, Inc., Publishers
Box 611, Jefferson, North Carolina 28640
www.mcfarlandpub.com*

Contents

Preface 1
Introduction 3
Glossary 7
Abbreviations 9

1. American Revolution — 11
2. The Fighting Tops — 19
3. Barbary Wars — 26
4. War of 1812 — 32
5. Between the Wars — 41
6. War with Mexico — 51
7. American Civil War — 60
8. China — 67
9. Colombia/Panama — 81
10. Spanish-American-Cuban War — 87
11. Philippine Islands — 91
12. Cuba — 95
13. Mexico 1914 — 102
14. Haiti — 105
15. Dominican Republic — 109
16. World War I — 114
17. Nicaragua — 141
18. World War II — 147

Notes 237
Bibliography 245
Index 253

Preface

The concept for this book came along a number of years ago and to the best of my knowledge no one has produced anything like it. It condenses the history of the Corps to just its battles. My intention is to provide a resource for anyone reading the history of the Corps which, generally, covers each battle with the necessary details, without the detailed overview. Or, perhaps, provides a quick reference point. This will allow further reading for persons interested in a specific battle or period. The Marine Corps has provided the best of that material in each of its later wars (see the bibliography), especially beginning with World War II.

Although this manuscript's purpose was to be a "complete" history of "every" engagement, I soon learned that goal was next to impossible to achieve. This book includes "almost" every engagement. A few of the small entanglements might have been overlooked. However, I believe you will be satisfied that I made an honest effort.

One of the areas I seemed to have ignored (but didn't) was the part played in World War II by Marine aviation. In fact, Marine aviators were all over the place, but played a part mostly as individuals. To have written about individuals would have taken up more space than I was allotted in this book. Only in certain encounters, like the support given the U.S. Army in its Philippine Campaign, and before that at Midway, has their part been developed. This is because they played an important role at Midway and the Philippines; in the latter, their role was solely that of Marines in an Army fight. The exception to this is their part in World War I, which was relatively minor, but that is where they developed their skills for future engagements, and the period is small enough to be covered in modest detail.

This book, like so many others, would have never been completed were it not for the support, without condition, of my wife of more than a half century, Jeanne J. D. Clark. So if you don't like what you find within, blame her.

My son Patrick T. Clark has been most supportive of my meager efforts for many years and there has been an occasional nod from my son Michael G. Clark and daughter Susan A. Evett and her family.

While most of the material you will find below has been derived from federal publications in my own collection, there are several people who have helped and encouraged me over the years. The list must include James T. McIlwain, MD, a friend and historian of many years; Col. Richard "Rich" Hemenez, friend, historian and author; Harry Tinney, a real support group all by himself; Comdr. Neil Carey, USN (Ret.), a friend of Marines, who, along with General Merrill B. Twining, created that marvelous tribute to the 1st MarDiv on Guadalcanal, *No Bended Knee*, and another long-time pal of mine; Lt. Col. "Pete" Owen, one of the Corps' finest and a splendid author himself; Col. Walt Ford, *Leatherneck*'s editor who has helped when asked; Gunnery Sgt. Richard "Dick" Gaines, who spreads the word; Maj. Gary Cozzens, and the many others who have kept me in business; and my *many* friends who also find the USMC in World War I the most fascinating period for military history.

Thanks to all.

George B. Clark

Introduction

Much of the early history of the very small body of men that made up what was known as the United States Marine Corps was about service aboard ship, for that was their primary reason for being. Marines, as they have been known throughout history, are soldiers of the sea, and they have been since ancient times. Greek and Roman warships carried marines, as did all other seafaring nations from the earliest times forward. Therefore the early histori-cal periods will, for the most part, be written about their history aboard ships. Later they served, frequently with the U.S. Army, in land campaigns against our own aborigines, or remained at sea fighting the usual troublemakers (British, French, Spaniards, Moors and others).

After their resurrection in 1798, the U.S. Marines were assigned to the War Department. Much later they were reassigned to the U.S. Navy Department. Thereupon confusion as to who "owned them" reigned. On occasion the U.S. Army leadership tried to command them and for many more years the chief of Naval Operations, or the equivalent position in earlier times, often tried imposing his will directly upon the Marine Corps, with an angry Marine commandant fighting it all the way. In recent times, both other services have backed off, at least temporarily.

Later, as the wars became ponderous, Marine service expanded to land engagements as well as those at sea. During the first war with Mexico Marines served with the U.S. Army in Mexico and in California. The Civil War saw them aboard ships but utilized, mainly by the U.S. Navy, as a landing force to attack Confederate installations. For the following near-forty years, the Marines were mainly a landing force in the Pacific islands where local natives offended our Navy, such as in Hawaii, Samoa, the Fiji Islands, as well as in China and Korea.

Then came the war in which the United States began to develop an empire. It was called various names but has more recently become the Spanish-American-Cuban War, and as far as the U.S. was concerned it was over almost before it began. The U.S. Navy destroyed the ancient Spanish fleet in Philippine and Cuban waters, the U.S. Army landed and took Cuba from Spain about four minutes after arriving ashore, while Marines also landed in Cuba, later at Guam in the Mariana Islands, and in and around Manila. However, the U.S. Army quickly gathered sufficient troops to displace those latter Marines, who soon returned aboard their ships.

From early in the 19th century our government insisted upon enforcing our doctrine, the so-called Monroe Doctrine.

Monroe Doctrine

This famous declaration was essentially a two-part document. John Quincy Adams wrote the part concerned with Russian aspirations in what we now know as our Northwest (Washington, Oregon and Northern California) in 1823. Other historians pull in President Monroe as the other author but more likely it was a staff functionary. At any rate, the declaration was really aimed against Spain, then trying to defeat the rebels in Latin and South America and retaking previously owned land. It was also a warning to France and a few other nations in Europe to keep their hands off any lands in the Western Hemisphere. Interestingly, the British were solidly behind the U.S., mainly because they wanted to keep the rest of Europe out of the Western Hemisphere without actually declaring that to the rest of the world. Although the doctrine had no legal standing in international law (until 1940), most nations didn't want a fight with the infant U.S. if it could be avoided. Consequently no serious trouble ever evolved because of it.

The Corollary to the Monroe Doctrine: Our very aggressive president Theodore Roosevelt decided to add to the doctrine in December 1904, when several nations, notably Germany and Great Britain, and later Italy, established a naval blockade about Venezuela. Many nations were owed substantial sums by the dictator of Venezuela, Cipriano Castro, and he refused to consider negotiations at The Hague Tribunal. With pressure brought by the U.S., however, the matter was eventually settled by arbitration at The Hague Tribunal and most of the nations were satisfied.

Essentially, at about the same period, the same sort of thing happened in Santo Domingo, whereupon the Belgian government recommended that the U.S. establish an administration and collector of custom income. These "improvements" satisfied the European nations and Roosevelt was in turn satisfied that none would try to physically impose its will on any American nation. It was justified as "protecting the nation from foreign intrusion" when in reality the U.S. desired to keep the Monroe Doctrine pristine. Roosevelt didn't desire to fight every nation which demanded that its bills be paid.

All of the above meant that the numerous times Latin nations wouldn't or couldn't pay their bills the U.S. was forced to intervene. When President Woodrow Wilson came upon the scene he would enforce the rules, "or else." In fact he used the doctrine or corollary to impose on Mexico (twice), Haiti (over an 18-year period), Dominican Republic (only eight years), and to continue the pressure on Nicaragua begun by Taft, his predecessor in 1912, until 1925. Fairly speaking, the United States made a load of enemies in the Western Hemisphere and even picked around a bit with Japan and, in 1917, with Germany.

Being an aggressive people, the Americans of the United States found themselves constantly interfering in other nations' affairs. This required a military force which could be on the scene and brought to bear when the local naval commander or the State Department thought it necessary. The U.S. Marines were that force. Though Marines never directed themselves to land anywhere, some people have placed the blame on them for doing so, which any right-thinking person must find ridiculous.

The Marines have fought in "every clime and place where they could take a gun" but it wasn't until the "Great War" in France that they found some real soldiers. The Germans gave the Marines and soldiers of the AEF a real fight and many casualties, following which the Marines went back to fighting small wars. Twenty years later they were once again engaged in a "real" war. This time it was an amphibious war, which was what Marines were trained for: from ships to land to fight. After World War II, in the war in Korea there was one amphibious landing; then the Marines were back to land warfare, which is mainly what they have been fighting ever since. Some might now call it a second Army, which the Army frequently does.

I'm not sure that the Marine Corps has or will have a reason for existence during the next two hundred years, but they certainly have been a ready force which the Navy can send any place at any time to enforce the will of the United States. It would seem to be an intelligent usage of a fine body of men in a world always in turmoil.

Glossary

Words used by Marines and their Corps are often different from common usage. The following brief rundown of some of those words, especially from later periods, might be helpful, especially if you have never been a member of the Marine Corps. There are others which should never be seen by decent company. I'm sure the later periods have other words, some unprintable, that relate to later events.

Advanced Base Force— The concept of taking and occupying distant islands in order to provide bases for the USN, protected by a small force of Marines using small caliber artillery.

Airdale— Naval or even Marine aviator.

BAM— Broad-assed Marine. Woman Marines did not take kindly to the insult. I have heard the theory that this unpleasant abbreviation came about because a QM Sgt. found that eight male Marines could be seated in the back of a truck whereas only six female Marines could be.

BAR— Browning Automatic Rifle. A quick-firing weapon that found great favor among Marines and soldiers. In its time, the major automatic infantry weapon.

Boondockers— Field shoes — to be worn out in the boondocks.

Boot— That common urchin who, according to senior NCOs, can ruin the Marine Corps when he or she goes to Boot Camp. Somehow, most manage to come out all right in the end.

CMC— Commandant of the Marine Corps. Also labeled as "MGC" for Major General commandant, or other rank such as "ColC" for earlier Colonel Commandants.

Corpsman— The guy who saved many a Marines' life. One swabbie who was always there when needed by a wounded Marine. Sometimes identified as "Doc."

Cruise— Usually, a four-year enlistment.

Defense Battalions— Their origin was in 1937, when it was deemed essential that the Corps provide coast defense and anti-aircraft protection for naval stations. They were heavily utilized at the beginning of World War II but later recognized as a less valuable usage of manpower. Their greatest contributions during the war were at the defense of Wake and Midway Islands. Abbreviated DF Bn.

Detachment— Nearly any size group that didn't easily fit in ordinary designated units like company, battalion, regiment, division. In use for a long time, with no parameters, up or down. Abbreviated MD.

Fire Team— A formation utilized late in World War II. It consisted of four men, a leader and three subordinates, one of whom carried a BAR. Three FTs were a squad, three squads a platoon. A marvelous innovation.

Fleet Marine Force (FMF)—Had its origins in the Advanced Base Force concept, in the early years of the 20th century. It was essentially a defense force to protect captured Navy installations with artillery and infantry. On 7 December 1933 it evolved into an amphibious striking force and was called by its current name, most frequently by its initials.

Gunny—Term for a gunnery sergeant, the most popular sergeant.

HAM—Hairy-assed Marine. The verbal response to "BAM," launched by women Marines.

JASCO—Joint Assault Signal Company. A group of Marine, Navy, and sometimes Army units to provide air-sea fire control to serve landing forces ashore.

Marines—Used to denote a regiment, individuals, or a collective group of Marines.

Mister—Term used when addressing junior Marine officers. Mister Brown, etc.

Navajo Code Talkers—Intelligent use of Native American language for communication between ground units, a language which the Japanese had failed to learn.

Pack-Howitzer—Lightweight artillery, designed to go anywhere that Marines could go. They were often, at the beginning of World War II, the only artillery the Marines had.

ParaMarines—Paratroops designed to provide services behind enemy lines. Usually there was little, if any, depth behind the enemy. They were, like Raiders, lightly armed and usually unable to contribute more than courage to an engagement. They were phased out early in World War II.

Raiders—Formed as a result of Roosevelt's decision to satisfy Winston Churchill's desire to see the United States emulate the commandos of Great Britain. Understaffed and under-weaponed, they performed miracles and paid the price for doing it.

Replacements—Those Marines that were brought in to replace those brought out.

Reserves—A valuable addition to the expanding Corps. The first genuine Marine Reserves was established on 29 August 1916 but didn't come into its own until the postwar period. Then the unpaid reserves were generally scattered around the country in company formations. Its history is too complex for this space, however it provided great value in World War II and has ever since. The 4th Marine Division was heavily composed of reserves.

Samoan Marines (Reserves)—Formed in that island group from natives around a cadre of Marines on 1 July 1941 to defend the island from any foreign (Japanese) invasion.

Seabees—Naval construction battalions mainly created from a stock of older but well-trained construction workers, whose help during tough times the Marines genuinely appreciated. They were "the goods."

Skipper—A term used for a company commander. Origins are obviously nautical.

Abbreviations

As usual, I have utilized those abbreviations which suit me best. All ranks, Army, Navy, and Marines, are reduced to a minimum. I have provided explanations for most of these abbreviations below.

AAA = Anti-Aircraft Artillery
ABMC = American Battlefield Monument Commission
ADC = Assistant Division Commander
AEF = American Expeditionary Forces
AF = Air Force
AG = Aircraft Group
ALP = Air Liaison Parties
Amph. = Amphibious
Arty. = Artillery
AWC = Army War College
BAR = Browning Automatic Rifle
BBD = Battleship Division
Bn. = Battalion
Brig. = Brigade
Btry. = Battery
CG = Commanding General
Chem = Chemical
CNO = Chief of Naval Operations
CO = Commanding Officer
Co = Company
Comm. = Communications
CoS = Chief of Staff
CP = Command Post
CT = Combat Team
DB = Defense Battalion
Demo. = Demolition
Det. = Detachment
Div. = Division
DMO = Division Marine Officer
DOW = Died of Wounds
D, P&P = Director, Plans & Policies
DUKW = amphibious truck
EBS = Engineer Boat & Shore
Eng. = Engineer (ing)
Exec. = Executive Officer
FA = Field Artillery
FMO = Fleet Marine Officer
Grp. = Group
H&S = Headquarters & Service
Hdqs. = Headquarters
Hosp = Hospital
How. = Howitzer
HQMC = Headquarters Marine Corps
IG = Inspector General
IJA = Imperial Japanese Army
IJN = Imperial Japanese Navy
IMAC = I Marine Amph. Corps
Inf. = Infantry (USA Regiment)
InfDiv. = Infantry Division (USA)
Intell. = Intelligence
JAG = Judge Advocate General (USN)
JASCO = Joint Assault Company
KIA = Killed in Action
Landing Craft:
   LC, Mk II = Landing Craft, Mechanized
   LCI = Landing Craft Infantry
   LCM = Landing Ship Medium
   LCP = Personnel
   LCT = Landing Craft Tracked
   LCV = Landing Craft Vehicle
   LCVP = Vehicle or Personnel
   LST = Landing Ship Tank
   LSV = Landing Ship Vehicle
   LVT = Landing Vehicle Tracked
   LVT (A) = Amphibious Tank
MAG = Marine Air Group
Main. = Maintenance
Maj. = Major
Marines = Marine Regiment

MarDiv. = Marine Division
MAW = Marine Air Wing; any variant
MB = Marine Barracks
MCG = Marine Carrier Group
MCS = Marine Corps Schools
MD = Marine Detachment (any place)
Med. = Medical
Mess. = Messenger
MG Co. = Machine Gun Company
MIA = Missing in Action
MoH = Medal of Honor
MOS = Marine Officer's School
MP = Military Police
MT = Motor Transport
Mun. = Munitions
NAD = Naval Ammunition Depot
NAS = Naval Air Station
NCO = Noncommissioned Officer
NG = National Guard
NWC = Naval War College
ONI = Office of Naval Intelligence
Ops. = Operations
Ord. = Ordnance
Para. Bn. = Parachute Battalion
PC = Post of Command
Pion. = Pioneer
Plt. = Platoon
Prov = Provisional
QM = Quartermaster
RB = Raider Battalion
RCT = Regimental Combat Team
Recon. = Reconnaissance
Rein. = Reinforced
RN = Royal Navy
Serv. = Service
Ships; Amphibious:
    AK = Cargo Ship
    AKA = Attack Cargo Ship
    AP = Transport Ship
    APA = Attack Transport Ship
Sig. = Signal
SNLF = Special Naval Landing Force
Sp. = Special
Sup. = Supply
IMAC = I Marine Amphibious Corps
IIIMAC = III Marine Amph. Corps
Tk. = Tank

Trac. = Tractor
Trp. = Troop (usually USA)
USA = United States Army
USN = United States Navy
VAC = V Amphibious Corps
WIA = Wounded in Action

Ranks — Marines and Army

Officers
  Gen. = general
  Lt. Gen. = lieutenant general
  Maj. Gen. = major general
  Brig. Gen. = brigadier general
  Col. = colonel
  Lt. Col. = lieutenant colonel
  Maj. = major
  Capt. = captain
  1st Lt. = first lieutenant
  2nd Lt. = second lieutenant
Enlisted
  SgtMaj. = sergeant major
  1st Sgt. = first sergeant
  GySgt. = gunnery sergeant
  PlSgt. = platoon sergeant
  SSgt. = staff sergeant
  Sgt. = sergeant
  Cpl. = corporal
  PFC = private first class
  Pvt. = private

Officer Ranks — Navy

Adm. = admiral
VA = vice admiral
RA = rear admiral
Comm. = commodore
Cmdr. = commander
Lt. Comdr. = lieutenant commander
Lt. = lieutenant
Mast. = master (earlier rank)
Lt. jg. = lieutenant (junior grade)
Ens. = ensign

1

American Revolution

Date: 9 May 1775 to 26 April 1784.
Location: Various colonies and in the Atlantic Ocean.
Involved: American colonies, France, and Spain versus Great Britain. Continental Army, Navy, and Marines; Militia, Navy, and Marines of various colonies, French army and navy plus some help from Spain.
Situation: When Great Britain ignored the demands of the colonies to stop "taxation without representation," among other offenses, the various colonies' patriots encouraged colonists not only to not pay taxes, but to prepare to fight for independence. Most colonies had a maritime connection and began making ready ships to engage British ships at sea. The original fighting crew and officers were, more or less, privateers. Their main interest was in capturing and selling for profit any ships they could easily take. Men were required to sail them, and men were also required to board and fight the crews of the opposing ships. The latter would be, and are, considered Marines.

Most maritime colonies (excepting New Jersey and Delaware) had their own navy and Marines. Later in the first year, when General George Washington took control of the army assembled around Boston, it was soon recognized that the British occupying Boston had convenient access to the sea, which allowed easy replacement of troops and supplies. Therefore, it was decided that Washington required a navy (and Marines, of course). Much of the naval action in this first year of the war occurred in and around Massachusetts Bay.

Because the war would frequently be fought between land armies, the naval actions have received somewhat less attention from historians. However, our interest is in the Marines' activities. Because Marines were in many guises, on land briefly, and at sea frequently, it is more difficult to present their entire story.

The first known action by Americans as Marines occurred on Lake Champlain in upper New York colony. The later traitor, Col. Benedict Arnold, led a seafaring force on that lake for several months, preying on the British ships. Most of his military force were volunteers from Massachusetts, and some were sailors. They began fighting on 9 May 1775 when they captured a sloop belonging to a loyalist and renamed her *Liberty*. Briefly successful, by mid–October at the Battle of Valcour Island, 11 of 15 American vessels were sunk in three days of fighting. Less than half the Americans survived, but it was acknowledged that the mainly Massachusetts men had fought gallantly against exceptional odds.

Survivors of Arnold's crew escaped to serve elsewhere. American Gen. Horatio Gates sent his thanks to Arnold "and the Officers, Seamen, and Marines of the fleet for the gallant defence they made against the great superiority of the Enemies Force." Gates also proclaimed that "such magnanimous behaviour will establish the Fame of the American Arms throughout the Globe."

Some of those Massachusetts Marines were later with Maj. Gen. Richard Montgomery in his winter invasion of Canada, where they helped capture Montreal and later attacked Quebec. They, like the rest of Montgomery's army, suffered privations from the weather, and many lost their lives on this ill-fated expedition.

During the balance of the war, there were many engagements in the Atlantic waters off North America between American-owned ships and those of the enemy.[1] The American ships were, frequently, privateers, but each had a small force of Marines, men who fought from the "tops" with muskets. Their main interest was to capture the opposing ship and sell it for prize money. In each encounter, Marines as well as sailors were engaged, unless the ships were merchant vessels engaged strictly in trade. Early on, before the Continental Navy was authorized, most of the various colonies had small navies. These had Marines as well as sailors. Not long after Gen. George Washington assumed command of the Continental Army before the British occupied Boston, he also added a fleet to his command, and Marines.

The *Hannah*, a 78-ton coastal schooner, became the first ship in Washington's fleet. He ordered some of his troops aboard to serve as Marines. They were "federalized" into Continental employment on 24 August, but not technically as Continental Marines. The Marines aboard *Hannah* were from John Glover's Marblehead Mariner Regiment. They were all professional seamen but organized and accepted as soldiers, and then credited as a Marine regiment, which they in reality were: Soldiers of the Sea.

Neither the Continental Navy nor its partner, the Continental Marines, had yet been created. Their subsequent roles would require service farther afield and against larger British craft. In addition to fighting at sea, there would also be the beginnings of amphibious landings against the foe. Some of the landings would be in the Canadian Maritimes — Nova Scotia and Newfoundland — and others would be in the West Indies.

Congress directed, on 13 October 1775, that two vessels be acquired for the Continental Navy. Crew, including Marines, were to be hired from men familiar with the sea. This is considered to be the birth-date of the Navy. And, on 10 November 1775 the Continental Congress formerly established a body of men to help man ships of the infant Continental Navy[2] to be called Continental Marines. The resolution read:

> Resolved, That two battalions of Marines be raised consisting of one colonel, two lieutenant-colonels, two majors, and other officers, as usual in other regiments; that they consist of an equal number of privates with other battalions; that particular care be taken that no persons be appointed to office, or enlisted into said battalions, but such as are good seamen, or so acquainted with maritime affairs as to be able to serve to advantage by sea when required; that they be enlisted and commissioned to serve first and during the war with Great Britain and the colonies, unless dismissed by order of Congress; that they be distinguished by names of First and Second Battalions of American Marines, and that they be considered as part of the number which the Continental army before Boston is ordered to consist of.

Samuel Nicholas of Philadelphia, the first Continental Marine officer, was commissioned a captain on 28 November. He would also become the senior officer of the new Corps and, many years later, be regarded its first commandant, though technically his title was "senior officer of Marines."

The first action of the new year in 1776 was one of the most important insofar as the Marines were concerned. It established the force as an amphibious assault unit, yet it would only be utilized as such a small number of times during the eight years the war endured.

Need for powder and ball for the colony's military forces, Navy and Army, was serious because at that time not much, if any, was being produced in the colonies. An ample supply for Britain's warships was known to be located in the British Bahama Islands. In January 1776 preparations were being made to send a fleet and an assaulting force to capture the needed material and to destroy the fortresses' ability to defend themselves. A second but equally important feature would be the diminution of those same items for British ships. It was known that the British had an island militia with, perhaps, a token regular army unit, and a few smaller naval ships in the several harbors.

In January 1776 Marines began loading onto their assigned frigates and sloops of war. Samuel Nicholas, officer in charge, Continental Marines, and his nine officers plus the now nearly 220 Continental Marines loaded aboard the operational commander Esek Hopkins' flagship, the *Alfred*. However, the balance of the fleet — the *Columbus*; *Andria Doria*; *Cabot*; and *Providence*— were still not yet ready for sea. On 17 February, after the ice had broken in the bay, the first Continental fleet cruised down the Delaware River to the Atlantic Ocean. But, before sailing to their target a number of deserters, sailors and Marines, had been rounded up and forcibly returned to their ships. *Semper Fidelis* was to them just two Latin words, neither of which meant anything special at that time.

Orders were given for the fleet to separate and reform in early March near Nassau, a city or town in the Bahama Islands. This was to be the first test of fleet and Marines in a combined operation ashore and the first amphibious landing by Continental Marines. It took place in the Bahamas at New Providence Island on 3 March. On this morning the fleet reassembled about ten miles north of Nassau. The fleet's appearance was soon discovered and the guns of Fort Nassau fired a warning shot. Hopkins realized that his fleet had been discovered and that surprise was now impossible. The officers gathered to discuss their options. It was soon decided to land the Marines on the eastern shore of the island, and instead of taking Nassau, to instead take Fort Montague. Nassau would have to be taken by the "back-door," a much more difficult task now.

The Marines and a force of 50 sailors to augment them were transferred to the *Providence* and two smaller, captured ships for the amphibious landing. Montfort Browne, the British governor, was subject to mild stomach disorders and, according to history, kind of mental condition. His militia and other island guardians were shunted about in delusive efforts to stop the incursion by the Americans. Overall, Browne was notoriously unsuccessful while the Americans were successful, to a point.

As Capt. Nicholas and his men moved toward the fort with a "prodigious thicket on one side and the water on the other," three guns at Fort Montague were fired upon them. Nicholas halted his column and gathered his officers to decide the best course of action. Lieutenant John Trevett was given a flag and told to make the fort aware of the intentions of the Americans to take it and to try to obtain its surrender before much blood was shed. Trevett met Lieutenant Burke, the fort's commander, coming from the other direction also under a flag of truce. Nicholas and Burke soon settled the matter because the fort had already been evacuated and the guns spiked. The Americans soon took possession of the fort and got a decent night's sleep. Nicholas had made Burke aware of what they wanted: provisions, stores, powder, weapons and the like. The next day Hopkins addressed a letter to the occupants of the island reiterating the same thing.

Hopkins, in a magnificent blunder, had not closed the entrance to Nassau harbor. The following day two British ships were loaded with powder and early the next morning they were directed to take the load to the British possession at St. Augustine, Florida. This was to ensure the powder would remain in the hands of the British.

Soon after Governor Browne was arrested and hauled aboard the *Alfred* and charged with firing guns at the Americans. Everyone knew that Hopkins was just getting even for the loss of the powder, which had been the main reason for the operation. On 16 March the many fewer captured stores had been loaded aboard the ships of the fleet, as were the Marines and attached seamen who landed with them, and the order was given to set sail.

The fleet arrived safely back in Philadelphia and the ship's detachment of Marines was soon temporarily ashore. They had all performed their jobs to the best of their ability in the very first combined operations amphibious assault in the history of the Continental Marines. It was not their fault that it had not been a complete success.

During the balance of the year the fighting at sea was constant, with successes and losses. As yet, the overwhelming power of Britain at sea had not yet been brought completely to bear in the Atlantic Ocean. Meanwhile several Navy men would become famous, like Capt. John Barry and later, Capt. John Paul Jones. The first was Irish-born, the second Scottish-born. Both would create a viable and successful naval appearance against a much larger, skillful, and dangerous opponent.

Captain Samuel Nicholas was promoted to the rank of major of Marines on the 25th of June. Sixteen other Marine officers were listed on the appointing order of this same date.

The Declaration of Independence was finalized and announced to the world on 4 July 1776.

By order of the Marine Committee dated 5 September, a uniform for Marine officers was adopted: "green coat faced with white, round cuff, slashed sleeves and pockets, with buttons round the cuff, silver epaulette on the right shoulder, skirts turned back, buttons to suit the facings; white waistcoat and breeches edged with green, black gaiters and garters." Green shirts were ordered for the men, if they could be procured.

Major Samuel Nicholas and three companies of Continental Marines were dispatched on 2 December from Philadelphia to reinforce Gen. Washington's army in its retreat from New York City to New Jersey. For the balance of the year sea-borne Marines continued fighting the enemy off Puerto Rico, Nova Scotia, and the New England coast.

As part of Washington's forces, Nicholas' Marine battalion plus other Marine companies from various ships participated in the Second Battle of Trenton on 2 January 1777. The successful defense of Trenton Bridge against the British army under Lord Cornwallis helped the colonial forces protect the Congress in Philadelphia. This appears to have been the first occasion when the Marines, as a land unit, fought a land battle with the Army.

The next day Maj. Nicholas' battalion and other Marine companies participated in the Battle of Princeton and helped capture the town. The next day, the Marines went into camp at Sweet's Town and later, on 1 February, went into winter quarters at Morristown, New Jersey. They and Army comrades suffered from the near starvation and lack of adequate clothing that was endured during this winter. These were truly times to try men's souls. Not long after, the Marines returned to ships.

On 14 June Congress adopted the 13 stars and 13 stripes as the national flag.

By the end of this year the British had severely brought the war to the east coast of the united colonies. Their army occupied Philadelphia, the seat of government, its approaches up the Delaware River, the new capital New York City, the Connecticut River, and Narragansett Bay. Their navy was decisively on the scene and things looked bad for the new nation.

On 27 January 1778, Marines and seamen landed once again on the island of New Providence to search for munitions. Just after midnight "twenty-six Marines 'all smart' filled their pockets with extra ball cartridges and prepared to go ashore." One very cautious Marine told Marine Capt. John Trevett, "I can not run." "You," said Trevett, "are the Man I should Chuse." So much for sick-bay commandoes in 1778.

Trevett, leading, found a fence picket still missing that he had removed in the 1776 visit. He crawled through the opening and soon became aware that the outpost watch was not much better than it had been two years earlier. Trevett returned to his men and got them through the fence. Waiting 30 minutes (he assumed the sentry calls went off with that frequency) and hearing the "all's well," he led his men in and quickly captured the only two sentries. Within a few hours they had managed to take Nassau Fort and for the first time planted the "Stars and Stripes" over a foreign stronghold.

The Marines immediately went to the already primed cannon and aimed them toward the main streets of the town. Trevett then sent Lieutenant Michael Molten with two Marines the four miles to Fort Montagu. His orders were to give the two-man garrison "no time to parle." They took Fort Montagu and, between the two occupied forts, covered the town of Nassau. Trevett was still not finished. They had come to New Providence to capture a ship, the 16-gun *Mary* which was loaded with munitions.

He led a midshipman and four just-released American prisoners and paddled out to the ship. He had a bit of trouble getting aboard, as the officer in charge at first refused him permission to come aboard. However, Trevett pointed out that the guns of both forts were trained on *Mary*. That settled it; they were then "welcomed aboard."

Notwithstanding their mission's ease, so far, the situation went downhill rapidly. A British privateer came up toward the fort, was warned away by the local residents, and circled about and later came up to Fort Montagu. Trevett realized that Molten couldn't hold the fort with but two Marines and ordered him to spike those guns and return to Fort Nassau. The perils were many but the captured munitions were safely placed aboard the *Providence* and within four days of arrival, on the 31st, the entire crew and released American captives were on their way home. After arrival, Trevett was sent to command the captive ship *Mary* while in harbor.[3]

In mid–April in France, John Paul Jones' ship *Ranger* had managed to obtain a complete crew and was now at sea to become the scourge of British shipping. Jones' various victories on land as well as at sea are well known and, because many of the "Marines" were technically foreigners, I will ignore most of his activities. It is sufficient to state that Jones and his sometimes mutinous officers and crew did a great deal of damage to British shipping. His attacks were ofttimes on shore, and the British were anxious to get him.

Fortunately for the American cause, France agreed to come into the war in February 1778. Her troops and fleet would help to balance the colonies' basic weakness against Great Britain. France's warships and loans would also make sure that the Congress would be able to continue the war.

On 24 July 1779, the Massachusetts ship *Tyrannicide* landed its Marine detachment on Fox Island (now Vinalhaven) in Penobscot Bay, Maine. This was a reconnaissance mission to destroy British efforts to build a fort near Bagaduce. Eventually, this was the beginning of a somewhat extensive operation in Penobscot Bay which required a relatively weighty Marine land participation, the largest in some years. For just about a month, between 26

July and 16 August, firing between American and British ships in the river continued every day. No serious damage was done to either side but the British moved further up the river to escape the minimal damage.

The Americans decided to land Capt. John Welsh and the Marines under his command on Banks Island, which was then occupied by the enemy. Twenty Royal Marines were the defenders. Though armed with four light guns, they elected not to defend but instead left their posts, abandoning the cannon. Additional Massachusetts militia under Capt. R. Davis landed in support of the Marines.

The following day the British defending the "fort" on high ground fired one shot blindly upon the island and managed to kill two Americans and wound three other. (It isn't clear if all or any were Marines.) Later that day a disagreement developed between the Navy and Army. The latter wanted the Navy to attack the three British vessels in the river first before any attempts were made to attack the fort. Commodore Saltonstall refused to endanger his ships by attacking ships protected by the guns in the British fort. He instead wanted the militia and Marines to attack the fort, and his position ultimately won out. There were 227 Continental and Massachusetts Marines, and 850 officers and men of the militia.

The landing began at midnight 27-28 July with Marine boats on the right and the militia on the left in three parts. The problem with the Navy plan was that both the Marines and militia would land at the base of a precipice with the British on top firing their guns down upon them. Confusion during the amphibious effort cost the Americans many lives and hours, and they were still offshore in broad daylight. It was about 0800 when the landing force was finally ready, with its boats just out of musket range. Four American ships opened fire on the fort's defenders, who returned their fire on the force as it was making its landing. Milling about, the militia troops ashore were trying unsuccessfully to form up in the usual line of battle.

Militiamen and Marines, in small groups and with muskets slung, made an effort to scale the cliffs. For some reason, the heavy fire from above seemed more directed at the Marines on the right of the line. The Marines, however, finally made it to the top and the veteran British troops took off. All but a handful under 2nd Lt. John Moore (later a heroic general in the Napoleonic Wars of Spain) stood their ground. Moore kept his handful in action and continued killing Marines. Their capable leader Capt. John Welsh, having made the top, dropped dead of a bullet to his head. Down below, at the base of the cliff, was Hamilton, his lieutenant, also severely wounded. After driving off Moore and his command the Marines counted noses and found they had suffered 32 casualties, 15 percent of their total force.

Marine 1st Lt. William Downe, commanding the Marines aboard the *Tyrannicide*, led his men toward the fort but they were without sufficient support to proceed any further. It was later learned that the British commander, Gen. McLean, was just about to haul down his colors and surrender when it dawned upon him that Comm. Saltonstall's ships not only were not coming upriver to bombard the British ships and the fort, but were retreating downriver. He changed his mind when he observed the confusion in the numerically superior American lines.

Though the Americans dug in and established defensive lines, over the next few days they had no leadership and by 5 August the morale of the now dug-in troops was at an all-time low. Noting the lack of activity and communication from Saltonstall, his superiors demanded that he take action. In the meantime a large British fleet consisting of one 64-gun ship of the line, several 32-gun frigates, and numerous smaller vessels was on its way.

On 14 August the American Navy made a dilatory effort to escape its entrapment, but by the end of that day most ships in the river were sunk, captured or useless. Saltonstall's caution was eventually destructive to this well-founded American offensive action. By 15 August the few ships that had managed to escape upriver were found and destroyed by British troops. The Americans on the ground, Marines and militia, were making their way home as best they could through the Maine woods. Losses were quite light compared to the actual potential, between 100 and 400 casualties. Marines were credited with professionalism and creditable performance throughout. Saltonstall was later tried and found guilty of dereliction of duty and was cashiered.

John Paul Jones, after nearly a year ashore, was now in his French ship, the *Bon Homme Richard*, and off the Irish coast. Not only was his ship (a very old merchantman) rebuilt by the French, but his crew was now heavily French, as were his Marines. They were all volunteers, from the Franco/Irish Regiment of Walsh, and wearing red coats.[4] The least that could be said about all of them was that "they were spoiling for a fight," especially against the English.

During the month of February 1780, the American command at Charleston, SC, Gen. Benjamin Lincoln, Army, and Abraham Whipple, Navy, decided that the expected forthcoming British attack upon Charleston required unusual preparation. Lincoln ordered Whipple to bring his ships into harbor and deny the British ships access to the town. When they finished their assignments, the British closed in, landed a large military force and forced Lincoln to surrender everything. A complete disaster.

A Spanish fleet was joined in mid–March by a few American ships for the planned attack upon Mobile, Alabama, now a strong British position. On the 15th, Continental Marines aboard the *West Florida* were sent ashore by the Spanish commander, Gen. Bernardo Galvez. He also landed his artillery just about a mile below the city, then the group headed towards Mobile. At 0800 on the morning of the 17th the guns opened fire upon the fort and at 1600 the white flag appeared and the British capitulated.

On 2 June the American 28-gun frigate *Trumbull* managed to stumble upon the 36-gun British letter of marque *Watt*. Under-gunned, *Trumbull* and her crew would be in for the fight of their lives. Marine Capt. Gilbert Saltonstall wrote a very descriptive letter which stated that *Trumbell* [sic] got a terrific walloping from the very beginning. "We were literally cut to pieces." The British hit them with everything, including the proverbial kitchen sink. Right from the beginning, most of the masts, sails and other navigational tools were gone.

Nonetheless, the *Watt* was also badly hurt during the engagement and decided to call it a day, pulling off after two and a half hours of this destructive punishment. She too had lost most of her masts and sails. *Trumbull*'s personnel losses were extremely heavy. Among the 13 officers and men killed were Marine Lts. David Bill, Jabez Smith, Jr., Daniel Starr and Sgt. Ezekial Hyatt. About 30 additional men, sailors and Marines, were wounded, including Saltonstall. Their ship survived and arrived at New York, somehow, on 11 June.

Later in the year, John Paul Jones, still afloat but now in the *Alliance*, was having a great deal of trouble with a French captain under his command named Landais. The latter would have been performing adequately, if he had been commanding a British ship. Because of him, Jones had mutinous officers, sailors, and Continental Marines. Jones somehow managed to survive this very serious threat and returned to the United States.

There were still ship actions in the Atlantic and Marines performing their duties in the year 1781. An example was when the U.S. sloop *Saratoga* engaged the 16-gun privateer *Resolution*, firing one broadside into her and having her then strike her colors. Not long after (hours or days?) the *Saratoga* engaged the letter of marque *Tonyn* for a full hour. The musket fire of Lt. Hugh Kirkpatrick's Marines was enough to satisfy the British ship that all was unwell and that she was finished. Her colors were lowered and the ship taken.

Captain John Barry had more than his share of fighting and defeats during the year. However, he too managed to survive and continue service for the newly established republic.

The senior Continental Marine officer, Maj. Samuel Nicholas, was directed to perform a most important project for the nation. He and a civilian, Tench Francis, with Marine guards, moved a gold shipment (a loan from Louis XVI) from Boston to Philadelphia during the months of October and November, avoiding the British in so doing. The route they followed is unclear but it is certain that traveling by oxcart over broken country as far from the coast as possible was a considerable task. The money arrived safely in Philadelphia on 6 November 1781.

Not much of import happened during the year of 1782 but Maryland's Marines did fight the Battle of the Barges in Chesapeake Bay on 30 November 1782. Captain Levin Handy, recently assigned to the unit, commanded. He was badly wounded, as was his brother, Capt. Joseph Handy, also of the states' Marines. Of the 60 Marines, 25 were killed or wounded.

In January 1783, Marines aboard the *Hague* participated in the capture of the final prize taken during the war, the British merchant ship *Baille*. And, on 10 March, the last naval battle of the war was fought between the British ship *Sybil* and the U.S. *Alliance* under John Barry. At 10 minutes to twelve Barry gave the order to fire. The broadside hits made *Sybil* shudder. Though her damage was heavy, the British ship managed to escape while *Alliance* went after two other British ships. But *Alliance*'s sluggish consort, the *Duc de Lauzun*, was unable to keep up so Barry was forced to turn back to protect her.

On 11 April 1783 the U.S. Congress formally proclaimed an end to the conflict between the infant United States and Great Britain. Then on 3 September the Treaty of Paris was signed by both Britain and the United States, effectively ending the war. That month, Lt. Thomas Elwood, the last remaining Continental Marine officer, was released from duty.

The date 26 April 1784 saw the last recorded mention of an enlisted Continental Marine, Private Robert Stout, who served aboard the *Alliance*. After nearly eight years of service, the Continental Marines ceased to exist, as did both the Continental Army and Navy. The Congress, finding no need for any military services, stopped funding them.

> *Results:* The colonial Americans, with help, especially from France, eventually forced the British to concede freedom to the colonies. Although the Marines were an important part, especially at sea, their numbers were always small. During the entire war, about 2,000 men served as enlisted Continental Marines and 130 as known officers. The probably larger numbers that served in the various states' navies, and even in George Washington's navy, are too difficult to ascertain. However, every ship, including privateers, carried Marines of one sort or another. And every engagement (many not listed above) between fighting ships during the war included Marines, possibly on both sides, except when the ships were merchantmen. Their few amphibious landings were generally successful, except at Penobscot Bay, which was the fault of the Navy's commanding officer. All in all, the Marines served the nation very well indeed.

2

The Fighting Tops

Date: 1785 to November 1811.
Location: On the Atlantic Ocean, Caribbean Sea, and Mediterranean Sea.
Involved: France and Great Britain versus the United States.
Situation: The infant United States had enemies on all sides and on many continents. Its attempts to trade with foreign nations had many interruptions and harassments. The outbreak of war in 1793 between revolutionary France and other European states greatly affected the American merchant fleet. Hundreds of ships were taken by various perpetrators, especially by the French and British when not fighting each other in the Caribbean.

After 13 U.S. merchant ships had been taken by Algerians in the Mediterranean (see "Barbary Wars"), and their crews imprisoned, enslaved, and otherwise mistreated, the Congress decided the United States did need a navy to protect its merchant ships in any part of the world into which they might wish to venture. Forthwith, the Congress passed a resolution in 1794 ordering that six frigates be constructed bearing between 36 and 44 guns, each carrying one officer and upwards of 54 enlisted Marines. Or roughly, that six officers and 310 enlisted Marines be hired as part of the Navy's shipboard complement. The new Navy, and its Marines, were to be under the secretary of war, since only the Army had been provided for by the Congress.

Part of the agreement among the disaffected members of Congress was that if a satisfactory treaty with Algeria become a fact, the Navy construction would be halved. After the U.S. paid a large financial bribe and conceded to pay an annual tribute, an agreement with the Dey of Algiers was signed on 5 September 1795. Consequently, the Congress instead authorized only three frigates with a Marine strength of only three officers and 155 enlisted Marines. Several other treaties — with Tunis and with Tripoli, under much the same terms — were signed the same year. Other than congressional approval, not much else had transpired.

By January 1797 at least one Marine officer had been commissioned, although the actual date is not known. There is mention that prior to this date Marines were serving aboard the newly built U.S. Navy ship *United States*, commanded by a hero of the Revolutionary War, Captain John Barry. However, the nation not being at war, it does not appear that those Marines engaged in any action during the period.

The secretary of war recommended to Congress the "raising of a regiment of infantry to act in the double capacity of Marines and infantry." This act was signed on 9 April 1798. Later that month, on the 30th, a separate Department of the Navy was established by Congress. However, for the time being it would continue to report through the secretary of the Army. On 22 May, legislation was introduced in Congress to raise a battalion of Marines for service aboard U.S. Navy ships. By the end of the fiscal year, 30 June, manpower strength of the Marine Corps was listed at 25 officers and 58 enlisted Marines.

On 1 July President John Adams signed into law legislation authorizing Marine strength at 5 officers and 161 enlisted men. Additionally, there had been Marines serving aboard revenue cutters, and this same legislation stipulated that there would be no more than 30 Marines and seamen aboard these ships. Duties of Marines aboard ship were established as providing security, maintaining discipline during peacetime, and manning the fighting tops, with seamen, when grappling with an enemy ship, to board or repel boarders.

On 24 August a Marine uniform was approved. It would include a blue cloth jacket, faced and edged with red, and red cuffs with one small button, with the high collar also of red material. The shoulder strap had red edging and there was a red belt around the jacket. The hat was of woolen material trimmed in yellow and turned up on the left side with a leather cockade. The officer's undress uniform was a plain blue frock with lapels with buttons which had an eagle with a shield on the left wing enclosing a fouled anchor. A white vest and breeches completed the uniform.

The nation had been having difficulties with revolutionary France. Since the French Revolution in 1793 that nation had been at war with practically every other nation in Europe. Because they were trying to interfere with ships delivering goods to European ports, French privateers were taking unarmed vessels, including numerous American ones. But then, they were doing exactly what British ships were doing to ships headed for France, also including American ships.

What has been labeled the Quasi-War commenced on 28 May 1798 when President Adams declared that armed vessels of the U.S. should make reprisals against merchant vessels of France. It would be a naval war that would continue until a treaty with France was signed on 3 February 1801.

In the opening gun of the war, the U.S. Marines from the sloop *Delaware* boarded the captured French schooner *Le Croyable* on the 7th of July, making the crew prisoners of the United States. Four days later President John Adams approved an act "establishing and organizing a Marines Corps." This is the true birth-date of the United States Marine Corps.[1] And on the following day, 12 July, President Adams commissioned William Ward Burrows as a major and as the first commandant of the U.S. Marine Corps.

For the next few months, the (now) U.S. Marines and crews of ships managed to take French merchant ships on a regular basis.[2] Unfortunately for the U.S., they weren't to have everything their way for long. On 20 November the U.S. schooner *Retaliation* was taken by two French warships, the frigates *L'Insurgente* and the *Volontaire,* 40 guns and 44, respectively. Two other U.S. ships escaped. Marines and crew went into captivity, but this would be the only ship the U.S. would lose during the entire war with France.[3] The officers were interred on a frigate but the men were held in a "loathsome prison" at Bassa Terre, Guadaloupe. The ship and crew were eventually returned to the U.S.

In a letter dated 7 March 1799 to Commandant Burrows, the secretary of the Navy stated that the French were complaining about the unruly behavior of the Americans. "You are requested to place two Centinels on board or alongside of the *Retaliation*, to prevent disorder, as the Frenchmen who now have her in care complain that they are interupted [*sic*] and insulted by some evil disposed Persons." (Marines? Evil disposed Persons? Highly unlikely.)

2. The Fighting Tops

February 1799 was a good month for the U.S. Marines commanded by Lt. Bartholomew Clinch aboard the *United States*. They assisted in sinking the French privateer *L'Armour de la Patrie* off the coast of Martinique on the third. Revenge! Just off the island of Nevis, near Basse Terre, Guadaloupe, the French frigate *L'Insurgente*, which had captured the *Retaliation* in November, was sent into captivity on 9 February, as was its crew, by the Marines and seamen of the U.S. frigate *Constellation*. And, on the 26th, the *United States* and its crew were providing the French with continued headaches in the West Indies. Off Martinique the ship and its crew participated in the release of the British ship *Cicero*, previously captured by the French. The U.S.'s enemy's enemies were its friends, at least for a while. President Adams also increased the strength of the Corps to one major, 40 other officers and 1,044 enlisted Marines. Regardless of the recruiting efforts, the Corps only had 25 officers and 343 enlisted men at the end of the fiscal year.

For the balance of the year, the U.S. ships took 17 French ships, mainly off French colonies in the Caribbean, so it was, overall, a great year for the small American war fleet.

On the first day of 1800, the U.S. schooner *Experiment* was becalmed off small islands in northern Haiti. They were then attacked by ten Haitian barges, "manned with negroes [*sic*] and mulattoes, and armed with muskets, sabres, and boarding pikes." Several of the barges, carrying at least 50 men, also carried 4 pounders and swivels in the bow. Hundreds of natives were trying to climb, or succeeding in climbing, over the rails. The Americans waited until they were close enough, and then the Marines opened up with their muskets, following it with grape shot from the ship. The attackers retired out of range to the island of Gonaive and there collected more boats and men. Their numbers eventually reached in excess of 1,500, with an estimated 40 barges, far outnumbering the Americans becalmed in those straits.

After an hour and a half they came on again. The Haitians opened fire as soon as they reached half-musket range. The captain of the *Experiment*, Lt. William Maley, had everyone hold their fire until the natives were all about the ship. He then gave the order and the guns opened up; the "fire of the Marines continued with great steadiness and activity," until "we at length succeeded in driving them off." A number of the barges were sunk, as were two smaller American vessels. The attacks continued but the Haitians were driven away each time. The ammunition was getting quite sparse, but by the end of the day the *Experiment* and the other vessels caught wind and were able to move out of the entrapment.

Captain Thomas Truxton, master of the U.S. frigate *Constellation,* flying English colors came alongside a "heavy French ship of 54 guns" at which he gave orders to clear the decks on the *Constellation*. This was the frigate *La Vengence* and this was to be a big fight on 1 February in which all hands would participate.

Truxton chased the enemy ship for hours until, at about 2000, he managed to speak through his megaphone and demand the surrender of *La Vengence*, at which the Frenchmen opened fire. Truxton's orders were to conserve ammunition by carefully firing only into the hull of the enemy ship. By 0100 the enemy's fire "was completely silenced." In his report he added "the Rascalls fought like cowards in firing at our Rigging to get away." The French ship did manage to escape but had to be run aground to avoid sinking. The American casualties totaled "15 killed and 25 wounded, all badly." One Marine, Pvt. Christopher McCormick, was killed and three Marines, Pvts. Cacie Branton, William Small, and George Carson, were wounded.

Truxton added, "I must transgress in favor of the brave Lt. B.[artholomew] Clinch of marines his corps was raw and never experienced such a scene; but by his manly deportment, he made them equal to the bravest; for when the enemy had manned his rigging and quarters to have boarded as a last refuge, the promising [Lt. John H.] Dent with his cannonades and Clinches' brave marines so well received them, that they fell back and damned the cause."

The French captain, F. M. Pitot, wrote his account of the fight, saying that the enemy's musketry fire [from Marines] was numerous and well supported the forecastle and "waist" batteries. "She had a very numerous crew and a *well-served musketry*" [emphasis added]. The ship and its crew, like Captain Truxton, were well-honored by Congress. So far it was the most important victory of the war.

On 11 May one of the Marine Corps' great heroes, Capt. Daniel Carmick, seconded by 1st Lt. William Amory, led a party of Marines in one of the war's eminent escapades. Silas Talbot, the captain of the *Constitution*, wanted to take a French privateer (sometimes listed as Spanish), the *Sandwich*, lying in the harbor of Porto Plata on the north shore of Santo Domingo. The water was too shallow for his ship so he decided to use the American sloop *Sally* to launch his attack. Into the harbor went the 40 Marines and 40 seamen, all hidden below decks, under Carmick and Navy Lt. Isaac Hull, another great Navy hero. It was Sunday morning and everyone, including the Spanish soldiers in the fort just above, were sleeping or at church. The *Sally* came alongside the *Sandwich* and in minutes the Americans were all over it. According to Carmick, "the men went on board like devils," however, little blood was spilled in the capture. Carmick and his men went up the hill and spiked the guns of the fort. Then they went back down to the boat, expecting to leave the port immediately.

The trouble was, the breeze wouldn't cooperate. While the aroused Spaniards were demanding surrender and threatening to open fire with their muskets, both Hull and Carmick negotiated (in bad faith) until a breeze finally came up at 0200 the next morning. The ship was able to move and join the *Constitution* outside the harbor. That ship was too big for the Spaniards to take on, so the Americans' risky venture was successful and they sailed *Sandwich* and *Sally* home.

The year was successful for the Americans at sea, with more than 20 French ships taken. Several other encounters of note occurred. French forces took the Dutch island of Curaçao and when the Dutch ship *Patapsco* entered the harbor, the French, who had taken the fort, were firing at her. The American response was to land Marines the following day to assist the Dutch in their efforts to retake the fort and repel the invaders. The French vacated the premises in the dark, surprising the Americans. However, a large British fleet moved in and took the islands for "His Britannic Majesty."

On 1 January the U.S. frigate *Chesapeake* captured the French privateer *LeJeune Creole* northeast of Bermuda.[4] James Fanning, late master of the *Hibernia*, which the same privateer had taken on 22 December, was freed from captivity. He learned that the French had already stripped his boat and sold it as a prize, and he subsequently filed a complaint.

The last French ship captured in the war, the *Marrs*, was taken off Antigua, West Indies, on 18 January. It was, however, returned to the captain, as was his crew, upon the discovery of a treaty drawn up between the United States and the Republic of France. The Treaty of Peace with France was ratified by the Senate on 3 February. On the 18th it would be proclaimed by the president.

One month later, when the nation was officially on a "peace basis," the Congress ordered all but 14 warships sold. Barely two months later, on 10 May 1801, the Bashaw of Tripoli would declare war against the U.S. because he felt short-changed in his tribute payment. This would once again require Marines ashore as well as afloat.

On 3 March, the Congress appropriated $20,000 for the building of a Marine barracks in Washington. The U.S. Navy was placed upon a peace establishment and it appeared, at that time, that the Marine Corps would continue in the future. On the last day of the month, Commandant Burrows and President Thomas Jefferson rode all over the Washington area to find a proper place to build the Marine barracks. They found it near the Navy Yard. On 21 June the land selected for the Washington, D.C., Marine barracks (at what is now 8th and "I") was purchased for $6,247.18.

After several years of demanding and receiving tribute, then attacking American ships, on 10 May 1801 the Bashaw of Tripoli declared war upon the U.S. and on 14 May had the flagstaff cut down before the American consulate. This was the formal beginning of the so-called Barbary Wars. War was declared by the Congress against Tripoli on 6 February and instructions were forwarded to Commodore Dale to begin operations against the Bashaw and his subjects (see Barbary War section). The Marine Corps, at this time, had 38 officers and 319 enlisted men. The Navy, as usual, was also under-manned in both ships and manpower.

On 20 December 1803 the French tricolor was pulled down and the American flag pulled up in the newly transferred city of New Orleans. Captain Daniel Carmick and his 105 Marines were landed to restore order amongst the recalcitrant French population. He, three lieutenants, four sergeants, two musicians, and 96 enlisted Marines settled the dispute in short order.[5]

The war off North Africa continued, still at sea, with several major losses to the U.S. ships. The *Philadelphia* had gone aground in October 1803 and its entire crew, including many Marines, were taken into captivity. Numbers of officers and crew made efforts to the ship's captain, Bainbridge, to fight back, but he instead decided to give up. Almost every American involved was ashamed. War was mostly at sea, with wins and losses, and that continued until 1805 when Marine 1st Lt. O' Bannon and his six Marines settled the hash of Tripoli that June.

On 14 October 1805 the secretary of the Navy directed that the Marine Corps change uniforms. Officers would wear navy blue coats with scarlet collars, and laced cuffs with a white vest and pantaloons. The hat would be cocked with a gold laced loop and leather cockade. Enlisted Marines would wear a navy blue short coat, white pantaloons, high crowned hats with a plume of red plush on the front and a brass plate with eagle. The hat band would be of red, white and blue cords, and the tassel of the same colors. Sergeants would wear a leather cockade on the left side of the hat with red plume.

The following year, 1806, was one of unpleasantness between the U.S. and Great Britain, with Napoleonic France's encouragement. The latter established a European blockade against Britain while Britain established one against France. If the U.S. attempted commerce with either, it would be in the wrong. This small nation had to continue commercial activity or die. Consequently its ships were always at a serious disadvantage. President Thomas Jefferson was against going to war and was willing to accept many insults, consequently the U.S. was subjected to many.

A British ship, the 52-gun frigate *Leopold*, stopped the American 39-gun frigate *Chesapeake* just beyond the three-mile limit off Norfolk, VA, on 22 June 1807 and demanded the return of four seamen they charged as British deserters. Captain Samuel Barron refused and the British opened fire. Barron was unprepared (and would later suffer courts-martial because of this) and three of his men were killed and 18 wounded. He then permitted the British to board the ship and remove the four men. Later, only one was determined to be British and was hanged. The Marines aboard suffered the indignities of the rest of the crew.

Finally fed up, President Jefferson issued a proclamation on 2 July, advising British warships to vacate U.S. waters. It wasn't until 17 October that the British government reacted to Jefferson's proclamation by announcing their intention to even more rigorously enforce their policy of impressing American seamen, which they did.

Napoleon issued a directive on 17 December that any nation that obeyed British orders to refrain from commerce with *his* Europe could expect to be treated as a belligerent and its ships would be taken by France.

Congress passed the Embargo Act on 22 December which forbade trade with foreign countries. This would create a nightmare for the government and its agents, the U.S. Navy and Revenue Service. Whatever affected either service also affected the U.S. Marine Corps. The following year was quiet, at least for the Marines, and on 3 March 1809, Congress authorized an increase to 46 officers and 1,823 enlisted Marines and from three-year enlistment contracts to five-year ones. The following day, the Marine Band played its first Inaugural Ball for the incoming president, James Madison.

Off the Bahamas, the British sloop *Moselle* fired upon the U.S. brig *Vixen* on 24 June 1810, later apologizing, claiming her captain thought the ship was a French privateer.

On 5 August Napoleon purposely misled President Madison into believing that France would stop interfering with American trade beginning on 1 November. As a result, Madison rescinded the boycott against France.[6]

The following year, in January 1811, a slave-led insurrection north of New Orleans was quickly put down by Maj. Daniel Carmick and his Marines. On the first day of May, the British 38-gun warship the *Guerrière* stopped the *Spitfire,* an American brig, off Sandy Hook and kidnapped an American-born seaman. This created an outcry in the nation. Commodore John Rodgers, just out of the Chesapeake Bay aboard the U.S. frigate *President*, spotted a ship which he believed to be the British *Guerrière*. He cleared his decks at 1430 and began the chase to "speak" to the captain of the British ship. The chase lasted until about 2030, when Rodgers asked "what ship is that." He was answered by a shot which hit a portion of the mast system. Captain Henry Caldwell, commanding the ship's Marine detachment, was standing nearby when he shouted "Sir, she has fired at us."

Rodgers tried to avoid fighting because he wanted to negotiate the return of an American ship and crew. However, the ship's captain (the ship's name was then still unknown but was in reality the *Little Belt*) was not in the mood. Fighting commenced and lasted as long as the ships could see each other. Musketry from the *President* was heavy and caused numerous casualties to the enemy ship. Regardless, the enemy kept going and Rodgers continued to chase her.

The next morning at approximately 0800, the ship was seen to be about 8 miles in the distance. The enemy ship was by now determined to be the 20-gun sloop *Little Belt*. A boat ran alongside to offer assistance but the British captain Arthur B. Bingham declined. He had severe losses; 13 were killed, including the lieutenant of Royal Marines, and the wounded included the acting captain and 19 other men. Rodgers' loss was one ship's boy wounded.

The *Little Belt* was allowed to continue its voyage to Halifax, while Rodgers pulled into Sandy Hook and sent Captain Caldwell to the secretary of the Navy with an account of the engagement. As the fiscal year ended, the personnel strength of the Corps remained over 500.

Negotiations between the U.S. and Britain over the *Little Belt* and the attack on the *Chesapeake* back in 1807 failed to resolve the main issues. Nevertheless, on 12 November, the British came up with a better offer of compensation on the *Chesapeake*, which was accepted later, but did not satisfy for the *Little Belt*.[7]

> *Results:* The U.S. managed to avoid losses, but had few gains during the entire period. It was a major struggle for this new nation and it ultimately led to a second war with Great Britain, one the European country encouraged so as to get even for its previous loss. Most of the fighting during the entire period was at sea and consequently Marines were included in every battle entry. Their most important role on land was represented by the Marines along the Great Lakes and at New Orleans.

3

Barbary Wars

Date: 14 May 1801 to 30 June 1816.
Location: North Africa.
Involved: Various North African nations, Algeria, Morocco, Tunis, and mainly Tripoli, versus the United States.
Situation: For many centuries, in order to sail the Mediterranean with as little harm as possible, most European nations paid tribute to various Barbary nations. Otherwise their ships would be attacked and captured, and their sailors made slaves; this sometimes happened even if they did pay. The U.S. was also forced to pay until 1816.

The U.S. *Enterprise*, with 12 guns and 90 men, was sailing the Mediterranean on 1 August when it fought its first action against the new enemy off North Africa. This was when it encountered the Tripolitan polacra[1] *Tripoli* of 14 guns and 80 men. Captain Andrew Sterrett was flying a British flag when he approached the polacra and requested information about what that ship's master intended to do. Admiral Rais Mahomet Rous told him, "I'm looking for Americans ... but haven't found a one." "You have now," responded Sterrett, raising the American colors and ordering a volley of musketry fire. Three times the Africans tried to board the *Enterprise*, but the Marine detachment's firing, led by 2nd Lt. Enoch C. Lane, was especially deadly at close range. The Marines are credited with sweeping the decks clear of the occupants each time they attempted to board. After three hours of bombardment and musketry fire, the Americans boarded the *Tripoli* and found the ship completely shot to pieces. The dead numbered 30, as did the wounded. Only 20 men remained able to serve the ship and its guns. After the enemy surrendered Sterrett took stock of his own ship and found that not one American had a scratch. After many years of insult and abuse, the Tripolitan's enemy was unwilling to take it any more.

Because orders did not allow taking prizes, as in the past wars, Sterrett set about abuse so grand that the admiral was publically disgraced upon returning to his home port. The enemy ship had all cannons rolled overboard, and all ammunition and weapons, including cutlasses, muskets, and pistols, were also thrown into the sea. The masts were chopped down, leaving but a single spar with a ragged sail, just enough to make it to the nearest port. News of the destruction spread and caused the Tripolitan sailors engaged in preparing new ships to hide, which effectively kept the Tripolitan fleet from sailing out to meet the enemy for an entire season. Only those already at sea were still dangerous to any American vessel.

Keeping an effective blockade on the port of Tripoli was difficult. Two Tripolitan gunboats attacked both the *Philadelphia* and *Essex* on 29 September in order to try to break up the "noose" closing in on Tripoli's importation of food and ammunition. The ships fought back and while the gunboats were damaged they managed to return to port. Congress recognized that the four-ship fleet of Comm. Richard Dale was not sufficient to close all the ports of North Africa and soon new ships were being prepared for sea duty off North Africa.

War was declared by the Congress against Tripoli on 6 February 1802 and instructions were forwarded to Dale to begin operations against the Bashaw and his subjects. Over the course of the next several months several ships joined Dale's little fleet, including the *Boston* on 16 May.

Morocco declared war upon the United States on 22 June, thereby adding a powerful foe to those the U.S. already had in the area. They controlled the entrance to the Mediterranean and would have a grave impact on the ongoing war with Tripoli. The U.S. ships, aided by the Swedish fleet, continued to have serious encounters with the Tripolitans all during this year. The Bashaw went so far as to parade his 6,000-man army on the beaches to frighten or at least to impress Dale, which failed its purpose. Commodore Richard Valentine Morris, newly commanding the Mediterranean U.S. fleet, decided on 9 May 1803 that it was long past time to be active against Tripoli.

Meanwhile, a Marine Lieutenant Presley N. O'Bannon wrote the commandant and let him know how disgusted he was with the whole affair of sitting in "that hell-hole, Gibralter" and how happy he was to be back close to the scene of possible action. Recently arrived Marines and shipmates aboard Capt. John Rodgers' ship *John Adams* were in for very busy period. They caught seven Tripolitan gunboats attempting to break the blockade and severely punished them. Then Rodgers and his men chased, caught, and captured the Moroccan ship *Meshouda*, bringing her back to Malta as a prize. Captain Rodgers led a three-ship excursion toward three Tripolitan merchantmen making an effort to escape, but they reversed direction and ran ashore. Marines and sailors were sent ashore as a landing party to destroy the three merchantmen. Naval Lt. David Porter (later to become one of the most famous of all Navy men and grandfather of a Marine hero) led the party ashore, destroying the ships, and they made their way back to the ships with few casualties, one being a wounded porter.

On 2 June Marines and sailors from the squadron were sent ashore to burn 10 more boats. Twenty days later the *John Adams* answered a signal flag from the *Enterprise*, located in the harbor of Tripoli. She had engaged a larger Tripolitan ship, a polacra of 22 guns, and needed help. *Enterprise* had been pumping shells point-blank into the ship, however, and within an hour the enemy crew abandoned the ship. *John Adams* had sent Marines and some crew to take the supposedly vacated polacra when all of a sudden she was blown up. Her hull split in two and down she went, taking the Americans with her.

Peace with Morocco was reestablished on 12 October, which made transit past its shores much easier for the American Navy. But, at the end of the month, serious trouble would happen. On the 31st the second-largest American ship in the Mediterranean fleet, the *Philadelphia*, ran up on an unmarked reef in the Tripoli bay. The smaller *Vixen*, which had been accompanying *Philadelphia*, had been set astray by a heavy wind and was 300 miles away off Cape Bon. It was soon evident to the Tripolitans that the *Philadelphia* was in trouble and small boats from shore were sent out to test her combat ability. Because of the ship's location and position upon the reef, the starboard side was not able to do anything, so the Tripolitan boats came in on that side. Captain William Bainbridge decided that there wasn't much they could do and that surrender was his only alternative. He ordered the ship to be scuttled but failure by the ship's carpenter to pierce the bottom sufficiently allowed the ship to be taken. The enemy also captured 235 seamen, 41 Marines and 33 commissioned and noncommissioned officers. The Marine officer in command was 1st Lt. William S. Osborne. Private William Ray, a Marine, later wrote that the men begged Bainbridge not to surrender but to fight and try to get the ship refloated, but the captain persisted. As a result, they spent 19 months in captivity.[2]

The rest of the U.S. fleet in the waters continued to fight most effectively. Covering all the ports of Tripoli constituted a huge problem for Comm. Edward Preble, aboard the *Constitution*, his lone 44-gun frigate now that the *Philadelphia* was gone. His much thinned-out Mediterranean fleet now consisted of but two brigs, *Argus* and *Siren*, 16 guns each, and three schooners, *Enterprise*, *Vixen*, and *Nautilus*, with 12 guns each. He had placed Tripoli under a blockade with his minuscule fleet, and was now in dire straits trying to cover all the exits.

However, there were some bright moments. On 16 February 1804 the *Intrepid* commanded by Lt. Stephen Decatur, with 60 volunteers, eight of whom were Marines led by Sgt. Solomon Wren, entered Tripoli's harbor and there boarded and burned the *Philadelphia*, which was still hung up on a reef. At least there was no chance the enemy would have it to sail and fight against its comrades. Incidentally, the U.S. offered $100,000 for the safe release of its men, which was refused.[3]

In the meantime, Preble had been assembling more boats and on 20 May had acquired gunboats with a 24 pounder and mortar boats, each with a 13-inch brass sea mortar, from the Neopolitan king's navy, and some of that king's subjects to help man them. Preble assigned sailors and Marines to each boat to carry the fight directly into Tripoli Harbor and divided his formation into two divisions. Lieutenant Richard Somers commanded the 1st Division and Lt. Stephen Decatur, the 2nd Division. Each of these boats was going up against better armed, with 18 to 26 pounders each, and more numerous enemy, but Preble was a fighter and this failed to deter him.

On 3 August Tripolitan boats began coming out toward Preble's fleet and he decided to make them "pay for their insolence." At 1400 Preble gave the command and each mortar boat pumped its shells down upon the oncoming enemy. The first boat to get into the action was that mastered by Decatur, which headed for nine Tripolitan boats. He had his Marines shower all with musket fire, causing the enemy heavy casualties. Commanding a boat in Somers' division, Lt. James Decatur, younger brother of Stephen, pulled ahead and joined Stephen's group. The four boats were soon up to their necks in Tripolitans. The first enemy boat taken was leaderless. The captain had been hit by numerous musket balls and left no one to command.

For the subject of various paintings, artists would later utilize the hand-to-hand fighting that ensued that afternoon. Casualties for the Tripolitans numbered in the hundreds while, at the end of the fight, Decatur's loss was but one dead, his brother James, and three sailors wounded. The boat that killed James soon fled but Decatur followed him. After Decatur caught the enemy boat they fought for about 20 minutes before he managed to kill the Tripolitan captain that he blamed for his brother's death. During the fight a Turk had been wrestling with Decatur and had him on the deck. He raised his scimitar but a sailor, Daniel Fraser, leaped between them and received the blow on his head. Meanwhile, a Marine raised his musket and killed the Turk before he could finish off Decatur or Fraser. Both men survived, the former to go on to greater glory in the years ahead. He was a real fighting sailor and pride of the U.S. Navy. From that date, 3 September, Marines participated in the constant shelling of Tripoli. Meanwhile, the next serious blow against Tripoli was going to be on land.

After several years of demanding and receiving tribute, then attacking American ships, on 10 May 1804 the Bashaw of Tripoli declared war upon the U.S. On the 14th he had the flagstaff cut down before the American consulate. This was the formal beginning of the so-called Barbary Wars. William Eaton, the local American consul and adventurer, promised to rectify the situation and persuaded president Thomas Jefferson that it would be easy for him to stir up a revolt against the Bashaw of Tripoli. The president was anxious to believe that and gave Eaton permission to make the attempt.

A Marine officer, 2nd Lt. Presley O'Bannon, had been assigned to him along with six enlisted Marines (names below). This part of the war would be the only land combat in the entire period.

In October 1804, O'Bannon, with the U.S. fleet at Malta, was transferred to the *Constitution* and three days later to the brig *Argus*, commanded by Isaac Hull. This ship had received special orders to pick up William Eaton and convey him and his "command" to Alexandria, Egypt.

At Alexandria, Eaton had brought along a willing O'Bannon, Navy officer Joshua Blake, two midshipmen, Eli E. Danielson and George Washington Mann, and a few assorted adventurers. He made arrangements to gather the deposed Tripolitan Bashaw Hamet, while O'Bannon recruited more adventurers in the sea-port town: 67 "Christian" (meaning Greek) mercenaries and 90 Arabs. Midshipman Pascal Paoli Peck and seven Marines from aboard the *Argus* constituted the entire "army."

For ten days the army moved westward along the northern coast of Africa toward Derna without encountering serious trouble. On the 18th Eaton had trouble with the camel

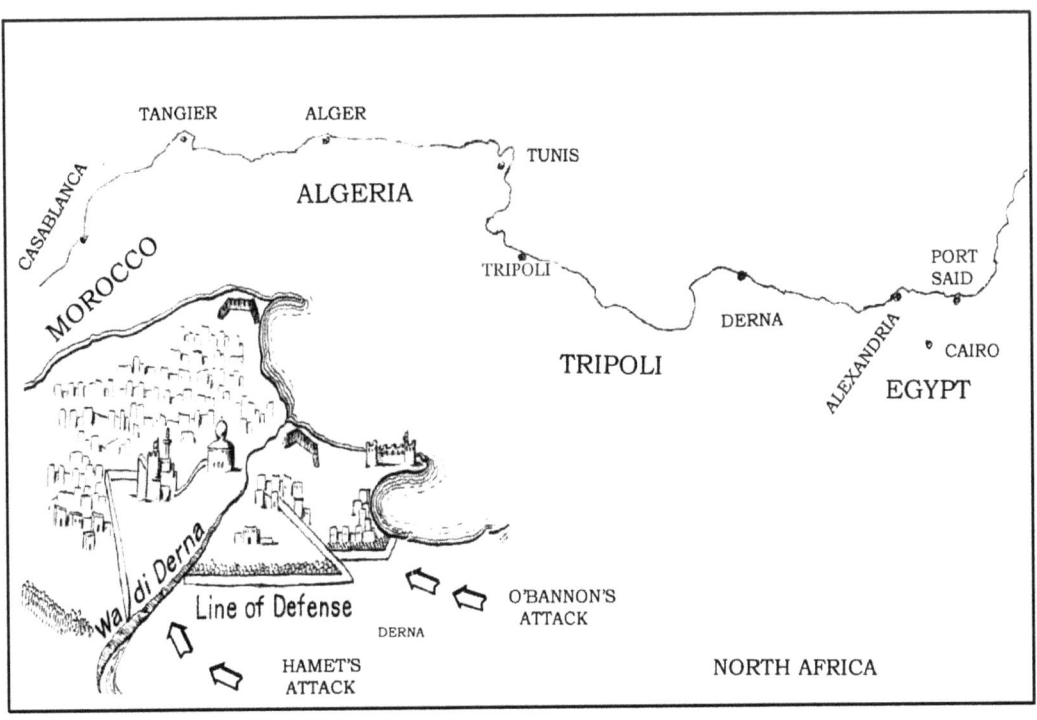

drivers. Several days later 230 Arabs on horse and foot joined them. As they moved westward, disputes with the Arabs were continuous, but each was eventually settled. At one point only the Americans and a few Christians stood between total revolt and continuing to advance. A few days later the Christians revolted because their food was gone and water was severely limited. By chance three American ships were off Bomba; provisions were landed and once again, all was well. So far the little expedition had traveled over 500 miles across deserts, frequently without water, and with little food.

Eaton requested another hundred Marines but Comm. Samuel Barron refused, although he did return the volunteers, Midshipmen Danielson and Mann. On 23 April their trek resumed. Meanwhile, the Bashaw became alarmed at Eaton's threat to the fortress of Derna and sent reinforcements from Tripoli. That discouraged Hamet and his Arabs, who had anticipated a bloodless victory. Eaton was forced to bribe them to go on. Two days later, on 25 April, Eaton and his motley force arrived upon the hills overlooking the walled city of Derna.

Eaton at once sent the Bey of Derna a note demanding surrender. The Bey, obviously sure of his 800 defenders, replied simply, "My head or yours." One field piece was landed via the offshore *Nautilus* and that was followed by gunfire from the three U.S. ships just a hundred or so yards offshore. Eaton placed the Christian forces under O'Bannon's command, and Hamet and his Arab horsemen in reserve.

The Marine lieutenant with his command of six Marines and 26 Greeks, plus a few Arabs on foot, were to be the assaulting force. Enemy artillery fire was soon canceled out by the ships' firing, and the small force charged the defenders. The latter believed in the old adage "There is safety in flight." O'Bannon and his Marines went over the walls and soon planted the national colors upon a fortress high above the city. There were, however, several counterattacks, all of which failed, and the remaining Marines forestalled any serious attempt by the defenders to stand their ground. The situation was far from bright. In his original attack, though O'Bannon had suffered a modest 14 casualties, three of those were Marines. With only six to begin with, the Marine casualty rate was 50 percent. As Eaton was to report, "The detail I have given of Mr. O'Bannon's conduct needs no encomium." He added, "it is believed the disposition our government has always discovered to encourage merit, will be extended to this intrepid, judicious, and enterprising Officer."

The month of May saw continued efforts to throw the Americans out of Derna, all of which failed. At the end of May, O'Bannon drove off a 50-man attack with his three remaining Marines supported by 35 Christians. A few days later O'Bannon led a feint which forced the Tripolitans to withdraw from the city entirely. Once more, on 11 June, the Bashaw sent another large force to retake Derna, which also failed miserably. On that evening the U.S. ship *Constitution* arrived with orders to Eaton: Peace had been signed and he and his men were to withdraw from Derna.

William Eaton was terribly disappointed, being sure that with one hundred Marines he could have easily taken all of Tripoli. Tobias Lear, American counsel at Alexandria, had negotiated the, as it later turned out, disadvantageous treaty. But at the time he made complimentary remarks about Eaton, O'Bannon and "our brave countrymen," meaning the six other Marines. O'Bannon and his three remaining Marines (names below) returned to the *Argus*.[4] In the summer of 1806 the ship set sail for the United States.

The previous March the Congress had passed a resolution praising the courage, valor, and zeal of the Americans involved. Kind words throughout but little else.[5] On 26 December 1805, O'Bannon's home state, Virginia, passed a resolution authorizing a sword be created and presented to him. It was designed after a bejeweled Mameluke sword which Hamet had presented to O'Bannon, but which subsequently had disappeared. That sword design is the origin of today's Marine officer sword. The original Virginia gift now resides in the Marine Museum.

The names of the Marines who accompanied O'Bannon on his hazardous tour are as follows: Acting Sgt. Arthur Campbell; Pvt. Bernard O' Brien; Pvt. David Thomas, wounded in action on 27 April 1805; Pvt. James Owens; Pvt. John Whitten, killed in action on 27 April 1805; and finally, Pvt. Edward Steward, who died of wounds on 30 May 1805.

Not all was victory; the U.S. was forced to pay a ransom of $60,000 to free the American prisoners from the capture of the *Philadelphia.* The terms did specify there would not be further harassment of American ships in the area.

President Madison approved an act of Congress on 3 March 1815 authorizing force against the Dey of Algiers because of depredations against American ships and the enslavement of their crews. It wouldn't be until the month of June that any serious counter-action would be taken against the Algerians. On the 17th Comdr. Stephen Decatur's squadron caught the Algerian frigate *Mashuda* off Cape de Gat and the Marines were especially cited by Decatur as providing excellent musketry fire from the tops. Two days later they took another Algerian ship, the brig *Estedio* off Cape Palos, where he again cited the effective fire of Marines as helping greatly in forcing the surrender of the Algerian ship.

At the end of the month, the Dey of Algiers realized that the game was up and signed a no question treaty with the United States.[6] Then, on 31 July, a peace treaty was signed with the Bey of Tunis. This was followed on 9 August with a treaty of peace signed by the Bashaw of Tripoli. These would effectively end all payment of tribute to the nations of North Africa. Decatur obtained a treaty on 30 June, another with Tunis on 26 July and another with Tripoli effective 5 August, all in 1816.

> *Results:* Warfare between the U.S. and various North African states lasted for more than 15 years and the final outcome was a barely visible victory. During the earlier years the USN, with a variety of commanding officers, did rather poorly trying to control access to and from the various nations being blockaded.
>
> A major success was the taking and holding of the city of Derna by O'Bannon until at least 11 June 1805. After numerous failed attempts to retake the city, the Pasha signed a peace treaty with the U.S. ending payment of tribute to Tripoli. The treaty subsequently faltered and was rehabilitated on 5 August 1816. However, it wasn't until that year, more than ten years after Derna, that the USN finally stopped payment of tribute.

4

War of 1812

Date: 18 June 1812 to 30 June 1815.
Location: North America and the adjacent seas, the Great Lakes, Atlantic, and Pacific.
Involved: Great Britain versus the United States.
Situation: Trouble between Great Britain and the newly created United States had been brewing ever since peace between the two was signed in Paris on 3 September 1783. Great Britain and its politicians did not take kindly to the successful breaking away of their former colonies and harassed this nation continually, from points north, south, and west, but especially at sea. This would continue for many years, though in slightly altered form.

Impressed British sailors jumped ships, frequently to join American ships. For this reason Great Britain assumed the power to return them to their "correct" duty. This meant stopping American ships anywhere they could and removing seamen, theirs and others, regardless of the protests of the American sailing masters. Even regardless of our nation's presidents' continual protests.

On 18 June 1812 President Madison approved an act of Congress which declared that a state of war existed between the United States and Great Britain. The war at sea was the most extensive, and, like its predecessors, included Marines in all actions.

Early in the morning of 23 June, the U.S. frigate *President*, Comm. John Rodgers, sighted the British frigate *Belvidera* of 42 guns. At 1600 both engaged in a running fight. *Belvidera* escaped but suffered much damage to spars and sails and lost two killed and 22 wounded while Rodgers' loss amounted to two killed and five wounded. Marine Pvt. Francis H. Dwight was killed and 1st Lt. John Heath was "slightly" wounded. Captain Archibald Henderson was the commanding officer of Marines aboard the *President* and 1st Lt. Henry H. Forde was his second.

Although the U.S. Marine Corps had an authorized strength of 1,869, there were but 10 officers and 483 enlisted men in the first year of this war. Eventually, before the war ended, the Corps managed to attract nearly enough men to fill most of those allowed slots.

Major Daniel Carmick, the Marine commanding at New Orleans, exchanged letters with Commandant Franklin Wharton between June and August. The letters were concerned with recruiting, discipline, and winter uniforms. The big problem though, was an attempt by Brig. Gen. James Wilkinson to merge Marines into his U.S. Army formation, to which Wharton responded "violently."

In June, the American brig *Oneida* captured the British schooner *Niagra* on Lake

Ontario. *Oneida* was noted as being "manned by an under strength crew and only a few Marines." On 19 July British ships attacked the U.S. naval base on Lake Erie at Sacketts Harbor, NY, but were driven off by the U.S. Marine defenders and the *Oneida*. This seems to have been the first land engagement of the conflict in which Marines participated.

The U.S. frigate *Constitution* engaged the British frigate *Guerrière* on 19 August in the North Atlantic. This was a battle between two giants, the first major fight between the two navies. The Marines aboard were heavily engaged in the hand-to-hand fighting and earned deserved accolades from the captain, Isaac Hull, one of the great fighting sailors of the period.

The *Guerrière* had already earned a reputation during the Napoleonic Wars and her captain, James R. Dacres, would not easily suffer the loss of the Royal Navy's reputation. They fought hard the first hour without either ship gaining an advantage. Then Hull closed to the very shortest range and in 20 minutes of magnificent gunnery the *Constitution* more than doubled the damage she received. Each side thought the other was going to board and it was the time for musketry. The Marines gave much better than they took. However, at this point, 1st Lt. William S. Bush, on the "taffrail," was shot in the head at close range while preparing to lead his men aboard the British ship. Hull would later exclaim, "In him the country has lost a valuable and brave officer." Bush's subordinate, 1st Lt. John Contee, later wrote to Wharton, "thus fell that brave and illustrious officer, who, when living, was beloved, and, now gone, is lamented by all. The conduct of the detachment was highly honorable to themselves and their country: and the execution, they did, is allowed, by the officers of Both Ships, to have been of essential service. Francis Mullen, Stationed in the Mizzen Top was the only Marine wounded."

Guerrière was the first major loss at sea for Britain, but it wouldn't be the last. After Dacres' surrender, Hull had the *Guerrière* scuttled. News of the victory beat Hull back to Boston harbor and upon arrival the ship was cheered and given an ovation by the huge crowd waiting by the wharves.[1]

During September, in order to strengthen Army Lt. Woolsey at Sackett's Harbor, Marines and sailors were being collected and rushed toward Rome, NY. Wharton had ordered Capt. John Hall, at New York City, to provide "three Sergeants, two Corporals, & Fifty privates ... in short, the Command ... must be as far as possible perfect in everything." Half would go to the *John Adams* on the Gennessee River and the balance, still commanded by Capt. Richard Smith, would report to Sackett's Harbor.

Marines aboard had little opportunity to utilize their muskets in the fight between the *United States* and the British frigate *Macedonian* on the 25th. The fight off Africa was a long-range gun duel with the odds in favor of the British ship, which had more and heavier gun power. However, Capt. J. S. Carden, RN, was hardly a match for Capt. Stephen Decatur, USN. Superior maneuvering and gunnery of the Americans placed more than one hundred shots in the enemy's hull, while also taking out a mast. *Macedonian*'s personnel losses were heavy while Decatur's losses were 12 men killed or wounded, of which two of the dead were Marines, Pvts. John Roberts and Michael O' Donnel. Private John Lalor was wounded. First Lieutenant William Anderson commanded the Marines with assistance from 2nd Lt. James L. Edwards. *Macedonian* was taken into Newport, Rhode Island, and later its flag joined that of *Guerrière* in Washington, where it was displayed at a grand ball.

By the end of the first year, the USN and their crews, including Marines, had taken 39 British ships as well as fought ten actions without firm results; they had had but one loss.

The following notice appeared in the British "Pilot," the authority for British naval affairs, early in 1813, "a third British frigate has struck to an American.... Lloyd's list contains notices of upward of five hundred British vessels captured in seven months by the Americans ... yet, down to this moment, not a single American frigate has struck her flag. They insult and laugh at our want of enterprise and vigor. They leave their ports when they please and return to them when it suits their convenience; they traverse the Atlantic; they beset the West India Islands; they advance to the very chops of the [English] Channel; they parade along the coasts of South America; nothing chases, nothing intercepts, nothing engages them but to yield them triumph." One very sad correspondent acknowledged that the "colonists" (damn them) were better at sea than the vaunted British navy.

Matters and location changed a bit during the month of March. Various ships of the U.S. fleet began to make the South Pacific Ocean a national "lake." The men of the U.S. frigate *Essex*, under Captain David Porter, had been giving British shipping an abusive time.[2] They had taken three whalers loaded with whale oil, two privateers and numerous prisoners, plus 80 additional guns. First Lieutenant John Gamble was the CO of all Marines in Porter's little fleet. Marines and crew of the *Essex* in small boats captured the British ship *Montezuma* in the Pacific on 29 April. Porter specifically detailed the attack and commended Gamble for his part in the capture.

Essex and her crew were taking British merchantmen and privateers in late May when on the 30th Porter took the British ship *Greenwich* in the Pacific Ocean and placed her into U.S. service as a part of his little fleet. This led to a very interesting period of history. The master placed aboard her by Porter was Capt. John Marshall Gamble, the first, and probably last, U.S. Marine to command a ship of the U.S. Navy.[3] This fleet would continue to torture the British for months to come.

Major Carmick was in command of a Marine detachment prepared to launch, on 16 April, an assault upon the Spanish-held town of Mobile (now in Alabama) when the Spaniards surrendered Fort Charlotte to him. In late April, Marines and U.S. soldiers were battling Indians in Florida in what was termed the Patriot's War (sometimes called the "First Seminole War"), which ended in May.

Meanwhile, Marines participated in the expedition led by Maj. Gen. Henry Dearborn, USA, and embarked in Chauncey's squadron, which landed in York, (Toronto) Canada on 27 April. While there, the Americans captured the 600-man garrison and set fire to the government buildings. A powder magazine exploded, however, and 320 Americans were killed in the explosion.[4] At the end of May, under the direction of USN Capt. Isaac Chauncey, Capt. Richard Smith and his Marines landed with their Army comrades of McComb's regiment and took Fort George on Lake Ontario.[5]

Though very ill-prepared — mainly with a new, untrained crew, and with officers limited in naval skills — Capt. James Lawrence decided to break the newly created British blockade off Boston with the frigate *Chesapeake* on the first day of June. His Majesty's Ship *Shannon*, one of the finest ships in the British navy, commanded by Capt. Philip Brooke, an equally good officer, was the target. Unfortunately for Lawrence, the *Shannon* had a record during the Napoleonic wars that was second to none.

Chesapeake came out like a tiger with Lawrence choosing to fight close up. Unluckily Lawrence missed on his first pass and *Chesapeake*'s broadside did little damage to *Shannon*. *Shannon* pulled around and blasted *Chesapeake* with broadsides that tore the American ship to pieces. Musketry fire was equally damaging, mortally wounding Lawrence and his second,

Lt. Augustus C. Ludlow, and the British boarded literally in minutes. Marines aloft fought the good fight but small swivel guns from *Shannon* cleared them from both platforms, killing most of them. Marines on deck fought until all were either killed or wounded, but the balance of the American crew was unable to withstand the volume of carnage and after but 15 minutes was forced to yield. One of the casualties was Marine 1st Lt. John Broom, who was killed in action. Lawrence's dying words were "Don't give up the ship" (or a variation), which had little effect. It was the first major American loss, but it would not be the last. The tide was beginning to turn for the heavier gunned British navy.

To help in defending the Gosport fort just below Norfolk, VA, 50 Marines under 2nd Lt. Henry B. Breckinridge were added to the seamen and Virginia militia on Craney Island. That morning of 22 June, 2,500 British Marines and infantry were landed about two miles northwest of the island in order to outflank the defenders. Then the British landed another 1,500 men from barges directly onto the island. The 700 American defenders were in for a busy time. "[When they] opened their fire, which was so well directed that the Enemy were glad to get off," the fire from the defenders sank three of the barges with their human cargo. Many prisoners were taken and the loss of life was considered to be great. Needless to state, the attempt failed.

Secretary of the Navy William Jones wrote a letter to Capt. Chauncey telling him of the manpower being sent for his forces on the lakes. He mentioned Capt. Robert D. Wainwright and 110 Marines from Sacketts Harbor which Chauncey "should expect to arrive by 15 July." This was about 20 percent of the total strength of the Corps at the time.

First Lieutenant John Gamble's ship *Greenwich* took a leading part on 14 July in Porter's little fleet action against three British ships, the *Seringapatam*, *New Zealander*, and *Charlton*, in the Pacific. According to his biographer, Gamble handled his ship like an experienced sailor. *Greenwich* hit the 14-gun *Seringpatam*, one of the best-equipped ships locally, with a broadside that toppled the mizzen-topmast and brought down the British Union Jack. Gamble's crew cheered, but the Britisher crowded all her remaining sail for the getaway, and Gamble did likewise to chase. Porter's ship, the *Essex*, hove into view, closing the escape gap, and *Seringpatam*, her captain not wishing another broadside, reduced sail and surrendered to Gamble. Porter signaled "Well Done."

On the last day of July, an American landing force of soldiers and Marines once again landed at York, on Lake Ontario, in Canada, and burned stores and the British military barracks. During much of August the U.S. arms were successful. On 12 August, anticipating landings by the British blockading force, Marines from the Washington barracks were sent to defend Annapolis, MD.

On 10 September, Captain Oliver Hazard Perry, possibly the most famous sailor of the U.S. Navy, was leading a small fleet of 10 jerry-built warships on Lake Erie against a superior-quality British fleet of six ships commanded by Capt. Robert H. Barclay. In the three-hour engagement, Perry, his sailors and Marines so badly defeated the British that Perry could not but proclaim, "We have met the enemy and they are ours." This decisive battle gave the United States complete control of this important lake and one big lift in spirits after so many defeats.

Marine casualties aboard their ships totaled one officer killed and one wounded, with 10 enlisted Marines killed and another 24 wounded. Fewer than 600 Marines, in all, were taking relatively severe casualties. But the following few weeks on the lakes saw some success for Chauncey's fleet.

In the Pacific Ocean, U.S. ships continued their aggressiveness during September. Sailors and Marines, under 1st Lt. Gamble, were landed on an island in the Marquesas on 29 October. From the journal kept by Midshipman William W. Feltus, "the savages shewed themselves about 11 O clock on the top of the Hill ... none of our men in sight but we can hear at times the report of their musketry." On the 4th of December, Cpl. Andrew Mahan, of Gamble's command, died as a result of close combat with natives in the Marquesas Islands on the previous day. On the 13th Porter left Gamble in charge of prizes collected during this long period in the Pacific. His orders were rather vague but essentially Gamble was to remain where he was in the Marquesas Islands until May 1814 and then sail for Valparaiso, Chile, with the two prize ships, *Seringapatam* and *Sir Andrew Hammond*.[6] The other ship, *New Zealander*, was placed in the hands of Master's Mate John J. King, but later was recaptured. On the day before Christmas, 1st Lt. John M. Gamble, now anchored off Nookaheevah Island in the Marquesas Islands with his three ships, landed part of his men and intimidated a hostile native force, regaining part of the property previously stolen by them.

When the year 1813 ended the USN had had many more conflicts with British ships than before. By year's end 61 British ships had been taken and another eight combats, undecided, were registered. Porter got whipped on 28 March 1814. Two British ships, the 53-gun frigate *Phoebe* and sloop *Cherub*, caught him and the *Essex* off Chile and after a three-hour battle captured him and the balance of his crew. Before their capture, *Essex* and its flotilla, including Gamble's little "fleet" then in the Marquesas Islands, had taken 40 British ships.

On land, in the area near Washington, D.C., Capt. Samuel Miller led a battalion of Marines from Washington to St. Leonard's Creek, about 12 miles from the mouth of the Patuxent River, to help stave off an expected British land attack from that direction. His force arrived there on 15 June to assist Comm. Joshua Barney's naval forces, then ashore. Captain Samuel Miller and soldiers of the U.S. Army managed to drive back the British fleet blockading St. Leonard's Creek. On the 28th, the British crew of the *Reindeer* attempted to board the American ship *Wasp* but the Marine detachment repelled them and then swept them away with musketry fire, causing numerous casualties amongst them.

On the 20th of July, Marines and soldiers on Lake Huron landed at the island of St. Joseph and attacked a fort of the same name. Few defenders were present, most had apparently fled and no one was present to surrender. Marines and soldiers landed at Mackinac Island on 4 August in an attempt to take Fort Mackinac, held by the British, with their Indian allies. However, after a bloody battle, they were repulsed. In his report, the army commander, Lt. Col. George Croghan, gave 1st Lt. Benjamin Hyde and his Marines credit for being steady and "ready to meet any exigency" while in reserve with the 28th Infantry. More Marines from Sinclair's squadron landed on 14 August with their army comrades at the mouth of the Nautauwasaga River on Lake Huron and captured a British blockhouse barricading further passage.

On the 24th of August, a rather extensive land battle occurred at Bladensburg, Maryland, in which U.S. Marines played an exceptional role. A British force, led by Maj. Gen. Robert Ross, was composed of veterans of the Napoleonic War in the Spanish peninsula. The American force, a small group of Army, Navy, and Marines, was gathered together to try to stop Ross, who was bent on capturing and destroying the new capitol at Washington, D.C.

This is a day which lives in Marine history as a superb example of the steadiness of

U.S. Marines under exceptional duress. As the British army landed, on the 23rd all American forces commanded by Brig. Gen. William H. Winder, USA,[7] had retreated, falling back toward Washington. On the 24th, part of Winder's soldiers, probably 5,000 men from the Army and militia, and Samuel Miller, with 103 Marines plus support from about 200 sailors of Comm. Joshua Barney's flotilla, moved toward Bladensburg to stand their ground against several attacks by the British army of regulars. About 1,400 American regulars against an estimated 7,000 British regulars.

The British came across open ground and were chewed up by the few but well-used artillery pieces and the regular's musketry. They tried again, this time against the Marines on the right flank. Again they were repulsed, losing heavily. After some time, Army forces began to retire, leaving the small force of Marines and sailors behind. Samuel Miller was placed in command of all remaining "infantry," including the sailors. Once again the British came on, this time managing to outflank the modest Marine-seaman formation but suffering huge losses. Barney, commanding the modest artillery, was wounded, as was Miller, and by now the overwhelming enemy numbers had completely surrounded the token American naval forces. Barney ordered his force to break out and retire without him because he and Miller and a few others were too badly wounded to move. They were captured but apparently were well-treated by the British. Also wounded was Marine Capt. Alexander Sevier, who may also have been captured. Marines suffered perhaps 35 casualties, and the naval flotilla men somewhat less. The enemy losses were 64 killed and at least another 185 men wounded, many of whom were senior officers, who were always prime targets.

Later, Captain David Porter, USN, who was directed to protect Washington, wrote a report to Secretary Jones commenting upon 1st Lt. Alfred Grayson (who received a brevet to captain) and Miller and "those veterans [Marines] who so much distinguished themselves under their Gallant though unfortunate commander [Miller] at Bladensburg." Other Marine officers who fought there were Capts. Anthony Gale and Samuel Bacon and 1st Lts. William Hall and Joseph L. Kuhn. They, their men, and the sailors made an indelible impression on all in attendance, including the veteran but casualty-heavy British army.

Marines and sailors ashore at White House, Virginia, shelled British ships on the Potomac River as they were withdrawing down the river on the 1st of September. The fighting U.S. sloop *Adams* had been withdrawn from the Atlantic, up to Hampden, ME, for repairs. Somehow getting wind of this, the enemy moved in a large force on 3 September and the local militia defense fell apart. Marines, commanded by Capt. Samuel E. Watson, and sailors defended the *Adams* and were exposed to enemy fire all around them. Captain Morris decided to fire his ship. With that, the survivors, in a desperate march, managed to make their way safely to Portland, ME.

The middle of September, from the 12th through the 14th, was another period of which Marines can be proud. The defense of Baltimore included the command of Marines by 1st Lt. Alfred Grayson, who, as seen above, was highly commended by Capt. David Porter.

The Marines were mainly with the battery of guns on both Hampstead and Loudonslager's Hills. (Present location now Patterson Park, Baltimore.) The British did not bring their ships that far up the Patapsco River when it was observed how well the city's defenses were arranged, and they soon withdrew.

On 16 September a landing party of Marines and soldiers went ashore at the pirate's stronghold on Grande Terre Island, LA. They killed or captured the defenders and wiped out the entire living space of what had been a serious nest of thieves. All but one of the pirates' ten vessels were captured or sunk. The pirates had been a boon to the economy of New Orleans but a hazard to peaceful shipping for many years. Nonetheless, they returned to this site on the 17th of October. Marines and soldiers came back and "wiped out the nest of vipers" once again.

Vice Admiral Sir Alexander Cochrane, RN, was charged with bringing Maj. Gen. Edward Pakenham's 6,000 veterans to capture New Orleans and control the outlet of the Mississippi River. They landed at New Orleans on 15 December 1814 and U.S. Navy Lt. Thomas C. Jones, commanding the U.S. flotilla of five gunboats on the lakes before the city, were the first subjects of the British attention. Thirty-five Marines aboard were part of the defense and as the five-boat flotilla withdrew from Pass Christian into Lake Borgne, they kept up a steady musketry fire that galled the British. British ships, large and ocean-going, were unable to move into the lake.

The British then improvised a fleet of small boats to move into the lake to clear it for the advance toward New Orleans. Jones held his fire until the British were within effective range and then had his men open up. The 15 barges and many more men of the British overwhelmed the fewer than 200 Americans. But, over several days, the small force had managed to delay the British, which consequently allowed Gen. Andrew Jackson to better prepare the defenses about the city.

Between 23 and 28 December the U.S. schooner *Carolina* opened up upon the British encampment prior to a probing attack launched by Jackson's forces. Although they badly hurt the British on shore, at least eight Marines were killed and another eight wounded during this encounter. That same night a company of Marines, led by Maj. Daniel Carmick, were part of Jackson's force in the spirited attack upon the British camp. The attack so upset the British that they were unable to regroup and launch an attack, thereby effectively saving New Orleans. Because of these savage "pinpricks" the British would be ineffective for at

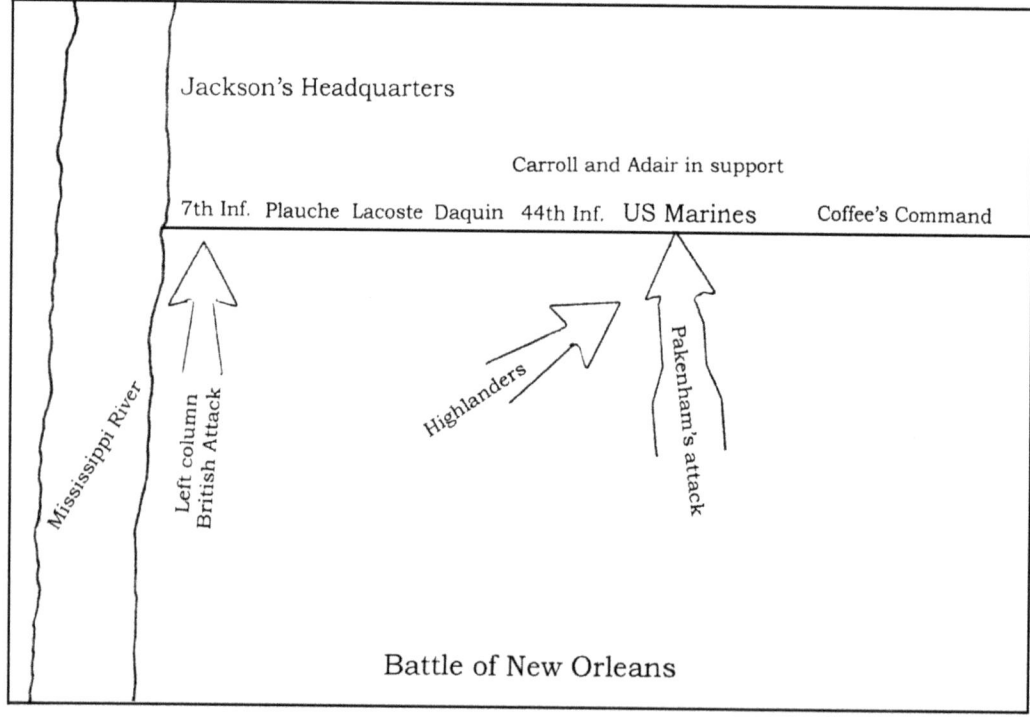

Battle of New Orleans

least a week and a half, giving Jackson more time to collect additional volunteers and prepare defenses.

When the year 1814 ended, the Americans at sea had taken 57 British ships and engaged in seven undecided actions. They had also lost two ships. Another one-sided year for the United States.

At daylight on 8 January 1815 Gen. Packenham formed up his army of 8,000 men for an all-out attack upon the American defenders, who numbered about 2,500. Among the latter, about the center of the line, was a detachment of Marines commanded by Maj. Carmick. The British came in a multi-line formation, initially undeterred by the accurate musket fire of the Americans.[8] Regardless, their ranks were rapidly depleted by the American musketry and by the time they arrived at the barricades, they were literally destroyed as a fighting force. At least 2,500 went down and many more were captured. Packenham and several of his generals were killed. American losses are said to have been 8 killed and 13 wounded. It was certainly a lopsided victory, one which counted for little since peace with Britain had already been signed at the Treaty of Ghent on 24 December, two weeks before. Unfortunately, the American agents at Ghent did not manage to obtain satisfactory results: the British still claimed the right to stop all ships and remove crew they could claim to be British subjects. That was a major reason the U.S. had declared war in the first place. That practice would provide more problems in future relations between the two nations.

Nevertheless, peace was still unknown in the middle of January 1815, when the *President*, ever-victorious until now, fell to four British frigates off Long Island. The *Endymion*, *Majestic*, *Pomona*, and *Tenedos* were the victors. During the fight the *Endymion* was badly hurt, especially taking heavy casualties from the U.S. Marines in the tops. First Lieutenant Levi Twiggs commanded the Marines aboard the *President*. Commodore Stephen Decatur later commended Twiggs and his Marines: "Twiggs displayed great zeal, his men were well supplied, and their fire was incomparable." Evidently the crew members went into British captivity.

News of the signing of the Treaty of Ghent, formally ending the war between the United States and Great Britain, finally reached the U.S. on 13 February, however the engagements between ships at sea continued for some time. The U.S. frigate *Constitution* captured the British ship *Susannah* off Lisbon, Portugal, and that same month captured two more British sloops, the *Cyane* and *Levant*, near Madeira Island. On 23 March the war at sea transferred south to just off the island of Tristan d'Acunha, midway between Argentina and Africa, where the U.S. sloop *Hornet* defeated the British brig *Penguin*. After a bashing, the latter signaled surrender, and then when *Hornet* drew close she opened fire, wounding Capt. James Biddle in the neck. He had difficulty, according to him, in restraining his crew from retaliating. A real surrender was concluded and *Penguin* fell into American hands. The British losses were heavy: 14 killed and 28 wounded. Biddle's loss was one killed and 11 wounded. After the Americans removed the wounded and prisoners the *Penguin* was scuttled.

In mid–June the "war" now switched to the East Indies off what is now Indonesia. The *Peacock* captured the British ship *Union* in the Straits of Sunda, the British ship *Venus* on the 21st, and the British ship *Brio de Mar* and the British brig *Nautilus* on the 29th and 30th, all in the same location. These appear to have been the last shots fired of that war.

> *Results:* The primary cause of the war was the continual harassment of U.S. commerce by the British fleet and the taking, with or without permission, of

sailors from American shipping. That was never really settled. Mostly it was warfare at sea, and, for the most part, the Americans held their own against a much larger navy. The Americans at Bladensburg were badly led, disorganized, and unprepared to face a veteran force. They were defeated, although the small naval force of sailors and Marines made a decent reputation, even among the enemy, for courage and ability under intense pressure despite being greatly outnumbered. The nation's capitol was burned down by the British in retaliation for the destruction of a few barns in the village of York, Ontario.

The war was in part because of Britain's previous loss to the Americans and its intention of showing the Americans who was "boss." The Americans badly defeated the British in the final land engagement of a war already ended, though this was not yet known to the participants. The British would continue to harass the U.S. for some years to come, until they eventually decided that they had enough of the Americans. They also began to need U.S. support and friendship.

5

Between the Wars

Date: 1816 to 1845.
Location: Nearly everywhere.
Involved: Pirates and slavers, Great Britain, Haiti, Creek and Seminole Indians, West Indies, Pacific islands. The United States was involved with nearly everyone.
Situation: During this period, the infant U.S. Navy and Marine Corps was kept busy, even though, generally speaking, it was less active on "foreign scenes" than it was previously or would be later. Most of the Marines, officers and enlisted, came from the coastal states, and their bloodlines were primarily from Britain and Ireland. Officers were commissioned directly from civil life, without any appreciable military service or experiences. The enlisted men were trained aboard their first ship or at their first duty station. They learned by doing.

In 1807 the Congress had finally passed a law prohibiting the importation of slaves into the United States. That act created an important duty for the U.S. Navy and Marine Corps. Following the war with Britain, the main task for the Atlantic fleet was the interception of slavers. Of course, that wasn't their only duty. Countering piracy in the coastal waters off North America, Africa, the West Indies and the East Indies took up sizable amounts of time as well. Fortunately, for a change, the U.S. was not officially at war. U.S. Marine manpower was less than 500 officers and enlisted.

In 1816, U.S. forces and American Indians engaged in several actions. In late July, at the request of the governor of Georgia, Marines from U.S. barges 149 and 154 assaulted, captured, and destroyed a fort on the Apalachicola River, FL. It had been manned by escaped slaves and their Seminole Indian comrades. Florida was still the property of Spain so this incursion could have, but did not, become an international incident. Exactly one month later, on 27 August, the U.S. schooner *Firebrand* was fired upon by a Spanish warship off Vera Cruz, Mexico. The Marines and crew stood to for possible further trouble, which did not occur.

On 3 March 1817, Congress passed the Peace Establishment Act, which set the strength of the military forces. The Marine Corps was set at 50 officers and 943 enlisted. Captain Samuel Miller was appointed the first incumbent of the newly created office of adjutant and inspector on the staff at Headquarters, Marine Corps. However, there were still fewer than 500 Marines.

Pétion, the ruler of the southern portion of Haiti, had seriously mistreated the U.S. consul in his district, and he had returned to the U.S. On 17 July, the State Department sent a replacement, Mr. Tyler, to reestablish relations. They provided him with 1st Lt. William Nicoll and 47 Marines from the frigate *Congress* to encourage Christophe, the dictator of northern Haiti, to accept the inevitable. Christophe, however, soon found that Tyler's written instructions were not "in due form," whatever that might have meant. So Tyler was turned away and he returned home.

Two days before Christmas, Marines from six Navy vessels joined their Army comrades in a joint Army-Navy operation that forced the surrender of pirates on Amelia Island, FL. Three days later, Gen. Andrew Jackson assumed command of the Florida contingents. He urged President Monroe to allow him to "conquer" Florida, which he claimed would only take him 60 days.

Jackson placed a heavy hand on Florida. In January 1818 he marched west and he took Pensacola on 24 May 1818. He also executed two British subjects who he claimed were aiding the enemy, escaped slaves and Seminole Indians. For this act, he was later condemned by Congress. Great Britain seethed but did nothing to retaliate. Late in 1819 it was declared that Jackson was only acting in self-defense and Spain was accused of aiding and abetting the hostiles. Spain gave up ownership of West Florida and also ceded East Florida to the U.S. in February 1819.

Sergeant McFadian commanded the Marine detachment from the U.S. sloop *Ontario* at Cape Disappointment, Oregon Territory, near the entrance of the Columbia River, as they raised the U.S. flag to signify ownership of the territory. This, on 19 August, was part of the ongoing dispute with Great Britain as to where the line between Canada and the U.S. should be.

Brevet Major Anthony Gale was appointed lieutenant colonel commandant of the Marine Corps on the 3rd of March 1819. His command included 21 officers and 664 enlisted men and he replaced acting commandant Brevet Major Archibald Henderson.

Off the west coast of Africa, during the first week in April 1820, Marines of the U.S. revenue cutter *Cyane* helped capture the schooners and crews of five slavers off Cape Mount and the Gallinos River. Two days later, in the same area, they took two more slavers.

Lieutenant Colonel Anthony Gale was held under arrest for trial by courts-martial on 30 August and Maj. Samuel Miller became acting commandant. On 18 September Gale faced trial and on 16 October was found guilty of the charges preferred (public drunkenness and carousing with loose women), and he was cashiered effective this date.[1]

From October to May 1822 three U.S. ships were stationed off the coast of South America to protect American commerce during the ongoing revolutionary wars being fought by various Spanish colonies against Spain.

On 2 January 1821, Brevet Major Archibald Henderson was appointed to replace Gale as lieutenant colonel commandant of the Marine Corps, retroactively effective back to 17 October 1820. Henderson, who would serve as commandant until 6 January 1859, would begin with a personnel total of 35 officers and 844 enlisted Marines. Nearly 39 years later he would have 47 officers and 1,804 enlisted Marines.

For the balance of the year Marines aboard the U.S. brig *Enterprise* would assist in the capture of six pirate vessels off Cape Antonio, Cuba.

5. Between the Wars

In the first and second weeks of April 1823, Marines and seamen from three U.S. vessels, the sloop *Peacock*, and the barges *Gallinipper* and *Mosquito*, landed east of Havana, Cuba, and chased pirates. A week later, the Marines and crew members captured a pirate schooner off Cuba. The same thing happened several times in July.

Led by Brevet Lt. Col. Robert D. Wainwright, 31 Marines from the Boston Navy Yard were called in on 12 March to suppress and subdue a mutiny in the local prison. This was one of the singular exploits of personal bravery by any Marine, during this year or after. Though cautioned by the guards not to enter, but to fire through the windows from outside, the Marines went into the building. There they found 283 prisoners holding a guard hostage against the release of three of their number who were to be flogged. The prisoners had managed to arm themselves with weapons taken from captured guards and, when the Marines arrived, they threatened to open fire if the Marines advanced.

This was the day of the single-shot musket; though it had a bayonet attached, one shot was all the gun could get off, and there were 31 Marines versus 283 highly agitated prisoners. Wainwright formed his men into two ranks and ordered them in front of the prisoners to load with ball, which gave the prisoners a concept of what lie in store. Wainwright ordered the prisoners to disperse and they responded with a roar of threats. Wainwright gave the order to level muskets and then took out his watch, telling the prisoners, "you have three minutes to leave this hall. If at the end of that time any man remains, he will be shot dead. I speak no more."

For two minutes not a person moved a muscle or made a sound. Then two or three men in the rear began to leave the group, a few more followed their example, and before the final half minute passed, the prisoners in that crowded hall had panicked and it was cleared of everyone who wasn't a Marine. This moment in history was recorded as a heroic event in what was a common textbook of the period, *McGuffey's Eclectic Reader*, and remained there for the next 75 years.

Several American merchant ships had been attacked and had their goods confiscated by pirates operating from Frajado, Puerto Rico. At the ships' owner's request, Navy Lt. Charles T. Platt of the U.S. ship *Beagle* landed at Frajado, a Spanish possession, and patiently awaited recognition from the senior official there. This was on 26 October.

He was then rudely treated, subjected to insults and physical assaults, and had his commission forcibly taken from him. It was called a forgery and he was accused of being a pirate. The Spaniards refused his entreaties for the commission's return and his release. Finally, with a boot, he was allowed to return to his ship.

As his ship was leaving the port they came across another American ship, the *John Adams*, with Comm. David Porter aboard. When Porter learned of what had happened, the two ships returned to the port and 14 Marines under the command of 1st Lt. Thomas B. Barton were disembarked with orders to spike the cannon in the fort looming above them. That mission was satisfactorily carried out and the Marines returned without further incident.

Porter waited until 14 November (possibly waiting for official sanction?), then landed with 200 Marines and sailors with a letter to the Alcade (mayor) demanding satisfaction for the affair concerning Lt. Platt. Navy Lt. Cornelius K. Stribling, under a flag of truce carried by 2nd Lt. Horatio N. Crabb and his 27 Marines, was dispatched to deliver the letter. Stribling, followed by the governor and the captain of the port, returned to Porter. They very humbly apologized and promised that no insults or harm would ever come to any U.S. officer ever again. Porter accepted the apologies and marched his men through the town "to see the sights."²

Most of the activity during 1827 was limited to October and early November and to the Aegean Sea, off Greece. Marines and sailors aboard the U.S. sloop *Warren* engaged, defeated, and captured two pirate vessels in the Cyclades (Kikládhes) Islands off southern Greece. A week or more later, the U.S. schooner *Porpoise* engaged 200 pirates in the Doro Passage, the Cyclades Islands. The following days she engaged several more Greek pirate vessels off Andros, in the same islands. At the end of the month, the U.S. sloop *Warren* and her crew members continued to be very busy with pirates in the Aegean Sea. On the 25th they captured a brig, and on the 29th they recaptured a pirate prize, an Austrian brig, in the Cyclades. On 1 November Marines and sailors landed and burned the town of Miconi, also in the Cyclades, and on 7 November they landed once again to capture pirate vessels on the island of Andros.

In December 1828, Marines and crewmen aboard the U.S. sloop *Eric* captured the Argentinean privateer *Federal* off the island of St. Bartholomew in the West Indies.

Marine Corps Headquarters' center building was destroyed by fire on 20 February 1829. Many valuable and irreplaceable records were demolished, especially those relating to heroic deeds by Marines for the previous 45 years. The Corps' total personnel were 43 officers and 852 enlisted Marines.

On 5 June 1830 the U.S. schooner *Grampus* captured a slaver, the brig *Fenix*, off Cape Haitien, Haiti.

In 1831 Argentine officials had been trying to establish a claim to the Falkland Islands; in the course of this effort they captured three American ships that were catching seals. They held the ships and the crews prisoner. On the morning of 1 January 1832, two Marine officers and 15 men were landed from the U.S. sloop *Lexington* to discourage that sort of behavior. Fifteen minutes later more Marines and sailors were landed to support the first group. The three vessels and crews were released. In the ensuing discussions it was learned that the American citizens on the island (20 men, 8 women, and 10 children) wished to leave. They were protected by Marines and conveyed to the ship for transport home.

Trouble was brewing in Buenos Aires, Argentina, and in mid-month Comdr. John P. Zantzinger had been in the harbor aboard the U.S. ship *Natchez* but without the necessary manpower or equipment to adequately do the job required. He requested back-up and on 21 October Comdr. M. T. Woolsey arrived at that port on the U.S. ship *Lexington*. Woolsey ordered 43 Marines and sailors ashore to protect American citizens and their property. The detachment remained ashore until 15 November, when it was determined that events had simmered down sufficiently for them to return to the *Lexington*.

—m—

Date: 24 December 1835 to 23 July 1838.
Location: Florida swamps.
Involved: Various Native American tribes — Creeks, but mainly Seminoles — and Black ex-slaves versus the U.S. Army and U.S. Marines.
Situation: The major military force in the Second Seminole War was the U.S. Army, but it included a large contingent of U.S. Marines and some U.S. Navy seamen. These forces were trying to "collect" the Indians for shipment west.

Hostilities broke out when Chief Osceola and his Indians refused to accept a treaty signed by other Indian chiefs, agreeing to a move from their home grounds to wherever the U.S. government decided to send them.

In Florida, on 24 December 1835 a U.S. Army column moving between Fort Brooke on Tampa Bay and Fort King was ambushed and massacred by Indians and escaped Black slaves living amongst them; this is considered to be the commencement of the real Florida Indian Wars. This war would continue for six years and require, in addition to most of the U.S. Army, the presence of many U.S. Marines, including the commandant. Odds against the Seminoles were heavy; an estimated 4,000 Seminoles, perhaps 1,000 of them warriors, were pitted against 17 million American citizens with an army estimated at 7,000, plus 1,000 Marines and Navy ships and sailors as offshore support. As we shall witness, the odds of eight to one weren't all that heavy, or, in most cases, even sufficient.

On the 28th of December Marines and sailors from the sloop of war *Vandalia* were landed at Pensacola to support the U.S. Army. On 1 January 1836, Marines and sailors began their journey from Pensacola to Fort Brooke at Tampa. The West India Squadron, commanded by Comm. Alexander J. Dallas, which included the frigate *Constellation* and sloop of war *St. Louis*, on 22 January landed their 57 Marines and seven sailors at Fort Brooke as reinforcement against anticipated Indian attacks. Their commander was 1st Lt. Nathaniel S. Waldron. The small force landed just in time to halt a serious Indian attack upon Fort Brooke and they remained at the fort until additional Army forces arrived to relieve them.

Marines and sailors from the U.S. sloop of war *Vandalia* on 17 March participated in a boat expedition on the Manatee River and around the keys of Tampa Bay. After modest success, they returned to their ship on 28 March. Meanwhile Waldron and his Marines accompanied an Army expedition on 22 March which had several skirmishes with Indians. On 31 March Waldron and his Marines plus seamen from the *Vandalia* proceeded from Tampa Bay to Charlotte Harbor, where they once again joined Army troops in an expedition up the Myacca River. Having engaged the Indians several more times, they returned on 27 April. On 18 May Comm. Dallas wrote to Maj. Keney Wilson, USA, requesting the return to their ships of Waldron's Marines but Wilson responded "the Marine force is still considered, by me, as a very essential part of this command." Waldron and his Marines would continue to support the various Army expeditions that summer and also to occupy Fort Brooke until August 1836.

President Andrew Jackson readily accepted Colonel Commandant Archibald Henderson's offer of a regiment of Marines to assist the Army in the southeastern U.S. Jackson then issued orders on 21 May for all available Marines to report for duty with the U.S. Army. Three days later Henderson reported to the War Department for duty in compliance with General Order No. 33, which directed that "all the disposable force on shore" proceed to Alabama. By reducing most shore establishments to a sergeant's guard and shipboard detachments to a corporal's guard, he had managed to assemble most all the available Marines in the Marine Corps.[3] At that time the total was 46 officers and 869 enlisted Marines, more or less.

Henderson, with the 1st Battalion, U.S. Marines, had proceeded via steamer to Charleston, SC, then by rail to Augusta, GA. After a march of 224 miles, the battalion arrived on 23 June at Camp Henderson for duty with the Army at Columbus, GA, to fight the Creek Indians in that area.

Lieutenant Colonel William H. Freeman, USMC, led the 2nd Battalion in reinforcing

Henderson's unit near Columbus, GA, on 1 July. He and his 160 officers and men were instead rerouted to Ft. Mitchell in Alabama. But in early October Henderson and his battalion were joined by Freeman and his men to form a Marine regiment of six companies at Ft. Brooke and Waldron's detachment left Brooke to return to its ships. It was decided that since the war with the Creeks was over, the Marines should be temporarily sent to Apalachicola, FL, to aid in fighting the Seminoles in that vicinity. Henderson and his regiment arrived at Apalachicola on 16 October and would serve in numerous engagements against the Seminoles under Gen. Thomas S. Jessup's general direction.

Meanwhile, on 13 October, two Marine officers and 95 Marines, plus 50 seamen from Commodore Dallas' West India Squadron, embarked aboard the *Vandalia*, sailed toward shore and then boarded small boats at Key West and voyaged up the Miami River to New River. During this period they too came under the overall command of Gen. Jessup, USA. They spent nearly two months searching for Indians but had no success, returning to their ships on 9 December.

Elsewhere, in northern Florida, Marines, soldiers, and their Creek Indian associates,[4] under the command of 1st Lt. Andrew Ross, were involved in a firefight with Seminole Indians at Wahoo Swamp, FL. Ross was mortally wounded during that battle, dying on 11 December.

Colonel Henderson and his command, along with Army troops, left Ft. Brooke for the interior of Florida on 3 January to search for Seminole Indians. They would continue serving in the field, not returning to Ft. Brooke until 18 May 1837. Meantime, on the 8th, Order no. 34, of the Army of the South, divided the Army into two brigades. Colonel Henderson was directed to command the 2nd Brigade.[5]

Later that month, Capt. John Harris (a future commandant), with his company of Marines, under the overall command of Lt. Col. Caulfield, USA, took part in a fight with Chief Osuchee and a large band of his Indians. The outcome was the death of Osuchee and several of his Indians, plus the capture of several more.

On the 27th of January one of the most important battles of the war occurred. The main body of Seminoles was engaged at Hatchee Lustee, near and in the Great Cypress Swamp, by Henderson and his brigade, which also included Army troops. The Marines bore the main part of the Indians' attack, with Henderson in the forefront. At the colonel's command, a fierce charge enabled the brigade to capture two dozen Indians and former slaves. A company of Marines was charged with protecting the captives while the main body continued the fight and followed the retreating Seminoles into the swamp. At nightfall, as the Indians disappeared into the swamp, Henderson gave up the impossible task of continuing the search. Two Marine noncommissioned officers and two privates were killed in this action and a number were wounded. This battle, however, was the end of the war, or close to it.

With the seeming end to the Seminole War, seagoing Marines returned to their various vessels in the vicinity.[6] But it wasn't until 23 May 1837 that Henderson and a part of his staff left Lt. Col. Samuel Miller as senior Marine officer on hand and returned to Washington.

> *Results:* Eventually, after many years and much bloodshed, the U.S. government was successful. However, it took many soldiers and a large number of Marines in addition to numerous USN vessels to finally defeat the Indians, at a cost of about $40 million and the loss of 2,000 white lives. The number of Native or Black slave lives lost remains unknown. Unfortunately, the surrendered

Indians were shipped west, never to see their beloved swamps ever again. Collected slaves were, when possible, returned to their "masters." There was a third Seminole war (1855–1858) but some of the Indians continued to refuse to move and it wasn't until 1934 that the last treaty with the Seminoles was finally signed.

Date: 7 and 8 February 1832 and 2 January 1839.
Location: Quallah Battoo (Kuala Batu), Sumatra.
Involved: U.S. Naval forces versus natives of the port.
Situation: The conflict was seen as retribution for the murder of American sailors in 1831.

The 7th of February was the day for retaliation. A year before, a mate and two seamen had been murdered by natives attacking the commercial vessel *Friendship* while at port in Quallah Battoo. Commodore John Downes and his ship the *Potomac* arrived at the port on the 5th to retaliate. The afternoon of the 6th he and numerous officers went ashore to reconnoiter the territory. Downes decided to attack, even though there were many natives that appeared to be well-armed and in a feisty mood.

At 0215 the landing party started ashore. It was composed of 250 Marines and sailors, all of whom were anxious to even up the score. Navy Lt. Irvine Shubrick was in overall command with 1st Lt. Alvin Edson commanding the Marines. The landing party arrived ashore at about 0515 and formed up into three divisions, two of sailors and one of Marines. Shubrick had Edson and his Marines advance first and attack a fort at the rear of the town while a division of sailors attacked the nearest fort. In two hours, after desperate defenses, both forts had been taken.

Meanwhile, the third division of sailors had attacked another fort. This third fort was the most difficult. After the Marines and sailors had completed their assigned conquest of the first two forts they arrived to lend a hand, helping to take that third fort. All three were demolished by fire, as was the town. It was then that another, fourth fort, was discovered. It too was taken by assault and by 0730 the American flag had been raised over it to signal the ship that the victory was theirs. No captives were taken because all the natives were either killed or had fled the attack.

The casualties for the Americans were relatively light. One Marine (Pvt. Benjamin T. Brown) and one sailor (William P. Smith) were killed while seven others were wounded, including two Marines (Pvts. Daniel G. Cole and James G. Huston). The dead bodies were properly disposed of at sea.

Shortly after midnight, Downes moved in closer to the shore and, at 1220 on 8 February opened fire upon the town. His bombardment lasted about an hour, after which the defenders raised the white flag. Downes decided to wait for daylight before moving in. That morning a few officers protected by several Marines boated in and looked about the town, returning aboard at 1430. That evening, at 1810, a native boat headed out for the warship. In it was a delegation of native chiefs who humbly expressed the "greatest penitence for their misdeeds." Adding "please no more big guns be fired." Downes warned them that further transgressions would bring consequent "rewards." They promised future kindliness to American seamen, and Downes was gratified that his mission was satisfactorily completed. He and his ships returned to his station in the Pacific Ocean.

The same sort of trouble at Quallah Battoo began once again seven years later, in late December 1838. On 25 December the U.S. frigate *Columbia* and corvette *John Adams* opened fire on that town. They waited until the late morning of the 28th, when the natives raised a white flag at 1000 and a chief came aboard and promised to refrain from hostilities. Three days later the ships arrived off Mucke, Sumatra, and Lt. Thomas Turner went ashore to discuss with the chiefs the attacks upon American ships and individuals. The results of his visit were unsatisfactory and Comdr. Thomas W. Wyman decided to shell the town, continuing until about 1130. Soon after, Marines and sailors from the U.S. sloop *John Adams* landed to obtain retribution for previous depredations. The situation was less than satisfactory, so that afternoon additional Marines and sailors from the U.S. frigate *Columbia* went ashore to support the earlier landing party. It is assumed that 1st Lt. D. D. Baker, USMC, was the Marine officer in charge ashore. Both units together destroyed the villages and while both ships continued intermittent shelling, the men returned to their vessels by 1500, bringing back prisoners. Commodore George C. Read was apparently satisfied that they had accomplished their task and his ships sailed away.

Results: Several native forts were destroyed and once again, the natives promised never to harass American ships or individuals.

Date: 12 July 1840.
Location: Fiji Islands, Samoa and the Gilberts.
Involved: Local natives versus the U.S. Navy and Marines.
Situation: Attacks upon American naval forces prompted military reaction by the same. A Naval exploratory force under Lt. Charles Wilkes, USN, received a very unpleasant reception at Sualib Bay in the Fiji Islands when it was fiercely attacked by the locals.

Marines, led by Quartermaster Sergeant Marion A. Stearns, and seamen from the U.S. sloops *Vincennes* and *Peacock* landed at the town of Sualib on 12 July 1840 to settle the hash of the natives. They proceeded to burn the 60 or so huts, then returned to their ships. On the 26th, while the ships' working crews were collecting provisions at that same beach, the natives attacked them, killing two naval officers and wounding a seaman. One of the dead was Wilkes' nephew. Enraged, Wilkes landed almost his entire force with himself leading and Stearns in charge of the Marines. Ashore, Wilkes divided his group into two columns, with Lt. Cadwalader Ringgold leading the second and he leading the first, they converged upon the town of Sualib. The natives defended their town behind coconut walls while Wilkes held back beyond the range of hurled spears and arrows, hurling rockets and burning the entire town down around them.

The American forces then burned down the other principal town, Arro. The next day the natives begged the Americans to grant them peace. Wilkes believed they had taught the natives a lesson and that henceforth American seamen would be treated decently. They would be for nearly 15 years.

Trouble occurred in Samoa on the 25th of February 1841 when several American seamen were murdered by the locals. Seventy Marines and sailors from the *Peacock* landed at Upolu, Samoa, and Lt. William L. Hudson, USN, demanded the murderers be turned over to him for trial. From the local chief he received a resounding "NO." The only recourse open to the Americans was the destruction of that town. The *Peacock* was brought about in order to fire a broadside or two and Hudson's force was again landed. The ship's fire and landing party destroyed all the buildings but the natives had long since disappeared. The ship's landing party was retrieved and then proceeded toward two other towns along the coast. The results were the same. Natives had disappeared but buildings were destroyed and all canoes found throughout the area were torched. It was then determined that the punishment for all murders had been sufficient.

The men of the *Peacock* were once again landed, this time on Drummond's Island, in the Gilbert Islands on 6 April, to rescue whoever remained from a vessel wrecked "some time previously."[7] The story related was that the natives had boarded the wrecked ship, slaughtered the captain and crew and taken the captain's wife and young son into captivity. Hudson took his ship within four miles of Utirod, the village where the catastrophe had occurred.

Ashore the small scientific body was well-received by the local natives, who provided access to most of the area. Inquiries about the white woman and her child were met with silence. Their observations were hindered when they attempted to enter certain huts. On the 7th another landing and four hours were also "wasted." When the sailors returned to their boats they discovered that Seaman John Anderson was missing. Inquiries about him brought forth hostility and obvious preparations for militant actions.

When Anderson failed to appear after two days, Hudson then sent ashore a party of 80 Marines and seamen under the command of Lt. William M. Walker, USN. About 800 natives met them and began threatening the Americans with a war-dance. Walker demanded the surrender of Anderson, which the natives paid no attention too. Then the natives pushed out into the water and threatened the landing craft. Walker ordered a retreat into deeper water and had a rocket fired directly into that crowd. They immediately fled, but their courage returned and so did they.

Out into the water they came, once again, and this time were met with volleys of musketry by the force in the boats. Many natives fell and the war-chief stood alone when all his remaining warriors took off once again. The Americans landed and began destroying the village. They succeeded in the destruction but failed to learn what happened to Anderson or the white woman and her child, none of whom were ever heard from again.

> *Results:* Firepower provided the necessary advantage and the U.S. emerged somewhat victorious, at least temporarily.

President Andrew Jackson issued orders on 10 April 1833 that the uniform of U.S. Marines be changed from blue with red trim to green with buff trim. That was for 853 enlisted Marines with, I suppose, the same changes for the then 43 officers.

Manpower totals in the Corps jumped by nearly 50 percent when at year's end (30 June 1835) there were 68 officers and 1,349 enlisted men on the Marine Corps rolls. The cause of the drastic increase was the act passed in 1834 to establish the Corps as part of the naval establishment. At the same time, Henderson was promoted to colonel.

During local unrest, on 10 December, four Marines from the U.S. ship *Brandywine* were sent ashore to protect the American consul's residence in Lima, Peru. Difficulties continued and a week later the entire Marine detachment was sent ashore, where it would remain until 24 January 1836.

Colonel Commandant Archibald Henderson issued orders on 4 July 1840 to alter the uniform colors of Marines from green to blue with red trim.

On 6 March 1843 Col. Commandant Henderson was awarded a brevet rank of brigadier general for his services in the war against the Seminole Indians. He was the first Marine ever to become a general officer and at that time he commanded 43 officers and 1,041 enlisted Marines.

> *Result:* There were none of any consequence. Marines and sailors did their duty for the several years after the war with Great Britain, but generally it was a down time, with nothing of major historical significance happening for several years. The next few years would find an entirely different United States, one which was usually at war.

6

War with Mexico

Date: 18 May 1846 to 17 June 1848.
Location: Mexico's east coast, west coast, and California.
Involved: Mexican Army versus the U.S. Army, Navy and Marines.
Situation: The Marines, regardless of the words of their hymn, were limited in their role in the war with Mexico. They played a larger role in the conquest of California and aboard ships plying the coastline of Mexico, landing east and west at various places. They also supported Gen. Scott's landing at Vera Cruz, and a relatively small number participated in the invasion of Mexico and performed extremely well at Chapultepec and entering Mexico City's gates, though the senior leadership (of all arms) was at times questionable.

East Coast

In order to help protect General Zachary Taylor's army's left flank, Marines and seamen from Comm. David Connor's Home Squadron landed at Port Isabel on 8 May and took the fort (renamed Fort Polk) at the mouth of the Rio Grande. This was the first war-like move by the U.S. against Mexico, and it happened four days before war was declared on 12 May 1846 by Congress. On 18 May a detachment of about 200 Marines and seamen from the *Cumberland* and the *Potomac* voyaged up the Rio Grande for about 15 miles to assist Army Lt. Col. Wilson's few men in establishing a post at Burrita on the south (Mexican) side of the river. These would prove to be the first troops to actually invade Mexico. When, two days later, the Mexican army retreated south, the naval force returned downriver to their ships. These moves were followed on 24 May by Marines participating in the attack by the U.S. sloop *St. Louis* upon the fortress of Tampico.

Marines participated in an expedition to Alvarado, Mexico, on 7 August. However, because the weather was bad, the landing force was withdrawn. The following month, on 7 September, Marines of the U.S. sloop *Warren* boarded and captured the Mexican brig *Malek Adhel* off the coast at Mazatlan. Then, on 15 October, Marines of Connor's squadron again landed to assault Alvarado, but overall accomplished little.

Captain Matthew C. Perry's portion of the squadron sailed for the entrance of the Tabasco River, arriving on 23 October and landing his Marines and seamen at Frontera. From the port his 200 Marines and seamen sailed up the Tabasco River for San Juan Bautista (aka Tabasco). Two days later, Capt. Alvin Edson, a long-serving Marine, led his 70 Marines and soon took the town. Soon after they were recalled to their ships.

At the request of the Army, Connor and Perry planned to attack Tampico, arriving offshore on 14 November. Shelling began at once and within minutes the townspeople raised a white flag. All Mexican troops had already been withdrawn from Tampico and it had been held only by civilians. Five days later it was learned that the Mexicans holding the town of Panuco had control of a large store of weapons and ammunition. Thus 20 Marines under Edson and 12 seamen boarded the steamer *Spitfire* and schooner *Petrel* and traveled 25 miles upriver to capture and destroy the town and its stores and weapons. Afterward, Edson and his command returned to Tampico.

Marines participated in Perry's squadron's taking of two Mexican ships on 27 December, the schooners *Amelia* and *Isabel* off Alvarado. This would be the last activity of the Marines until the following year. Meanwhile, action was taking place on the west coast, in which Marines were involved (see below).

Major General Winfield Scott, USA, commander in chief, U.S. Army, was finally allowed to lead a field army in this war. Politics had previously interfered, but now his greatly expanded army of mainly volunteers were ready for insertion into Mexico proper.

Connor had brought Scott's force to Vera Cruz, and on 9 March 1847, they were landed and began a siege of the city. A battalion of more than 200 Marines, commanded by Capt. Edson, was attached to the Third Artillery Regiment as part of the 1st Division (Brig. Gen. William J. Worth) and played an important role in the nearly month-long siege. Upon landing, the division moved forward and occupied a line of hills about a mile and a half inland to protect further landings. Edson and his men continued serving for the month-long siege.[1] On 18 April Edson's force, composed of over 160 Marines from the various ships in Perry's squadron, were part of the naval landing force which captured the Mexican city of Tuxpan. After destroying the city's various weaponry, the Marines were withdrawn to their ships. Fleet Marines were kept busy during this period. Marines from the *Mississippi* were part of a force from Perry's squadron which landed and took Ciudad del Carmen on 15 May 1846.

Secretary of the Navy George Bancroft ordered the formation of a Marine regiment to serve with Scott's army in the invasion of Mexico. On 21 May the force of six companies, composed of 23 officers and 291 enlisted, was organized into two battalions, with Lt. Col. Samuel Watson in overall command. The 1st Battalion was commanded by Maj. Levi Twiggs and the 2nd Battalion by Brevet Maj. William Dulany. It was noted that upon arrival, they might see soldiers from Scott's army incorporated into the "regiment" to fill it out. Being Marines, this would have been a sore point.

Edson's battalion, now numbering about 230 officers and men, went ashore on 14 June with a naval landing force from Perry's squadron and proceeded up the Tabasco River to participate in the taking of the town of San Juan Bautista during this second Tabasco expedition. Approximately 1,100 men participated in this exercise. The Mexicans had fortified several places before reaching Tabasco and the fighting was raging (temperatures also soared under the broiling sun) but at each encounter, the Mexicans were forced to flee. Perry's ships came upriver and shelled San Juan Bautista, forcing it to surrender. Though Perry decided to garrison the town, he only had 44 Marines and about 50 seamen. Losses and yellow fever caused Perry to recall them on 19 July. During much of this period, Col. Commandant Henderson made numerous unsuccessful efforts to have Perry release his fleet Marines to join Watson's formation when they moved towards Mexico City.

Watson's Marine regiment arrived off Vera Cruz on 29 June and was soon joined by an additional 66 officers and men from some of the ship detachments. Scott's army had already moved toward Mexico City and Watson's force rapidly moved to join them. They managed to make contact in mid–July and Watson's force was assigned duty with Brig. Gen. Franklin Pierce's brigade. Pierce placed Watson and his men in the rear of his formation to protect his animal train and rear. Their accelerated movement soon brought them up with the advance forces under Scott.

The advance by the Americans was subjected to intense attacks along their line of march. Pierce later wrote that due to the Marines' efficiency, he lost neither men nor animals en route through the guerrilla-infested countryside.[2] Marines defeated an attempt by the Mexicans to destroy the National Bridge crossing the Antigua River, which made the Army's crossing possible.

For the continued march the Marines were attached to Maj. Gen. John A. Quitman's 4th Division, and Watson also assumed command of a detachment of the 2nd Pennsylvania Regiment. The Americans had two days of rest before continuing their march on Mexico City.[3]

During the balance of August and early September, Scott's army proceeded toward Mexico City, suffering daily harassment from guerrillas. Climbing mountains and marching down into valleys, the army had a long arduous journey. After arrival in the immediate vicinity of Mexico City, Scott made the mistake of agreeing to an armistice in order to stop the fighting and killing. However, erroneously believing weakness on Scott's part, Santa Anna violated the conditions and on 6 August the armistice was over. Pierce and his brigade, including Watson's men, joined Scott's army at Puebla, Mexico, on 6 August, but because the Marine regiment was very short of manpower it was downgraded to a battalion.

Scott, realizing that the Castle of Chapultepec held the key to Mexico City, made the decision to take it first. September 13th was the big day for the American forces. In Quitman's division, two storming parties, each of 250 Marines, were formed and commanded by Maj. Levi Twiggs and Capt. John G. Reynolds. They were supplied with scaling ladders, pickaxes and crowbars for going over the walls. Another detachment of Marines under Capt. George H. Terrett of Watson's battalion joined with a small U.S. Army force under 1st Lt. U. S. Grant to advance and force entrance through the San Cosme gate at Chapultepec. Major Watson continued to command the balance of the Marines not yet engaged.

Because the ground was exceedingly swampy, the assaulting force was forced to stay on the causeway leading to the fortress. Concentrated, they were prime targets for the snipers on the walls. Because of the extremely heavy and intense fire, Twiggs and his men were forced to drop down beside the causeway. From there they returned fire. As Twiggs attempted to lead his men back up onto the causeway to again advance, he was shot dead and the surviving Marines did not leave their protective cover. Watson received orders from Quitman to remain where he was. Watson obeyed Quitman's command and refused to budge.[4]

Meanwhile, Terrett's few Marines were far in advance and continuing to lead. His subordinates are to be noted: 1st Lts. Jabez C. Rich, William Young, John D. Simms, and 2nd Lts. Edward McD. Reynolds, Charles G. McCawley, and Charles A. Henderson.[5] Gathering stragglers as he advanced, Terrett and his command continued forward, chasing Mexicans that were retreating from Chapultepec. Finally, along with Grant's men, he took the San Cosme Gate which was the key to Mexico City. Terrett was now down to about 15 or 20 men. The Army and Marines continued to advance right into the city, becoming the first American troops to enter Mexico City.

In the meantime, Watson's Marines had entered the fortress of Chapultepec, capturing about 30 Mexicans who remained. They then were ordered by Quitman to advance to support those troops taking the San Cosme Gate. All Marine officers engaged were later promoted one rank by brevet.[6] Essentially, this was the end of the fighting. The sometime military leader, Santa Anna, had disappeared to someplace north and wouldn't return until many months later, after the Americans left.[7] The few Mexican leaders remaining in the city chose to agree to an armistice. On the morning of 14 September, Quitman's division marched to the Grande Plaza in Mexico City and the Marines were assigned as guards at the National Palace—known as "The Halls of Montezuma."

This ended the serious fighting on the east coast. Negotiations between representatives of the United States and Mexico began nearly at once. There was constant trouble in the streets of Mexico City between the conquered and conquerors, but nothing extraordinary considering the natives' natural attitude toward the occupation of their capital by foreigners. Unaware that peace was being negotiated, the U.S. naval forces on the west coast continued to harass the Mexicans.

In March, Maj. John Harris, USMC, and his battalion were ordered to occupy Alvarado.[8] His total force included four companies of 90 men each in addition to ten officers.

West Coast

One of the most embarrassing occurrences for the U.S. in the 19th century happened on 21 October 1842. Marines and seamen from the U.S. frigate *United States* were landed in Monterey, CA, at the direction of the captain, Comdr. Thomas ap Catesby Jones.[9] Jones had sailed into the harbor and, under the erroneous impression that the U.S. and Mexico were at war (which most Navy personnel had been expecting), demanded the surrender of that town. Facing Marines and their muskets and bayonets, the town leaders complied at once. First Lieutenant George W. Robbins, USMC, and his men raised the Stars and Stripes over the city hall as the local Americans cheered. It was then that the local American Consul Thomas O. Larkin brought several newspapers out to Jones, showing clearly that the war had not yet begun. Jones apologized to the local alcalde and had his force return to the ships. Surprisingly, and fortunately, Mexico didn't make a great issue out that situation.

Three years later, on 18 October 1845, President Polk met with 1st Lt. Archibald H. Gillespie, USMC, and gave him secret orders and documents to deliver to the American Consul Thomas Larkin, and others to deliver to Capt. John C. Fremont, USA, then exploring somewhere in California. In time, this would be a very important association involving the eventual adoption of California as a state within the union.

After a relatively hazardous journey through a seething Mexico, one of the least credited individuals of the entire period, Gillespie, arrived at Monterey, CA, on 17 April 1846 with a secret message for the American Consul Thomas Larkin. The message from the State Department gave him instructions on how and when he should begin to turn the current discontent among the locals, Anglos as well as natives, against the Mexican government. Within a few weeks Gillespie journeyed east and north to find the explorer Capt. John Fremont on 7 May, delivering to him a confidential message from President Polk and his father-in-law, a U.S. senator. Essentially, that message was to encourage Fremont, then on a "geographical study," to raise a force of so-called "Anglos" and lead a revolt against Mexican authorities. Now captain, Gillespie would remain in California during the entire period and provide superb services to the American cause, earning a brevet to major effective on 6 December 1846.

When Captain John D. Sloat, USN, arrived at Monterey Bay on the 5th of July, he went ashore to discuss the situation with Consul Larkin and both agreed that the Americans should capture the town. On the 7th, 250 Marines and seamen from Sloat's Pacific Squadron, which now included the *Savannah*, *Cyane*, and *Levant*, landed at Monterey, occupying the town without resistance, and declared California to be part of the United States. The 85 Marines were commanded by Capt. Ward Marston with 2nd Lts. Henry W. Queen, Lt. William A. T. Maddox, and Orderly Sgt. John McCabe. Maddox and a detachment of Marines remained ashore to garrison Monterey.

Marines and seamen aboard the U.S. sloop *Portsmouth* were landed at Yerba Buena (now San Francisco) on 9 July and occupied that town, raising the U.S. flag, all without opposition. First Lieutenant Henry Bulls Watson, USMC, and 14 Marines, later increased to 26, remained behind to defend their conquest. That same date, Lt. James W. Revere, USN, of the *Portsmouth*, was sent to Sonoma with news of the unopposed capture of Yerba Buena.

Between 22 and 23 July Maj. Fremont and his second in command, Capt. Gillespie, arrived at Monterey with the Bear Flag Mounted Riflemen, raring to go.[10] Meanwhile, on the 23rd, Comdr. Robert Stockton, described as a "vigorous officer," replaced an ailing Sloat in command of the squadron. On the 25th Fremont, Gillespie and their fighting men boarded the *Cyane* for a trip down to San Diego, where they arrived on 29 July. Soon after landing, the ship's Marines, Mounted Riflemen, and a detachment of seamen took possession of that town and a Mexican ship lying in the harbor.

During the month of August the U.S. naval forces and their loyal land-based friends caused the Mexican government grief. It began on 4 August when Marines and seamen from the frigate *Congress* landed and took possession of Santa Barbara. Stockton was aboard and directing the entire operation. Then, on the 6th, further south near Los Angeles, at San Pedro, 1st Lt. Jacob Zeilin and his Marine detachment landed and raised the American flag.[11] Nonetheless, the town was not permanently held and Zeilin and his men returned to their ship.

After a march overland, Stockton's Marines and the California Battalion strode into the town of Los Angeles on 13 August. General Jose Castro, the leader of the Mexican Californios revolt, and his provincial force dissolved and retreated south upon the arrival of Stockton.[12] The Castro forces and supporters wanted an Anglo-free California and began preparing for a fight.

Gillespie, who in the meantime had been governing San Diego, arrived at Los Angeles on 31 August and was installed as military commandant of the Southern Department.[13] Acting as mayor, judge, and sheriff, he installed martial law and irritated the natives sufficiently to cause himself great problems. By the end of August most of his men had been moved to other locations and when Fremont marched north on 11 September Gillespie remained in LA with just 48 men.

Beginning on the 23rd of September, a revolt against U.S. (Gillespie's) authority in Los Angeles took place. The disorganized rebels were, however, easily dispersed by Gillespie's men. But their anger was at such a boiling point that tomorrow would be a different day, with a different outcome. Gillespie now had an estimated 500 irate Californios up in arms; he and his men tried to continue to hold the town, but after a week of near starvation, Gillespie was forced to ask the rebels for terms.

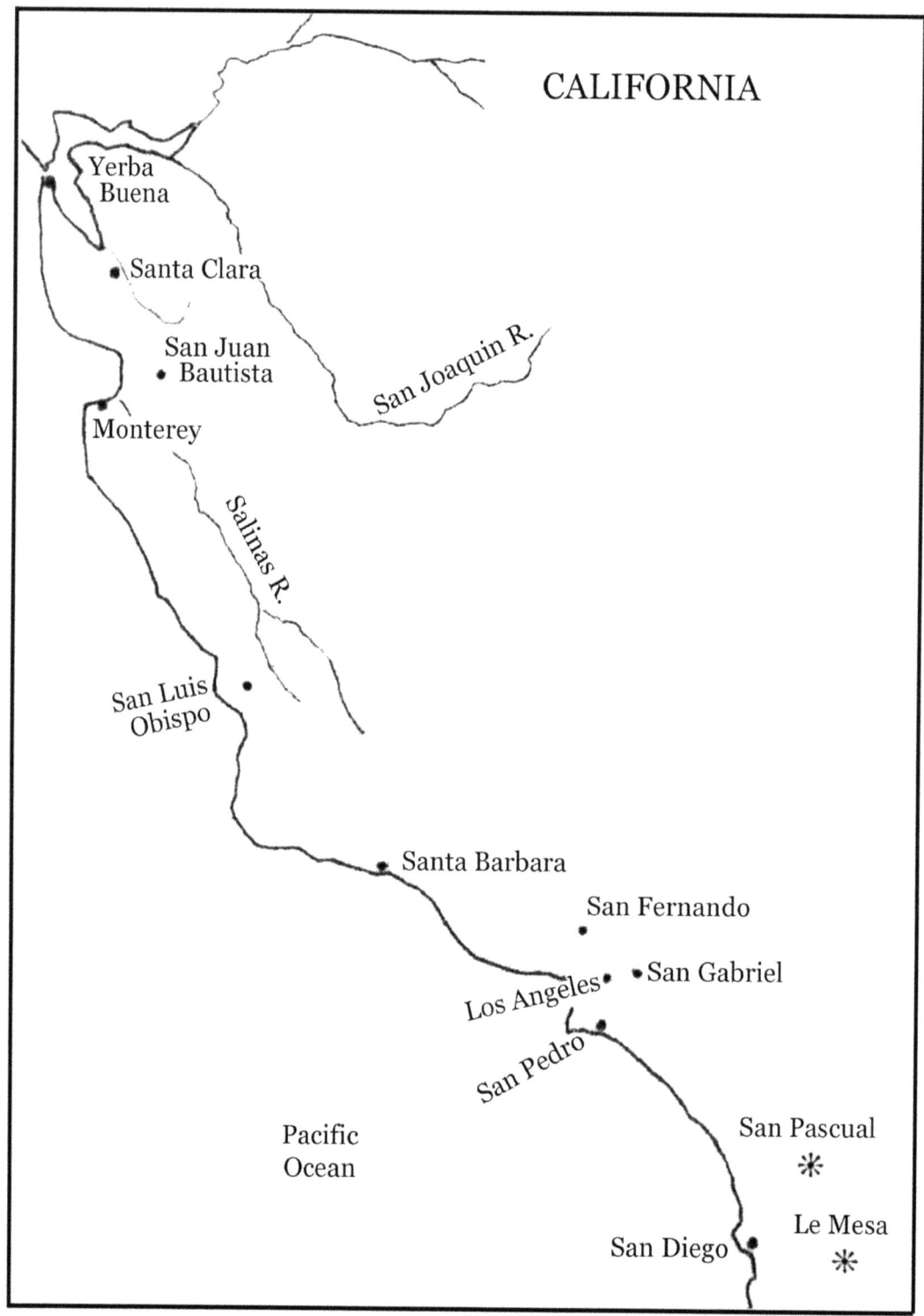

Though some rebels wanted to continue to fight it out, the leaders of the rebel group had sense enough to recognize that Gillespie and his modest force would cut them to ribbons if they attacked Gillespie behind his barricades. Therefore, on 30 September he and his men, under arms, were allowed to march out of Los Angeles to San Pedro, where they would board the American merchantman *Vandalia*.

Captain William Mervine, USN,[14] of the U.S. frigate *Savannah* led his ship's seamen and Marines, under command of Capt. Ward Marston, ashore between the 7th and 8th of October in an attempt to relieve the city of Los Angeles. Gillespie and his men joined them. On their route they were attacked in a narrow defile and Gillespie and his men charged up the hills and dispersed them. Mervine blamed Gillespie for "wasting ammunition — we can't spare caps." As they neared Los Angeles, Mervine was faced by a huge crowd of rebellious Californios and was soon forced to retreat to San Pedro. Meanwhile an angry Gillespie denounced Mervine's reluctance to engage the crowd, an engagement which he believed they could have easily won. This was the beginning of some difficult personal relations between the two men.

Stockton returned to assume command of the naval forces in the area on 27 October. On the 26th he had ordered Gillespie and his Marines, with a landing force of seamen, to retake San Pedro. On this date they took the high ground and planted the U.S. flag, which discouraged the Californios, who retreated. But Stockton, realizing he wasn't prepared to retake Los Angeles just yet, recalled his ground force aboard their respective ships and sailed away for San Diego. There they found that the garrison was in a bad way. Gillespie landed and resumed command. In a period of about a month, he had found sustenance and cattle for the garrison and San Diego was once again secured.

At sea, *Cyane* and its crew were still giving the Mexicans a bad time. Beginning on the 1st of October and continuing for the balance of the month, they took a dozen Mexican vessels off Lower Mexico. Otherwise matters appeared to be quiet and nothing of consequence occurred for nearly a month.

On 18 November the Californios launched a well-planned attack upon the forces at San Diego from the surrounding heights and the plains below. Gillespie launched a counter-attack with his men and charged up the hill, driving the Californios back a "great distance" and retaining possession of the ground taken. One gun was mounted on the high ground, soon hurting their foe and keeping them from launching another serious attack. Two weeks later came word that Gen. Stephen W. Kearney was in the vicinity with 100 mounted U.S. dragoons.[15] This was what the American forces had been waiting for since the beginning of summer. On 5 December, Gillespie with his men and 10 sailors under Lt. Edward F. Beale, USN, met Kearney at his camp and planned the next day's battle.

The Battle for San Pasqual, the momentous encounter between the U.S. forces and the Castro-led Californios, took place on 6 December. While on the trail Kearney and his followers met a large force of California lancers. Kearney ordered Gillespie to protect the baggage in the rear. The order went out to the Army to "trot" but was somehow altered to "charge." The lancers fell back, or so it seemed, and then fell upon the advancing but disorganized Americans, causing great carnage. Gillespie raced to their aid and in the process was attacked by four mounted lancers. Wounded in the chest, he fell from his horse. As he tried to stand he was hit on the back of his head by a lance and fell once again. At the battle's end, somehow the Americans held the field but they had suffered severe losses, 19 dead and many wounded, including both Kearney and Gillespie. The following day Kearney made his way toward Stockton but was forced to pitch camp after ten miles. Don Andres

Pico, leader of the lancers, had formed a friendly relationship with Gillespie and sent him medicine, then brought Gillespie to his camp for treatment by his doctor. (That kind of thing happened in those times.)[16] Nearly a week after the battle, Lt. Andrew Gray, USN, and Capt. Jacob Zeilin were leading a force of Marines and sailors, 215 in all, which had been dispatched by Stockton to assist Kearney in reaching San Diego. They arrived to join him on 12 December and with their aid Kearney reached San Diego.

Stockton's expedition left San Diego and on 29 December recaptured Los Angeles. Captain Jacob Zeilin became the officer commanding the 1st Division, which was composed of the merging of all Marines from the squadron.

In December 1846, Lt. Washington A. Bartlett, USN, and five sailors in the San Francisco area were buying beef for the naval detachment when a local chief of the Californio rebels, Francisco Sanchez, and his men captured them. They were offered as a trade for a captive Californian. Commander John B. Montgomery, USN, refused and prepared to effect a rescue.

Captain Wade Marston and his Marines from the U.S. sloop *Dale* were a part of the rescue team that encountered Sanchez on 2 January 1847. The Californios were driven back and hid in the nearby mountains. Sanchez decided to discuss the matter with Marston and soon both men agreed on an armistice until the matter was settled. Though criticized by Cmdr. Montgomery for not killing the rebels, events proved that Marston was right. The prisoners were released when Sanchez and his men surrendered.

A battle at San Gabriel on 8 January ended in victory for the Americans, with Capt. Zeilin and his Marines and Gillespie and his volunteers. Upon contacting the Californio forces of Jose Flores, Comm. Stockton formed his men into a square with cattle and supplies in the center and awaited the enemy. Flores had been the officer who accepted Gillespie's surrender back on 30 September. Gillespie and his varied force were the guard of the day and protectors of the rear, while Marston and Zeilin and their Marines were positioned in various other parts of the square.

Stockton maintained his square formation even as his forces advanced toward the enemy. Second Lieutenant Henry B. Watson, USMC, held the most delicate part of the formation. He and his men from the *Portsmouth* were on the exposed left flank. Various attempts were made by the Californios to break the formation, but to no avail. Zeilin and his Marines on the right flank deployed forward with two pieces of artillery. When the enemy attempted to turn Stockton's right flank, Zeilin and his men quickly broke up the attack and forced them to retreat.

Stockton prepared his men to attack the heights which now lay before them. As his men went up the hill his artillery pounded the enemy, forcing them to retreat before this overwhelming force. It was Stockton's victory and there were only two dead and nine wounded, including Gillespie, once again.

The next day brought another battle. Stockton's forces began an advance toward Los Angeles at 0900 and soon came under fire from forces on a hill, effectively blocking any further progress. Artillery on both sides were the main part of the ensuing battle. Eventually Stockton's guns were better handled and they drove off the Californios and their guns, quickly followed by their troops. Losses that day for the Americans at the Battle of La Mesa were one killed and five wounded. Kearney entered Los Angeles at about noon on 10 January and Gillespie elevated the same flag over the Government House that he had been forced to lower the previous September.

For the balance of the year 1847, all activity that the Marines engaged in was from their ships on or off the west coast of Lower California, which would remain the property of Mexico. All encounters were against Mexicans, not Californios. Several Mexican ships were captured, as was a British blockade-runner. On the 30th Marines and seamen from the *Portsmouth* landed and captured San Jose, at the very tip of Lower California, Mexico. In Lower California, the *Portsmouth* landed her Marines and sailors at various locations, being successful in each encounter. Later, on 20 October, Marines from the *Portsmouth* and the U.S. frigate *Congress* landed and captured the town of Guaymas in the Gulf of Lower California.

During the month of November, beginning on the 1st, Marines participated in the expedition to take the town of Todos Santos. These same Marines were ordered to return to garrison San Jose on 7 November. Then on the 11th Marines and seamen from the U.S. sloop *Cyane*, frigate *Congress*, and the razee *Independence*[17] landed and took the town of Mazatlan, Mexico. The defender, Col. Rafael Telles, realizing he would be unable to defend the town against superior numbers, fell back to a position up the Puerto Viejo bay to Palos Prietos. On the 17th, still holding Guaymas, the Marines and seamen from *Dale* defended the town from several attempts by Mexican forces to regain it. Two days later a major effort by Mexican forces to recapture San Jose was repelled by Marines. The attempts continued until 21 November but were all unsuccessful.

Marines and sailors defending their conquest of San Jose were under siege by Mexican forces beginning on 22 January 1848, and that would continue until mid–February. Later that month, on the 30th, Marines and seamen landed from the *Dale* and captured the town of Cochon.

A Treaty of Peace was signed at Guadalupe Hidalgo on 2 February, which concluded the war between the United States and Mexico, but elsewhere men weren't aware and continued fighting. Eleven days later Marines and seamen from *Dale* landed at Guaymas and advanced to Bocachicacampa and there dispersed a small force of Mexican irregulars. Two days later Marines and seamen from *Cyane* landed and fought their way through the besieging Mexican forces at San Jose to relieve the American garrison. It appears as though that didn't settle anything because on the 15th of March Marines and sailors were once again landed from *Dale* to reconquer Cochon. On 9 April the final engagement on the west coast took place when Marines and seamen landed from *Dale* at Guaymas and marched inland 12 miles to capture the town of Empalme. On their return they had a serious encounter with Mexican forces.[18]

> *Result:* The war with Mexico was an outstanding success for the United States, but was a disaster for Mexico. For the most part, its badly led military forces were everywhere defeated. Only the Californios occasionally defeated the Americans, and they desired a separate nation run by them, not the "anglos" or the Mexican government. Mexico's primary general, Santa Anna, was another disaster. He ran faster than the Americans and they couldn't catch him. Mexico was fortunate that the American politicians in Washington that desired the complete incorporation of Mexico into the U.S. were in the minority. In fact, there were some senior Mexican officials that desired that to happen. The U.S. kept California, Arizona, and New Mexico in addition to Texas. Mexico was shorn of about one-third of its territory.

7

American Civil War

Date: January 1861 to 15 April 1865.
Location: United States east and Gulf coasts.
Involved: Eleven Confederate states versus 22 Union states.[1]
Situation: When the war began, the Marine Corps' total strength was at 1,801: 46 officers and 1,755 enlisted. There were never more than 3,800 officers and enlisted men during the entire war.

Marines provided the core of the naval landing forces, manning the secondary guns aboard ships in battle, and maintaining order and discipline among the ships' crews. The Navy's role was significant, especially in the blockading of ports, and Marines played their roles aboard ships or as landing parties. Still, their part in the war was limited overall.

In early 1861, Marine detachments were moved around to provide instant protection in case of Southern attempts to attack naval installations. An attack was anticipated at the Brooklyn Navy Yard, NY, and the Marine guard was placed under arms as early as 22 January. Marines at the Navy Yard, Washington, D.C., were assigned to the defense of the main gate on 1 February.

On the 14th of April 1861 Marines manned howitzers preparatory to the defense of the Navy Yard, Washington, D.C., which was deemed a serious target for southern sympathizers, of which there were many in Maryland, Virginia, and the District of Columbia. The date the war began is officially listed as 15 April, and the greater part of the Marine Corps would serve aboard ship.[2]

On 21 April, 150 Marines commanded by Maj. Augustus S. Nicholson reinforced the Gosport Navy Yard, Norfolk, VA. Upon arrival they found most buildings and ships had already been destroyed. They were soon joined by Lt. Col. James Edelin, with the station Marines, and numerous others from ships based nearby.[3] The position was eventually destroyed, as were the unfinished ships and a large supply and weapons cache, before the local Virginia militia could take possession of it. On 22 April, President Lincoln approved the increase of 550 privates for the Marine Corps.

During the First Battle of Bull Run a battalion of 12 officers and 353 enlisted Marines, commanded by Maj. John C. Reynolds, was assigned to protect U.S. Army Capt. Griffin's Flying Battery.[4] On the way toward their encounter with the Confederates on 16 July, the battery moved out on horses and the Marines had to double-time in an attempt to keep up. Exhausted at the end of their trip, they were then assigned to support the 14th New York Regiment (Brooklyn).

They took their position on the far right of the line on 21 July. Under continually accurate artillery fire, they were forced to fall back, but they returned to their positions again. Major General Irvin McDowell, commanding the Union forces, became convinced that the Confederates were falling back and ordered his army to advance. The Marines were ordered to follow Griffin's battery, which they did, taking up a position to its rear. An error in judgment allowed the 33rd Virginia Infantry to get close enough to Griffin's battery to shoot down most of the gunners. So far the Marines had come through in reasonably good shape. In fact, so had the entire Union army. The loss of this battery, however, was the beginning of the end for McDowell. His army started to dissolve. The Marines were recruits, and, like the rest of the Union array, they too became part of the flotsam and jetsam. In other words, they all ran. Marine casualties were extensive; nine killed, 19 wounded, and 16 more missing in action.

Marines from the U.S. frigates *Minnesota* and *Wabash* and the U.S. sloops *Cumberland* and *Susquehanna* joined soldiers of Gen. Benjamin Butler in landing at Hatteras Inlet, NC, on the 28th of August, resulting in the capture of Forts Clark and Hatteras. A total of 237 Marines were landed, making it to shore in a poorly organized and managed amphibious landing. There they remained in a precarious position. Fortunately, the Confederates decided to vacate the premises. Marines, sailors and soldiers entered and occupied the fort and the national flag rose above Fort Clark. The following morning, the rebels, after taking a pounding, raised a white flag at 1110 above Fort Hatteras.

On 14 September Marines led by Capt. Edward N. Reynolds, and at least 100 seamen from the frigate *Colorado*, rowed into the harbor of Pensacola, FL, to board and burn the Confederate privateer *Judah*. At 0330 the force went aboard and during an especially desperate defense by the crew and from shore guns, drove them from the ship. Private John Smith, the first man to board the *Judah*, was accidentally killed, Capt. Reynolds and Pvts. Savillan Coburn, Terence O'Dowd, and Charles Carberry were wounded.

On 2 November a disaster occurred to Maj. John C. Reynolds' 300-man Marine battalion. While embarked on the chartered steamer *Governor* and headed for Port Royal, SC, the crew and passengers were forced to transfer to the U.S. frigate *Sabin* as the *Governor* sank in a gale off Cape Hatteras, NC. Many of the Marines were saved, except for a corporal and six privates, who drowned.[5] Five days later, a detachment of Marines, commanded by an unnamed sergeant and with seamen from the U.S. frigate *Santee*, attempted but failed to capture the Confederate steamer *General Rusk*. But after being repulsed in that attempt, they did succeed in seizing and sinking the Confederate ship *Royal Yacht* at Galveston Bar, TX. The following day, 8 November, the Confederate Comm. Tattnall, with a relatively tiny fleet, was unable to defend Fort Walker against the encroachment of the federal forces before he withdrew. Six hundred and fifty U.S. Marines and seamen, commanded by Maj. Reynolds, landed from the frigate *Wabash* at Hilton Head, SC, to occupy Fort Walker on Hilton Head and Fort Beauregard on Bay Point. They remained there until Army Gen. Thomas W. Sherman could bring in Army troops to replace them.

That same date, Marines and seamen aboard the *San Jacinto* boarded the British steamer *Trent*, east of Havana, Cuba, and carried off the Confederate diplomats John Slidell and James Mason, plus a Mr. Eustis and Mr. McFarland. Captain John Schermerhorn commanded the Marine detachment aboard the *San Jacinto*.[6]

Marines and sailors from ships of Adm. Samuel F. Du Pont's fleet went ashore on Tybee Island, GA, on 24 November, and finding it abandoned, the naval leader Cmdr. John Rodgers left a small detachment of Marines to occupy it, at least temporarily. On the 26th

Tattnall brought his fleet downriver, shelling the island but also being shelled in return by Du Pont's fleet, and then withdrew from the area. Three days later Marines from the *Savannah* were landed on Tybee Island at 0800 but were forced by shell-fire from Fort Pulaski to retreat to their boats at 1130. On the 28th, 1st Lt. Philip C. Kennedy and his Marine Guard from the *Savannah*, accompanied by 30 seamen, returned to Tybee Island and occupied the local Martello Tower.

Dale's Marines, led by Orderly Sgt. Patrick Lomasney, transferred to the *Isaac Smith*, and on 10 December came under the command of Lt. James W. A. Nicholson, USN. They then landed on Otter Island and took control of an abandoned fort which Nicholson then turned over to the U.S. Army. Two days later Sgt. Lomasney's detachment of Marines landed to reconnoiter Fenwick's Island Fort, NC, and while there, they burned the headquarters of a Confederate cavalry at Mosquito Creek Junction, NC. On the 26th of December, Lomasney's Marines drove off Confederate troops at the mouth of the South Edisto River, SC.

On the 31st, Marines from the *Niagara* commanded by 1st Lt. George Butler, and joined by the Marine Guard from *Massachusetts*, plus seamen, boarded the *Henry Lewis* and, after joining with the *Water Witch*, steamed up to Biloxi, MS, demanding the surrender of the town. To enforce the demand, Marines and seamen landed at Biloxi, MS, which surrendered to this party from the U.S. ships. After they destroyed a small battery of two guns and a captured schooner, the party returned to its ships.

This ended the first year of the war. Marines from the U.S. steamer *Hatteras* landed at Cedar Keys, FL, to successfully raid and burn Confederate stores on 13 January. In addition to burning military stores, the Marines also destroyed two large guns, plus several Confederate schooners loaded with cotton which were ready to run the Union blockade. Three days later, the same crew landed at the same location and, with gunfire support from its ship, destroyed a Confederate battery and captured a detachment of Confederate troops. They also managed to destroy seven blockade runners loaded with cotton and turpentine, a railroad depot and wharf, and a telegraph office.

On the last day of January, one officer and 27 enlisted Marines were assigned to the river gunboat *St. Louis*, flagship of the flotilla which later supported Army Gen. Ulysses S. Grant's attack on Forts Henry and Donelson on the Tennessee and Cumberland Rivers, respectively.

Marines assisted Army troops in the seizure of Confederate positions on Roanoke Island, NC, and in the capture of 2,500 Confederate troops on 7 February.[7] Two days later the Marine detachments of 14 United States vessels took part in the pursuit of a Confederate naval fleet up Croatan Sound from Roanoke Island, and in the occupation of Fort Cobb and Elizabeth City, NC. On the 19th, the Marine detachments of ships of the Atlantic Squadron took part in the Battle of Winton, NC.

Major John G. Reynolds commanded a battalion of Marines that landed on the 4th of March from the transport *McClellan* to occupy the town of Fernandina, FL. Another company of Marines and seamen from the U.S. sloop *Mohican* occupied Fort Clinch, GA. Flag Officer Du Pont then stated, "our principal and ultimate object ... to take control of ... the whole line of the sea-coast of Georgia [would] control the whole state of Georgia." Then on the 8th, 25 Marines from the U.S. sloop *Mohican* and the U.S. steamer *Pocahontas* landed at Brunswick, GA, which surrendered without a struggle. That same day, Marines were serving aboard the U.S. frigate *Congress* and the U.S. sloop *Cumberland* when they were attacked by the Confederate ironclad ram *Merrimac* in Hampton Roads, off Norfolk,

VA. The Marine detachment, commanded by 1st Lt. Charles Heywood, distinguished itself but suffered grievous losses. The first shot from the *Merrimac* killed nine Marines aboard the *Cumberland*. The Marines got partly even; they managed to fire the last shot at the *Merrimac*. The next day Marines were serving on board the U.S. frigate *Minnesota* when she was taken under fire by the *Merrimac*, also in Hampton Roads. This was soon to become the world-famous "Battle between Ironclads" when the Union's new ship the *Moniter* arrived on the scene, the so-called Cheese-box on a raft.[8]

Marine detachments from U.S. gunboats took part in a combined Army-Navy expedition up Slocum's Creek, NC, to capture the towns of New Bern and Washington, NC. The troops, U.S. Army and Marines, were landed on the 13th and proceeded up the river, arriving at New Bern in the evening. On the 14th the National Flag was raised over captured Forts Dixie, Ellis, Thompson, and Lane; a costly deprivation for the Confederacy.

Major Isaac T. Doughty and a detachment of Marines and seamen from the U.S. sloop *Mohican* and the frigate *Wabash* landed and occupied the town of St. Augustine, FL, on St. Patrick's Day.[9] On 26 March, the Marine detachments of the U.S. steamers *Mercedita* and *Sagamore* took part in an expedition against Confederate vessels and stores at Appalachicola, West Florida.

Marine detachments continued serving main battery guns in ships of Adm. David G. Farragut's squadron in actions against Forts St. Philip and Jackson and against Confederate gunboats below New Orleans, LA. The bombardment, which began on 24 April, continued for 144 consecutive hours, at the end of which, on 28 April, the Confederates surrendered.[10] The same day Marine detachments, all sergeant's guards, of the U.S. steamers *Daylight*, *State of Georgia*, and *Chippewa*, and the bark *Gemsbok*, participated in the reduction and occupation of Fort Macon, NC.[11]

On 29 April, 200 Marines formed in four companies, commanded by Capt. John L. Broome, proceeded to occupy New Orleans, LA. They first marched to the custom house, about a mile distant, and confiscated the quarantine station, raising the U.S. flag at both. They also managed to capture a large number of Confederate prisoners, both officers and enlisted men. When Broome and his command were joined by a detachment of sailors with two howitzers, then ordered to proceed another half mile to take the city hall, Capt. Alan Ramsay and his 50 Marines from the *Richmond* were left behind.

By this time the Confederate troops had vacated New Orleans, but the streets were filled with excited mobs which verbally abused the Marines as they marched along. Reaching the city hall, 2nd Lt. John C. Harris and some Marines entered and lowered the state flag, while the remainder circled the building.[12] Not long afterward, all of Broome's command, except Ramsay's detachment still holding the custom house, returned to its ships. Ramsay and his command remained at their post until the U.S. Army relieved them on 1 May. Three boats of Marines from the U.S. steamer *Iroquois* landed at Baton Rouge, LA, on 9 May, taking possession of the U.S. arsenal and raising the American flag over it. Marines manned secondary guns aboard the advancing Union flotilla on the Mississippi River, repulsing an attack by Confederate ships off Fort Pillow, MO, on 10 May.

While serving aboard the *Galena* during an engagement with Confederate shore batteries at Drewry's Bluff, VA, Marine Cpl. John Mackie was the first Marine to be awarded the Medal of Honor. He was commended for fearlessly maintaining his musket fire against the rifle pits along the shore on 15 May. When ordered to fill vacancies at the ship's guns, "caused by enemy fire, he manned his gun with skill and courage, and accuracy."

On 24 June 60 Marines from the U.S. steamers *James Adger*, *Keystone State*, and *Albatross* boarded the gunboats *Hall* and *Andrew* to serve as sharpshooters during raids up the Santee and Wahamau Rivers, SC. Firing continually as they followed Confederate cavalry on shore, the Marines debarked at the private home of an English citizen named Blake, and there found evidence that it had been used as quarters by the Confederates. They captured weapons found there and fought a brief battle with the cavalry, but failed in their effort to capture an enemy battery in the nearby woods. They burnt the home of Mr. Blake and then returned to their boats with two Marines wounded.

Marine detachments aboard Union ships above Vicksburg, MS, manned secondary guns in action against the Confederate ram *Arkansas* on 15 July. Two days later, 28 Marines and 20 sailors joined the steamer *New London* in an expedition to capture or destroy several Confederate vessels loaded with cotton at Pascagoula, MS. They succeeded, but the strong enemy forces made them retire to their ship.

Ninety-five Marines with two officers, from the U.S. ships *Wabash* and the *New Ironsides*, took part on 8 August in setting up large naval guns on Morris Island, SC. On 23 August, Capt. David K. Cohen and a force of Marines from the Navy Yard at Brooklyn, NY, quelled a riot among Army recruits of General Spinola's "Empire Brigade."

Between the 3rd and 9th of October the USN bombarded Galveston, TX, forcing the city to surrender on the 9th. Meanwhile, Adm. Farragut complained to the secretary of the Navy, "the failure to have a sizeable effective Marine Corps to send ashore in conjunction with fleet operations reduced considerably the effectiveness of the Navy and may have lengthened the war."[13]

Four officers and 88 enlisted Marines from Headquarters in Washington, D.C., were sent west on 4 November to occupy the new naval station at Cairo, IL, and supplement those Marines aboard the ships of the naval flotilla when required. On that day, one officer and 38 Marines went aboard the flagship *Black Hawk*.[14]

A major disaster occurred when a company of 150 Marines, commanded by Maj. Addison Garland, was captured on 7 December 1862 aboard the schooner *Arid*. They were en route to Mare Island, CA, when they were seized off Cuba by the Confederate raider *Alabama*. Captain Jones of the *Arid* rightly realized that the women and children aboard would suffer if he allowed the Marines to repel boarders, so he surrendered his ship and all passengers. While negotiations for ransom proceeded, Garland was allowed to arm his Marines in order to protect the liquor stores aboard. Upon payment of the ransom, the Marines, including Garland, were paroled and allowed to proceed with the ship, to be exchanged on 27 December while at Mare Island, CA.[15]

Marine detachments of the *Hartford*, the *Richmond*, and the *Monongahela* took part in Adm. Farragut's attack upon Port Hudson, LA, on 14 March. Captain Alan Ramsay was particularly selected for notation: "[He] deserves special mention ... in charge of the Marine division of great guns, had nearly a whole gun's crew swept away by a single cannon shot." Losses were heavy. On 19 March and again on 25 March, ship detachments of Adm. Farragut's fleet were active in the bombardment of Grand Gull, MS, and again just below Vicksburg at Warrenton, MS.

On 9 June 1863 a blockade-running sloop was captured and put into U.S. service as a scout for other Southern blockade runners. She was manned by Orderly Sgt. Christopher Nugent and his command of six Marines. Floating six miles up the Crystal River, they discovered a Confederate position. With four of his Marines, Nugent went ashore on the 15th and stealthily crept up to their position. Seeing 11 Confederates and a woman, Nugent ordered the Marines to fix bayonets and to charge. As the Marines came on them, the Confederates took off into the nearby swamp. Their officer turned and fired, hitting Nugent, but the bullet glanced off his waist belt. Nugent ordered his men not to hit the woman as they returned fire. Nugent and his men then gathered together all the pertinent material and weapons left behind and brought them back to their ship. For this exploit, Nugent, born in Ireland and just 24 years of age, was the third Marine awarded a Medal of Honor. He received it on 16 April 1864. As the fiscal year ended, the Corps finally reached 3,000: 69 officers and 2,931 enlisted men.

A battalion of Marines, about 180 strong and under the command of Capt. John C. Grayson, was part of a naval brigade which helped restore order on 13 July during draft riots in New York City. They were dispersed throughout the sections of the city which were the more disorderly, and after two weeks order was restored.[16]

At midnight on the 17th of July 1st Lt. George W. Collier and 20 Marines landed at Pascagoula, MS, and destroyed telegraphic installations between that town and Mobile, AL. He tried to move up the river but ran into an ambush where Confederate cavalry and infantry ashore peppered his boat. His small command of eight Marines and 14 sailors took severe casualties, three Marines and five sailors. After a spirited defense, Collier and his command returned to their ship.

On 21 July, Orderly Sgt. Christopher Nugent took his boat on a midnight reconnaissance into the harbor of Bayport, FL, returning the following day with information that no enemy boats had been sighted. On the 30th Nugent and his small command rescued three refugees in a boat coming from Bayport. Rear Admiral Theodorus Bailey wrote the letter to Welles recommending the Medal of Honor for Nugent.

A Marine 500-man battalion, commanded by Maj. Jacob Zeilin,[17] on 10 August landed on Morris Island, SC, to provide artillery support for forces ashore. Dahlgren ordered Zeilen to "be ready to move on instant notice; rapidity of movement is one of the greatest elements of military power."[18] From that force, 100 Marines, now commanded briefly by Capt. Edward McD. Reynolds, seconded by Capt. Charles O. McCawley,[19] plus 300 seamen, took part on 8 September in an ill-fated attack on Fort Sumter, SC. The Confederates were well prepared; they had the USN fleet's code, which had been taken from a sunken USN ship. Waiting for the assault boats to come close to shore, the Confederates then opened devastating fire with muskets and shore batteries. The Union attack was repulsed with the loss of about one hundred of the landing party, and with numerous Marines and seamen captured.

On the first day of 1864, heavy seas interfered with a landing prepared by Adm. Dahlgren in which 100 Marines plus seamen were to have used "corrective measures upon Confederates" who had been troubling his fleet in the inlets off South Carolina. A detachment of 30 Marines and seamen from the South Atlantic Squadron landed at Murrell's Inlet, Charleston, SC, and sank a Confederate schooner loaded with turpentine and destined for a breakout.

On the 5th of May, Marines aboard the U.S. ships *Metabesett, Myalusing, Sassacus*, and *Whitehead* took part in the action against the Confederate ram *Albemarle* in the coastal waters off North Carolina. After three hours *Albermarle* broke contact and fled upriver. A week later Col. John Harris, sixth commandant of the Marine Corps, died in office.[20]

Secretary Welles decided to "retire the Marine officers who are past the legal age and to bring in Zeilin as Commandant of the Corps" and on 9 June Zeilin was promoted to colonel and appointed the seventh commandant of the Marine Corps.[21] He was a very satisfactory replacement for a rather weak Harris.

Marines were serving aboard the U.S. steamer *Kearsage* when she captured the crew, excluding Capt. Raphael Semmes, and sank the Confederate raider *Alabama* off Cherbourg,

France, on the 10th of June. The Marine detachment was commanded by Orderly Sgt. Charles T. Young, and all officers and crew were credited with "special mention."

In early August the Marine detachments serving aboard ships of Adm. David O. Farragut's squadron participated in the bombardment of Forts Morgan, Gaines, and Powell on the shores of Mobile Bay, AL. Then on 6 August, 25 Marines commanded by Capt. Charles Heywood, from the *Hartford* and the *Richmond*, occupied Fort Powell, Mobile, AL.[22] Heywood was brevetted a lieutenant colonel for his actions.

Late in the month of October a Marine battalion of 182 men was part of the naval brigade which, with Army troops, was repulsed at Boyd's Neck in an attack near Honey Hill, SC, on the Charleston-Savannah rail line. When the Army brigade was driven back Marines on the left flank, led by sergeants, were forced to fall back in order to avoid being out-flanked.

The following day, a naval brigade of ships of the South Atlantic Blocking Squadron, composed of 150 Marines and 350 seamen led by Comdr. George H. Preble, joined in an Army attack upon Honey Hill. This was to enable Gen. Sherman to continue his march toward Savannah. On the 30th the Marines and seamen played a significant part in the ensuing battle, after which they entrenched along the Grahamville Road.

A Marine detachment, commanded by 1st Lt. George O. Stoddard, was part of the Federal force which on 6 December attacked Confederate troops at Tullifinney Crossroads and Derang's Neck, SC. Stoddard and his command managed to drive the Confederates back to within a mile of the railroad, but were once again stopped by the Confederates' desperate defense.

Two days before Christmas, Marines serving aboard ships of the South Atlantic Squadron manned secondary guns in the bombardment of Fort Fisher, NC.

Mid-January in 1865, 400 Marines from Admiral David D. Porter's Union squadron were part of the naval brigade which reinforced Army troops in the second attack upon and capture of Fort Fisher, near Wilmington, NC. The naval landing party consisted of 2,000 sailors and Marines, while the Army contributed another 8,000 men.

On the 13th at 1500 the assault upon the fort began. Four thousand Army troops went to assault the western face of the fort while the 2,000 men of the naval brigade attacked the northeast bastion. The Army had a wooded area between them and the fort but the naval attack was in the open. The gunners in the fort fired at point-blank range, plowing lanes through the naval brigade. Losses were heavy — officers and men, sailors and Marines — but by absorbing that punishment, the Army was able to more easily approach the walls and ultimately succeeded in taking the fort. More than 30 sailors and four Marines were awarded the Medal of Honor for their bravery on these dates, two aboard ships and two in the landing party. The fight began on the 13th and lasted through most of the 15th of January.

On 26 February, six companies of Marines, again commanded by Stoddard, occupied Georgetown, SC, until Army troops relieved them on 1 March. This, I believe, was the last important fighting effort of the Marine Corps during the Civil War.

Marines, commanded by Capt. Frank Monroe, on 15 April assumed guard over those persons accused of conspiracy in the assassination of president Abraham Lincoln.

> *Results:* The Marine Corps played a relatively small part during the Civil War, fighting alongside Navy shipmates at main batteries. When fighting between ships, or when engaged ashore, Marines were almost always on landing parties from their ship assignment. Occasionally several detachments, usually with sailors, served together. The Union eventually won.[23]

8

China

American naval vessels had been patrolling off the coast of China since at least the early part of the 19th century and seamen and Marines went shore on infrequent occasions to protect American interests. On 18 June 1844, a Chinese mob attacked and destroyed an American concession in Canton, China. Marines were sent ashore to protect the Americans in the area, remaining ashore until things quieted down. They returned to their ship, the *St. Louis*, on 20 July. This was shortly after the U.S. opened serious relations with China, though trade had been conducted since 1783.

Date: 4 April 1854 to late 1855.
Location: East coast of China, primarily off the city of Canton.
Involved: Chinese navy, army and pirates, versus U.S. naval and Marine forces.
Situation: Chinese troops and particularly pirates had been mistreating American sailors and ships for some time. The Chinese were having serious problems, especially with the British and French fleets. Weak Chinese attempts to prohibit foreign vessels from forcing their trade upon China were mostly unsuccessful, and therefore the Chinese were harassing any foreigners. There were several incidents in which American lives were threatened and prowling USN ships close off-shore were called upon to squelch the more serious incidents.

On the evening of 4 April 1854 the USN ship *Plymouth* received a signal from shore requesting assistance. Lieutenant John Guest, USN, along with a landing party of 60 Marines and sailors, went ashore. The British also sent a force, creating a total of about 150 men ashore. Thirty-five members of the U.S. Marine detachment remained ashore to provide a consulate guard, and 11 more protected the local Protestant mission until 15 June 1854. One American sailor was killed and two Marines and another sailor were wounded during the fracas.

On 19 March 1855 Marines were again landed to protect U.S. citizens from rampant piracy. First Lieutenant James H. Jones and 41 men from the *Powhatan* went ashore and remained there for two days. Although available records are scant, it appears that nothing ominous occurred during that period.

But a few months later, Jones and his Marines would be engaged in some real activity. In August he and 26 Marines, along with seven naval officers and 66 sailors, went ashore at Hong Kong to join with other forces in attacking a large group of pirates gathered nearby. The *Powhatan*'s skipper, Capt. William J. McCluney, included four days' provisions and an appropriate volume of whiskey to complete their stores. The Americans joined a shipload of British Marines and sailors and then both groups proceeded to Ty-Ho Bay. There a battle ensued in which the combined Occidental force was again victorious; the allies captured 17 pirate junks and many of their crews. Two U.S. Marines and nine sailors were casualties, three of the latter were killed in action and the others were seriously wounded. The two wounded Marines, Pvts. Adamson and Mullard, later died aboard the British hospital ship and were buried at Hong Kong. Within 48 hours of their departure the American forces were back aboard the *Powhatan*, minus their stores and whiskey.

> *Results:* Conflict in China was an ongoing problem that would never really be settled as long as foreigners continued forcing their way upon the Chinese, who would, rightfully, continue to fight back for many more years.

Date: 22 October to 22 November 1856.
Location: The Barrier Forts on the Pearl River, Canton, China.
Involved: Imperial Chinese army versus the U.S. Navy and Marines.
Situation: The next serious altercation in which American Marines were engaged began on 22 October 1856. It turned out to be a most serious fracas. The American consul at Canton sent Comdr. Andrew H. Foote, commanding the sloop *Portsmouth*, a message that American interests were in great danger and asking him to "please help."

The next morning, at a little after 0600 Foote took five officers and 78 enlisted men ashore to Canton. Second Lieutenant William W. Kirkland commanded the 18 Marines sent ashore, which constituted most of the ship's detachment. Foote also took along a field howitzer, which gave his small force a loud and imposing source of firepower. But it soon became evident that the small force was not sufficient to provide the protection required for the American community at Canton. Therefore, on 27 October Comdr. William Smith ordered his detachment of Marines and a complement of sailors from the sloop *Levant* to assist Foote at Canton. Marine 2nd Lt. Henry B. Tyler went ashore with his Marine detachment and a group of sailors, proceeding up the Pearl River to Canton, where they joined the landing force from *Portsmouth*. The Marines were soon established as sentinels on rooftops and behind newly created barricades. From that vantage point they fired their muskets at any moving Chinese target. That was what Marines were hired to do and were usually quite successful in doing. Again, on 3 November, the Marine sentinels engaged in another spirited exchange of musketry fire with Chinese soldiers. But this time there were no reported casualties on either side.

The steam frigate *San Jacinto* arrived off Whampoa Island on the morning of 12 November with Comm. James Armstrong aboard. As senior officer present, he assumed local command. On 14 November he ordered Brevet Capt. John D. Simms to take 28 Marines ashore to join Foote and assist in the defense of the "factory." After Foote arrived at what appeared to be a satisfactory agreement with the Chinese authorities, the following day most of the force was ordered back to the *Levant*, leaving a few Marines at the American compound. Foote, the senior American officer ashore, had developed a plan with the Chinese commissioner Yeh, based on the promise to provide protection for American citizens in and about Canton. But the *Levant* would remain anchored off Canton as a place of possible refuge for the consul or other Americans. As Foote was rowed back to Canton to carry out the plan, his boat was fired upon from the first barrier fort. This forced him to return to Whampoa Island to fix matters once and for all. In those times, whenever an American soldier, sailor, or Marine was fired upon, it was believed that American honor required a military confrontation to adjust matters between the two nations.

Armstrong was furious, as was the always irascible Foote. The commodore ordered both the *Levant* and *Portsmouth*, to which he transferred his flag, to proceed up the river to attack the four Chinese forts. Before her guns could be brought into action *Levant* went aground. That left *Portsmouth*, which went forward alone. The four forts were equipped with a total of 176 modern European guns, which ranged in caliber from 8 to 10 inches (some records say 11-inch, a German caliber) and were mounted behind granite walls eight feet thick. In addition, at least 5,000 Chinese regular troops were included in the "strongest defenses of the Empire." The American sailors might have been very angry, but no fighting seaman worth the name should ever go up against a granite fortress with his wooden ship. They did and somehow it all came out right in the end.

The fire from the forts was accurate and it wasn't long before *Portsmouth* was hit several times, losing some of her rigging and receiving a badly wounded Marine casualty. Herculean efforts were made and *Levant* was finally moved off the sandbar. Shortly after midnight, as soon as it became light enough, she was in position to help her sister *Portsmouth* take on the forts. But instead a three-day lull followed while the Navy repaired the damage to *Portsmouth*. In the meantime Armstrong became ill and turned command over to Foote, admonishing him not to fire unless the Chinese attacked. Then on 19 November Armstrong ordered Foote to take any action necessary to forestall a Chinese attack. Foote made the decision to seize and level the forts. The defenders had 5,000–6,000 men behind the walls of the four forts, while Foote could only gather together possibly 500 Marines and sailors. He must have considered the odds just about right.

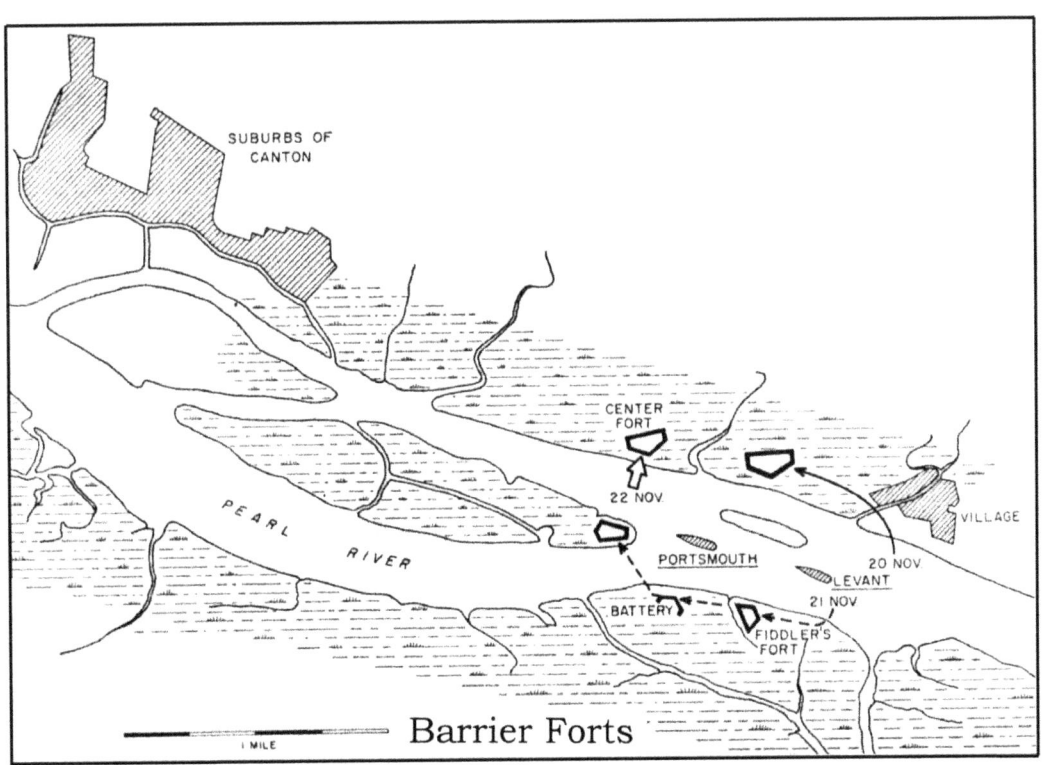

Early the next morning both ships were in position and at first light began their bombardment on Fiddler's Fort, the fort (no. 2) on the south bank of the Pearl River. Along with his Marines, Captain Simms and six naval officers and sailors were landed and ordered to proceed upriver to attack the first Chinese fort (no. 1) on the north bank of the Pearl River. The nearly 300-man landing force was forced to first navigate through swamps in order to reach a village to the rear of the fort. They rather easily brushed aside Chinese resistance and with accurate and destructive musketry soon drove off the defenders, killing upwards of 50 as they fled. The Marines occupied the fort and raised the American flag. The next nearest fort upriver (no. 3) opened up on them and the Marines used the captured guns to reply. Soon after, Chinese troops, which had re-occupied the village, began putting pressure on the Americans in the fort. A Marine detachment from fort no.1 was ordered to retake the village and drive them away. At this point the Chinese troops fell back into rice fields, making further pursuit difficult. Simms brought his men to a halt and then retired toward the fort.

The Chinese, assuming that the Marines were retreating, followed them with approximately 2,000 soldiers. The Marines turned on the advancing force and delivered another blast of fire so deadly that the Chinese again broke and ran. Simms and his little force then returned to the captured fort to re-assume their interrupted duties, which was spiking the captured guns. Some were instead thrown down the rise into the Pearl River. The river was quite deep at that point and the guns were not retrievable.

By this time the Chinese leaders in the city of Canton had gotten their act together and sent a force of about 5,000 additional Chinese troops the four miles to the captured fort. This large host made three assaults upon the defending Americans, but each time the deadly accurate musket and howitzer fire drove them back. The final attack soon turned into a bloody rout. For the balance of that day and through the following night a portion of Simms' Marines held fort no. 1, while the balance of the landing party returned to the ships from which they came.

The next morning at 0300 the no. 3 fort began firing upon *Portsmouth*. For some reason it would be an additional three hours before the two American ships would return the fire. That morning Simms and his landing party were embarked in landing boats. As the forts fired upon the ships, they also began working over the small boats occupied by the Navy/Marine landing force. One of the boats was raked by a medium-sized shot, killing or wounding most of the Bluejacket occupants. Shortly afterward the balance of the landing party commenced its assault upon fort no. 2, also known as Fiddler's Fort, which lay on the south side of the river. Though the landing party was forced to cross waist-deep ditches filled with what could be euphemistically called "dirty" water, they soon successfully stormed the fort. The Marine casualty during that assault was Pvt. Thompson, who was seriously wounded but managed to survive. Corporal William McDougal planted the Stars and Stripes on the fortress walls in the face of fire from thousands of Chinese soldiers. Simms and his party soon captured the fort and promptly turned the guns upon Center Fort (no. 4), which lay on the tip of Napier Island, just to the west of Fiddler Fort.

As soon as Fiddler Fort had been taken, Center Fort had turned its destructive fire upon Simms' group. It was also able, because of its location, to work over the landing force at the fort on the northern bank as well. The Marines were now spiking the captured guns in Fiddler's Fort. They also burned the carriages and dumped the tubes into the river to permanently forestall any attempts by the previous occupants to reintroduce them in another engagement. In small boats, Simms' group now advanced across the river toward Center

Fort. Quickly landing, the sailors and Marines advanced up the slight incline and came upon a breastwork which held seven guns. Simms' Marines soon captured it and then promptly turned those guns upon Center Fort. The enemy presently counterattacked but the Marines easily repulsed them, retaining ownership of the redoubt. Then, as he advanced, Simms left 2nd Lt. Kirkland behind with a small detachment. Their instructions were to destroy the remaining guns and to hold the breastwork against any attack as long as possible before withdrawing. Simms took the balance of his Marines and joined a Navy landing team which was then forming.

Under cover of the ship's guns, the landing force composed of sailors and Marines had successfully landed on Napier Island and with modest difficulty captured the well-constructed Center Fort. Once again it was Cpl. McDougal who planted the American flag on this Chinese stronghold. The victors took and rapidly spiked 38 additional guns. And, as elsewhere, the guns were dumped into the river. From that position the Navy ships began an artillery duel with the remaining fort (no. 3), which was on the north bank and before the city of Canton. Most guns were utilized — ship's guns, howitzers of the landing party, and those guns still remaining at Fiddler's Fort. Firing didn't cease until darkness entirely blanketed the place of battle, making observation and accuracy impossible.

The following morning the storming of the final barrier fort took place. The landing party, covered by the guns of the two ships and Fiddler's Fort, made its way forward. They were unable to land close to the fort and were forced to wade quite a distance under the most adverse conditions. Once again they were successful in storming and capturing that 28-gun fort. The Chinese army counterattacked, but, as before, they were easily routed, this time with exceptionally heavy losses. The guns were destroyed and carriages burnt, then dropped into the river. The forts were entirely denuded of weapons and then had to be flattened. Mining operations included digging beneath the walls while the Americans inserted powder in the holes drilled in the granite itself. Unfortunately, a spark from one of the crowbars hit on the granite set off a major explosion, killing three men and wounding nine others, all U.S. sailors. Eventually the granite walls came tumbling down. In effect, nothing now stood between the Americans and Canton, that most important Chinese port.

That was the end of the attack upon the barrier forts but during the very brief encounter the U.S. naval force had managed to capture four extremely powerful forts, killing an estimated 500 Chinese troops and routing their army. This was accomplished at a cost of seven men killed in action, three of whom died because of the explosion at the fort, plus 32 wounded. No Marines were killed in the fighting, but a Pvt. William Cuddy later became ill and died, and six Marines were wounded. They were Cpl. William Boyce and Pvts. Patrick Mahon and Joseph McNeil from the *Levant*, and Cpl. James Linus and Pvts. Patrick Melvin and John G. Thompson of the *Portsmouth*.

Two years later Comdr. Foote, now executive officer of the Brooklyn Navy Yard, began a project to create a monument to those sailors and Marines who were killed defeating the empire of China in its own backyard. It was dedicated late in 1858 with a list of 12 names. One name chiseled into the marble was that of "John McBride, Corporal of Marines." There was no John McBride on the muster rolls of any of the ships, nor for that matter, was there a sailor named Thomas McCann. Faulty research?

> *Results:* Temporarily, the U.S. naval forces and Marines managed to interfere with the efforts of the Chinese government to halt trade with the United States. But this wasn't the end, the Chinese were dogged and refused to accept defeat.

Date: June 1871.
Location: Korea (part of China at this date).
Involved: Korean fortress soldiers versus U.S. naval forces.
Situation: The American minister to China (Korea was then nominally a part of the Chinese empire), Consul Frederick A. Low, ignored by the Korean government when he complained about the treatment of American seamen, requested a naval response, which was forthcoming under the command of Comm. John Rodgers. The USN had orders to stop the outrages committed upon the American seamen who had been attacked and even killed when their ships floundered in Korean waters.

On 30 May 1871, Rodgers' five ships anchored at Inchon. On 1 June he sent a surveying party up the Salee River which was fired upon by the occupants of one of the five forts covering the entrance to the Han River. Rodgers demanded an apology and, after ten days in which none was received, he ordered the landing of a naval brigade.

On 10 June the *Monacacy* and *Palos* with four steam launches carrying a battalion of 109 Marines commanded by Capt. McLane Tilton, as well as a brigade of 542 seaman with seven field pieces, sailed up the Salee toward the forts. The forts opened fire but their guns were quickly silenced by the guns aboard the two gunboats.

The Marines steam launches were cast free and the Marines, followed shortly by the sailors, landed in deep water and mud. The landing site was a mud flat and at first the going was difficult. Their assault was further harassed by small arms fire from the redoubt on their right flank. The Marines went right after those Koreans in the fort, who rapidly placed space between them and the Americans. The Marines went in, spiked the heavy guns and proceeded to dismantle anything likely to cause future trouble. The sailors soon came up and the two groups worked hard at ruining the fort. The combined Navy/Marine force spent that night on top of a nearby hill.

The next morning on the 11th, the Marines, followed by the sailors, made their way to the second line of Korean defense, renamed Fort Monocacy. After going over the walls they found the defenders gone. That fort, too, was rapidly dismantled and the thoughts of the Americans turned to the Citadel, the Koreans' main defense. It was perched upon a conical hill that began at least 150 feet above the bottom of a ravine. The climb was steep and the walls had no break in them — the Marines were going to have great difficulty piercing them. As luck would have it, the howitzers aboard *Monacacy* and *Palos* managed to break the walls into rubble. The Marines went up under heavy small arms fire, managed to burst into the Citadel and engaged in hand-to-hand combat with the defenders who remained. It wasn't until the last of the Koreans were dead or wounded and the Koreans in the other forts had fled that the fighting ceased. The final blow was when Tilton, with Cpl. Charles Brown of the *Alaska* and Pvt. Hugh Purvis of the *Colorado*, made their way through the crowds of Korean soldiers and cut down the huge yellow Chinese-lettered flag. At this, the sailors and Marines cheered. Later, Brown and Purvis were each awarded a Medal of Honor. Navy commander Lewis A. Kimberly, in overall charge of the ground operations, later gave Tilton and his Marines their due in his report:

> To Captain Tilton and his Marines belong the honor of the first landing and last leaving the shore, in leading the advance on the march, in entering the forts, and in acting as skirmishers. Chosen as the advance guard, on account of their steadiness and discipline, and looked to with

confidence in case of difficulty, their whole behavior on the march and in the assault proved that it was not misplaced.

In capturing the three fortresses, the Americans took 480 pieces of ordnance and 50 flags (important in those times) and killed at least 250 of the defenders, not counting the many wounded. The sailors were apparently sans casualties but one Marine, Private Dennis Harrigan, was killed and Private Michael Owen was wounded. Soon after, the Americans, who were convinced they had made their point and won the battle, went back to their ships. The Koreans, however, believed the Americans had retreated and had in effect lost the battle to them.

> *Results:* The USN landed Marines and sailors to take the forts located on the banks of the Salee River, which was accomplished in two days. That was the end of the cruelties and violence against American seamen, even though the Koreans refused to believe they had been defeated.

Date: May to October 1900.
Location: North China — Tientsin and Peking.
Involved: Chinese Imperial government and Boxers versus portions of the armies and navies of most European Powers and the U.S. Army, Navy, and Marines.
Situation: A secret society, known as the "Righteous Fists" or the "Boxers," became active in 1899 in north China and began destroying Christian missions and killing Chinese Christians and foreign missionaries. In May 1900 the foreigners in their legations at Peking began demanding their own governments' military support to protect the legations. With its naval forces nearby, among the first to respond was the United States.

On the 24th and 28th of May, the USN deposited two separate Marine ship detachments and a few sailors at Taku, the nearest naval port. The group then moved on to Tientsin and eventually to Peking.

Captain Bowman H. McCalla, USN, commanding 47 Marines plus a few sailors and various small foreign contingents, left by a Marine-operated train from Tientsin, making the 83-mile trip in three hours and reaching Peking about 2000.[1] The Marines, commanded by Capt. John T. Myers and seconded by Capt. Newt H. Hall, were first to disembark and at 2100 marched to the legation in the Tartar City at the head of the column. Leaving Myers in command, McCalla returned to Tientsin on the 2nd of June to wait for more troops to support those already at Peking.

Over the next three weeks the arrival of the various contingents gave each an opportunity to make plans to defend each legation according to its ability. Early on it was decided that the British Legation was the best location for a final defensive. It was the largest and most remote within the legation compound.

On 9 June a large party composed of British, Japanese, Russian, and a small number of American sailors, plus a few Marines led by a sergeant, made a move toward Peking from Tientsin to relieve the legations. Their attempt was a disaster. They had barely made 25 miles in nine days when they were forced by 60,000 Chinese regulars and Boxers to retire on 18 June. The American force was composed primarily of sailors from the various American ships at Taku, except for about 23 enlisted Marines led by Gy. Sgt. Patrick Stewart (MoH).

The entire force, with many wounded, was forced to take refuge on 21 June in a Chinese arsenal, where they remained until rescued. On the 25th, Seymour's badly handled column, still in the Chinese arsenal in which they had holed up, was relieved by Waller's 1st Battalion of Marines and some Russian soldiers.

On 18 June an international force of ships (less the American Navy) shelled and captured the forts at Taku. The Chinese government thereupon declared war upon the allied powers and gave the legation members 24 hours to vacate Peking. The Occidental powers replied that they were unable to comply. Trains were not running and there were many elderly and sick who would not be able to make the 90-mile trip in carts and other conveyances. Soon after, a call was sent out for all civilians to fall back upon the British Legation, the time being considered opportune, and perhaps not yet too late.

It wasn't long before the Chinese forces climbed the Tartar Wall surrounding the legation quarters and began firing down into the compounds. For some reason the Marines and their German Marine neighbors hadn't considered defending the wall. But under fire, they soon mounted the wall and drove the offending Chinese back to the Chien Men (gate). Boxers continued to use the parapet at the Chien Men to attack the Marines, now based on the wall. To the east of them the German Marines also attained control of their portion of the wall and they too erected a barricade, facing the Hata Men. Most important, as long as both groups of Marines controlled that wall, both the legation's buildings and personnel were safe from direct artillery and rifle fire.

On the 27th, in broad daylight, the Chinese sallied from behind their barricade at Chien Men and advanced on the run toward the U.S. position. They suffered substantial losses and it was the first and only time the Chinese launched a daylight attack on the American positions. Nevertheless, fighting continued all day and into the night of the 28th and also incessantly during the 29th and 30th. During the dark nights, the Chinese managed to advance their barricades on the wall until they gained a position at the corner of the bastion opposite that occupied by the U.S. Marines. On 30 June, the lines were only about 30 yards apart.

By this time, Myers had been on duty steadily for five days when he was relieved by Hall. The next day the Chinese had pushed their barricades within a few feet of the Marine position and were also building a 15-foot tower overlooking the Marine position. Myers returned to the wall at dusk on 2 July, but, to his dismay, he learned that during the preceding night and day the Chinese had succeeded in building a wall into and across the bastion. They were busily engaged in erecting that tower directly on Myers' left flank, the fire from which, when completed, would reach and rake all parts of the Marines' position.

To assist the Marines in taking the Chinese barricades, the Russians sent five men and the British about 20, both groups arriving at about 0300 on 3 July. The attack proceeded as scheduled but Myers was struck in his leg by a spear which inflicted a painful wound. Soon, however, the Chinese were completely defeated, an estimated 40 having been killed, and the balance were driven back some hundred yards, once again to Chien Men. However, the fight cost the lives of two U.S. Marines, an Englishman, and a Russian.

Although Myers was now seriously incapacitated, he retained overall command until 21 July. In actual fact Hall was now responsible for the American defense, and as Myers' already infected wound got worse he would remain so for the balance of the siege.[2]

From the 4th through 6th, there was only an intermittent slackening of fire by the enemy during the day. The allies hardly replied, for fear of wasting their ammunition supply.

United States Navy Gunner's Mate Joseph Mitchell found an ancient cannon barrel in the ruins of an ironmonger's shop on the 7th. Shortly afterwards he had it cleaned and mounted upon an Italian one-pounder gun carriage using discarded rickshaw wheels. Russian sailors found shells that didn't quite "fit" and although the first round dismounted the barrel from the carriage, further adjustments were made and soon it was doing a fine job for the entire legation. It was the beneficiary of many nicknames: "Betsy" and "The Old Crock" were two, but the final name became "The International Gun." According to one Englishman, it and the Marines' Colt machine gun "killed more men than all the rest put together." Presumably and hopefully he meant more Chinese.

About 2100 on 15 July, Hall took Pvt. Daniel J. Daly with him as they went out to reconnoiter the bastion. This was with the understanding that if they were not attacked ten minutes later the coolies were to come up with sand bags. The coolies did not come at the appointed time, and Hall considered his options. According to Hall's report Pvt. Daly requested permission to remain in the bastion while Hall returned below to look for the coolies. Hall found them and returned with them to the barricade but, without a satisfactory interpreter, had difficulty in directing their work. For some reason they couldn't or wouldn't stay, and Hall went back down with them. Daly, who was on that wall all night alone, managed to hold off several heavy attacks and disposed of numerous enemy as he held his position. He was the most famous man to earn a Medal of Honor during the entire period.[3]

Somehow, and there is no explanation as to how and why, a sort of armistice was instituted, though the defense of the legations went on. By the middle of the month it appeared that serious trouble for the Chinese government was on its way westward. Cooler heads among the Manchu bureaucrats had suddenly come to the conclusion that the Boxers were a "broken reed." Thus began a period of "not peace, but not war."

During all of this period, the Foreign Settlement at Tientsin had been under siege by the Chinese. Allied forces had to first protect them before venturing onward to Peking. The 1st Battalion of U.S. Marines, Maj. Littleton W. T. Waller, CO, arrived at Taku on 19 June and immediately began trying to make its way through to Tientsin. In a few days Waller and his force, along with a large force of Russian soldiers, proceeded to within a short distance of Tong-ku, a place nearly halfway to Tientsin. But their combined force of less than 550 fighting men was attempting to push back or through an estimated 50,000 Chinese. Several times the Russian formation was badly hurt and retreated while the small Marine contingent protected their withdrawal. Waller decided that his handful of Marines could "not lick the whole Chinese nation" and they too fell back. In all, they had advanced 30 horrific miles with numerous Marine casualties and heroics.

A small British force and more Russians arrived and Maj. Waller decided to act in cooperation with the British Marines who were under the command of Comdr. Christopher Cradock, RN. The entire force, including a few Japanese and Italians, now totaled about 2,000, with half of them Russians. On the morning of the 23rd more German soldiers arrived.

On the morning of the 24th they all moved toward Tientsin. They were met by thousands of Chinese, but nevertheless drove them steadily backward until the combined force entered the Tientsin Foreign Settlements, relieving the besieged Europeans. These were the first foreign troops to arrive after the siege of Tientsin had begun and as they entered the concession Marine buglers played a loud rendition of a then very popular American song. American occupants of that city related their joy, relief, and pride when the Marines came marching in under the American flag. Later, in Herbert Hoover's personal memoir, he related how those Marines looked to him coming in: "I do not remember a more satisfying musical performance than the bugles of the American Marines entering the settlement playing *There'll Be a Hot Time in the Old Town Tonight.*"

Captain Bowman H. McCalla, USN, was still on his feet even though he had been wounded three times. Feeling weak, McCalla decided to give up and turn over total command of U.S. naval forces in China to Waller. Fighting around Tientsin continued. Finally, after several disappointments, on 9 July the allies agreed to attack the west arsenal in two columns. Waller, with 2,000 men, later reported that his duty was to cut off the Chinese retreat beyond the arsenal toward the city. The allies attacked the left flank of the Chinese army. Within an hour the international forces drove the Chinese westward, all the while being subjected to weighty shell fire. Proceeding to the arsenal, Waller's force was met by very dense rifle fire and reported losses of 45 men, Marines and sailors, of whom 7 were killed.

Attacks on the Chinese walled city at Tientsin continued; the next on 13 July would be the crucial attack. Colonel Robert L. Meade, USMC, with a group of 318 American Marines, arrived at Tientsin about midnight on 11–12 July. Upon arrival he replaced Waller as officer in command of the naval forces ashore in China. The Marine composition, with Waller's men, was considered to be two infantry battalions, regimental headquarters and an artillery company which included three 3-inch guns and three Colt machine guns. This was all compressed into about 420 Marines. The Marines did big things in a small way in those years.

Arriving on the 12th, the 9th Infantry of two battalions, Col. Emerson H. Liscum, USA, CO, was brigaded with the 1st Marine Regiment, under Col. Meade, who was senior officer. The Americans, in turn, were brigaded with a British force of over 2,000 men. All told the foreign troops now numbered 5,650, of which more than half were Americans and British.

It was soon decided that before the foreign troops could march on Peking, the Chinese-occupied walled city of Tientsin had to be conquered. The date decided upon was 13 July, and that morning Meade provided 1,000 men. The 9th Infantry would furnish 666 officers and men and the Marines 333, "including the artillery serving under me." At 0300 Meade marched out of the encampment with his Marines in the forefront. At approximately 0630, 7,000 allied troops began an assault against the walled city defended by about 50,000 Chinese Boxers and Imperial troops, which were well supplied with artillery and well trained to use their Krupp guns by European military experts. British and Americans moved against the southern side of the wall. During this day, the U.S. Marines would be called upon to support the Royal Welch Fusiliers on the extreme left of the line. Their front was swamp and included huge grave mounds, used to great advantage by the enemy snipers, and the Marine casualties increased dramatically. It has been recorded that the temperature in that area might have gone as high as 140 degrees Fahrenheit that day. The ground between the allies and Chinese was composed of rice paddies, graves, salt mounds and sewer muck from the old city, all of which contributed greatly to the overall discomfort of the allied forces. At this point Capt. Austin R. Davis, USMC, was killed by a stray bullet. He was the highest-ranking Marine to be killed during this war. Overall, the attack was unsuccessful.

As they retired, 1st Lt. Smedley D. Butler and two other Marines picked up a wounded Pvt. I. W. Partridge and began carrying him to safety. While so engaged, Butler was wounded. With supplies from his first-aid packet he covered the torn flesh and found that even though it "hurt like hell" he could still walk. Butler, Charles G. Long, and William

B. Lemly all received minor wounds in the battle, but each recovered in only a few days. But 1st Lt. Henry Leonard suffered the loss of his right arm. Most of the enlisted men who were wounded also recovered.

The day ended with the majority of Marines having expended all 180 rounds of their rifle ammunition as well as their meager allowance of artillery shells. Most of them were physically exhausted by their exertions in the day's heat. During this hectic day, six Marines earned the Medal of Honor and several Marine officers earned a brevet promotion, which was then their highest possible attainment.[4]

During the night of 13–14 July, Japanese infantry unsuccessfully attacked across the causeway leading to the city gates. At 0430 the Chinese artillery had opened fire and it became so severe by 0500 that the men were ordered out of their forward trenches. The Chinese infantry moved forward and occupied a burned village within 600 yards of the Marines' position. Marines re-occupied the trenches, and in the process, five more were killed and 23 wounded.

At 0600 a Japanese engineering officer blew himself and the south gate to bits, but effectively opened Tientsin to the allied forces. The defenders were by now completely demoralized and, according to Butler, fled in all directions, assuring the relatively easy capture of the city. The American forces had, however, been quite heavily hit in the process.

Because of rheumatism, Col. Robert L. Meade was declared unfit on 23 July 1900 by a board of medical survey and relieved. For the next few weeks Maj. Waller succeeded to the command of the 1st Regiment of Marines.

August 1 was the date originally scheduled for the advance on Peking. Newly arrived Maj. Gen. Adna Chaffee and other allied commanders, however, made the decision not to advance in force upon Peking and relieve the besieged legations until 4 August. Chaffee assigned a detachment of six Marine officers and 177 men, supported by two Navy surgeons, to remain and protect Tientsin, or at least the International Settlement. Captain Melville J. Shaw was the officer left to command the detachment. As a consequence, just two Marine battalions of the 1st Regiment accompanied the relief column.

But Chaffee wasn't finished with the Marines just yet. He had the 2nd Battalion, led by Capt. Franklin J. Moses (he would arrive with Biddle), assigned to the onerous duty of guarding the pack train. That left just the one Marine battalion for the anticipated fighting.

On 3 August, the 4th Battalion of Marines, now under the command of Maj. William P. Biddle, had arrived from Cavite at Taku. Biddle, now the senior Marine officer in China, relieved Waller of command of the 1st Regiment of Marines. According to the records, 650 Marines were in China, of which 29 officers and 453 enlisted men, or a total of 482, went to Peking.

It would be ten days before the allied column of 16,500 reached Peking. The heat on the march was intense, and the ensuing casualties slowed down the entire column. Being at the rear of the column doesn't allow for much activity, but on 6 August the Marines became involved in action with the Chinese. At Yang-tsun they provided infantry support for Reilly's Battery of the 5th Artillery, U.S. Army. The front was occupied by Waller's 1st Battalion of Marines, with the 2nd Battalion (Moses) in reserve. Chinese cavalry appeared on the right flank but the accurate Marine rifle fire soon repulsed them.

Now without serious opposition, the Marines went in and took the village. The all-important river crossing, which the Imperial troops had been protecting, was now in the possession of the Marines. Marine Sgt. Frank Keeler wrote in his diary on the 7th, "3 P.M. two-thirds of the command were missing." The men who couldn't keep up during the day came into camp that night. Second Lieutenant William C. Harllee witnessed soldiers of the column fall and die from convulsions, stricken by heat, dysentery and typhoid. He admitted that he had hoped to be wounded during the battle for Yang-tsun, therefore being relieved from the agonies of the march.

Even though they were but a few miles from Peking on the 13th, the entire allied force agreed to take a day of rest. It was to be, nonetheless, a day of reconnoitering as the attack upon the walls of Peking was being developed. However, because of movement by the Russians, everything changed dramatically. Chaffee later reported that the international forces heard firing from near the city of Peking beginning at about 2100 that evening. It was later learned that the Russians had advanced and the Chinese army had counterattacked them and the legations with an unexpected violence which died down by morning. It was, it seems, a last gasp by the Chinese, but the Russians were driven off and were of less use to the allied force.

Although the plans made for each nation's assault were now compromised by the early move of the Russians, each group did its best to live up to and follow the plan agreed upon. Biddle and his Marines moved out at about 0600 in what was then a driving rain. Instead of dust, it was mud the Marines and soldiers of the 9th Infantry were forced to march through. By 0700 the Marines were just before the Peking walls. Major Waller issued orders for part of Companies A and H to move forward to put an end to the Chinese firing from the wall.

At 1230 Biddle repositioned his men to a place nearer the Sha-Huo Gate. It would be their job to break through at this point and move through the Tartar City toward the legations. He then ordered two platoons of A Company to climb the walls and drive off the Chinese that were firing upon the relief force. It was here that Capt. Butler and two privates, G. P. Farrell and F. W. Green, were wounded, but fortunately all the wounds were slight. A bullet had grazed one of Butler's buttons and ripped out a small piece of flesh, deleting a portion of Latin America on his chest tattoo of the globe, eagle, and anchor. In spite of Butler's wound in the chest and his two previous wounds, after a few body repairs he would resume his place in line and continue to command Company A.

The British had not yet arrived when the Americans began assaulting the walls. But when they did arrive, their artillery blew a hole in the Sha-Huo Gate, and at the same time a sepoy from the 24th Rajputs had climbed the wall and opened the gate from inside. The British sepoys made their way to Hata-Men, where a German Marine sentry welcomed them in through the Imperial Canal water gate. As they entered they met a party of Marines cutting through the bars of the sluice gate to get into the legation quarters and helped them squeeze through. At about 1400 the legations were relieved. Two hours later the rest of the U.S. command followed and much later the Japanese and Russians came in. Finally, after 55 days, the legations were relieved.

The allies fought a few battles against die-hard Chinese forces in the Imperial City, but for all intents the occupation of Peking began on the 15th of August. What the allied forces did while there was to become a grave embarrassment for Europeans and Americans alike. The cost of the destruction of valuables, art, and artifacts, as well as theft, ran into the millions. And the Americans, including the Marines — and Biddle and Waller and the other officers and men — were a large part of the worst of the depredation.

For some reason, one can only wonder why, on 4 September Maj. Gen. Chaffee put a battalion of Marines in each of the Army brigades. To keep them apart, perhaps, or to strengthen the Army units? Ten days later Waller was appointed provost marshal of Tartar City.

The 49 officers and 1,151 enlisted Marines at Peking were desperately needed elsewhere and on 28 September Rear Admiral Charles C. Remey, USN, commander of all U.S. naval forces on the Asiatic Station, received a telegram from the secretary of the Navy advising him that Maj. Gen. Chaffee had received orders to withdraw all American forces from China save a legation guard. Remey was directed to withdraw all of his Navy and Marines in China and to ship them back to Cavite in the Philippines as soon as possible. On 10 October, the 1st Marine Regiment embarked aboard the *Indiana*, *Zafiro*, and *Brooklyn*. The day before, Colonel Henry C. Cochrane, USMC, had received an appointment as district commander of the Cavite Peninsula and commanding officer of the 1st Brigade of Marines in the Philippines. The 1st Regiment would soon be in his department.

Sixty soldiers, sailors, and Marines earned Medals of Honor in China, of which 4 were USA, 22 were USN and 33 were Marines. Of the latter, 18 were at Peking, 6 were to members of the 23 Marines in Seymour's column, and 9 were divided between Waller's battalion and the balance of Meade's 1st Marine Regiment while fighting for Tientsin.

> *Results:* Though there were five parts to the entire affair, the engagement lasted less than 90 days in all. Eventually, of the total U.S. participation (approximately 5,500 men) the Marines numbered about 1,200 officers and men. Their part at the defense of the legations at Peking was outstanding and crucial, for it was they who were primarily responsible for keeping the Boxers, and later the Chinese army, from taking over the legation compound. Saving the civilian personnel was, after all, the primary reason for the expedition.
>
> The U.S. Marines were withdrawn in early October for service in the Philippines, while the balance of the foreigners remained in occupation for many months to come. The defeat drove the Empress away from Peking and eventually a new Chinese Imperial government was created.

From the Philippines a detachment of 100 Marines, commanded by Capt. Harry Lee and 1st Lt. Thomas Holcomb, relieved troops of the 9th Infantry as the legation guard at Peking, China, on the 12th of September, 1905. This state of affairs had been a bone of contention between the U.S. Marine Corps and the U.S. Army. At the conclusion of the Boxer Rebellion the latter had been assigned this duty by Maj. Gen. Chaffee, but the duty was normally a responsibility of the USMC. It would remain within their purview until 8 December 1941, when the legation Marines would be forced to surrender to overwhelming Japanese forces.

> *Date:* October 1911 to November 1912.
> *Location:* China.
> *Involved:* Chinese nationalists versus the Imperial government; U.S. Marines.
> *Situation:* Millions of Chinese people, fed up with the royals that had been ruining China for so many centuries, were in an uproar all over the nation and the Americans and Europeans were frightened. There had been some deaths, cruelties, and destruction, mainly among the Chinese, and consequently forces

were being collected from all over the world. On 9 October 1911, a bomb built by Chinese revolutionaries exploded, sheerly by accident, at the Russian Concession in Hankow. That act, however, was given as the commencing of the Chinese revolution, after which President Sun Yat Sen became the first president of a republic after thousands of years of imperialism. During the period, there were many occurrences of violence against citizens of China and some foreigners, and U.S. Marines were frequently called in to protect their own.

Ten Marines and seamen from the *Helena* landed at Hankow, China, on 13 October 1911 to protect Standard Oil Company property from violent elements. Those Marines, 27 of them, and 23 Bluejackets, with two Colt machine guns, were sent ashore to help German Marines in guarding and defending their concession. Four days later they went ashore to help in defending the Japanese concession. On 4 November 24 Marines from the *Albany* and *Rainbow* landed at Woosung (near Shanghai), China, to guard two cable stations (12 each at Great Northern and Commercial) during a period of political disturbance. They returned to the *Rainbow* on the 14th. And on 29 November a company of Marines from Shanghai sailed on the *Saratoga* for Taku, China, to protect missionaries during a period of political upheaval.

The following year, on 4 March 1912, two companies of Marines, commanded by Maj. Philip M. Bannon, departed Olongapo, Philippine Islands, on the *Cincinnati* and *Abarenda*, for Taku, China, to protect American lives and property in north China during a period of political unrest. On the 11th that detachment, temporarily at Taku, moved to Peking to relieve a detachment of the 15th Infantry as embassy guard.[5]

A Marine detachment from the *Rainbow*, commanded by Capt. Thomas C. Turner, landed on Kentucky Island, near Shanghai, on 24 August 1912 to protect American lives and property from local revolutionary elements. Two days later the same detachment landed at Camp Nicholson, near Shanghai, China, to protect American interests.

Then from Guam, in November 1912, a detachment of 36 Marines under 2nd Lt. Harry Schmidt landed at Chefoo, China, remaining ashore for a few days to reinforce the Marines protecting American interests during the continuing local unrest.

> *Results:* Marines landed to protect American lives and property whenever they were threatened, but nothing more. This would essentially be the relationship between U.S. forces and Chinese troops for the following 36 years. A Marine brigade, the 3rd, would be sent to "protect American citizens" in 1927 but would leave in 1929, leaving behind the 4th Marines, which would occupy a portion of Shanghai from 1927 until November 1941. There would be many confrontations during that period but none of any serious consequence, that is until the U.S. Marines were sent to north China following the end of World War II in the Pacific. There they were to assist the Nationalist forces versus the Communist forces. The former lost, and the Marines left China forever in 1949.

9

Colombia/Panama

Date: 7 to 17 May 1873.
Location: Panama City.
Involved: Colombian army, Colombian (Panamanian) rebels, U.S. Marines and U.S. Navy.
Situation: A rebel faction captured and imprisoned the governor of the state, after which the faction established an independent Panamanian provisional government, which local Colombian troops refused to recognize. Then the war began.

The USN South Pacific Squadron's commander RA Charles Steedman arrived in Panama City on 7 May aboard his flagship *Pensacola* and accompanied by the *Tuscarora*. A landing force was soon sent ashore. This was at the request of American consul O. M. Long and "a number of influential Americans" in residence. First Lieutenant Henry J. Bishop led ashore 44 Marines and Lt. Comdr. Theodore F. Jewell with 160 Bluejackets and four pieces of artillery. Their job was to protect the consulate, American citizens, and the American-owned railroad.

The Colombian troops had a somewhat modest responsibility, but in about ten days the rebels laid down their arms and the rebellion was over. The American forces were then withdrawn.

Results: The American residents, railroad, and consulate were protected throughout the period of unrest.

Date: 24 September to 9 October 1873.
Location: Panama City.
Involved: Colombian army, Colombian (Panamanian) rebels, U.S. Marines and U.S. Navy.
Situation: The same rebel faction rose in rebellion again.

Upset over what it perceived as its ill-treatment, the same rebel faction again took up arms against the Colombian government. The U.S. ship *Benicia* under the command of Capt. Albert G. Clary arrived and was soon followed by the *Pensacola* with RA Steedman aboard. The shooting had become dangerous to people ashore, and Mr. Long once again requested a landing force. On 24 September *Pensacola* Marines under the command of Capt. Percival C. Pope with 2nd Lt. James V. D'Hervilly and 2nd Lt. Henry G. Ellsworth with Marines from the *Benicia* landed with Bluejackets, and two howitzers, all under the command of Capt. Aaron K. Hughes, USN.

By 4 October conditions had improved and the landing force from *Benicia* returned to its ship. Those from *Pensacola* returned to their vessel on 9 October. The ships remained in port until 24 October (*Pensacola*) and 14 December (*Benicia*).

>*Results:* The American residents, railroad, and consulate were protected throughout the period of unrest.

>*Date:* 16 March to 25 May 1885.
>*Location:* Aspinwall, Colombia (now Colon, Panama).
>*Involved:* Rebels, composed mostly of imported Haitian workers; U.S. Marines and U.S. Navy.
>*Situation:* Unrest at the Atlantic port of Aspinwall required U.S. intervention to protect citizens and the American-owned railroad. This would constitute a major landing of the Marines during the nineteenth century.

Though 12 years had elapsed since the previous altercations on the Pacific side of the isthmus, serious trouble raised its ugly head on the Atlantic coast after the New Year in 1885. On 16 January Cmdr. Lewis Clark in the *Alliance* arrived at Aspinwall and was immediately visited by Consul Robert K. Wright, Jr., who reported the current conditions ashore. He requested that a Marine guard come ashore to protect the railroad and Clark had the CO of the Marine detachment, 1st Lt. Louis J. Gulick, select a suitable number of Marines for duty ashore. On the 18th Gulick and his command were ashore but because the situation had quieted down, they were withdrawn on the 19th.

More trouble and, on 11 March, the *Galena* under the command of Cmdr. Theodore F. Kane, arrived. After discussions with Consul Wright, Kane had 2nd Lt. Charles A. Doyen take 16 Marines ashore on the 16th of March for the usual protection of "American citizens, railroad, and consulate." A bit later that day another Marine officer (unnamed) and 12 Marines were sent ashore in support of Doyen. On the 17th and 19th more Marines and officers were sent ashore.

On 30 March a most serious action came about which could have triggered more conflict than had so far occurred. An American ship, the *Colon*, in port at Aspinwall, flew the national ensign union down, the sign of distress. Kane sent Lt. Charles H. Judd, USN, ashore to learn the nature of *Colon*'s difficulties. He returned and reported that the ship carried arms and ammunition which the rebel chieftain, Prestan, a Haitian Negro, had demanded be handed over to him. The ship's captain had refused and Prestan had threatened him, his crew and his ship if he failed to comply.

Kane then sent Judd ashore with Naval Cadet Richardson (later Ensign Walter G. Richardson) to discuss the matter with the American civilian agents of the Pacific Mail Steamship Company. In the process, Richardson reported back that Prestan had arrested Judd, Consul Wright, and both representatives of the steamship company, demanding, in exchange for their release, the arms and ammunition. Prestan also made it known to Richardson that if the USN fired upon him and his men, the prisoners would be immediately shot. Kane, the father of future Marine officer Theodore P. "Tippy" Kane, would not, under any circumstances, suffer that kind of ultimatum.

Kane ordered his starboard battery loaded with grape and aimed toward the pier on which the rebels were gathering. That changed the complexion of Prestan's demands. Less than a hour later Judd, Wright, and the two civilians were released. Kane sent a crew aboard the *Colon* to bring her out of the harbor and then brought all the Americans aboard the *Galena* for their protection.

The following day, 31 March, Kane sent Doyen and 18 of his Marines, along with several naval officers and a detachment of Bluejackets to the strength of 126 men, to guard American property. Soon after going ashore the Colombian army arrived and began beating upon the rebels. The rebels soon were pressed back into the city and the fighting turned hot and heavy. A fire broke out and soon the city was in flames. The Marines and Bluejackets ashore tried to prevent looting as well as they could, with modest success.

Meanwhile, the trouble spread widely, and by the first week in April American Marines and Bluejackets were landing at Panama City. By the 10th both the *Alliance* and the *Tennessee*, with RA James E. Jouett aboard, had arrived at Panama City. In the meantime an expeditionary force of Marines and sailors had been made ready for duty on the isthmus. Marines under the command of Maj. Charles Heywood arrived at Aspinwall on 10 April.

On 11 April Heywood and his command were dispatched by rail to Panama City. It was Heywood's job to protect the American-owned transit. By 25 April he would command 685 Marines spread throughout the isthmus, mainly grouped at key points along the rail line. That was about one-third the total personnel of the Corps. On the 15th Cmdr. Bowman H. McCalla, a fighting sailor frequently associated with the Marines, was in overall command of the situation ashore. In those days the Navy made sure a sailor was in command ashore as well as aboard ship. McCalla was capable and a better man than many others when it came to problems ashore.

By the 21st most of the activity was centered in or around Panama City, where the insurgents, under "Gen." Aizpuru, had congregated after being driven from Aspinwall. McCalla was concerned that he and his followers might destroy the city as they had Aspinwall and called for the concentration of all Marines at Panama City. This included the numerous Marines from ship detachments assembled in the harbor. There were several confrontations between the Marines there and the rebels, but nothing of consequence came from them. On 28 April a confab between the parties involved took place and Aizpuru concluded a surrender to the Colombian army. There no longer being need of American forces ashore, they began the return to their ships and away from the isthmus, for the time being. There was a minor disturbance in 1895 in which few Marines were involved.

> *Results:* The conflict was settled eventually but not peaceably. Threats of shelling by the USN, a major landing by Marines, and the final return of the Colombian army were required to put down the rebellion. This appears to have been the largest action of Marines between the Civil War and the war in Cuba.

———m———

Date: 24 November to 4 December 1901.
Location: Panama City and Aspinwall (Colon).
Involved: Panamanian rebels, Colombian army, U.S. Marines and U.S. Navy.
Situation: More insurgency. Rebels from the isthmus declared their independence from Colombia. With both forces engaged in a fierce struggle for supremacy, the warships of several foreign nations, including Great Britain and France,

were on the scene to protect their nationals. This made the U.S. government uneasy, therefore it sent two small fleets to both the Atlantic and Pacific sides of the isthmus. The Pacific fleet arrived on 23 November and the Atlantic on 26 November. Both American fleets sent Marines and Bluejackets ashore.

Captain Albert S. McLemore and 2nd Lt. Edward A. Greene commanded their Marines and seamen from the *Iowa* and sergeants (unnamed) led their detachments from the *Machias* and *Marietta* at Panama City, Colombia, on 24 November to protect American citizens and their property. The following day, a battalion of Marines and seamen were landed from the *Concord*. They remained ashore until 4 December, when all were withdrawn to their ships. During this time, until 4 December, the Marines were also utilized as guards aboard the trains of the Panama Railroad, crossing the isthmus. By 28 November an agreement was signed between the opposing factions and by 4 December all Marines were withdrawn.

Results: With interference from U.S. forces, the rebels were forced to capitulate.

Date: 16 April to 18 November 1902.
Location: Aspinwall and Boca Del Toro (area north of Aspinwall).
Involved: Panamanian rebels, Colombian army, U.S. Marines and U.S. Navy.
Situation: More insurgency. Rebels from the isthmus once again declared their independence from Colombia. More difficulties ensued when rebels made moves threatening the area of Boca del Toro. This is where the United Fruit Company had its major shipping ports. On 16 April two officers and 28 Marines and Bluejackets were landed to provide protection.

Commander William P. Potter and his ship *Ranger* arrived at Panama City on 18 May, ostensibly to land Marines to protect American lives and property during a political disturbance. He soon learned that conditions ashore did not require a landing force, but Potter and his ship remained on watch. By the 18th the Liberal forces (read rebels) had signed an agreement ending the conflict with the government.

On 17 September Marines were landed at Aspinwall to guard the railroad, but by 21 September they were withdrawn permanently. By midday on the 19th government troops had arrived aboard ships. At first they threatened to shell the area, but agreed, with pressure from the USN, not to do so. Then, as the Colombian troops were being landed from their transport, Cmdr. McCrea landed the same force of 28 men on the 20th. Conditions at Aspinwall settled down and nothing untoward happened.

Commander Thomas C. McLean of the *Cincinnati* led ashore Marines and seamen at Colon, Panama, on the 17th of September to protect American lives and property. As usual, part of the detachment was diverted to protect the trains running across the isthmus. The detachment returned aboard each night and went ashore each morning. A few days later, on the 22nd, a battalion of 325 Marines, commanded by Lt. Col. Benjamin R. Russell, arrived at Colon aboard the *Panther* to protect American lives and property during this period of civil strife. On the 25th it went ashore and into camp. The battalion would remain there until it returned to the *Panther* on 18 November.

Meanwhile, the USMC commandant received orders from the Navy secretary to form an expeditionary battalion for service in Panama with Lt. Col. Benjamin R. Russell in command of 16 officers and 365 enlisted Marines. The force landed at Aspinwall on 22 September and went into camp, remaining there until 18 November 1902. The Liberal revolt eventually was brought under control by government forces and the U.S. presence was no longer required.

Results: Marines landed to protect U.S. citizens, but mainly to protect the American-owned railroad, and immediately went into camp for an extended period.

Republic of Panama

Date: 4 November 1903 to 21 January 1912.
Location: Colon (formerly Aspinwall), and other areas throughout the Republic of Panama.
Involved: Panamanian rebels, Colombian troops, U.S. Marines and U.S. Navy ships.
Situation: Panamanians declared independence from Colombia on 3 November 1903. In reaction, Colombian troops landed at Colon on 3 November. The U.S. president, Theodore Roosevelt, virtually recognized the new state on 6 November.[1]

Marines from the *Nashville* led by Lt. Comdr. Horace M. Witzel landed at noon on 4 November to protect American citizens and the railroad offices. This was followed by numerous other landings by Marines during subsequent weeks. The *Nashville* had arrived off Colon on 2 November, quickly followed by a Colombian troop transport, which disembarked its 500 troops on the morning of the 3rd. Their ultimate destination was to be Panama City but the American naval officer, Cmdr. John Hubbard, "persuaded" him to not proceed further. This in effect ensured that the Colombian troops could not take passage to Panama City.

On the evening of 5 November the USN transport *Dixie* arrived and the Colombian troops boarded a ship and left for ports unknown. That afternoon two companies of Marines under the command of Maj. John A. Lejeune went ashore and relieved those from the *Nashville.* Over the next few weeks more Marines arrived and were landed under the command of Capts. Norman G. Burton and Wirt McCreery and 2nd Lt. Fred A. Ramsey. Eventually Lejeune and his men went to Empire to establish a camp.

In the meantime, other Marine units were being assembled at Philadelphia, and on 11 December Maj. Lewis C. Lucas left there with a battalion of Marines, arriving at Colon on 24 December and going into camp. A regiment under Col. Littleton W. T. Waller left Philadelphia on the 28th and arrived at Colon on 3 January. The Brig. Gen. Commandant, George F. Elliott, arrived with Waller's regiment, as did Maj. James E. Mahoney, CO of the 1st Battalion, and Maj. Eli K. Cole, CO of the 2nd Battalion. Mahoney and his men went to Bas Obispo while Cole and his command went to the camp at Empire. On 15 February, Lucas and his command re-embarked for the destination of Guantanamo Bay.

Camp Elliott, Canal Zone, was opened on 20 December to provide a base for Marine forces operating in the area. Earlier in the month Marines had arrived aboard the *Yankee* under the command of Lt. Col. Thomas N. Wood. They landed and were the first Marines to occupy the camp.

On 20 May 1906 Maj. Lejeune led a battalion from Philadelphia for expeditionary duty in Panama. Traveling with him was the regimental commander, Col. James E.

Mahoney. Upon arrival they went into camp with Maj. Charles G. Long's battalion, already at Bas Obispo.

A battalion of 19 officers and 706 enlisted Marines was sent in June 1908 to the newly created state of Panama to prevent disorder during the election process. It were led by Lt. Col. Eli K. Cole and shipped out on the *Idaho* and *New Hampshire*. In order to be able to respond to any disruption, Marines were distributed to three locations. Trains were standing by each location for a quick trip to wherever they might be needed in a hurry.

The Marine battalion commanded by Lt. Col. Eli K. Cole, originally sent to Panama in June to prevent disorder during elections, departed the republic on 31 July aboard the *Idaho* and *New Hampshire* for the United States without any unpleasant happenstance.[2]

> *Results:* The U.S. established a protectorate over the new state for the main purpose of establishing and protecting a canal through the isthmus. Marines, with various changes in personnel, would remain as guards in the Isthmus of Panama until permanently relieved by the U.S. Army on 21 January 1914. The United States retained its protectorate over the canal until the administration of President Jimmy Carter, when he returned control to Panama.

10

Spanish-American-Cuban War

Date: 1 May to 3 May 1898.
Location: Philippine Islands — Manila Bay.
Involved: Spanish fleet versus the U.S. fleet.
Situation: Commodore George Dewey, USN, of the Asiatic Fleet, received a telegram from assistant secretary of the Navy Theodore Roosevelt, notifying him to be prepared to take out the Spanish fleet based at Cavite in Manila Bay, Philippine Islands. Dewey was ready, as was the U.S. Navy.

On 1 May the U.S. Asiatic Fleet was in Manila Bay, near the Cavite Naval Station, home of the Eastern Spanish Fleet. That morning Marines manned the secondary batteries aboard ships of Comm. George Dewey's squadron during the Battle of Manila Bay. At 0505 1 May 1898, the flagship signaled, "prepare for general action," and as the signal flags were hauled down the Stars and Stripes broke out from the masthead of every ship in the fleet and the bugles and drums sounded the "Call to Quarters." On the *Baltimore* the Marine detachment manned main battery guns nos. 1, 3, and 5. The no. 1 gun was an eight-inch forecastle gun, the no. 3 a six-inch gun in the waist on the main deck, and the no. 5 was an eight-inch gun on the poop.

The ships of Dewey's fleet at Manila Bay all carried Marines and they were distributed as follows: *Olympia*, flagship of the Asiatic Station, carried an MD of 45 men commanded by Capt. William P. Biddle.[1] Captain Biddle was the fleet Marine officer of the Asiatic Station at the time of the Battle of Manila Bay. The *Baltimore*, ordered to join the Asiatic Station on 25 March 1898, carried an MD of 52 men commanded by Capt. Otway C. Berryman, with 1st Lt. Dion Williams as the junior officer of the detachment. The *Raleigh* carried an MD of 30 men commanded by 1st Lt. Thomas C. Treadwell. The *Boston* carried an MD of 30 men commanded by 1st Lt. Robert McM. Dutton. The *Concord* carried an MD of 18 men commanded by 1st Sgt. Charles Bonhert. The *Petrel* carried an MD of 9 men commanded by 1st Sgt. Richard E. Burton.

All men in the U.S. fleet, sailors and Marines, were the instruments of a complete victory over the unprepared Spanish fleet on this date. The Spanish casualties were huge, and the fleet was no more. American losses were minuscule: just six seamen were slightly wounded. On the next day the Spanish commander elected to surrender the Cavite Naval Station.

The morning of 3 May brought information from shore that the Spanish land forces and the naval personnel ashore at Cavite from the sunken ships had evacuated the Cavite arsenal and the town of Cavite. Comm. Dewey ordered the captain of the *Baltimore* to land an MD to take charge of the arsenal and town at Cavite and to protect property there.

That morning a detachment of *Baltimore* Marines, commanded by 1st Lt. Dion Williams, landed at Cavite, establishing a guard over the station and especially the arsenal.

As soon as order was restored in the arsenal and town the Stars and Stripes were hoisted on the flagstaff at the arsenal while the Marine guard presented arms and the bugler sounded "To the Colors." This was the first flag hoisted on Spanish soil in the Spanish-American War and the halliards were manned by Sgt. James Grant and Cpl. Joseph Poe. The flag was preserved and afterward turned over to Dewey, who sent it to the Naval Academy with a letter stating the facts concerning it.[2]

> *Results:* It was a slaughter. The U.S. fleet easily destroyed the enemy fleet. This was the beginning of the conquest of the Philippine Islands, which would become much more difficult as the months and years went by.

Date: 11 May to 13 August 1898.
Location: Cuba and the seas offshore.
Involved: Spain and the U.S. Army, Navy and Marines.
Situation: Wild newspaper reports instigated a war with Spain, especially after the destruction of the battleship *Maine* in Havana harbor, which everyone blamed on Spain. Supposedly it was over the issue of freedom for the Cuban people. Perhaps that was what the Cuban and American people desired. More likely it was intended to drive Spain entirely out of the Western Hemisphere.

On 11 May Marines and seamen from the *Marblehead* cut the transoceanic cable off Cienfuegos, Cuba, but the enemy had a Maxim machine gun which created severe problems for the naval force in the boats. Five American seamen were wounded, three seriously, and Lt. Cameron M. Winslow, the officer commanding, received a slight wound to his hand. The Marines, however, had two Marines mortally wounded: Patrick Regan and Herman W. Kuchneister. The latter, plus nine other Marines, was awarded a Medal of Honor for his bravery.

On the following day, during the bombardment of San Juan de Puerto Rico, Marines served the secondary batteries aboard ships of the North Atlantic Squadron. The secondary batteries of the *Iowa* began the fight at 0517 when the six-inch guns fired at Fort Morro. Captain Robley D. Evans reported three men wounded: Marine Pvt. G. Merkle and two seamen, J. Mitchell and R. C. Hill.

On the last day of May Marines serving with Adm. William P. Sampson's fleet assisted in the bombardment of the Spanish fortress at Morro Castle, Santiago-de-Cuba. This bombardment continued for much of the month of June.

The 1st Marine Battalion, under the command of Lt. Col. Robert W. Huntington, embarked for Cuba on the *Panther* from its temporary camp at Key West, FL. The same day, Marines from ships of Adm. William P. Sampson's fleet landed at Playa del Este, Guantanamo Bay, Cuba, and destroyed a cable station. On the 10th Huntington's 1st Marine Battalion, composed of 23 officers and 623 enlisted Marines, landed at Guantanamo, Cuba, together with the Marine guard of the *Oregon*. While on outpost duty, 1st Lt. Wendell C. Neville[3] and his platoon of Company D were attacked by Spaniards. Two privates, William P. Dunphy and James McColgan, were killed.[4] The platoon was reinforced by that of 2nd Lt. Melville D. Shaw, which came rushing up at the sound of gunfire. That attack was beaten off, but the Spaniards would continue shooting in the direction of the Marines for several days to come.

On the 12th the Marine guard of the *Texas* reinforced Marines ashore at Guantanamo Bay and assisted in the defense of Camp McCalla.[5] On this date at about 0230, 1st Sgt. Henry Goode was killed just outside his tent, and sometime that night Sgt. Charles Smith and Surgeon Blair Gibbs, USN, were killed in action. Private Goode Taurman was also killed that night, but his body disappeared and it was much later that the Marines learned that he had fallen into the water and his body had been retrieved by a boat crew of sailors nearby. Additionally, four more Marines were wounded. All the losses were suffered by Co. D. Eventually, five companies with four Colt machine guns and the artillery company with three 3-inch rapid-fire field guns manned the outpost line.

Having had enough of the Spaniards shooting and killing or wounding Marines, three officers and two companies of Marines, C and D, commanded by Capt. George F. Elliott of Co. C, with three Colts and 50 Cuban volunteers, prepared to react. Later a reinforcement of a platoon of 50 men from Co. A, under 2nd Lt. Louis J. Magill, joined Elliott. This group of Marines, aided by Cuban rebels, defeated a large Spanish force at Cuzco Wells, near Guantanamo, Cuba, and captured the only Spanish water source near Guantanamo Bay. The enemy's post was in a valley and in order to get near them, the Marines had to climb a very high and steep hill.

As they reached the top of the hill, Marines of Co. C saw Spanish soldiers coming up from the opposite direction. The fight between both forces lasted about an hour. In the meantime, at the request of Elliott, the nearby U.S. ship *Dolphin* had been firing over the hill into the Spaniard's valley, but now that was dangerous for the Marines as they moved down into the valley. Elliott ordered Pvt. John Fitzgerald to go to the highest point and signal the ship to cease and desist. He did and was, much later (1910), awarded a Medal of Honor and promoted to corporal. Later that morning, because the ship continued intermittent fire, Sgt. John H. Quick, of Co. C, was also ordered to flag the *Dolphin*; he too was awarded a MoH, but much sooner (1898).[6]

After the hand-to-hand fight and the dispersal of the Spanish troops, Cpl. Frederick Rahn from Co. C was ordered to take a detail down the hill to burn a Spanish blockhouse and destroy their well for drinking water. He did so and was promoted to sergeant. Essentially the fight was over in that corner of Cuba. According to the 18 Spaniards captured, their losses had been severe: two officers and 58 enlisted men killed or wounded of the estimated 500 in the action on Cuzco Hill. In addition to the four Marines and one surgeon killed, 11 more Marines were wounded.

On 3 July the greatest sea-battle of the war around Cuba was fought. Admiral Pascual Cervera y Topete decided that his fleet, tied up in the harbor of Santiago, was not doing its job. On this morning he and his ships, badly outclassed and out-gunned by the American North Atlantic Fleet, waiting just offshore, made a dash for safety. They were forced to beach or were destroyed in short order by the superior firepower of RA William T. Sampson's fleet.

Marines manned the secondary guns aboard most of the vessels and were highly commended by the captains of their ships. Captain Charles E. Clark of the *Oregon*, later admiral, listed his commendations, "hoping that it may be of service to them." These included the CO of the Marine detachment, Capt. Randolph Dickens, "in charge of four 6-pounders," and 2nd Lt. Austin R. Davis, "in charge of four 6-pounders and one 1-pounder." He is also stated, "Every man in the guard had an exposed station, and the only reluctance ever shown by any of them promptly to obey was when ordered to take shelter behind the turrets, while the alacrity with which they ever sprang to their posts showed that they were all animated by the spirit that has given the Marine Corps its reputation for bravery and faithfulness during a full century."

Captain John W. Philip of the *Texas* commented, "The performance of all duty of the Marine guard under 1st Lt. [Cyrus S.] Radford met with my approval and commendation." He then added that when he asked Radford to provide 15 Marines to assist in the boiler-room, so as to keep up their speed, those selected rushed to be first. Captain Henry C. Taylor of the *Indiana* complimented Capt. Littleton W. T. Waller and his Marines for their "efficient work and excellent marksmanship in the destruction of Cervera's fleet." Also, as would be expected, Capt. Paul St. C. Murphy of the MD *Brooklyn* and 1st Lt. Rufus H. Lane of the *New York* added their admiring words about their detachments during the fight.

On 27 July, Lt. Greenlief A. Merriam was sent in a boat with a flag of truce toward the town of Playa del Ponce, Puerto Rico. There was a delay of a day between the demand for surrender and its acceptance. Additionally, 1st Lt. Henry C. Haines was sent with the MD from the *Dixie* which landed on the 28th, seizing the custom house and, for the first time, raising the American flag over the island. Both officers, Merriam and Haines, were highly commended by Cmdr. Charles H. Davis.

The 1st Marine Battalion sailed from Guantanamo Bay, Cuba, on the *Resolute* for Manzanillo, Cuba, on the 9th of August. They arrived on the 12th, but the Marines remained aboard ship in anticipation of surrender. Meanwhile, the following day, 1st Lt. John A. Lejeune, leading 37 Marines, landed from the *Cincinnati* at Cape San Juan, Puerto Rico, to protect a lighthouse previously seized by U.S. forces. On 13 August the First Marine Battalion on the *Resolute* was in the process of landing to take the town of Manzanillo, Cuba, when word of the armistice ending the Spanish-American-Cuban War was received.

Fourteen enlisted Marines were awarded the Medal of Honor during this war. Twelve were shipboard and two were with Huntington at or near Cuzco Wells.

> *Results:* The antiquated Spanish fleet was unable to effectively fight a modern U.S. fleet and could not stop the U.S. from landing troops, including Marines, in Cuba. Its fleet was completely destroyed at Santiago, which was the real reason the war was so easily won.[7] The Marines under Col. Robert W. Huntington defeated several attempts by Spanish troops near Guantanamo Bay to drive them back to their ships. For later Marine interventions in Cuba see the section "Cuba."

11

Philippine Islands

Date: 25 March 1899 to January 1901.
Location: Luzon and Samar, Philippine Islands.
Involved: Natives versus U.S. Army, U.S. Marines and U.S. Navy.
Situation: The natives had, with help from U.S. military forces, successfully driven the Spanish occupiers from their soil, only to find the U.S. replacing Spain as the occupier. They fought against the U.S. occupation for a number of years but most of the fighting was within the first several years.

The first record indicating a Marine presence on land in the Philippines was on 25 March 1899, following the end of the Spanish-American War. Until 31 March 1899 a Marine squad with a Colt automatic rapid-fire gun rendered invaluable support to the artillery of the 8th Army Corps during operations at Marialo River, Guiguinto, and Malinta-Novaleta, Philippine Islands. Corporal Thomas F. Prendergast and Pvts. Howard M. Buckley and Joseph Melvin, commanded by Ens. Cleland Davis, USN, were the individuals. This small unit was highly commended by Gen. Arthur MacArthur and a number of other USA officers, including Col. Frederick Funston.

It was soon apparent to Admiral Dewey's victorious U.S. Navy (see Spanish-American-Cuban War) that it would require many more Marines to serve at and protect overseas naval bases. Consequently the Naval Personnel Act of Congress provided for an authorized Marine Corps strength of 211 officers and 6,000 enlisted men, exclusive of the Marine Band. (Additionally, Col. Commandant Charles Heywood was promoted to brigadier general.) However, in fact the Corps then had a total of 3,142, 76 officers and 3,066 enlisted men. The Navy realized the need for a permanent Marine guard to protect the Cavite Naval Station against Filipino insurrectos and on 9 March 1899, Adm. Dewey cabled the Navy Department requesting a battalion to be shipped as soon as available. Colonel Percival C. Pope and the 1st Battalion of Marines arrived on 23 May 1899. The battalion was composed of 15 officers and 260 enlisted men and they were equipped with four 3-inch field pieces and two Colt machine guns. The men were also armed with Lee 6mm rifles.

The 2nd Battalion of Marines led by Major George F. Elliott with 16 officers and 362 enlisted men arrived at Cavite on 21 September on the U.S. Army transport *City of Sydney*. A few days after arrival, Elliott's men were able to relieve the U.S. Army detachment which had been guarding the station with Pope's men. The garrison now totaled 30 officers and 622 enlisted Marines. More Marines were coming, in fact, a lot more.

Seventy Marines and a detachment of seamen from the *Baltimore*, *Concord*, and *Charleston* landed at Olongapo on 23 September to destroy a large rifled gun mounted at the mouth of the Kalakan River. There were 34 Marines from the *Baltimore* and 18 from each of the other two ships. Led by Lt. John D. McDonald, USN, this force speedily destroyed the gun. Rifle squads led by Sgts. George Herbert and Louis Sample quickly took out the surrounding rebels with effective marksmanship.

On the 3rd of October Capt. Henry C. Haines, plus four officers and 84 enlisted Marines from Cavite, and Capt. John T. Myers with 20 Marines and 24 seamen from the *Baltimore*, joined the United States Army forces in a skirmish with Filipino insurrectos at Siran, Luzon. Five days later, while serving with U.S. Army troops, the 2nd Battalion of Marines from Cavite — 20 officers and 360 enlisted men, led by Lt. Col. George Elliott — launched an attack and soon took the town of Noveleta. Marines and soldiers were supported by fire from the *Petrel*. In the course of the action, which proved to be extremely difficult, Elliott was forced to divide his force into two columns, the left led by Haines and the right by Capt. Ben H. Fuller.[1]

The advance was through terrible terrain, mostly swamp with a narrow causeway running through it, but Elliott's Marines managed to advance about a mile. There they ran into a considerable number of insurrectos, but effective rifle fire soon broke up their formation. Through muddy swamps and rice fields they continued their advance another 250 yards, where they found shelter in rifle pits and managed to reorganize their by now mixed-up formations. From there they fired into enemy positions and, when favorable ground presented itself, charged them, gaining a foothold in their positions. The Marines continued their advance as the Filipinos melted away, but some of the latter remained hidden until the Marines passed them and then opened fire from the rear. Meanwhile the Army continued its advance from a different direction, and, caught between the two forces, the Filipinos dropped their weapons and ran away. Elliott had 11 casualties, one of whom later died. This was the first substantial encounter between Marines and the insurrectos.

The U.S. Army was then beginning movements across the entire length and breath of Luzon. As it moved westward, 50 Marines and a detachment of seamen, commanded by Capt. Dion Williams, landed from the *Oregon* on 26 November and advanced three miles to Vigan (in the north), capturing the town. About 100 Spanish prisoners gladly surrendered to the Americans and were sent out to the *Oregon*. Two days later an Army column marched in and relieved the naval forces in the town. Williams and his command then returned to their ship.

Major Littleton W. T. Waller arrived at Cavite on 15 December with the 3rd Battalion of Marines. This formation included 15 officers and 325 enlisted men and would later make a name for itself in China, and, after their return to the Philippines, on the island of Samar. This month, Capt. Herbert L. Draper, supported by 1st Lts. George C. Thorpe, Logan Feland, and James W. Lynch, with 117 enlisted Marines, was sent from Cavite to Subig Bay to clear the countryside of insurrectos. This operation would continue for several months. On 6 January 1st Lt. Logan Feland led a Marine scouting party which burned an insurgent signal station near Olongapo.

On 16 February, a small Marine detachment from Draper's company, commanded by Cpl. Wallace A. Sullivan, became engaged in a serious skirmish near Banictican. Sullivan and Pvt. C. M. Welsh were killed, and the timely arrival of seven more Marines led by Sgt. H. Harvey saved the rest of the detachment from annihilation. The following day Draper went looking for the insurrectos that had killed his men. He went to the village of Morong, and failing to find them but finding ammunition, destroyed the town. A few days later on the 23rd, Draper was still determined to punish the insurrectos for killing his men. He landed with more Marines and, supported by naval gunfire, destroyed the town of Banictican.

Elsewhere on the 27th the insurrectos had taken the town of Perez in the Gulf of Ragay, and with it 460 Spanish officers and enlisted personnel, 10 American prisoners, and an assorted group of Catholic priests, totaling 522 people in all. Twenty Marines led by 1st Lt. Philip S. Brown landed at Perez to rescue the prisoners of the Filipino insurgents. The task took 16 hours in all.

Led by Capt. Draper, a detachment of 45 Marines from Olongapo embarked on the *Nashville* on 5 March and landed at Bogac. With the help of an Army detachment approaching from the other direction, they soon captured the town. Afterward, Draper sent patrols out in different directions looking for insurrectos. Sometime in the early part of this month another company of Marines was added to the garrison at Olongapo. At this time, 1st Lts. Hiram I. Bearss, Charles S. Hill, and Logan Feland joined Draper's command. All continued to be very active for the balance of this year, fighting insurrectos nearly every day on the island of Luzon.

The Marines returning from China in October 1900 had rejoined their comrades and found themselves up to their proverbial ears in insurrectos. The constant patrolling and frequent ambushes kept both Marines and the U.S. Army engaged. The rebels had begun to slow down a bit on Luzon, however, after losing many engagements.

Captain Rufus H. Lane led a small detachment from Olongapo after two especially dangerous insurrectos. First Lieutenants Hiram Bearss and Frederic Wise, plus 2nd Lts. James T. Buttrick and John W. McLaskey, were part of his command. Lane split his force into two and appointed Bearss to command one, which, with Fritz Wise, was successful in capturing one of the rebels on 18 July.

At the request of the U.S. Army leadership, and especially Brig. Gen. Jake Smith, who commanded the area, on 20 October a battalion of Marines, composed of Companies C (Robert H. Dunlap), D (Bearss), and H (Arthur J. Matthews) from the 1st Marine Regiment, and Company F (David H. Porter) of the 2nd Regiment, boarded ships for the island of Samar, where the natives were in a constant state of insurrection. The Moros had virtually wiped out Company C of the 9th Infantry at Balangiga on 28 September and the Marines, who had been comrades with the 9th in China, wanted revenge. On the 24th the Marines arrived off Basey, where Cos. C and D were landed, then Cos. H and F were landed at Balangiga, relieving a detachment of the 17th Infantry, USA.[2] Four days later Porter and 75 Marines from Co. F went aboard the *Vicksburg* and, with 12 Marines from the ship, then landed at Guinan, where they destroyed the town and burnt the hemp.[3] They were not left alone; a substantial body of natives attacked them from the nearby jungle, but the Marines' return volley put them to flight.

Marine patrols were constant and it wasn't long before the burnt villages and destruction of edibles caused an outcry from the locals. This continued well into the month of November and produced many more enemies for the Americans. Continual reports kept coming to Waller that disaffected natives were finding their way inland to a spot they said was unapproachable and, if reached, would be unassailable. It was located above Basey up the Sohotan River. A few patrols had gone that way, so the Marines weren't entirely unaware of the forbidding terrain.

In mid–November Waller decided he had to take the "fortress" at Sohotan in order to overawe the Moros and force them to surrender. He left Basey with two companies, choosing to boat partway up the river and then, when still some distance from the "fortress," to all go ashore. On the 16th Waller split the command into two columns, Porter with one and Bearss leading the other, each on opposite sides of the river while he remained in the river aboard a boat. Both were to move as rapidly as possible but under no circumstances to begin a major battle until he was on the scene. Both columns fought natives as they made their way forward. That night they were below what was obviously the main part of the famed fortress and both groups decided to take a rest.

The next day, both groups set out without waiting for Waller, and as they advanced toward the main position they kept running into various traps indicating they were getting close to their target. Porter's group ran into a strong position on the left side of the river and he immediately set up his Colt machine gun and began firing into the rebels, who were apparently unaware of the presence of the Americans. Thirty of the Moros fell and the rest fled. Porter and his command then crossed the river to Bearss' side and both groups then proceeded to climb every available bamboo ladder or even the sheer rock face of the cliff. All the way up they were fired upon by the natives above, and had to dodge the boulders dropped down upon them. Somehow they all made it to the top and then the Moros made tracks for points unknown. By capturing the cliff top, they had accomplished a feat the natives sincerely believed was impossible. Waller was furious that they hadn't waited for him but Porter and Bearss were both recommended for the Medal of Honor. Being Marine officers, they weren't entitled to receive it.[4]

In December Brig. Gen. "Hell-roaring" Jake Smith, USA, Waller's overall commander, gave him orders to search a path across the island of Samar in order to erect telegraph lines. Even though various other Army officers who had spent considerable time in and around Samar warned Waller not to attempt the trip, he ignored all advice; an order was an order. Waller and a selected party of officers and men landed on the 24th at an Army base on the east coast of Samar at Lanang. Waller stubbornly refused to listen to the several senior Army officers who tried to talk him out of this venture, and after modest preparations, the Marines began the ill-fated march across Samar. It dragged out until the 18th of January. This story is not combat-related so will not be delved into any further.[5] The losses in men were horrific.

Though Marines were represented in the islands for many years, this was the end of their major impact, insofar as fighting natives was concerned. From now until they were no longer combatants, it was the U.S. Army's job, which they competently completed, generating numerous heroes along the way. Captain John J. Pershing was one notable hero. The 4th Marines in the Philippines later is, however, included in the section on World War II, "Corregidor." The assistance provided the U.S. Army by Marine artillery and air forces during the landing and fighting on Leyte will be included in that section.

> *Results:* This was, essentially, a guerilla war. The Filipino patriots realized that, unlike the Spaniards, the U.S. military forces could fight them in the same fashion. Eventually, the rebellious natives were defeated and the U.S. held the islands until, as promised, returning them to the natives following World War II. What is not generally known is that Germany and Japan both wanted the islands and the former was nearby when Dewey finished off the Spanish fleet.

12

Cuba

Corollary to the Monroe Doctrine

Platt Amendment: That the government of Cuba consents that the United States may exercise the right to intervene for the preservation of Cuban independence, the maintenance of a government adequate for the protection of life, property and individual liberty, and for discharging the obligations with respect to Cuba imposed by the Treaty of Paris on the United States, now to be assumed and undertaken by the government of Cuba.

In 1904 President Theodore Roosevelt further extended the right of the United States to intervene in the affairs of Latin American nations. The various protests of foreign nations, mainly concerned with non-payment of debts, and their threats of intervention was Roosevelt's reason for implementing the corollary. It was justified as "protecting the nation from foreign intrusion" when in reality the U.S. desired to keep the Monroe Doctrine pristine. Meaning that Roosevelt didn't desire to fight every nation which demanded that its bills be paid.

Date: 12 September 1906 to 23 January 1909.
Location: Cuba.
Involved: Cubans rebels versus U.S. Marines, U.S. Navy, and the U.S. Army.
Situation: The Moderate party under the first president, Tomas E. Palma, then in power, faked a near total win in the December 1905 election even though the Liberal party was by far the stronger. The Liberals rose in revolt in August 1906. The panic-stricken Palma government urgently requested U.S. aid under the Platt Amendment. President Roosevelt reluctantly ordered the Navy to intervene and U.S. Marines began landing on 12 September.

At the request of Cuban President Palma, President Roosevelt had the U.S. Navy dispatch the cruisers *Des Moines* and *Tacoma* to Cuban ports to "protect American lives and property if endangered." In June a battalion of Marines had been established aboard the transport *Dixie* for service in the Caribbean. Major Albertus W. Catlin commanded and his force was strengthened by the addition of two officers and 110 enlisted Marines by September.

An estimated 8,000 insurgents threatened the city of Havana, consequently six officers and a mix of 124 Marines and Bluejackets were landed from the cruiser *Denver* at Havana on 13 September, at the request of Mr. Sleeper, the American chargé d'affaires. Navy Lt. Comdr. Marcus L. Miller was in overall command but this unit was withdrawn the following day after Sleeper received directions to NOT land "armed forces under any circumstances." Something must have changed because the following day a detachment of both Marines and Bluejackets was landed from the transports *Dixie* and *Marietta* at Cienfuegos to protect American-owned plantations in that area. Meanwhile, 400 Marines were being gathered together at Norfolk and Philadelphia Navy Yards for service beyond the seas. In the next few days small detachments of Bluejackets were dispatched in and around the ports closest to Havana.

On 18 September, at Cienfuegos, Maj. Catlin sent 1st Lt. William E. Parker ashore with a detachment of 50 Marines to guard the Costancia sugar plantation. Second Lieutenant Ralph L. Shepard went ashore with a detachment of 25 Marines to help guard the Soledad plantation and Catlin went ashore with four officers and 125 enlisted men to establish headquarters at the Hormiguero plantation, leaving 25 Marines aboard the *Marietta* for temporary duty. A few days later, on the 21st, a detachment of Marines and Bluejackets from the *Marietta* were also landed at that port to join Catlin. In the meantime, with sufficient Marines now ashore to guard most American property, most of the sailors were back aboard their ships. One naval officer, Lt. John V. Klemann, was quite active during this period, landing at or near Cienfuegos with detachments of Marines and Bluejackets several times, then returning to the *Marietta* as each situation demanded. When word came that the Cuban Central Railroad was being threatened with destruction on 21 September, Klemann with 32 Marines and Bluejackets went ashore to Sagua la Grande, stopping any destructive action. He did so again on the 25th at Palmira.

In the meantime, Roosevelt appointed William H. Taft to head a commission to look into the Cuban problem. The commission recommended that the Liberal party be installed and that more American troops be dispatched. Meanwhile, on 28 September, a detachment of 30 Marines, commanded by 2nd Lt. Gerard M. Kincade, was landed at Havana to guard the treasury at the special request of the Cuban government.

One battalion assembled in Boston under the command of Lt. Col. Franklin J. Moses and sailed aboard the *Prairie* on 30 September, and another, under the command of Maj. Edward R. Lowndes, was ordered to assemble at Havana; the latter group was transported from different ports and arrived there at various times. On 1 October 804 Marines, officers and enlisted, assembled from six of the Atlantic Fleet ships' detachments, arrived at Havana aboard the *Kentucky* and *Indiana*. These Marines and all those ashore were commanded by Col. Littleton W. T. Waller, whose orders directed him to organize them into the 1st Provisional Brigade.

The brigade was composed of two Marine regiments; the 1st Regiment was commanded by Lt. Col. George Barnett and included four battalions: 1st Bn., Maj. Theodore P. Kane (4 companies); 2nd Bn., Maj. Dion Williams (4 companies); 3rd Bn., Maj. Edward P. Lowndes (3 companies); 4th Bn., Maj. Albertus W. Catlin (4 companies). The Second Regiment was commanded by Lt. Col. Franklin J. Moses and included three battalions: 1st Bn., Maj. Wendell C. Neville (6 companies); 2nd Bn., Capt. William N. McKelvey (3 companies); 3rd Bn., Capt. Philip M. Bannon (4 companies). They had a total strength of 97 officers and 2,795 enlisted Marines, approximately a third of the total force of the Corps at that time.

During the early days of October several Marine detachments were landed at several points along the Cuban coast to protect American property. Early in the month, at least 2,000 Marines were in Cuba. Between the 7th and 10th of October, 333 officers and 5,064 U.S. Army troops sailed for Cuba, landing on 10 October. In his 1906 report the secretary of war stated, "the Army landed without opposition." He failed to indicate that the Navy and Marines had already pacified the entire nation, or at least the coasts. The Corps was also requested to provide additional men for the Army of Cuban Pacification. On 1 November the 1st Marine Provisional Brigade was disbanded, the Marines from various ship detachments mostly returning aboard, while a 1st Provisional Regiment had been formed and under the command of Col. George Barnett arrived to serve with the now established Army of Occupation under U.S. Army command. The Marine regiment consisted of about one-fifth the total of the U.S. Army but occupied 11 posts to the Army's 18. The regiment remained in these posts until 23 January 1909, when it was released from Army control and returned to the United States.

On 3 December 1906 President Roosevelt made the following address to the Congress: "It was owing in large part to the General Board that the Navy was able at the outset to meet the Cuban crisis with such instant efficiency; ship after ship appearing on the shortest notice at any threatened point, while the Marines Corps in particular performed indispensable service."

Results: A Liberal government was installed on 1 February 1909, which settled the revolt, temporarily. There would be, however, additional interventions based upon the Platt Amendment over the next few years.

In the Meantime

The 1st Regiment of Marines, commanded by Col. George Barnett, was organized on 8 March 1911 aboard the *Prairie* while at Philadelphia for service, as part of the 1st Provisional Brigade in Cuba. In fact, it was organized to intimidate rebels in Mexico, by showing how quickly the U.S. could respond to any threat. It was disbanded in Philadelphia by 22 June.

A detachment of 22 officers and 666 enlisted Marines from 11 ships of the Atlantic fleet, commanded by Maj. George C. Thorpe, landed at Guantanamo, Cuba, on 13 March to protect American interests in the face of impending civil unrest.

Date: May 1912 to 2 August 1912.
Location: Oriente Province, Cuba.
Involved: Negro Cuban rebels under Estenoz versus the local militia and Marines.
Situation: The large Negro population of Cuba, always angry at being treated unfairly by the white population, especially by the government, seethed, and in May 1912 exploded into an armed rebellion. Evaristo Estenoz, the leader of the "colored party" (his own term) revolt, threatened to destroy American property, especially in Oriente Province, thereby trying to induce the U.S. to intervene according to the Platt Amendment. The Liberal president, José Gomez, was at first against American intervention, but as the revolt became more intense and violent, he agreed and requested the same.

Secretary of state Philander C. Knox (who initiated the concept of "Dollar Diplomacy"), unwilling to wait for Cuban authorities to put down the rebellion and anxious to protect American property, especially the copper mines, railroads and sugar plantations, reacted immediately. The very concerned American minister to Cuba, Mr. Beaupré, relayed reports (most were unreliable) to Knox of the destruction of American property. On 23

May the latter had already requested that the Navy send ships and Marines and that they be prepared to land in the eastern portion of the island. He advised the Cuban government on 29 May that if the revolt was not quelled soon, U.S. troops, including the U.S. Army, would be landed.

The 1st Provisional Regiment of Marines was formed at the Philadelphia Navy Yard with a strength of 32 officers and 777 enlisted Marines in Headquarters Co. and eight infantry companies, A through H, under the command of Col. Lincoln Karmany. The regiment sailed immediately, landing at Deer Point, Guantanamo Bay, and went into camp on 28 May.

The 2nd Provisional Regiment of Marines, under Col. James E. Mahoney, with 40 officers and 1,252 enlisted men, organized into Headquarters Co. and ten infantry companies, was assembled at the New York Navy Yard and at Hampton Roads. They sailed aboard ten battleships of the Atlantic Fleet and arrived at Key West, awaiting further orders. Its first battalion was sent to Guantanamo Bay on 5 June and the second battalion to Havana on 10 June. Karmany and his headquarters remained at Guantanamo with the remainder of unassigned Marines. Following which, all Marines of both regiments were organized into the 1st Provisional Brigade with Karmany in overall command.

The rebel Estenoz was rapidly losing control of his organization. Separate units with different leaders began the destruction of American property. Demands for Marines to protect the various plantations and mines began to pour into headquarters. One faction burned down an American-owned sugar mill at La Maya. Gomez then requested that his Congress give permission to establish martial law in Oriente Province, which was readily granted. Nevertheless, the rebels threatened to burn another plantation at Belona, then property near Santa Cecilia, both American-owned. They set fire to railroad buildings there and burned nearby cane fields. Large bands of rebels were menacing plantations and individuals in the vicinity of El Cobre and Siboney. It was obvious that vigorous action was required immediately.

Company A of the 1st Regiment debarked from the *Paducah* on 7 June and proceeded to Siboney and environs, where the Daiquiri mines had been damaged. One company was not sufficient to restore order and 50 additional Marines from the First Regiment were sent to reinforce the Santiago area. Another 125 were sent to El Cobre and 60 more to Siboney. On the night of 9 June the Marines at El Cuero were attacked, but without loss to either side. On 10 June Lt. Col. John A. Lejeune went to establish his command of all Marines in the district, with headquarters at Santiago.

At Guantanamo City, Lt. Col. Lewis C. Lucas arrived with three companies of the 1st Regiment, which were soon split up to cover and defend ten towns in the vicinity. Lucas soon received the two remaining companies of the 2nd Regiment at Guantanamo as support. Meanwhile, ship detachments of Marines and Bluejackets were being landed at various ports as reports of depredations, many exaggerated, poured into American hands. Several groups remained ashore much of the month of June before being relieved. The Americans' major role was to defend American property while allowing Cuban troops to round up the rebels.

Marines guarded the railroads and trains in the area. After the affair was resolved and the rebels disbanded, the U.S. government received a bill for transport costs of the Marines who rode them as guards. As was the situation in previous encounters of this kind in the Caribbean, various foreign governments requested their nationals and property be protected by the U.S. forces. Britain and Brazil were the foremost and Karmany, the brigade CO, soon issued the necessary orders to comply.

During the month of June, the Cuban government forces were actively engaged in attacking rebel forces, dispersing large bands (Estenoz's total force was now estimated at about 1,800). Although the rebels continued their activity and threatened to attack Marines at several locations, no attacks actually occurred. That month the Gomez government offered amnesty to all rebels that surrendered by 22 June and many did. Estenoz refused and with a large group assaulted the area around Soledad and San José. He was, however, killed during an altercation at Miraca, and his body was brought to Santiago for identification. By the end of June, after many rebels had surrendered or just gone home, Ibonet, a major rebel, remained. Although he remained in the field, he was soon being driven about and by mid–July was deep in the mountains. Refugees were returning to their homes and the government soon announced that the Marines were no longer needed.

Many Marines had returned to their ships and were on their way in early July, while others of the brigade were evacuated, the last group leaving aboard the *Prairie* on 2 August, bound for stations in New England. Karmany was highly praised for his control of the situation, much the opposite of the situation during the Marines' previous excursion to Cuba in 1906.

> *Results:* Though the rebels threatened to make life difficult for the American owners of property in Cuba, hoping that it would bring in the American military, nothing of consequence really happened. With the death in action of Estenoz, the Negro forces broke up into small factions and were defeated, most eventually returning to their homes, no better off than before. The Marines were on hand to protect American-owned property, which they accomplished as usual.

> *Date:* 1 January 1917 to 6 February 1922.
> *Location:* Guantanamo City and eastern Cuba.
> *Involved:* Many Marine units became involved in Cuba, while some companies were drained off to be a part of the 4th Brigade in France. Other companies were created and became a part of the intervention, then were withdrawn. Early on, it was the fleet Marines ashore, then the 7th Marines, then the 9th Marines, after which they became the 3rd Brigade. With the addition of the 8th Marines and later the 1st Marines, it became the 6th Brigade.
> *Situation:* In 1917, the United States government was certain that agents of the Central Powers (i.e., Germany and Austria) would sabotage the sugar production in the island. It consequently moved Marines into Oriente Province to ensure that there would be no interruption of sugar production. This intervention was known as "the Sugar Intervention." There was, however, the usual clashes between the two political parties, Liberals and Moderates, with the Liberals out and the Moderates in. This political upheaval was the major cause of the intervention and there was much activity during the entire period.

Trouble between the two major political parties in Cuba had caused a warning from the U.S. State Department "that the U.S. would only support a legally constituted government in Cuba." Former President Gomez ignored that warning and marched on Havana with his Liberal rebels. President Menocal fled. Some loyal troops defeated rebel efforts and Menocal returned, then he managed to gather sufficient troops to capture Gomez and most of his followers. All this caused several sugar mills to close down, greatly affecting the Allied war effort. Because the U.S. was preparing to declare war on Germany, this was the cause for intervention.

Meanwhile, as early as 1 January 1917, the Navy Department issued a report that there were 300 Marines in Cuba and another 100 on the way. As early as 12 January the 55th Co., aboard the *Maine* offshore at Guacanayabo Bay, was prepared to land if needed to protect American interests. Complaints to the naval commander at Guantanamo by American plantation owners brought instant action. He ordered the station's Marine detachment plus the *Montana* ship detachment to occupy Guantanamo City on 25 February and preserve American property in the vicinity. He then notified the CO of the Atlantic Fleet of his actions, which were approved. On 1 March various ship detachments were landed, mostly in Oriente Province: *Connecticut*, ashore from 1 to 19 March; *Machias*, 1 to 31 March, and again from 1 to 11 April; *Michigan*, 1 to 3 March; *Montana*, 1 to 22 March; *New York*, 3 to 7 March; *Olympia*, 8 to 16 and again 18 to 22 March; *South Carolina*, 3 to 4 and again 7 to 16 March; and lastly, *Texas*, 7 to 10 March. Additionally, the 24th Co., based at the Naval Station, Guantanamo, was in the interior of Oriente between 1 and 27 March.

During the month of March, numerous Marine units were being shipped from current stations to Cuba. These included the 7th, 17th and 20th Companies from Haiti on 4 March; the 49th and 51st Cos. from the *Jupiter* which landed at Santiago on the 9th; and the following day the 43rd from *Jupiter* landed to support the other two companies. Finally, the 55th Co. aboard the *Maine* landed at Guantanamo Bay on 22 March.

For the most part, during the spring and summer of 1917, protection for Americans and their property was furnished by the Marine companies mentioned above. The largest problem for the Marines in Cuba was retaining as many of them on site as could be managed. This was a time when the Corps was recalling units from the Caribbean area to form the 5th Marine Regiment at Philadelphia. Of those companies in Cuba, the 17th, 20th, 43rd, 49th, 51st, and 55th Cos. became part of the group. This left but several companies in Cuba before the arrival of the 7th and 9th Regiments, later in the year.

On 14 August 1917 the 7th Regiment was organized at Philadelphia. The regiment was composed of the 93rd and 94th Cos., the 37th joining on 15 August, the 18th and 59th Cos., then on 20 August, the 71st, 72nd, 86th and 90th Cos. On 21 August Col. Melville J. Shaw and his 7th Regiment embarked aboard the *Prairie*, destination, the Naval Station at Guantanamo Bay. On 24 October the regiment moved into the interior of Oriente and was stationed at San Juan Hill, Bayamo, Camaguey, San Luis, and Guantanamo City. According to the official documents, these movements were only intended to minimize the impact of foreign agents in the area, not to interfere in local activities.

Later in the year, on 20 November, the 9th Regiment was organized with, initially, Maj. Rush R. Wallace in command, followed on 25 November by Lt. Col. Frederic L. Bradman. Wallace assumed command of 1/9, Maj. Edward A. Ostermann joined 2/9 on 1 December, then Maj. Ross E. Rowell, on 16 December, assumed command of 3/9. The following companies composed the 9th Regiment: the 14th, 36th, 100th, 121st, 122nd, 123rd, 124th, 125th, and 126th.

On 19 December 1917 the regiment's 1,000 officers and men embarked aboard the *Von Steuben* at Newport News, VA, and sailed for Guantanamo Bay, Cuba. On 24 January 1918, Col. Thomas C. Treadwell joined the regiment and assumed command from Bradman. The latter became, more or less, G-3, before there was such a post. On 31 July, the regiment lost the 36th and 100th Cos. and adopted the newly created 154th, 155th, and 156th Cos. on 13 August 1918.

Upon the arrival of the 9th Regiment, the Marines in Cuba, plus the addition of a headquarters unit, now composed the 3rd Brigade of Marines. On 24 December Col. James E. Mahoney arrived and assumed command of all Marines ashore on that island. For the balance of the period of the Sugar Intervention there was a coming and going of units and officers.

On 31 July the 9th Regiment was moved to Galveston, Texas, to join the 8th Regiment to form the 3rd Brigade along the Mexican border. Colonel Thomas C. Treadwell, with the 1st Marine Regiment, landed at Guantanamo Bay on 8 November 1918 and, along with the Marines that remained, organized the 6th Marine Brigade. The 6th Machine Gun Battalion, Maj. Julian C. Smith, joined them on 26 January 1919. Treadwell's brigade soon after began its withdrawal from Cuba. Major Smith's 6th Machine Gun Battalion was first to leave in June for the U.S. Then the 1st Regiment and Brigade Headquarters were next. The 7th Regiment remained until August, when just two companies were left behind at Camaguey. That occupation continued until the Marines left that station and withdrew into the naval station at Guantanamo Bay on 6 February 1922.

Although the U.S. did not intervene in Cuba, even though there was a series of revolutionary activities brought about by a series of corrupt governments, the Platt Amendment was junked in 1934 by the incoming administration, ending a 30-year "protectorate" over that island nation.

Results: No agents of the Central Powers, nor the rebels, interrupted the growth of sugar cane nor the production of sugar during the entire period. There may have been inadequate agents on the island, but they were not capable of interfering with production. It was one more example of the U.S. State Department jumping to conclusions.

13

Mexico 1914

Date: 21 April 1914 to 23 November 1914.
Location: East coast of Mexico and especially Vera Cruz and environs.
Involved: Mexican troops versus U.S. Marines: 1st Marine Regiment with eight companies; 2nd Regiment with seven companies; 3rd Regiment with six companies; 4th Regiment with nine companies; and an Artillery Battalion of three batteries; USN and U.S. Army.
Situation: At Tampico, Mexico, a mail boat from the U.S. fleet with three American sailors plus a USN mail courier was detained and the people on it were arrested, which consequently delayed a State Department dispatch. Rear Admiral Henry T. Mayo, whose fleet was offshore, demanded an apology. President Woodrow Wilson backed him up and another fleet off Vera Cruz, under RA Frank F. Fletcher, also got into the act.

The real reason behind the ensuing problem was that Wilson had made up his mind that president Victoriano Huerta must go. Consequently, under Huerta, nothing the Mexican government did would satisfy Wilson. Huerta had to go and nothing else would suffice. This was just one instance of Wilson's interference with the Mexicans while he was president. There were many more.

In the meantime, the USN had been quite active in and about Vera Cruz, selected because it had a great harbor and had been utilized once before, in 1847, for the invasion of Mexico. On 31 January 1914 the *Minnesota* returned to a post off Vera Cruz. A plan was in the making. Eventually, Maj. Smedley D. Butler, CO of the Marine detachment, would go ashore with six enlisted Marines in USN uniforms and go to the U.S. Consulate. They were told their job was to protect Mr. John Lind, unofficial ambassador to Mexico.[1]

Two Marines were to accompany Lind wherever he went, two were on guard at the consulate, and the other two were off duty. Those to accompany Lind were also to prevent him from saying too much when he was around and about town. For this reason, at one point, when he became aware of what Wilson was doing, he began to blab the recent news before the two Marines hustled him away.

Sometime after 1 March, Butler was sent to spy out the proposed travel path to Mexico City. He traveled in civilian clothes as "Mr. Walter Garvin" and when he had seen all that seemed necessary, returned to Adm. Fletcher to report. It appears that Butler and Fletcher had been making plans to land Butler's battalion at Vera Cruz to invade Mexico as far as Mexico City.[2]

13. Mexico 1914

Mexico's government refused the insulting demand to fire a 24-gun salute to the U.S. flag. That caused Wilson to order Marines to land and, if necessary, for the USN to open fire upon shore stations. He also asked Congress for permission to do so, which was granted the day after the Marines landed. At the request of the State Department, on 15 April 1914 the 1st Marine Regiment and 1st Advance Base Brigade, composed of 24 officers and 810 enlisted men, commanded by Lt. Col. Charles G. Long, boarded the transport *Hancock* at Philadelphia, bound for Tampico, Mexico.

However, Vera Cruz, 250 nautical miles south, was the nation's major port of entry. Control of its custom house would effectively interdict Huerta's supplies and arms from overseas. It would also cut his government off from its major income source. Besides, it became known that a German ship, the *Yperanga*, which carried huge stocks of machine guns, rifles, and ammunition, was headed for that city.

Fletcher, subordinate to RA Charles J. Badger, who commanded all local naval forces, had received Badger's orders to proceed. Fletcher then warned the local Mexican General Maas that his men would be going ashore and, if fired upon, that Fletcher's fleet would bombard Vera Cruz until it was destroyed. The first troops ashore from the fleet offshore at Vera Cruz were the 2nd Marine Regiment. Commanded by Lt. Col. Wendell C. Neville, the regiment landed from the *Prairie* on 21 April. Their first task was to take the custom house.[3] At 1300, Long's 1st Marine Regiment and Headquarters, 1st Marine Brigade, landed at Vera Cruz from the *Hancock*. Colonel John A. Lejeune, commanding the brigade, landed and assumed command of all Marines ashore. Marines then proceeded to clear the streets and advanced well into the town. Later, they were followed ashore by Butler's battalion from the *Minnesota* and other ships at anchor.

The 2nd Regiment and support continued to move through the city. They spread out, moved about a half-mile, and managed to take the railroad terminal and assorted other buildings when fired upon by Mexicans at about noon. Continuing their forward movement, they took a railroad roundhouse lying west of the city. During the day, Marines and Bluejackets ashore moved through the city rather easily until they ran into nests of snipers, but they ran into real trouble at the military academy. Although most of Huerta's regular army had vacated the city, the bravest of the cadet soldiers gave the advancing Americans a bad time. Guns firing 3- and 5-inch shells from the *Chester* and *San Francisco* were a bit more than the nearly leaderless cadets could handle and they were wiped out or left their defenses under extreme pressure.

During the night, Maj. Randolph C. Berkeley's battalion held the right flank of the defensive line while Maj. George C. Reid's men held the left. That night at 0330 Butler and his "Panama" battalion reported to Neville at the railroad terminal. They went into the lines as support for Berkeley and Reid. Meanwhile, Maj. Albertus W. Catlin, fleet Marine officer, was made CO of the 3rd Regiment, composed of Marines from the various ships' detachments assembled off Vera Cruz. It went ashore that evening as support for both regiments. That night a naval brigade also began going ashore to help the Marines.

The next morning the naval forces became active once again. One serious problem occurred when the untrained Bluejackets began firing at anything that moved. Consequently, U.S. Marines were frequently their targets and victims. It is said that more Marines became casualties from USN firing than from Mexican weapons.

More Marines and sailors were landed on the second day and the Americans continued clearing the city of any patriots. Every building had to be searched in order to clear them of snipers so the Americans could continue forward. On the 24th a battery of artillery from

Pensacola was landed from the *Minnesota* in addition to the balance of the 2nd Marines already ashore. On the 25th Reid's battalion was pushed forward to occupy the city waterworks at El Tejar, about ten miles from Vera Cruz. Additional posts were established on the outskirts of the city, and by the end of the fourth day the Americans had pretty well occupied most of the city and important environs. On the 27th the city was considered pacified. Because the Mexican civil authorities had vacated the city, Fletcher appointed Navy and Marine officers to their posts.

On the 29th of April another regiment of Marines arrived. It was the "real" 3rd Marine Regiment, composed of eight officers and 861 enlisted men commanded by Col. Franklin J. Moses, and they landed from the *Morro Castle* on 30 April to replace Major Catlin's fleet Marine force, which was still ashore. They then returned to their own vessels. Later that day Maj. John H. Russell's battalion relieved Reid and his men at El Tejar.[4] The 1st Marine Brigade consisted of three infantry regiments and an artillery battalion, all told 84 officers and 2,321 men. Colonel Littleton W. T. Waller had also arrived and replaced Lejeune in command of the brigade.

In the meantime, the *Yperanga* had been stopped off the coast by the *Utah*. It became unnecessary to remove the cargo because the German captain placed his ship under U.S. control. Later it was allowed to remove itself and then landed its arms and ammunition at another Mexican port. For several months the U.S. Army had been planning to intervene in Mexico and by now had collected a sizable force, approximately a brigade, near the Mexican boundary at Galveston, TX. This organization, with Brig. Gen. Frederick Funston in command, left Galveston on 23 April and five days later arrived at Vera Cruz. On the 30th he and most of his men debarked.

On the following day, 1 May 1914, the 1st Marine Brigade was detached from naval jurisdiction and was attached to United States Army forces commanded by (now) Maj. Gen. Frederick Funston, USA, for occupation duty. They would remain under Army jurisdiction until Vera Cruz was evacuated on 23 November 1914. During the entire period, Marines suffered the loss of three men killed in action and 12 wounded. The USN's loss was much more severe; 16 killed in action and 58 wounded.

Three companies of the 4th Marines embarked at San Diego on the *Colorado* on 17 June 1915 for expeditionary duty in Mexico. That proved to be unnecessary and they returned to their home base.

However, because the U.S. was expecting the Mexican government to create difficulties during American participation in France during World War I, in November 1917 the government had the newly created 8th Marines stationed at Ft. Crockett, near Galveston, TX. They were there to be available to intervene at Tampico in the oil fields, should the State Department deem that necessary. Later the 9th Marines would join them in the newly created 3rd Provisional Brigade, in August 1918. No incidents with Mexico occurred and eventually both regiments were withdrawn.

> *Results:* This was the second, and very nearly the third, time the U.S. aggressively forced its will upon Mexico. It was successful twice, but at the cost of antagonizing a near neighbor without true cause. The Mexicans have never forgotten, and neither should the U.S. Essentially it was ugly aggression in the 19th century and not much better in the 20th. Unfortunately, Woodrow Wilson was successful in undermining Huerta, who was soon replaced, but he never received the demanded 24-gun salute from Mexico. Hooray for the Mexicans.

14

Haiti

Date: 29 January 1914 to 15 August 1934.
Location: Haiti, on the island of Hispaniola.
Involved: Mobs of individuals, later called Cacos, versus U.S. Marines and U.S. Navy.
Situation: Although the government of Haiti, always in debt, had managed to borrow 65 million francs from American, French and German bankers in 1910, there was no way it could repay the loans. Haiti's government, then led by the president, Theodor, had long been in disfavor by most nations and it is a wonder that any money could be found to loan to such a disreputable government. On 29 January 1914 Marine detachments from a number of foreign ships lying offshore in the harbor at Port-au-Prince, including British, French and German ships, landed to protect their consulates from the ever increasing mobs threatening the government.

First Lieutenant Andrew B. Drum led the *South Carolina* Marines ashore, where they remained until 9 February. When the situation ashore settled down all Marines were withdrawn; the Americans were the last to leave.

The Marine detachment of the *Wheeling* landed at Port-de-Paiz, Haiti, on 16 February 1914 to protect local Americans and foreign citizens as political unrest continued. It landed once again on 21 February at Cap Haitien for the same purpose.

President Theodor was overthrown by Vilbrun Guillaume Sam, who then became president; in Haiti that was a normal transition of power. The big problem was when a new revolt under the leadership of Dr. Rosalvo Bobo broke out but four months into the new administration. Sam had the entire leadership of the enemy party arrested and imprisoned. He gave orders to Gen. Oscar to have all of them killed if the revolutionists succeeded in driving him from office. In Haiti, overthrowing a government and even imprisonment were acceptable, but killing your replacements was a no-no. Meanwhile, on 9 July a detachment of Marines under the command of Capt. George Van Orden landed from the *Washington* at Cap Haitien to protect U.S. citizens threatened by the rebellious mobs.

The mob in Port-au-Prince, bent upon getting to Sam, chased him out of the regular offices of government. He took refuge in the French Embassy and Oscar had 167 prisoners killed. The mob, notwithstanding, forced their way into the French Embassy on 28 July and removed Sam. The mob beat him to death, tearing his body to pieces in the process, then decapitated him and placed his head upon a pike, which they paraded about the city of Port-au-Prince.

Rear Admiral William B. Caperton, U.S. naval officer in charge of the area, moved his ship, the *Washington*, to Port-au-Prince, arriving on 28 July. After Sam's death, he landed Capt. Giles Bishop and his company of Marines, along with the ship's detachment and a large group of Bluejackets. Caperton then radioed for "at least a regiment of Marines as soon as possible."

On 31 July, Col. Theodore P. Kane and five companies from the 2nd Regiment of Marines embarked aboard the *Connecticut* and sailed for Port-au-Prince, arriving on 5 August. Meanwhile, Capt. William G. Fay and the 24th Co. landed on the 29th and were based at Guantanamo Bay. Caperton was still not satisfied and cabled for more Marines. In response, Col. Littleton W. T. Waller in command, with Col. Eli K. Cole, CO of the 1st Regiment of Marines, sailed for Haiti aboard the *Tennessee* on 10 August. Upon their arrival on 15 August, they became the 1st Brigade of Marines. It also included "Tippy" Kane's five companies of the 2nd Regiment, and added later Maj. Robert H. Dunlap's artillery battalion, which did not sail until the 24th.

During this period a new president of Haiti was elected by the assembly and sworn in on 12 August. His name was Dartiguenave and one of his first duties was to negotiate a treaty with the U.S. in which U.S. Marines would establish and train a new police force. That proved to be the Gendarmerie d'Haiti (later changed to the Garde d'Haiti), which was to be the saving of the nation (at least temporarily). Eventually, after organization, training and being led by Marines (officers and enlisted men), the police force, later to be led entirely by Haitian officers, maintained law and order that hadn't been experienced by the nation of Haiti since it had broken away from France.

During the intervening time, Marines from the 1st Brigade began patrolling and on 18 September encountered a group of about 75 Cacos near Gonaives, exchanging a few shots. This was the first clash between the two groups. The bandits, and the Cacos were certainly considered that, had been terrifying the local inhabitants, in particular by shutting off the supply of incoming food. Major Smedley D. Butler soon arrived at Gonaives to assume command of the Marines stationed there. Leading his command on a vigorous campaign several days later, he began to get rid of the Cacos and to reestablish incoming supplies and restore the flow of water into the community.

While Butler and his Marines were successful, that success, in effect, drove the Cacos to the coastline, where things became worse. Not long after, in September, the Cacos began diverting supplies from entering Cap Haitien. By the 18th, however, a detachment of Marines sent out by Cole managed to eliminate that interference and soon supplies returned to the area. For some reason the Cacos, generally, did not interfere with the Marines on the scene. In one case, the Marines argued with an outpost of Cacos' chief and were allowed to exit without further ado. Rameau, the headman, decided that the local chief was too lenient and chopped his head off with a machete. The following day when the Marines, five squads led by Capt. Frederick C. Barker, tried to pass that area, they were fired upon. Captain Chandler Campbell and six squads of Marines were on patrol nearby and moved to the scene, as did another patrol out of Cap Haitien. The large group of Marines, when assembled, was soon surrounded by hordes of Cacos, whose firing wounded 10 Marines.

Colonel Cole heard the sounds of firing and left Cap Haitien with the remainder of his Marines. They soon engaged the Cacos, driving them off. After they were gone, 40 dead Cacos bodies were counted. On 27 September Cole then went on to the Cacos headquarters at Quartier Morin, soon captured it, and left a Marine guard to hold it. Afterward he and his command marched throughout the area without encountering any resistance. The Cacos were stopped dead in their tracks and the flow of incoming supplies to Cap Haitien was immediately reestablished.

The area was now considered relatively quiet; nevertheless, problems with Cacos at Petit Riviere caused a troop of mounted Marines to be sent there. Once they arrived, the Marines were soon engaged in a firefight and Sgt. John Platt, the first Marine killed in Haiti, fell. Not long after, the situation assumed a new face. Colonel Waller decided that trouble in the north required different tactics. Taking active control, he obtained a substantial sum of Haitian funds to buy off many of the Caco leaders, who agreed to cease and desist their tactics and to give up their weapons. Many of the "enlisted men" failed to live up to the leader's bargain and instead broke off contact and retreated into the hills, with weapons intact. Several hundred rifles had been turned in, however, so the attempt to buy off the Cacos wasn't a complete loss.

Waller, leading the 11th Company of Marines, then went to the farthest east, where a command of about 400 loyal troops, nearly naked and starving, were still holding Ft. Liberte on the Dominican border. He paid them off and sent them all home, leaving some of his Marines in their place, and on his return to Port-au-Prince he managed to pick up another 1,000 rifles.

Strong bands of natives still held out in the hills and Waller decided to actively pursue those bands until they were wiped out. The 13th Co. was moved to Grande Riviere; Capt. William P. Upshur and his 15th Co. went to Ft. Liberte; and the 11th Co. concentrated at Ouanaminthe. A detachment of the 13th Co. under the command of 1st Lt. Thomas E. Thrasher then went deep into the countryside and occupied Bahon, soon after which the balance of the 13th Company arrived to reinforce him.

Cole, accompanied by Maj. Butler, took more Marines and moved his headquarters to Grande Riviere. Following this, Butler, with several other officers and 40 mounted men, made a six-day reconnaissance covering about 120 miles. During this excursion, he and his men had possibly the most successful and interesting fighting period in the Haitian story. Butler later described how, on the evening of 24 October as his command was crossing a river, they were suddenly fired upon from three sides. He estimated there were about 400 Cacos located but 100 yards from Ft. Dipitie. He and his men fought their way into decent positions and managed all night to keep the "wolves from the door." Meanwhile a gunnery sergeant named Daniel J. Daly went down to the river and after diving in several times managed to remove a machine gun and ammo from the dead mules, bringing them to the Marines position on the hill. He set the gun up and then reported its position to Butler.

In the morning, Butler divided his command into four sections, one under Upshur, a second under 1st Lt. Edward A. Ostermann, a third under Daly's command and the fourth group under himself. The three detachments attacked the enemy that morning, pushing in three directions and killing and wounding many of the Cacos. This assault by trained troops was more than the natives could handle and they fled in all directions. Then Upshur and Ostermann attacked the fort and captured it when the 13 Marines put the garrison to flight. They then demolished and burned the fort and all the nearby houses from which fire had erupted during the fight. All three leaders were later awarded a Medal of Honor, the second for Daly.

Next came Ft. Riviere, about eight miles south of Grand Riviere, believed by the Cacos to be impregnable. Three more Medals of Honor were awarded to the first three men who went into that fort under heavy enemy fire. Three companies, the 13th on the east side, Marines from the *Connecticut* detachment on the south and the 15th Co. on the west, moved on the fort. Butler was with the 15th and his group was chosen to enter the fort under support fire from the other two groups. It happened that an entrance on the west made that feasible — all they had to do was enter against waiting Cacos. On the morning of 18 November at a signal from Butler, all three units advanced while firing. The automatic fire from the Benet-Mercie machine guns shook up the Cacos, many of whom tried to go over the walls. Most were gunned down before they made it. It is reported that Sgt. Ross Iams, closely followed by Pvt. Samuel Gross and Maj. Butler, entered first, after saying, "Aw! The hell with it, I'm goin' in." The three were soon followed by the rest of the company and the Cacos fell apart after strong initial resistance, with the Marines killing or wounding many and eventually taking the "impregnable" fort.

For some reason, Secretary of the Navy Josephus Daniels, upset at the reports of bloodshed in Haiti, decreed that operations against Cacos should be less bloody. Marines then reduced their activities to those necessary to guard themselves or innocent civilians. The fact that they had pretty much won the battle before Daniels' order was received probably engendered some humorous remarks from the Marines in Haiti.

The war against the Cacos continued for a number of years, at a much lower effort than formerly, although there were several times when fighting flared up, especially post–World War I. The successful training of the Garde allowed a great reduction in the number of Marines in Haiti, with many being siphoned off for the May 1916 intervention into the neighboring nation of Santo Domingo (later known as the Dominican Republic) and in 1917 for duty with the 5th Marine Regiment in France. Brigadier General John H. Russell was appointed American high commissioner and the personal representative of the president of the USA on 11 February 1922. This was the first time a Marine officer had ever held a high position in a normally civilian capacity, and he continued to hold that post until 12 November 1930. Soon after the ascension of president Franklin D. Roosevelt, on 15 August 1934 the U.S. Marines were withdrawn from Haiti.

> *Results:* Eventually, during the following 20 years, the rebellious natives were pacified, or at least made reasonably law-abiding. The Garde d'Haiti created by U.S. Marines was presumably non-political, and it managed to bring about peace among the various factions, at least temporarily.

15

Dominican Republic

Date: 1 to 19 April 1903.
Location: Santo Domingo City.
Involved: Dominican rebels and U.S. Marines from the *Atlanta*.
Situation: The American consul-general at Santo Domingo City, Mr. Campbell Maxwell, asked Cmdr. William H. Turner of the *Atlanta* for a Marine guard to protect Americans ashore and the consulate. Turner ordered 1st Lt. Richard G. McConnell, CO of the ship's Marine detachment, to take 25 men and proceed to the consulate to protect it and anyone within its confines, including any foreigners taking refuge during the ongoing political upheaval. The Marines remained ashore until it appeared that the consulate was no longer threatened and returned to the *Atlanta* on 19 April.

Date: 3 January to 11 February 1904.
Location: Puerto Plata, Sousa, and Santo Domingo City.
Involved: Forces and insurgents of Santo Domingo versus U.S. Marines and U.S. Navy.
Situation: Trouble began in late September 1903 when the local government refused to allow passage of various American commercial, then naval, ships into harbors already established in agreements as viable destinations. Several landings of Marines and Bluejackets in early to mid-January had little effect, as did verbal and written complaints. On 11 February the firing upon a USN launch from the *Yankee* by insurgents at Santo Domingo City that killed a member of the crew was the direct cause of the following intervention. It was a flagrant violation of an armistice existing between the contending parities, which included the United States.

The various American naval officers, in a conference, decided to open fire upon the city and then land Marines and Bluejackets to enforce the agreements. Captain Richard Wainwright, commanding the *Newark*, opened fire at 1525 and ten minutes later the troops left for shore. These troops included Captain Albert S. McLemore, from the *Newark*, along with 160 sailors and Marines; 1st Lt. Henry D. F. Long with Marines from *Columbia*; and Lt. Comdr. James P. Parker from the latter ship, commanding both groups. As the boats moved toward shore, they were soon taking small-arms fire from the insurgents ashore but the boats reached the shore at 1630 without any casualties. Meanwhile, the *Columbia* and soon after the *Newark* fired 4-inch shells at the insurgents' positions until 1700. The naval force encountered no opposition on shore and returned to their respective vessels between 2100 and 2200 hours.

> *Results:* The agreement previously signed was adhered to by the insurgents and government forces and the Naval/Marine force returned to its respective ships and continued in force thereafter.

> *Date:* 5 May 1916 to 17 September 1924.
> *Location:* Santo Domingo, later known as the Dominican Republic.¹
> *Involved:* Dominicans, insurgents and government troops versus U.S. Marines and Navy.
> *Situation:* From 1911 until 1916 fights between both factions provided physical threats to U.S. and foreign civilians. Additionally, much property was owned by U.S. citizens, as well as some by European nationals. The Roosevelt Corollary required the U.S. to solve that problem by intervening in Latin America, which, at this time, the State Department directed the Navy to mend.

Contending forces in Santo Domingo City were firing widely. The American Consulate buildings were in a direct line and were struck several times. Mister William W. Russell, the American minister, requested the USN to dispatch a naval force to the area in order to protect all foreign nationals, especially American citizens and property. A real or sensed problem was the belief that the Central Powers, Germany and Austria-Hungry, were trying to establish submarine bases on that part of the island of Hispaniola. No records were later found to prove that as a fact.

Rear Admiral William B. Caperton, commanding the USN cruiser force and all naval personnel in the area, ordered the Marines of the 6th and 9th Cos. in Haiti to board the transport *Prairie*. From there they were taken to Santo Domingo City and landed on 5 May along with the Marine detachment from the cruiser *Castine*. Soon after they were joined by the 4th, 5th, 13th, 14th, 19th, and 24th Cos., and Santo Domingo City was occupied. Marine detachments from the *Louisiana* occupied Monte Cristi on 26 May and those from the *Rhode Island* and *New Jersey* landed at Puerta Plata and occupied that town on 1 June.

Difficulties ashore were beyond the scope of the austere 600 Marines and Bluejackets already ashore. Arias and his rebels had removed themselves from Santo Domingo City in order to avoid confrontation with the U.S. forces and were located within the hinterland. Various efforts were made by the Americans to get the government leaders to select a candidate for president who would be a willing pawn of the U.S. State Department, but those failed. In fact, the deliberating body instead intentionally selected a candidate loyal to Arias. Caperton decided there was nothing to do but conquer the country. He therefore requested a regiment of Marines be sent to his command.

The 4th Marines, then based in San Diego, CA, were selected. Commanding the 4th Marine Regiment was Col. Joseph "Uncle Joe" Pendleton. Beginning on 6 June, Pendleton moved his men by rail across the U.S. to New Orleans, LA, from which three days later they embarked on the transport *Hancock*. Uncle Joe landed his force at Monte Cristi, on the north shore, on 21 June 1916 and thereupon assumed command of all naval forces ashore. This included Marine ship detachments already ashore.

The outspoken anti–American rebel leader, Gen. Desiderio Arias, minister of war, and his men held the city of Santiago, located in the southcentral part of the country. Santiago was exactly where Pendleton planned to go. Two ship detachments and the 4th and 9th Companies of Marines, under the command of Maj. Hiram I. Bearss, moved with supplies by rail south from Puerto Plata to Navarette, a dozen miles out of Santiago. There they were to meet and supply Pendleton's column, which would by then be badly in need of food and ammunition.

The main column, reinforced by artillery and led by Uncle Joe, moved southeast on 26 June. A 15-man mounted detachment led the column while "Fritz" Wise and his supply wagons took up the rear. The column moved quite well the first day, only encountering a few snipers, until they reached the village of Las Trencheras. There they ran into a hornet's nest when they found a ridge of entrenched Dominicans. Col. Pendleton decided to wait till morning so his tired men could get some sleep before fighting against a well-entrenched and prepared enemy.

On the 27th some of the Marines reconnoitered the positions the Dominicans held before placing their artillery. Pendleton planned a direct assault with two battalions abreast, one led by Maj. Melville Shaw and the other by Capt. Arthur Marix. Orders were issued at 0800 for the battalions to advance to their line of departure. However, the ground had some severe obstacles, including cactus, heavy brush, etc. On the right flank the 32nd Co. came upon a swamp directly in its line of advance. The 27th Co. on the left flank had been having dysentery problems, and would have trouble maintaining its place in line. At 0845 the machine-guns and artillery opened fire and it was not long before the rebels deserted their front-line trenches. The attack stalled when Shaw was forced to wait for Marix's wing to catch up with it. The rebels saw their opportunity and began a heavy fire upon the exposed Marines' flank. An anxious Pendleton sent Maj. Robert Dunlap, an old warrior, forward to take overall command. Dunlap proceeded by truck, taking along a machine-gun and crew.

Just as Marix came up, Dunlap's machine-gun crew had set up and began spraying the rebel's line with drumfire. Dunlap then ordered both battalions forward. As the rebel fire decreased, Dunlap ordered "bayonets fixed" and the Marines charged forward with a cheer. The fight lasted about an hour and when it terminated, one Marine and five Dominicans were dead, though it was known that the Dominicans always carried off their dead.

By 1300 the column was able to continue its march into Santiago but after it had reached a point about 25 miles from Monte Cristi, it encamped for the night. Trouble began as soon as the sun went down. The rebels apparently were as unprepared for night fighting as the sleeping Marines. A machine-gun unit of the 13th Co. opened fire and scared the rebels off. The "sprinkler guns," as the natives called them, would frighten anyone, Dominican or American. For some reason the uneducated rebels were convinced those guns could not fire at night, but they soon learned otherwise.

The next day two bridges crossing 40-feet deep gorges had been destroyed and the Marines had to put them, or at least one of them, back together again. It took several hours and then the Marines were able to continue their march on Santiago. Pendleton, knowing his reliance on a supply train with its return to Monte Cristi, had the 8th Co., 1st Lt. Holland Smith in command, remain to guard the repairs to the bridge. The column only made another five miles or so and had to stop for the night.

The next morning, 30 June, the rebels had moved up in the night and taken positions in the dense foliage around the camp. They opened fire, to which the Marines replied. The "sprinklers" drove them off, but at about noon they tried again and the same thing happened.

Pendleton and his command were unable to make many miles forward that day. Their supply lines were now stretched to their limits and Uncle Joe made the decision to cut off his lines and proceed forward, hoping to live on the country and rely on the Bearss column for necessities.

Bearss was meanwhile having great difficulty as he advanced. He and his smaller detachment were running into constant delays, including a dismantled bridge over which their train could not proceed until repaired. Along the line, the rebels would disrupt the tracks at the most disadvantageous points and effectively stop the train from proceeding. While repairs were being made, they would attack. Hiram was able, with his skills and fortitude, to shoo them off in every engagement and his train kept moving forward, albeit somewhat more slowly than anticipated.

Meanwhile, Uncle Joe had to consider his animals, whose food supply was just the nearby grass growing; grazing slowed the column down considerably. Another serious problem was the ammunition used for the machine-guns. The ammo was old, from 1907, and the cartridge cases had been reloaded so many times they expanded during firing, consequently the Benet-Mercie guns frequently jammed. And always at the wrong time.

On 3 July, during this march on Santiago, the most important altercation happened. Pendleton's column had moved but 4 miles when the point was fired upon by pickets. They were driven off, but ahead lay the main body of rebels near the village of Guayacanas. Uncle Joe ordered Shaw and his 2nd Battalion to deploy and attack. Skirmishes reported the enemy lines to be much stronger than at Las Trencheras. The rebels were well-entrenched on heights, couldn't be easily seen from where the Marines were to approach them, and had cleared their front of all vegetation for 200 yards, providing an excellent fire path. Lying about 150 yards before the first trench line was a barrier created from felled trees across the road. That road ran between the hills and in two lines the Dominicans were dug in on the tops of each.

At 0900 the 2nd Battalion advanced with companies abreast, supported by the 28th Co.'s machine-gun platoon and the 13th Co.'s artillery. The dense underbrush not only hampered the advance but served to blind the artillery layers; shrapnel was soon falling on the advancing men. However, no injuries were reported and their advance continued. The rebels commenced a fast and furious firing on the advancing Marines and didn't give ground.

Seeing that the infantry needed some heavy fire support, Dunlap did the same thing he had done at Las Trencheras. He led a machine-gun unit forward to where the felled trees lay and they began firing on the rebels. But they were in a spot; they were too far forward with little support themselves. Then Cpl. Joseph Glowin brought his machine-gun up and began firing. He was hit only moments later, but doggedly stuck with his gun and continued firing. He was hit again and refused to leave until forcibly removed. He was later awarded a Medal of Honor. Dunlap himself took over the gun, but, being a Benet-Mercie, it jammed almost immediately. Another crew ran forward and began firing, but that gun also jammed. Repairs on both were performed at the site, which was, of course, heavily doused with rebel fire.

The enemy continued concentrating on those machine-guns, making it impossible to affect repairs. The rest of the Marines were poised to advance against this very difficult position, but the leaders were hesitant to send them into what might be a disaster of the first magnitude. First Sergeant Roswell Winans ran up with more machine-guns, which attracted more attention from the rebels. They poured in a concentrated fire that was difficult to avoid in the Marines' exposed position. Winan's first gun crew was wiped out in a few minutes, its gun captain, Cpl. Frazee, was killed and the rest wounded. Winans had a spoke-wheeled Colt machine-gun moved up and it began firing. Not long after, this gun also jammed and he stood up to clear it, expecting to be hit, but he continued his work. For this he too was awarded the Medal of Honor.

Within a few feet another Marine died and seven more were wounded. Two more Colts were brought up and soon, with three guns firing, the Marines gained fire superiority, forcing the enemy to keep their collective heads down. The infantry moved forward and advanced to within 150 yards of the front trenches. Companies 27 and 29 cut through the underbrush and flanked the trenches. They then yelled and, with bayonets fixed, charged and drove the enemy out of their hole. The rebel commander had been killed, which took the heart out of any further resistance. The rebels ran for unknown parts.

With the fighting over, the column again began its move forward toward Santiago. However, the rebels had sabotaged the road and they spent many wearying hours moving a very short distance. Uncle Joe decided to camp and clean up for the next day, the 4th of July.

That morning some local doctors from Santiago had driven forward to care for their wounded, and with blindfolds they were allowed forward with Marine guards. As the column moved into Navarette, the Marines' travail greatly dissipated. The linkup with the rail line would now allow them to travel in comfort to Santiago. And better yet, the arrival of Hiking Hiram and his train loaded with badly needed supplies spread good cheer.[2] Colonel Pendleton made the wise decision to rest his weary force during the 4th and send the wounded back to Puerto Plata on Hiram's train.

The next day, 5 July, a train arrived with welcome reinforcements, including the 24th Company. A surprise visit by agents of Arias from Santiago City also brought with interesting news. Caperton and Arias had negotiated a settlement. The latter would surrender and he and his fellow rebels would be pardoned as well as receive amnesty. Uncle Joe was hesitant to accept this on face value and pondered his next move. The city was known to have an extremely strong defensive system, especially in a fort atop a hill. Pendleton, with his relatively weak force, had been considering what he must do to lay siege to it. Uncle Joe wasn't thrilled with the idea of continuing and an armistice would be pleasant news, if it were real. He later found out that it was and the Marines moved into and occupied Santiago.

From that point, the Marines were placed around the nation in strategic sites as guards to ensure orderly behavior by everyone. Trouble didn't just go away, though. The nation had been in a constant state of political upset for many years, and that continued. The U.S. continued to maintain a large force of Marines there, even during World War I, when every Marine might have been utilized in France. The Marines also created and trained a police force, the Guardia Nacional Dominica, which continued long after the Marines were withdrawn in 1924. It was that police unit from which the future dictator Rafael Leonidas Trujillo Molina emerged before he gained power and badly ran the country for so many years.

> *Results:* While the Marines remained in the country they were engaged periodically, supported fairly well by the Guardia, in trying to squelch various factions. Nothing of any real consequence happened during the period, but on occasion it was deadly for a few Marines and their opponents. After eight years in occupation, the U.S. government decided to withdraw its occupying force.

16

World War I

When the U.S. Congress declared war against Germany on 6 April 1917, the military forces of the Republic were in terrible shape. The Navy wasn't all that bad, but the Army was in dire need of rehabilitation. It had some intelligent and reasonably well-trained individuals but its numerical size and equipment was extremely limited. The Army didn't have an acceptable machine gun and the war in Europe, nearly three years old, had shown that was an absolutely essential infantry weapon. Heavy weapons were badly lacking; smaller field guns were a humble 3-inch model. The Marines, a modest military force intended solely to project the State Department's interest wherever desired, was a small and well-experienced fighting machete made up of individuals without formal military training.

The MGC Barnett managed to have one regiment, the 5th, included in the first troops going to France. That recently reactivated regiment collected together companies from various Caribbean islands to be transported to France with Maj. Gen. Pershing in May–June 1917. Pershing, however, had four regiments in his 1st Regular Division, and the Marines were sidelined to perform various onerous task: unloading ships, guard duty, etc. Meanwhile, the Army underwent a transformation from a three-company battalion to a four-company one. This was an American innovation, thought to be better for the man-slaughtering style warfare that was then in progress; more manpower means more staying power. Little thought was given to altering the style of the war then being fought.

In late 1917 another regiment of Marines, the 6th, began to arrive. By February 1918 it was complete, as was a newly structured machine gun battalion, the 6th. Pershing was desperate for trained troops and finally set aside his personal prejudices and accepted a Marine brigade formation, the 4th, from Marines in France for his 2nd Regular Division. Merged with a group of "regular" Army units, the 9th and 23rd Infantry, and various technical units, the division was born in France and began training.

Verdun

Date: 14 March to 14 May 1918.
Location: Toul Sector, near Verdun.
Involved: German army versus the French army, supported by the 2nd Division, USA, including its 4th Marine Brigade.
Situation: Since September 1914, when the World War had begun, and some severe losses from artillery and machine guns, the troops and leaders of both sides made the decision to go to ground. Fighting from trenches became the

mode of operations, with occasional attempts to go over heavily barbed wire emplacements and conquer the other fellow's trenches. The occasions were never completely successful, and the men continued to fall.

Even though Gen. John J. Pershing had intelligently decided the Americans would "never" fight in trenches, the French and British insisted they must train for it. So, when it was decided that the 2nd Division had been "completely" trained, they were sent into a quiet sector "to get the feel of it." The area around Verdun was, in 1917, as quiet a sector as could be found in the line. Each 2nd Division brigade would be directly responsible to, and under orders of, a French division, rather than responsible to its CO, Maj. Gen. Omar Bundy. The latter and most senior officers of the division would simply "observe."

The 4th Marine Brigade, which consisted of 280 officers and 9,164 enlisted men,[1] remained in the Bourmont training area until 14 March, when it commenced movement into subsectors of the Verdun front. Theirs was to be in the Toul sector.

On Friday, 13 March, 2/5 had entrained at Damblain and was the first Marines to move toward the enemy. On the evening of 14 March the battalion arrived at Dugny, detraining at 2200 hours a short distance from the front lines. A German aviator spotted the train unloading and called in his artillery and it wasn't long before the gunners got the range. They plastered the station with high explosives, hurting no Marines but destroying a lieutenant's trunk and nearly all the regiment's band instruments. Otherwise that was all the Germans could claim for their efforts. It impressed the Marines, however.

The balance of the brigade arrived within the following four days, and by 17 March 1918, all Marines were in assigned barracks or in trench dugouts. They then marched to Camp Nivolette; on the march, the entire force was subjected to artillery fire for the first time. The Germans were diligent.

The first Marines to enter the lines were those of 2/5. It was in the Montgirmont sector during the night of 16-17 March. One/five was placed in support near the center of the corps sector, Montgirmont, while 3/5 went into camp a little further back and continued its training. Two/five's semi-official history describes what was, in the beginning at least, rather little activity:

> Here nightly patrols and wiring were carried out. There was intermittent machine gunfire at night and an occasional bombardment, especially on rear positions and communicating trenches. Much information and experience was obtained especially in correct ways in organizing a position and patrolling in darkness. It was in this sector that we saw and felt the explosion of a tremendous land mine.[2]

On the night of 28 March, 2/6 relieved 3/6, occupying the towns of Mensil, Bonzee and Mont-sous-les-Cotes. The French relieved the 5th Marines of their section of the line on the evening of 29 March. The next evening, having marched northward all day, but still on the Verdun front, the regiment took over the subsector Eix-Moulainville-Chatillon. On the following night, 1 April, 3/6 relieved elements of the French army just to the right of the 5th Marines. That same date, Headquarters of the 4th Brigade was established at Post of Command (PC) Moscou. For the balance of the entire month both regiments occupied themselves with the same tasks. It was also at about this time that Marines began changing uniforms. Jackson mentions that the morale wasn't at its highest because "a lot of the boys were ragged ... by ragged I do not mean a little worn." While the 95th Co., 1/6, was at rest at Champignuelles it "discarded [uniforms] for new army clothes."[3]

Major Berton W. Sibley and 3/6 relieved the French on the night of 18–19 March at

Mont-sous-le-Cotes. The 82nd, 83rd, and 84th Companies were posted on line and the 97th Company was in reserve. There they had another French battalion between them and 2/5 on the front line. The plan was to leave each battalion in the front line for about ten days and then relieve them. Therefore on 28 March, 2/5 and the 8th MG Co. were relieved by 1/5, and 2/6 relieved 3/6. During this time the Germans launched a very aggressive attack upon the British at a point near where the British and French armies joined. Major adjustments all along the line were made and the French soon were moving divisions from the Verdun front further north to meet the threat. This resulted in a significant additional responsibilities for the Marines. The 5th Marines and a French regiment were assigned to hold a divisional position east of Verdun, relieving a French division at that point.

The arrangement was as follows: 1/5 occupied the extreme left flank and 3/5 the right. They were supported by 2/5 in reserve. The 6th Marines remained where they were but took over the original positions of the 5th Marines in addition to their own. Several new administrators replaced old ones at headquarters, Maj. Holland M. Smith became adjutant, with Capt. Henry L. Larsen, assistant adjutant, and 1st Lt. Benjamin S. Goodman became intelligence officer and Brig. Gen. Doyen's aide-de-camp. Captain George K. Shuler was regimental adjutant to Col. Wendell C. Neville, CO, 5th Marines, and Maj. Edward A. Green became CO of 1/5 until 13 March, when Maj. Julius S. Turrill returned and relieved him. Major Charles T. Westcott was CO of 3/5, until relieved by Maj. Edward W. Sturdevant on 26 March, and the latter was in turn relieved on 1 May by Maj. Benjamin S. Berry. The 6th Marines remained much the same, with few changes except for the 25 April relief of Maj. Robert E. Adams at 1/6 by Maj. Maurice E. Shearer. Adams joined the 38th Infantry, 3rd Division, to command a battalion.[4] Major Berton W. Sibley, who became ill, was relieved of command of 3/6 for the period between 29 March and 6 April 1918.

The 5th Marines were assigned the subsector Montgirmont-Les Esparges, PC being located at Ravin, and the 6th Marines the subsector Mont-sous-les-Cotes, PC at Bouee. Special Order no. 2 assigned the 6th Machine Gun Battalion companies as follows: the 77th to 1/5; 23rd to 3/5; 15th to 1/6; and 81st to 2/6, with the regimental machine gun companies (the 8th of the 5th Marines; the 73rd of the 6th Marines) taking position to support 2/5 and 3/6. The machine gun companies participated, along with the regular Marine infantry, in repelling raiding parties, patrolling no-man's-land, and constructing gun emplacements and trenches, as well as providing indirect and harassing fire.

Every day Brig. Gen. Doyen toured his sector, covering about eight miles of muddy, slippery trenches. Additionally, the weather was bitter cold that winter and the men were ill-prepared for its ferocity. According to a memoir of this period, two Marines died of exposure. Possibly there were more. The falling snow was soon waist high. In fact, it was on record as one of Europe's worst winters.

Until 13 May, each and every battalion took its place in the front line, with active patrolling or raiding parties every night. They also established listening posts, temporarily captured machine gun positions, wiping out the gun's effectiveness, and participated in all other activities that would gain the troops experience. The reserve troops were also busy digging reserve, or repairing existing, trenches.

The Germans always seemed to be aware of a change in the occupants of sections of the line, and this time was no different. Shortly after the 4th Brigade took up its part of the subsector, enemy artillery and aviation began to actively harass the Marines, as did the German infantry. Raiding parties and patrol encounters occurred on a regular basis, earning much credit for training the relatively new troops in the line.

During this period several casualties amongst the Marines occurred. The first Marine killed in action in France was Pvt. Emil H. Gehrke, 82nd Co., 3/6. On 1 April 1918 Gehrke received several shell fragments through his chest, killing him instantly. At the same time, Privates John R. Gabriel, Anton F. Hoesli, and Harry R. Williams, all of the 82nd, were wounded. Williams died of his wounds on the following day.

It was at this time that the 6th MG Battalion undertook to establish the field arrangement it would utilize for the next eight months. Each of four rifle battalions would have one machine gun company assigned to it. In the Verdun area the 15th Co. was assigned to 3/6, the 23rd Co. went with 2/5, the 77th Co. with 3/5, and finally, the 81st Co. went with 2/6. The 8th MG Co. would serve 1/5 and the 73rd MG Co. supported 1/6. Because enemy air activity was so intense, no outdoor drills were held. Even the animals had to be protected, so they weren't exercised until after dark. Other after-dark activities included the digging of machine gun emplacements and trenches.

Five U.S. Army infantry second lieutenants, straight from the Second Corps School, joined the 6th MG Bn. to take up duties as junior officers of that specialty service. They may have been the first to come, but it wasn't long before the Marine Brigade had upwards of 60 Army officers serving as platoon leaders. They generally performed at the highest possible level until most of the survivors were transferred out of the brigade after Soissons. Many friends were made during that four-month period.

Doyen, required by general orders to take the physical examination of all officers of the AEF, left for General Headquarters, AEF. He was back at brigade headquarters by 11 April, unaware that he didn't meet the physical standards established by Gen. Pershing. He would soon be relieved of command of the brigade he had led since it was formed in late 1917.

It was at about this same period when the Germans delivered a heavy bombardment of gas shells to the 4th Brigade. On 12 April, 1/6, and especially the 74th Company then in reserve at Camp Fontaine St. Robert, was heavily shelled, primarily with gas shells. The accurate fire caught many men in their billets before they could escape and nearly the entire company, 220 men and all of the officers, were evacuated in serious condition. In all, the 6th Regiment had nine officers and 305 enlisted men gas poisoned and evacuated to a hospital area, with 19 eventually dying.

A patrol on the night of 17 April 1918 of 5th Regiment Marines and French soldiers encountered a German patrol and earned a commendation in General Order No. 35 for their successful attack out of Eix, near Demi-Lune.

On the morning of 21 April, the 45th Co. of 3/5 (Maj. Berry), in particular a platoon commanded by 2nd Lt. Hope, which had just finished relieving 1/5 at Eix at night, was on the extreme left of the divisional and corps sector on a commanding ridge. The Germans desired that ridge and after a severe bombardment they launched a massive, well-planned raid on that section of the line. The specially trained raiding party left two German officers and two enlisted hanging on the wire after the Marines finished with them. Observers reported that the enemy carried a large number of wounded Germans back with them when they retired. But Hope's losses were also heavy; three Marines were killed and 11 were wounded, all from artillery fire and the raiding party. The French recognized the implications of this success and awarded the Croix de Guerre to a number of the officers and men who had participated in the brawl. Their French liaison officer, Lieutenant Viaud, reported to command that "our troops behaved admirably."

The 84th had a similar experience. A raiding party, loosely identified as the "Hindenburg Circus," raided its trenches with flamethrowers and grenades that same night. That raid was also repulsed with rifle fire and grenades and there were no Marine casualties reported. German losses, if any, weren't noted.[5]

The supply company of the 5th Marines was shelled on the night of 22 April and two men were killed and three were wounded. Losses in horses and mules were very heavy. The next night the Germans again shelled the same company, killing another Marine and wounding two more. Stables were destroyed, along with two horses and 13 mules. Two U.S. Navy men, Dental Surgeon Alexander G. Lyle and Pharmacist Mate, 1st Class Tony Sommer, were cited in General Order No. 35 for acts of bravery during the incidents, Lyle being awarded a Navy Medal of Honor.

General Order No. 3, the Brigade, dated 1 May, designated Maj. Edward B. Cole as brigade machine gun officer. And on the same date, five Marine officers were detached from the brigade and ordered to the 3rd Division, which had just arrived in France. The 3rd was listed as a "regular" division but was short of senior officers, especially officers with combat experience, and the 4th Brigade had more field officers than they could utilize at the time. Major Robert L. Denig was assigned to command the 1st Battalion, 30th Infantry; Maj. Edward W. Sturdevant the 3rd Battalion, 30th Infantry; Maj. Robert E. Adams the 3rd Battalion, 38th Infantry; Maj. Harry G. Bartlett the 2nd Battalion, 7th Infantry; and Maj. Littleton W. T. Waller, Jr., the 8th Machine Gun Battalion. Denig and Waller would both return to the 4th Brigade, although the former only temporarily.

The brigade had spent the better part of two months in trenches on the front lines when it was withdrawn on 14 May and transferred to an area around Vitry-le-Francois, in an area northwest of Paris. Not many of the Marines ever got any closer than the 30 or so miles to that great city, but spent what little of the free time they had in the towns and villages around them in open warfare training. One of the towns close by was named Marines, a fact that wasn't lost on the members of the brigade, and the name remained in many memories of those that survived the very dark days ahead.

There was a certain level of rancor in the brigade when Doyen was relieved. Not only was he well-liked, he was well-regarded professionally. It was he who had pulled together and trained the team which would go on to such fame in the future.

Brig. Gen. James Harbord got the brigade, and, according to his memoir, Pershing had told him that he was getting the best brigade in the AEF and "if it fails I'll know where to place the blame." It didn't fail. The brigade made him look very good, even though it paid a heavy price to do so.

Fourth Brigade opened headquarters at Venault-les-Dames. It wasn't long before the area was deemed unsuitable for training, so the brigade moved by train and a two-day road march to Gisors-Chaumont-en-Vixen, which was just north and slightly west of Paris. Headquarters was located at Bou-des-Bois. It was while in this relatively quiet zone that the division received its call to proceed to the Chateau-Thierry sector without delay.

> *Results:* During the two-month "training period" the 4th Marine Brigade learned little, as did their Army comrades of the division. Basically, they learned how to duck and patrol through barbed wire, which is what all the armies had been doing for three and a half years, without success.

Northwest of Chateau Thierry (aka Belleau Wood)

The Gettysburg of the war has been fought!
— General Pershing, referring to the success at Belleau Wood

Date: 1 June to 5 July 1918.
Location: Northwest of Chateau Thierry, the Bois de Belleau, between the towns of Lucy-le-Bocage, Bouresches, Torcy, Bussaires, Belleau, and Vaux.
Involved: German armies versus French armies and the 2nd U.S. Division, including the 4th Marine Brigade.
Situation: This was the first time the German army had gotten close to Paris since 1914, when the French forces in Paris taxicabs rode into history. Paris, the hub of France, from which extended the spokes of all commerce, supplies, and just about every item necessary for France's continuance of the war, had to be won. If the Germans continued their advance, Paris would have fallen. If Paris had fallen, France would undoubtedly fall, and if France should fall, the armies of the Allies must fall, too. There would be no tomorrow.

The 2nd Division was rushed eastward from its rest and training areas just north and west of Paris. The French were more hopeful that they would kill Germans than that they would halt their victorious armies. All day long the camions rushed as rapidly as possible, always through crowds of civilians pushing loaded carts or driving horse- or mule-drawn wagons. There were also many French soldiers, often without their arms, yelling to the Americans that the war was *Fini!* The sight of the poor, mainly women, children and the elderly, trying to escape the dreaded "Boche" remained with most of the Americans for balance of their lives.[6]

Major General Omar Bundy, CG, and Col. Preston Brown, the chief of staff of the 2nd Division, raced ahead to receive orders from the French command for the placement of his infantry brigades. They managed to locate Gen. Dégoutte, who was beside himself with the problems he faced as CG of the 6th French Army. Dégoutte explained what he planned for the Americans, which was to thrust them in anywhere, just to plug holes. Bundy and Brown told him they wouldn't place their men in the lines until their machine guns and artillery appeared. Finally, after much acrimonious discussion, the Frenchman gave in. He then asked Brown, "Can the Americans really hold?" and Brown replied, "General, those are American regulars. In a hundred and fifty years they have never been beaten. They will hold." And Brown was right; they did hold.

When the 2nd Division arrived at its stations on 1 June 1918, it began taking up positions north and south of the Paris-Metz Highway. A change in plans placed the 4th Marine Brigade north of the highway and the 3rd Infantry Brigade south of it. By the afternoon of the 2nd day, both infantry forces, including two of their machine gun battalions, the 5th and 6th, were on line. Their four regimental machine gun units and the artillery brigade were still en route, as were the supply wagons and, most important, the food and cook wagons, with the latter being most troublesome.

In the 4th Brigade, the two regiments of the 5th and 6th Marines and the 6th Machine Gun Battalion arrived. First on the scene was 2/6 (Maj. Thomas Holcomb), which occupied the ground running from the Paris-Metz Highway north up to and including Triangle Farm.

Major Edward B. Cole and his 6th MG Battalion arrived next and took up a position just to the rear of 2/6 and began deploying its guns at once. When 1/6 (Maj. Maurice E. Shearer) arrived, it moved behind the machine gunners and spread from Triangle to beyond Lucy-le-Bocage. With German shells falling on that village, they continued northward till nearly reaching the village of Torcy.

Last of the 6th to arrive was Berton W. Sibley's 3/6, accompanied by the regimental commander, Col. Albertus W. Catlin. He led them into the village of La Voie du Châtel and to the woods just beyond to serve as regimental back up. By 1850 Catlin could report to the brigade that his regiment was occupying a line three miles in length. There were two battalions on line and one in support and Catlin added that he was near the French 43rd Division of Infantry, which was attempting to hold the line at the Clignon Brook.

Next to come in was Col. Wendell C. Neville, leading the 5th Marines. They were assigned to a rear position at Triangle Farm. There the regiment went into a bivouac in the fields nearby. Within a few days Neville changed his headquarters to a position in the Carrières quarry not far from the village of Marigny.

Lieutenant Colonel Frederick Wise and 2/5 were sent northward to continue the line of the brigade to the west. They eventually occupied the western part of Hill 142, making contact with 3/6 on their right and extended their line westward through Les Mares Farm and beyond. There the Americans stood their ground for several days. Encounters on 2 and 3 June, between 2/5 and a large German force, preserved the line to the west at the Farm.

Meanwhile, 2nd Division Engineers began developing fortifications for the Marines, working westward from Lucy-le-Bocage. For the balance of the fighting in and around the area, those engineers would be right there with their Marine buddies, fighting and digging.[7]

Meanwhile, back at Les Mares Farm, Wise and his command were preparing for what they knew they would soon receive from the Germans. They too would find it interesting, not having yet run into the Americans.

On 3 June the Germans decided to advance southward toward Les Mares Farm, expecting to pierce the defensive line and easily outflank the 2nd American Division and any French units that might still be there.

As the Germans came forward the Marines spread out in a line with none of the four companies retained in support, the 18th Co. (Capt. Lester S. Wass) to the far left with the 43rd Co. (Capt. Charlie Dunbeck) to their right and continuing with the old fellow Capt. John Blanchfield with the 55th Co., and to the far right, the 51st Co. (Capt. Lloyd Williams). Lem Shepherd, 1st Lt. of the 55th, was out front with a small detachment to interdict any Germans that got that far forward.

To the Germans' very great surprise, Marines with well-aimed rifle fire began knocking them off long before they could see the defenders. This happened as the Germans tried to move forward, were forced to fall back, and tried again and again until their nerve failed completely and they fell back, never to come forward again.

In so doing the Marines created what later became known in the AEF as the *Bloody Angle of the AEF*. It has been recognized as a crucial spot, which, if lost, would have placed the 2nd Division in extreme jeopardy. Should the Germans have pierced the line at that point, they would have been able to envelop the division, and, most likely, in short order would have been able to force its surrender.

In the meantime, the hard-pressed French forces kept pulling back, behind the Marine and Infantry's lines. In so doing, they gave up possession of one vital location, the Bois de

Belleau, aka Belleau Wood to the Americans. The Marines would spend nearly an entire month trying to drive the well-entrenched Germans out of it. In so doing, their losses would total more than half the brigade.[8] Admittedly, their tactics were antiquated, but because of the enemy's strong positions and the division's lack of high-angled artillery concentration, regaining the ownership of Belleau Wood was believed to be absolutely necessary.

The CG of the 2nd Division, Maj. Gen. Omar Bundy, and his CoS, Col. Preston Brown, made the decision to only fight one of their brigades at a time, and they selected the 4th Brigade. A look at the map explains their reasoning. The woods were where the Germans were, at the center of the line. By this time the 5th Marine Regiment was on the line opposite the wood and the 6th Marines were a southerly position from the 5th's right to near the Paris-Metz Highway. To their right was the 3rd Brigade.

Marines launched the initial group of attacks, beginning on 6 June. First was an attack at 0345 by a portion of 1/5 under Maj. Julius S. Turrill from Hill 172 down to Hill 142, which was a salient into the northern sector. Turrill had but two companies and some engineers, plus a platoon from the 6th MG Battalion, to make the assault upon a very strong German position.

It was a bloody beginning. The whistles blew and down the hill they went. It was a narrow front and within the first hour almost all the officers and many of the men were casualties. Somehow the Marines, now under the overall command of Capt. George W. Hamilton (49th Co.), drove the well-entrenched Germans off that promontory and survived numerous counterattacks. Eventually, the two missing companies of the 5th Marines collected on that hill and helped to preserve the day's success. Turrill and his men withstood attacks on several of the following days, never losing what ground had been gained. Hamilton was the outstanding officer.

Harbord and his staff at brigade headquarters had made plans for two separate attacks that day. The second involved two battalions launched later that afternoon at 1700, 3/5 and then 3/6. The former attacked the southwestern face, just north of Lucy-le-Bocage, and the latter along the southern edge of Belleau Wood. At about the same time 2/6's target was the village of Bouresches, the most important position on the battlefield.[9]

The first attack by 3/5 was a complete disaster. It was shattered as it moved across open ground against formidable machine guns firing into them from three sides. What was called the Marines' "perfect parade ground formation" destroyed 3/5. Their leader, Maj. Benjamin S. Berry, lost an arm, and many of his officers and men remained where they had fallen in the wheat field. The remnants of 3/5 were forced to retire, even those few who had actually gotten into the woods.

Major Berton W. Sibley, leading 3/6 into the southerly part of the woods and against intense machine-gun fire, managed to get far enough inside to dig in and fight off numerous counterattacks that day and several following. His losses were also catastrophic. Albertus W. Catlin, the CO of the 6th Marines and in overall command (though Berry never accepted or acknowledged that fact) got too far forward and was badly wounded a few minutes after the attack began. He was out of the war. Meanwhile, Maj. Thomas Holcomb's 2/6 sent a divided force eastward toward Bouresches. Two of his companies (79th, Capt. Randolph T. Zane, and 80th, Capt. Bailey M. Coffenburg) went into the eastern portion of Belleau Woods, extending 3/6's line and covering the left flank of the 96th Co. (Capt. Donald F. Duncan) as it made its way to the village. The fourth company (78th, Capt. Robert E. Messersmith) was to the south of the 96th, covering their right flank. The 96th went across the open space, along the dirt road, and as it moved east, it lost most of the company, including the CO, Capt. Donald F. Duncan.

Remnants of the 96th Co. (approximately 22 men and an officer, 2nd Lt. Clifton B. Cates) fought their way forward against a heavy concentration of Maxims and rifle fire, with some artillery dropping in amongst them. Casualties had been extremely heavy but they managed to get in and take Bouresches, driving most of the German defenders out. The village would continue to be the subject of German attention for the balance of the month. June 6 finally ended with four Marine battalions shot to pieces. Nonetheless, there were still two more to be used, 2/5 and 1/6, and it wouldn't be very long before the brigade CO would find a way to do so.

After taking heavy losses, on 8 June Sibley and his exhausted men were finally allowed to vacate their tenuous hold on the southern part of Belleau Wood. On 10 June, 1/6 (Maj. John A. Hughes) entered the woods where 3/6 had once been, but the newcomers made nearly no progress. They would remain pretty much where they were, having taken much abuse, especially from gas shelling, until the Marine brigade was finally relieved after two and a half weeks in action. Even the French, who were notoriously low on manpower, wouldn't leave their men in combat longer than a week. The Americans still had a lot to learn.

Meanwhile, Fritz Wise's 2/5 was the next Marine unit to attack. On 11 June it entered the woods where 3/5 had nearly been wiped out with only somewhat better fortune. Wise's formation was badly hurt going in, with one company, the 55th, nearly finished because its right flank was exposed to German fire as they entered. A company from Hughes' 1/6 was supposed to have been there to protect Wise's flank but wasn't. However, 2/5 went in further and remained in the woods despite intense pressure from the Germans that were still in residence. Essentially, it was Wise and his battalion that saved the key position, and this was the beginning of the end for the German occupation of Belleau Wood.[10]

Wise and his command managed to continue to make life unpleasant for the enemy. By the time relief was coming, 2/5 had gotten further north than the "X-Line" set by Harbord for the first day's attack (6 June). It had continued pushing the Germans further north until it, like the rest of the 4th Brigade, was finally relieved.

An untested American infantry regiment, the 7th from the 3rd Division, was assigned to relieve the Marine brigade in the woods and began doing so on 15 June, though it took nearly a week to complete it. The story of the 7th is sad. That one regiment was unable to take the place of a brigade, shattered though it was, and consequently the infantry lost considerable ground, which infuriated the Marines when they returned a week later. Marine returnees began coming in on 22 June and were entirely recalled by 24 June. What happened to the 7th that week, however, isn't part of our story.

For the next few days the 4th Brigade endeavored to recover the ground lost. On 23 June Maj. Maurice E. Shearer, now CO of 3/5, devised a plan to drive the balance of the enemy out of the northern portion of the woods.

At 1900 on Sunday, 23 June, the attack began. Captain Robert Yowell's 16th Co., plus a platoon from the 47th (Capt. Philip Case) was on the left. To his right were Capt. Richard Platt and his 20th Co., plus 50 men from the 45th Co. (Capt. Peter Conachy). They were using what was to them a new tactic, sending forth small groups of Marines with grenades and their superior marksmanship to soften up any entrenched German positions lying before the advancing units. From the woods across the road the companies moved forward, spreading out upon entering the wood. Not long after they entered and advanced, both of the second line companies, the 45th and 47th, spread to the left and right to cover any enemy that remained behind the advance. The heroes that day are so numerous it is almost unfair to cite any one person. In fact, the heroes during the month included nearly every officer and enlisted man, as well as their Army comrades of the 3rd Brigade, and of course the brave Navy medical personnel.

Marine casualties soared as they drove deeper into the enemy's lines. While the Marines were moving forward, killing off all the interlocking machine-gun nests, German artillery was dropping high explosives and gas shells, hurting the Marines as well as the Germans. Slowly they inched forward and just as slowly the Germans fell back. During the night efforts were made several times to reinforce 3/5. On the night of 23–24 June, Sibley's 3/6 sent a couple of platoons forward to help the 20th Company. Neville's report to headquarters spelled it out: "Things are rather bad. One company (20th) almost wiped out."

Shearer's command held its ground that night while the high command discussed what to do next. Several suggestions were made, including the pulling back of the Marines and a high intensive shelling of that portion of the woods still held by the enemy. Reports coming in were definite: "The enemy seemed to have unlimited alternate gun positions and many guns. Each gun position covered by others. I know of no other way of attacking these positions with chance of success than [the] one attempted and am of opinion that infantry alone cannot dislodge enemy guns. Water is difficult to obtain and scarce. Men and officers very tired but retain their spirit."[11]

On Tuesday, 25 June, the same battered companies, supported by the always venerable 2nd Engineers, continued digging out the Maxims and gunners. Enemy snipers were adding to the rolls of Marines put down, but it wasn't all one-way. The Germans suffered many men killed, wounded and taken prisoner. To them the war was nearly over and they weren't reluctant to surrender. In fact, one lone Marine private, a runner, became lost in the woods and almost fell into a trench occupied by a company of Germans. Henry Lenert, a Chicago lad with plenty of gumption, was brought before a German captain and interrogated. Who asked, more or less, "How many units out there?" Henry replied, "the 5th Marines." When the captain asked what was behind them, Henry replied, "the 6th Marines." The captain then spoke to his fellow officers and, turning to Lenert, said, "Will you take us prisoner?" Henry wasn't about to refuse an officer anything and replied, "absolutely." They then moved westward through the forest, through company, battalion, regiment and finally to division headquarters, where his 83 prisoners were finally accepted. Henry Lenert's reward was a Silver Star citation instead of a well-earned Distinguished Service Cross.[12]

On the 26th Shearer's beat-up battalion, still moving forward, finally put "paid in full" to the German defense and Maurice could send a message to Brig. Gen. Harbord, "BELLEAU WOODS NOW U.S. MARINE CORPS ENTIRELY." That night 2/6 relieved 3/5, which went into a much-deserved rest behind all the lines.

Next came the 3rd Brigade's opportunity to prove its mettle. Tired of hearing how wonderful the Marine brigade had been, it successfully assaulted the town of Vaux on the highway, thereby eliminating any enemy troops across their line, north or south.

Many plaudits, most from the French and high-ranking U.S. Army officers, were spread about, but, in my opinion, the most important, because of who said it and what was said, is from Lieutenant General Robert Lee Bullard, CG 2nd, U.S. Army, who wrote:

> "With the help of God and a few marines," was a phrase descriptive of the halt of the march on Paris, which was not fair to other units. The marines "didn't win the war here." *But they saved*

the Allies from defeat. Had they arrived a few hours later I think that would have been the beginning of the end: France could not have stood the loss of Paris. So today at Belleau Wood stands perhaps America's finest battle monument.[13]

A second comment, written many years later by the English military historian Basil Liddell Hart, is also important: "The appearance and fierce counter-attack of the 2nd American Division at the vital joint of Chateau-Thierry was not only a material cement, but an inestimable moral tonic to their weary Allies."[14]

> *Results:* The 2nd Division of American regulars would be rightly lauded for slamming the door shut in June 1918 to the German army and, in the process, inflicting a defeat on at least four German divisions. The Marines, especially, were applauded everywhere, and their Army comrades hated them for it (and some still do).
>
> Though not exceptionally well led from the top, the Battle of Belleau Wood demonstrated the tenacity and overall courage of the modern Marine Corps. It thrilled the French, who initially were sure, as so many of their retreating troops yelled at the advancing Americans, that *la guerre est Fini*. Paris was saved in June 1918 by Americans, many of whom were Marines. The war was not finished, not just yet, but the Americans would play a great part in ending it. The commanding general of the 6th Army, in recognition of the great turnaround at that point, ordered that henceforth the Bois de Belleau would be known as the Bois de la Brigade de Marine. In later years, it has become the place to visit in June of each year, even for the busy commandant of the Marine Corps and his staff.

Soissons

> *Date:* 16 July to 20 July 1918.
> *Location:* Soissons environs.
> *Involved:* German army versus French Colonial DI, 1st U.S. Division (Regular) and the 2nd U.S. Division (Regular).
> *Situation:* In order to eliminate the huge salient caused by the German advances at Chemin des Dames (May–June), the French army planned to destroy one side of the penetration, at the proverbial armpit, weakening the whole structure. Additionally, more U.S. and French divisions would successfully advance at the southern end of the salient.

The Marines of the 4th Brigade participated in two distinct attacks in the Aisne-Marne Offensive, in which 270,000 American troops were engaged.[15] In the first, which started at 0430 18 July, the 5th Marines were in the attacking line with the 6th Marines in reserve; after a brief respite, another advance began at about 1800 18 July, and the 5th Marines were again in the attacking line. The second attack took place on the morning of 19 July, and the 6th Marines were in the attacking line. Marines in the first two days of these operations suffered so severely in deaths and wounds that they had to be withdrawn from the front lines.

On 11 July 1918, Brig. Gen. James G. Harbord, CG of the 4th Marine Brigade, received notification of his appointment as a major general, and two days later left on a five-day leave of absence. As Col. Neville had been evacuated to a base hospital after leaving the Château-Thierry sector, Lt. Col. Harry Lee, commanding the 6th Marines, assumed temporary command of the 4th Brigade. Major General Harbord and Col. Neville both returned in time to enter the Aisne-Marne Offensive (commonly known as Soissons), the former in command of the 2nd Division and the latter in command of the 4th Brigade.

On the night of 16 July 1918, the 4th Brigade of Marines moved in camions (open trucks) from the neighborhood of Nanteuil-sur-Marne to south of Soissons. After a terrible ride, the 5th and 6th Marines arrived during the afternoon and evening of 17 July, in the Bois de Retz, and the 6th MG Battalion about 0300. On 17 July 1918, the 1st Moroccan Division and the 1st and 2nd Divisions of American regulars were hurriedly and secretly concentrated during a terribly fatiguing ride in camions and then a forced night march over roads jammed with troops, artillery, and tanks, through rain and mud, in the Bois de Retz, near Soissons. Headquarters of the 4th Brigade was established at Vivieres.

The process of getting to the "jump-off" on time for this first counteroffensive of Marshal Foch will always have a place in Marine Corps history as an unmitigated horror, despite the illustrious victory that followed. It was so terrible for the personnel engaged that none ever forgot the experience. How the men exposed to these merciless conditions were capable of advancing, fighting, and winning a great victory that first day is still a mystery.

The Aisne-Marne Offensive lasted from 18 July to 6 August 1918, but the 2nd Division and 4th Brigade's parts terminated on 20 July. Generally speaking, the Americans were not led by their own divisional officers, Harbord being barely on the scene and having little input, about which he later complained. However, he didn't "jump-in" at that time and his division was wrecked.[16]

The division was a part of the III Corps (U.S.), but for this campaign was transferred to the XX Corps (French), which was part of the 10th French Army. French staff officers managed the whole thing, and as usual, severe losses were sustained by all units engaged.

The 1st and 2nd American Divisions, with the 1st French Moroccan Division between them, were employed as the spearhead of the main attack, driving directly eastward, through the most sensitive portion of the German lines, to the heights south of Soissons.

On 18 July the advance began without the usual brief warning of a preliminary bombardment, and these three divisions at a single bound broke through the enemy's infantry defenses and overran its artillery, cutting or interrupting the German communications leading into the salient. A general withdrawal from the Marne was immediately begun by the enemy, although they still fought stubbornly to prevent a complete disaster.

The attack was made by the following troops in line from right to left: 23rd Infantry, 9th Infantry, and 5th Marines; Corps Reserve was the 6th Marines. The direction of the attack to the first objective was generally northeast. Then its course turned more to the southeast. This was planned by the French staff officers, and the change of direction caused a serious intermingling of some units which was unavoidable. Additionally, since the troops were rushed into action, no reconnaissance of the ground had taken place. Therefore they were unaware of what they would be running into. Also, the force's machine gun companies were not available, and there was no opportunity to supply the troops with the auxiliary weapons of the individual soldier, so the attack was made with rifle and bayonet and the automatic rifle. All of the troops were in position or going into position when the attack started at 0445. The Germans' first warning was a heavy barrage, which rolled ahead of the troops at "the rate of 100 metres in two minutes." It was a complete surprise, and by 1300 both the first and second and most of the third objectives had been taken, but the "sunken town" Vierzy was not taken until later in the day. Another attack late in the evening carried the line forward to a point about a half-mile east of and beyond Vierzy.[17]

In a later report, Lt. Col. Logan Feland, CO, 5th Marines, inadvertently forgot to mention the distraction of his 17th Co. (Capt. LeRoy Hunt). Moroccan troops, on their left flank, weren't there and the Germans and German Maxims were directed toward the Marines, which they didn't like. With help from the 55th Co. (1st Lt. Elliott Cooke, USA) both went far enough northeast (and out of their sector) to take the town of Chaudun.[18] Additionally, the 1st Battalion, 9th Infantry was headed in the same direction, but didn't go quite as far. Going into the middle of the lines helped the Moroccans who weren't keeping up with the 2nd Division in their advance, however they did manage to eventually catch up.

Major Julius Turrill, CO, 1/5, gave some more details in his report. He described his command activity:

> With the 66th Co. (Capt. William La. Crabbe) on right and the 17th Co. on left, the 67th Co. was in support. The 49th Co. came up about ten minutes later and went to the left to establish liaison with Moroccans. We covered the front in the woods from the National Road to the Route Chretiennette. A few Frenchmen were seen, and some trenches where we started our deployment. Our barrage commenced while we were deploying.

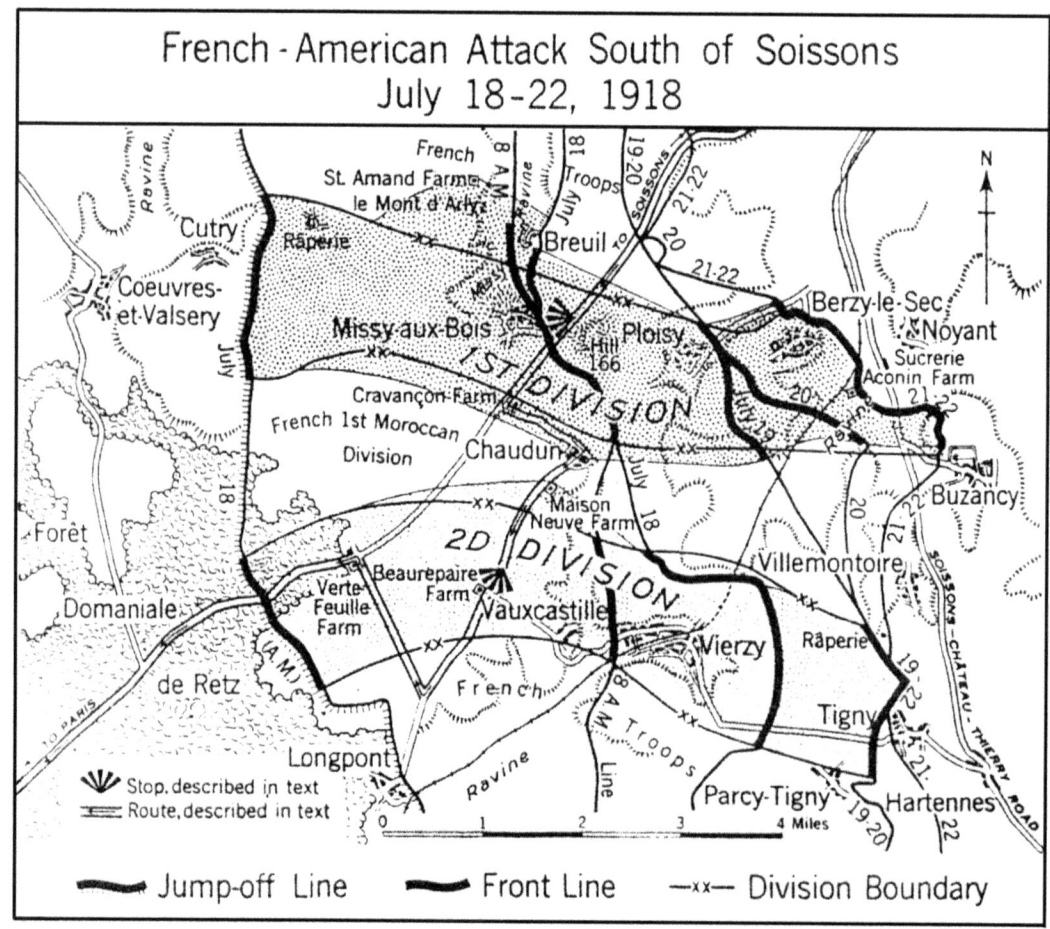

Then the 2nd Battalion came up on Turrill's right. The German barrage was hitting the 5th Marines at this time. Twenty minutes later Turrill issued orders to advance. Captains Richard N. Platt, CO of the 20th Company and Robert Yowell's 16th company, both in 3/5, came up as a support for 1/5. The 67th Co. (Capt. Frank Whitehead) had been sent into line about 0800. Platt's and Yowell's companies, with some of the 49th Co. (Capt. George W. Hamilton), formed a new support.

Major Ralph S. Keyser, CO of 2/5, took up positions to the right of 1/5. The disposition of the battalion from right to left was as follows: 51st Co. (Capt. William O. Corbin), as liaison with 9th Infantry on the right, 18th Co. (Capt. Lester S. Wass), 43rd Co. (Capt. Joseph B. Murray), and 55th Co. (1st Lt. Elliott D. Cooke, USA). Captains Wass (KIA) and Murray and Cooke were casualties. Captain Corbin was the last in. His company came under heavy artillery fire shortly after leaving an ammunition dump and went off to the right of a road into woods and failed to get in contact with the 23rd Infantry. French guides took the two left companies (43rd and 55th) too far to the north, as they were both on the north side of the Paris-Maubeuge Highway. Captain Murray discovered this and changed direction in time to practically cover his sector. The 55th Co. advanced along the north of the highway. The 66th Co. (Capt. Crabbe) of 1/5 was in the rear of Keyser's left and advanced through it and his left companies were too far to the left of the 2/5 sector. There was some opposition encountered in the woods, but after the tanks had been along the edge of the woods opposition ceased. Most of the enemy surrendered from their dugouts as Marines advanced. The Verte Feuilles Farm was taken by 2/5 and the advance continued to the first objective, which all of the companies reached, except the 51st Co. (liaison company on the right).

When Murray was wounded Wass assumed command of both companies in a ravine and soon after Cooke was stopped by machine guns across a road on his right. He sent men across the road to clear it and make contact with the 43rd Co. The 66th Co. came by them momentarily. It was about here that the battalion ran into our artillery fire and was badly scattered, 1st Lt. Cooke and some of his company going northeast toward Maison Neuve Farm and the remainder going to the southeast. All of the officers of the 18th Co. were casualties. Keyser gave high praise to the work of the tanks, which he thought was remarkable.[19]

Major Maurice E. Shearer, CO of 3/5, reported that his battalion advanced as the reserve component and occupied the French trenches in the rear of the jumping-off line. Later they moved to an advance line of trenches. At the request of Keyser, the 45th Co. (Capt. Thomas Quigley) (less than 10 men) was sent in to reinforce the 55th Co. at about 0800. After a reconnaissance, the 20th Co. and 16th Co. were sent to support 1/5. At Harbord's order a provost guard of two officers and 30 men was established at Cre-de-Montgobert from 47th Co. (Capt. Raymond E. Knapp). The balance of 47th Co., 3/5, was used to escort prisoners to the rear and bring ammunition forward.

The battalion PC was then moved to Verte Feuille Ferme with orders to Maj. Shearer to prevent all straggling to rear and collect and forward all men to the front line. This duty continued until 0300, 20 July 1918, when the 2nd Division was withdrawn from the lines. Shearer's battalion joined the balance of the 5th Marines in position in the woods at Cre. Fourneaux.

What happened to Capt. John H. Fay and his 8th Machine Gun Co. is a superb example of how confusing orders can be during the "fog of battle." Fay received orders from Col. Feland, CO, 5th Marines, at 2200 on 17 July to join the regiment and take over 3/5's rear. Further orders were that two platoons of the 8th Co. would join 2/5 and another platoon would join 1/5 in the attack. This order could not be complied with as machine guns and ammunition were not received until about 1800 on 18 July.

After receiving machine guns and ammunition Fay received an order from the chief of staff, 2nd Division, to proceed forward and support the attack. While en route he received orders from the 3rd Brigade CG, Hanson E. Ely, to report to him for orders. From Ely, Fay received orders to proceed to Beaurepaire Ferme and await further orders. At 1500, on 18 July, he received orders from the CG of the 3rd Brigade to "take the town of Vierzy." While en route to comply with the above orders, Fay met 1/5, which was also moving forward in the same mission. The town was taken at about 2000, 18 July.[20] Six machine guns were placed on the east side of the town and six on the northeast side in compliance with the CG's order.

The following day, 19 July, the French plan was for the advance to continue. Only this time the 2nd Division advance would be made entirely by the 6th Marines. What had required three regiments abreast on the 18th would only require one regiment on the 19th, according to the planners. Not only that, but the 6th Marines, because of various foul-ups not of their making, did not jump off at 0700 as ordered but at 0830, missing entirely the artillery barrage laid down for their support at 0600.

The regiment was to attack from east of the village of Vierzy. At 0830, with 1/6 on the right, 2/6 on the left, and 3/6 in support, the regiment went forward. Tanks were in the forefront and were slow, therefore the infantry moved across the open wheat fields at a slower than normal pace. German heavy guns were not only ready, but well-prepared. After all, they had an enemy artillery barrage a few hours before which informed them an attack was coming. The Marines, more than the tanks, caught a lot of incoming fire and paid the price. An official history of the regiment was vague about the time element and the whirlwind the regiment faced. The *History of the Sixth Regiment* describes the operations of 19 July in the following words:

"When the front lines were passed then enemy machine guns proved most troublesome.... What *remained* of the regiment took shelter in a line of semi-complete entrenchments constructed by the Germans [in other words, shell holes], where from 10.30 A.M. until dark the regiment was subjected to artillery, one-pounder and machine gun fire" (emphasis added). Someone discovered a gap in the lines. Consequently several companies from 3/6, notably the 83rd (Capt. Alfred H. Noble) and 84th (Capt. Horatio P. Mason), were sent to fill in.

At 1545, Col. Harry Lee, CO of the 6th Marines, sent the following message by runner to the three battalion commanders, to those of the Hdqrs. Co., and to the 1st Bn., 2nd Engineers.

"The Division Commander [Harbord] directs us to dig in and hold our present line at all costs. No further advance will be made for the present. He congratulates the command on its gallant conduct in the face of severe casualties."

Conditions were bad, no food or water could reach them, and the men's canteens were empty. As mentioned, the losses were horrendous. The 1st Battalion had three officers killed and eight wounded; 2/6 was even worse off, with only three officers on their feet when relieved; and 3/6 lost 39 percent of its officers. Of the 2,450 officers and men engaged, 1,300 were killed or wounded that day.

On 19 July at 2200 Fay received orders from Col. Feland of the 5th Marines to proceed 900 meters northwest of Beite-Feuille Ferme and then to proceed into the woods about 600 meters and take up a reserve position. At midnight the regiment was relieved by Algerians and withdrew to a position far behind the lines. While in a bivouac on the 20th, German artillery fire followed them into the forest and the remnants suffered more casualties, many dying from falling tree branches. The Marines remained where they were until dark, when 3/5 was brought up to provide them with some protection as they withdrew. The 2nd Division was finished, though the battle wasn't.

> *Results:* The results at the northern armpit of the salient were extraordinarily successful. The enemy retreated. Once again the 2nd Division, including its 4th Brigade, suffered heavily. The 2nd Division had taken another beating. This was the second while under French command, and there would be a third, at Blanc Mont in October. Meanwhile, the division would be put into a quiet sector where it would have few firefights and no serious opposition. It was known as the Marbache sector and would allow the Marines, with substantial replacements, to rebuild the division.

St. Mihiel and Marbache

Date: 8 August to 16 September 1918.
Location: Marbache (until 18 August), Favieres (until 2 September), then St. Mihiel on 11 September.
Involved: German forces occupying the St. Mihiel sector versus the 1st American Army, including the 2nd Division.
Situation: After the bloodbath experiences at Belleau Wood and Soissons, the 2nd Division was allowed a respite in the Marbache sector for ten days. A limited amount of fighting in that sector between infantry and enemy patrols occurred and the Marines suffered a very few casualties, although the exact numbers are not known.

The division was then transferred to the neighborhood of Favieres to train for the forthcoming assault upon the St. Mihiel sector. The latter began when the division was moved to the line just about at Limey on the night of 10–11 September. This was on the eastern or southern part of the salient, which was located south of the Verdun area.

It was to be a massive production, with a total of 12 and a half divisions on line and 5 and a half in support. Of this total, two American divisions, the 4th and 26th, would be at the western or northern armpit with several French DIs. The main thrust would come from the American divisions in two corps, I and IV, on the south side. These included the 2nd Division, whose first objective would be the high ground between Jaulny and Xammes, with the latter partly in the 89th Division's zone.

Artillery support on the morning of 12 September was enormous and intense. It began at 0100 and more or less continued until 0500, when the attack began. Then the artillery was to provide the infantry with a rolling barrage as they moved forward. The division moved out with the 3rd Brigade in the lead and 4th Brigade in reserve. Within an hour Feland's 5th Marines were to follow the 9th Infantry, which supported the leading 23rd Infantry. But for some reason Feland was having minor difficulty bringing his battalions forward. Light French tanks assigned to the 4th Brigade were also having difficulty in the terrain, which would cause the Marines some of their problems.

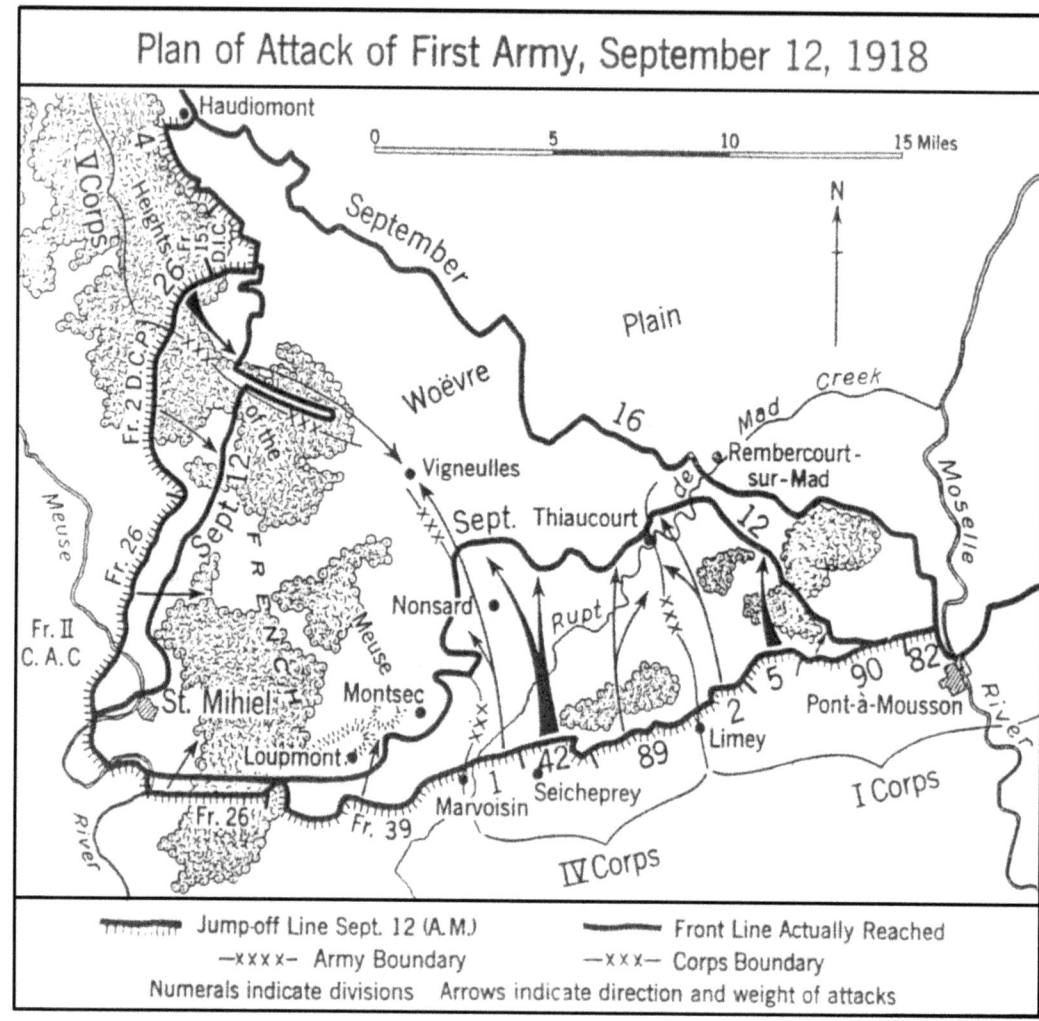

Factually, the 2nd Division had a reasonably easy go at this sector, with the 4th Brigade having the easiest time of all. The 3rd Brigade made its objectives that day, passing through Thiacourt at 1700 and then practically at 1st Army's objective. What was causing this easy time? Simply that the Germans had been planning to vacate the sector and the attack caught them as they were moving to the rear. However, according to various reports from the 3rd Brigade, their losses were nearing the 50 percent range, a number which later proved to be terribly incorrect.[21]

The fighting continued as the Germans fell back and the 2nd Division was pulled out of the line on 16 September, a bare four days later. The division had further obligations to serve the French army in a planned advance to begin in early October. The 1st U.S. Army continued for a few more days, until it was obliged to move northward toward the Argonne forest to begin another attack on 26 September.

One additional piece of interesting material which isn't exactly about the 4th Marine Brigade but is rather about an individual Marine, happened on the opposite side of the salient. Colonel Hiram "Hiking Hiram" Bearss was an officer of the Marine Brigade who was called off to serve in command of the 102nd Infantry, 26th "YD" Division. He was an aggressive officer who had seen service in the Philippines, Haiti, and Santo Domingo, and in several other hot spots, earning a Medal of Honor citation, later issued after his retirement.

Hiram's responsibility on 12 September was to drive through the salient and meet the venerable 1st U.S. Division at Vigneulles, which was coming from the opposite side of the salient. Hiram selected an ancient pathway, known as Le Grand Tranchee de Calonne, apparently underutilized by the Germans in that sector. He and his regiment, with bayonets fixed and orders not to shoot, advanced under cover of this heavily overgrown pathway, completely avoiding Germans as they proceeded at Hiram's speed toward their objective. Hiram, with his aide, a captain, and a sergeant, proceeded in advance and as they arrived at the village found a German machine gun company preparing to get underway. Hiram yelled out (in German?) to halt and surrender their weapons. Used to obeying orders when given, the Germans halted and dropped their weapons. He then ordered them to form in ranks, which they did, officers included. Then he spotted a German preparing to hurl a grenade at him and he punched the man in the face, knocking him down. That seemed to be the end of the "rebellion" and just then the balance of the 102nd Infantry made its appearance, which ended any further attempts at escaping.

It wasn't until the next day that the 1st Division arrived in a nearby village, and was dismayed to find the National Guardsmen already there.[22]

The period between Soissons and the upcoming Blanc Mont was a time, more or less, of recuperation for the 2nd Division and its fighting men of both brigades. Unfortunately, they would soon pay for this respite.

> *Results:* St. Mihiel was a first victory for American arms in France. It was important because it reclaimed a large sector which Germans had taken earlier in the war and pointed at the heart of unoccupied France. Yet overall, it was a rather easy go, and only Gen. Pershing's broadcast of its worth impressed the folks back home. The upcoming events would have a much larger contribution to ending the war.

Blanc Mont

> *The taking of Blanc Mont is the single greatest achievement of the 1918 campaign—the Battle of Liberation.*
> —Marshal Pétain

Date: 1 October through 10 October 1918.
Location: Blanc Mont and environs.
Involved: German army versus the 2nd Division, 36th NG Division and the French Army.
Situation: In the fall of 1918, the Allied High Command, meaning Marshal Foch, but in this case also the British commander, Field Marshal Haig, decided to launch a sustained offensive all along the line. The French army was greatly reduced in manpower, mainly because of numerous badly designed offensives since the war had begun. Britain's army wasn't much better but its government had retained military manpower in Britain so Haig wouldn't be allowed to "waste them" in his "frivolous" attacks. But, upon their release, Haig imme-

diately wanted to use them to attack. Foch, an exponent of attack, agreed to a plan which called for the British army at the north end of the line, the French army in the middle, and the newly arrived AEF, now in substantial numbers, at the right or south end of the Allied line.

The German army had advanced into France in 1914 and had taken several positions which would cause the French army many problems as it attempted recovery. One, the worst, was a section in the Champagne district known to the locals as "Blanc Mont." It was the south end of a rather flat promontory extending northward to the Aisne River. This south end caused headaches for the French. Besides providing the German army with a magnificent and picturesque southerly view of 180 degrees over the Marne valley, it was also controlling the cathedral city of Reims. That city's historical cathedral was of prime importance to France and had to be protected before the enemy could destroy it. They had actually tried, without success, several times.

The Blanc Mont height itself was only about 200 feet over the nearby village of Somme-Py, but any previous assaults by French troops had always resulted in massive death. Heavy fortifications and a large number of well-located and protected artillery and machine-gun sites did not allow the advancing French troops much chance for survival. It was a long gradual climb that looked relatively easy, until one appreciated what the German defenders on top observed.[23]

Meanwhile, the French realized that in the forthcoming planned attack, they would require additions to their formation in order to take that most difficult position in the entire line. They needed manpower, and the only available troops were those of the AEF. Foch and Pétain both requested (almost begged) Gen. Pershing to provide them with three of his well-tried and heavy divisions for this one exercise.[24] Agreeing to support the French army, on 23 September Gen. Pershing allowed the transfer of the 2nd Division (regulars) and the 36th National Guard Division (newly arrived in France) to French control. Eventually, Maj. Gen. John A. Lejeune and the 2nd was assigned to Gen. Gouraud's 4th French Army and later to the XXI French Corps. Lejeune's first orders were to relieve the exhausted 61st French DI near Somme-Py during the night of 1 and 2 October.

Although the 2nd Division arrived at its sector in parts and pieces, it was the 4th Brigade of Marines that was the first on the scene. Its arrival in the area was on 1 October and that afternoon Operations Memo No. 9, 4th Brigade, spelled out the brigade's responsibility, which was to move forward that night and be in readiness north of Somme-Py to attack on the morning of 2 October. From the very beginning there was great confusion at XXI Corps headquarters. Division attack orders for the morning of 2 October were not issued until 2350 hours the previous night. Those orders stated that the 21st French DI, in liaison with the 2nd Division on their right, "will attack at 1150 hours after an artillery preparation, the duration of which will be fixed later." The position of the 3rd Brigade was such that it was nowhere near its assigned positions at that time. In fact, it would barely be able to make the advance of 3 October, because it had to drive the Germans out of its starting point before it could even begin.

The next morning (2 October) Maj. Gen. Lejeune was at Corps Headquarters, "presumably for orders," and the exact sector to be occupied was, "of course, unknown." For some good reason the attack on 2 October did not come off as scheduled.[25] At 1600 hours, Memo No. 10 called for the brigade commanding officers to send officers out to make the necessary reconnaissance of the country to their front and obtain whatever information they could from the French troops then holding the line.[26]

Brigade field orders issued at 1820 on 2 October gave a brief description of where heavy weapons should be placed in the forthcoming fight and stated that Maj. Gen. Lejeune's headquarters would remain at Suippes. It was from his PC near that town that Lejeune would direct his division, about eight miles from the division's objective. Those were the days before radio, and telephone communication was almost non-existent. Eight miles from the action was obviously not conducive to good management, but there he was and there he stayed.

Lejeune tells us in his memoir that the task on 2 October for both the 2nd Division and the French 21st Division was to clear out the occupied Essen and Elbe trenches to their front. On that day the Americans were successful with their section but the French were not, a situation which did not bode well for the next day's attack.

Fifteen men from the 6th Marines were casualties from fire on their left flank, at the Essen Hook, but the 5th Marines on the right flank had a relatively easy time taking the German trenches lying just before them. Colonel Harry Lee of the 6th Marines reported to division that a reconnaissance of the Elbe and Essen trenches, directly to his regiment's front, had found them to be unoccupied, but that the strong points northwest of the subsector occupied by the 6th, notably the Essen Hook (i.e., in the 21st French Division sector) were able to completely control any ground that his regiment would advance over. He added that for his troops to attempt to overcome these strong points before the advance scheduled for the following day would do irreparable damage to his lead battalion. He suggested that the position be neutralized by artillery fire when his troops were in their jump-off positions.

Late on the 2nd of October, Lejeune was instructed to report to XXI Corps Headquarters for attack orders. He brought with him both of his brigade generals: Ely, of the 3rd, and Neville, of the 4th. When they arrived they were made cognizant of plans that the corps commander, Gen. Naulin and his staff, had developed. Lejeune reportedly rejected that plan outright and suggested that he and his two generals would come up with a better one. In a very brief time they returned to Naulin with their plan. What they had come up with was two brigades separated by about a mile until reaching the Blanc Mont ridge, then their sectors join for the balance of the campaign. Ground occupied by enemy troops between the two brigades was to be "cleaned-up after they had taken Blanc Mont Ridge."

On 3 October corps and division artillery placed a bombardment upon the approach terrain and then at 0530 the two brigades advanced. Brigadier General Wendell C. "Buck" Neville commanded the 4th Brigade. Colonel Harry Lee commanded the 6th Marine Regiment with Lt. Col. Thomas H. Holcomb as his second in command. Battalion commanders were Maj. Frederick A. Barker, 1/6; Maj. Ernest C. Williams, 2/6; and Maj. George K. Shuler, 3/6. Colonel Logan Feland commanded the 5th Marine Regiment with Lt. Col. Julius S. Turrill as his second in command. The battalions were commanded by the following officers: Maj. George W. Hamilton, 1/5; Maj. Robert E. Messersmith, 2/5; and Maj. Henry L. Larsen, 3/5. Maj. Littleton W. T. Waller, Jr., commanded the 6th Machine Gun Battalion.[27]

The formation of the 4th Brigade, as assigned for the attack in a column of battalions, was as follows:

Front:
2nd Battalion 6th Marines and 81st Machine Gun Company.
12 light French tanks.
1st Battalion 6th Marines and 73rd Machine Gun Company.
12 light French tanks.
3rd Battalion 6th Marines and 15th Machine Gun Company.
Rear:
2nd Battalion 5th Marines and 23rd Machine Gun Company.
3rd Battalion 5th Marines and 77th Machine Gun Company.
1st Battalion 5th Marines and 8th Machine Gun Company.

Each battalion moved in a two-company advance, with two in support. The guns continued their rolling barrage at a pace agreeable to walking troops. The 6th Marines ran into difficulties immediately from harassing fire coming from their left flank, out of the Essen Hook. The French 21st DI was not advancing and the left sector was wide open, with Germans giving the Marines a positively bad time. It wouldn't be long until the 5th Marines, following the 6th, sent one of their companies, the 17th of 1/5, over to eliminate the problem. It did so in relatively short order, then turned the terrain over to the 21st DI, which lost it to the Germans again that afternoon.

The 6th Marines made it to the top in three hours and at 0830 started to spread out as each battalion came up. Two men from 2/6 each earned a Medal of Honor during that climb, Pvt. John Kelly and Cpl. John Pruitt, both from the 78th Co. Later that day John Pruitt was killed in action. Like the 6th Marines, the 5th Marines had to fight Germans to their left flank all the way up to the ridge. Not having moved, the French remained below and had left that entire flank wide open. Enemy fire concentrated on the advancing 6th Marines, which also had to face the Germans before them as they climbed.

The ridge was taken, but the knob on the left flank of the 4th Brigade's sector, known as Blanc Mont, still remained in the hands of the enemy. It would remain so for several days to come, as would the French sector to the Marines' left. Both situations would help to create horrific casualties to the 4th Marine Brigade on this date and especially again on 4 October. Late in the day orders were issued for the 5th Marines to pass through the lines of the 6th Marines and advance on St. Étienne, a few miles further north. Conditions would not allow this to happen. Because they were still trying to protect the left flank of the 6th late in the day, the 5th Marines were discombobulated and spread about. Assemblage of that regiment was near impossible in the time allowed for a further advance.

The next morning, however, the 5th Marines were ready for what was coming to them. Passing through the lines of the 6th, the regiment advanced by battalions, two companies leading, one in support, up the road toward St. Étienne. Major Henry L. Larsen and 3/5 led, followed by Maj. Robert Messersmith's 2/5, and with Maj. John Hamilton's 1/5 as support, they began their ascent toward the town at just after 0600. Larsen nearly immediately ran into heavy artillery and machine-gun fire, much of the latter coming from the knob of Blanc Mont. After taking a beating, at 1100 Larsen requested assistance to his left from Messersmith and Hamilton. Messersmith moved and spread out while keeping liaison with Larsen's left flank. Hamilton and 1/5 were next and they moved farther to the west, where they were then greatly exposed to enemy fire coming from the right flank.

The day became a complete, that is the word, *complete* disaster for the 5th Marines.

Within a few hours 1/5 was reduced to about 130 officers and men from the nearly 1,000 that began the day. They and 2/5 were caught in what has been called by many surviving members of the battalions, "the Box."[28] As far as the 5th Marine Regiment was concerned, it was finished at the Battle for Blanc Mont. The regiment retired back to the road where it could spend the night, but regardless of where they were, the Marines were still under constant enemy fire. On 5 October the remnants of the regiment were pulled back behind the 6th Marines at the ridge, where they would remain in "support" for the balance of the time at Blanc Mont.

For the 6th Marines and their comrades of the 3rd Brigade, the war continued, even though all of them had also been badly hurt. At 0615 on the morning of 5 October, 3/6 successfully moved against the remnants of enemy troops on the knob and ridge, capturing more than 200 dug-in prisoners and 65 machine guns. The French had finally come up on the left sector and flank protection was no longer necessary, relieving that pressure. As the 6th Regiment continued its assault upon the enemy, 2/6 was still in the lead, even though it had held the same position on 3 October. Colonel Lee decided that evening to put 3/6 in the front, backed up by 1/6 and with 2/6 in support.

The next morning, 6 October, an artillery barrage of one hour preceded the proposed advance scheduled for 0630. For a time, it was more dangerous to the 6th Marines than the enemy, with shells falling upon that regiment instead of the Germans. They tried to advance but as 3/6 jumped off it was almost immediately caught by German Maxims. Yet Maj. Shuler, 3/6, reported at 0930 that he and the 23rd Infantry to his right had both attained their objectives. Within another half hour Col. Lee could report to Neville that the French 22nd DI was to their left, and the 23rd Infantry to their right, and all were in line. In the meantime, orders were emanating from brigade headquarters to perform various tasks, behind the lines, which Lee responded to with uncharacteristic sarcasm. "Use the 20 percent hold-back for behind the line work." The farther back from the front the orders originated, the more ridiculous they became.

On this date, the brand-spanking-new 36th Division's 141st Infantry, of the 72nd Brigade, arrived and was being blended into the 3rd Brigade's regiments. Later, when the 71st Brigade's 142nd Infantry arrived and moved into the lines, 1/6 remained with them and both 2/6 and 3/6 were pulled out of the line. According to the records, on the night of 6–7 October, the 36th Division assumed responsibility for the front. However, Maj. Gen. Lejeune remained behind, still in command, as did the division's machine gun battalions and 2nd FA Brigade to provide those services to the 36th Division.[29]

Meanwhile, the infantry units of both brigades that were left behind continued their fighting and assistance to their new comrades. One story told by Warren Jackson, a Texas Marine in the 95th Co., 1/6, very well describes what happened in the next few days.

> I think it was October 7 that a regiment of the 36th Division came up and leap-frogged us.... This was their first trip to the front and they had just passed through our lines. A lieutenant of that division became so excited that he committed the most unparalleled blunder of advancing his men under fire in a column of squads, or some other close formation. As they advanced "Pop" Ansel, a 95th man who was a private by choice, hollowed [sic] out to the looie: "What the hell are you pulling off there?" he demanded. The men who witnessed this swore that the lieutenant begged Ansel to come out and get the men in proper formation for making the attack, which request Ansel ignored.[30]

Fighting for control of the promontory and to the Aisne River continued with members of the 2nd Division continuing their support to the Texas/Oklahoma "cowboys" for a few more days. However, they were used up in taking the high ground and it was now up to their replacements. Second Division artillery and machine guns continued fighting until the entire sector was conquered in late October. The 36th Division took some hard knocks, but the men were of stalwart stuff and they gave back as good as they got, pushing the reeling Germans back many miles. Blanc Mont was finally taken for the French army.

> *Results:* As usual, the 2nd Division bore a heavy burden but managed to take the "impossible position." But, as mentioned, it paid a heavy price in so doing. The 5th Marines were shattered, the 6th Marines weren't much better off, and both the 9th and 23rd Infantry regiments were in equally bad ways, as were most of the machine-gun units. This was especially true on 4 October for the 5th Regiment's 8th MG Co. During the balance of October, the entire division required exceptional personnel replacement in order to be ready on 1 November for the Meuse-Argonne campaign. Incidentally, the AEF literally ignored the battle for many years after the war, and the U.S. Army barely acknowledges it today. After all, it was "only" a French operation.

Meuse-Argonne

> *Date:* 1 November to 11 November 1918.
> *Location:* West of the Argonne Forest and east of the Meuse River.
> *Involved:* German troops versus the 2nd U.S. Division (regulars)
> *Situation:* Beginning in late September, several attempts by the 1st U.S. Army to drive the enemy out of the Argonne Forest had failed. Relieved by the French army and rested, sort of, the 2nd Division then became a part of the 1st U.S. Army and was assigned to the V Corps to serve with the 89th Division near the center of the Army's line. They were there to provide stability to a line almost entirely composed of inexperienced divisions, and a few that had already been badly handled by the Germans in September/October.

Most of the AEF units assigned to the operation were in place by 31 October, with the 2nd Division located between Landres-et-St. Georges, two villages on the road, about a half mile apart.

The attack formation was as follows: 23rd Infantry on the right beyond St. Georges, with two battalions forward and one in support. The 6th Marines were on the far left at the village of St. Georges and the 5th Marines were in the center at Landres. On the division's right was the 89th, already bloodied while serving with the British on the Somme. They were, as the saying goes, "good people." On the left was an untried 80th Division that proved to be not bad for "rookies." The morning was as expected, cool and foggy. Artillery was slated to fire from 0300 to 0550 and then place a rolling barrage before the troops, which eventually jumped-off at 0530.

On the right, the 23rd Infantry's task was to break up a strong formation just to the east of the town of Landre-et-St. Georges. But the 4th Brigade was to be in the lead until reaching both objectives for the day. Lee's 6th Marines, with Maj. Frederick A. Barker's 1/6 in the lead, had a more difficult time than did Hamilton's 1/5. Both, however, had to advance first down into a ravine then up it, all the while fighting Germans at the opposite crest. By 0800 Hamilton reported that he was taking heavy losses, with five officers down, but not doing so bad with the enlisted Marines. At 0830, Capt. Charley Dunbeck and 2/5 leap-frogged Hamilton and pushed beyond Landreville, which had been the division's first objective. Meanwhile, at 0800, Maj. George K. Shuler's 3/6 relieved 1/6 and assumed the lead at Landreville, with Maj. Ernest C. Williams' 2/6 in support. The 23rd Infantry, having accomplished its mission, then fell behind the 9th Infantry in a reserve formation.

Both Marine regiments continued forward, taking prisoners and numerous machine guns, plus a few 77 artillery pieces and their gunners. At about noontime, 3/6 had reached beyond Bayonville, the division's second objective, and rested. The 5th Marines were keeping abreast and at 1430 that afternoon, Maj. Henry L. Larsen sent a message to Feland that he had passed the third objective, beyond Barricourt Heights. When the 4th Brigade stopped further forward movement that day, the point reached for the 6th Marines was nearly the Foret de la Folie and the 5th Marines held Buzancy on the left and Barricourt on the right. The 89th Division had kept abreast, but the 80th on the left flank had various problems. Major George Stowell, who commanded a mini-battalion composed of the 95th Co., a machine-gun company and a platoon from the 80th Division, was charged with maintaining liaison between the 2nd Division and the 80th. He found it difficult. The 6th Marines had to occupy Imecourt, in the 80th Division's sector, to protect their flank (shades of Blanc Mont) until the 80th came up late in the day. Advancing far beyond the anticipated point, the division was maintaining its illustrious reputation, but the troops were tired.

The following day, 2 November, the division mostly rested, although the 6th Marines were kept busy. Especially busy was 1/6, which was battling with the enemy in the Bois de la Folie, and 2/6 was entertaining the Germans in and around the village of Chennery, lying just south of Bayonville. Orders were received late in the day for the 3rd Brigade to assume the leadership of the advance, with the 9th Infantry going forward first. On 3 November the 9th Infantry did just that. It pushed ahead on a narrow front, avoiding the Bois de Belval to the right of the division's sector, with the 23rd Infantry following closely behind. In the meantime, the 5th Marines were pushing over into the 89th Division's sector to protect the 23rd Infantry's right flank and advance.

On 5 November it was the 23rd Infantry in the lead with the 9th following, and more progress was made. The 3rd Brigade continued to hold the lead position, with each of the infantry regiments alternating lead and support. This continued until the division passed several important towns on its way toward the Meuse River, its ultimate destination. Mainly, the 4th Brigade was used to protect the right and left flanks of the sector, pushing forward when either the 80th or 89th Divisions were not up with the 3rd Brigade.

The night and early hours of 6 November witnessed the Germans falling back from around the town of Beaumont and crossing the river to escape the 2nd Division "racehorses."[31] Following the 236th German DI to the river line, the 9th Infantry extended its lines to Villemontry and the 23rd moved north to around Mouzon. Somehow part of the 5th Marines managed to arrive at a position east of Létanne, which lay near a bend in the river, and there they overlooked the village of Pouilly. Several companies of the regiment engaged in cross-river excursions but returned that night to the west side of the river.

That evening both Marine regiments received orders removing them westward from the area about the river, the 5th to the Bois de Grand Dieulet, west of Beaumont, and the 6th to the Bois du Fond de Limon, west of Villemontry. They were also advised that within the next few days they would make a major move.

On the morning of 7 November, the 6th Marines, now known to be the choice to cross the river, had only 72 officers and 1,728 enlisted Marines out of an AEF-established 3,000-component command. That night the 1st Division (regular) had moved up and relieved the 80th Division to the west of the 2nd Division. This was to be the beginning of one of the weirdest moments of the AEF in France.³² On 8 November, boundaries were altered so that the French could take Sedan.

Crossing of the Meuse River was delayed because bridging equipment was not available and would not be available for several days. Part of the reason was the terrible traffic jam on the roads leading into the various sectors. It was so bad, the many wounded couldn't be taken to hospitals in the rear. It was not a good time for the AEF. Fortunately the 1st Army had pushed the enemy farther back than either of their two Allies, and could afford to wait a few days.

German troops on the opposite bank were doing everything possible to keep the river from being crossed. Their main concentration was opposite the town of Mouzon, and in fact they occupied the town until 8 November, when they crossed the narrow, short bridge and assumed positions on the east bank. There they remained, with the area entirely covered by heavy weapons and Maxims well-positioned for any attempt by the Americans.

In the afternoon of 10 November orders were issued from 2nd Division headquarters directing the 6th Marines to the town of Mouzon and from there to cross the river that night. At the same time the 5th Marines were directed to cross the river on bridges then being built by the 2nd Engineers between Létanne and Villemontry. Even as late as 1730 that afternoon neither orders specified a time. At any rate, the orders directed the 6th Marines, with 3/5 as reinforcement, northward and they marched in the dark to within three miles of Mouzon, where they waited for orders to cross. Major George Shuler, CO of 3/6, was in overall command.

The 5th Marines had different orders. Dunbeck's 2/5 was selected to cross with support by one battalion from the 89th Division, 2/356, under command of Maj. Mark Hanna. Hanna, through no fault of his own, didn't make it to the site, and instead Hamilton's 1/5 was selected to do the honors. Then the order was rearranged so that 1/5 would cross, followed by 2/5. Artillery was to begin laying down an hour's barrage, after which the Marines would cross as a rolling barrage, beginning at 2130, preceded them. Their initial target was a huge forest, the Bois d'Alma-Gisors, just opposite their crossing point. There was some open ground leading up to it, with a farm lying across their pathway.³³ If the 5th Marines had been allowed a bit of time to reconnoiter, they might have seen the numerous German machine-gun emplacements in that immediate area. But, as usual, there was no time allowed for anything like that.

Engineers of the division worked under stressful and violent conditions as they attempted to cross the river just to the north of Mouzon, but the enemy artillery destroyed each before they were useable. This went on during the evening hours and continued until the early morning, when Shuler made the brave decision on his own. A daylight crossing of the river would be disastrous for his regiment. He called the crossing off.³⁴

A few miles away, the orders were finally issued. The 5th Marines, less 3/5, would begin the crossing as soon as the engineers finished one bridge.³⁵ From the heights above the river the men of the 5th came down in a narrow passageway, often sliding down as best they could. When assembled on the bank where they were to cross, Maj. George Hamilton, one of the bravest officers in the war, led his battalion across the river. Many Marines died on that narrow pontoon bridge and very few made it across. Upon reaching the other bank,

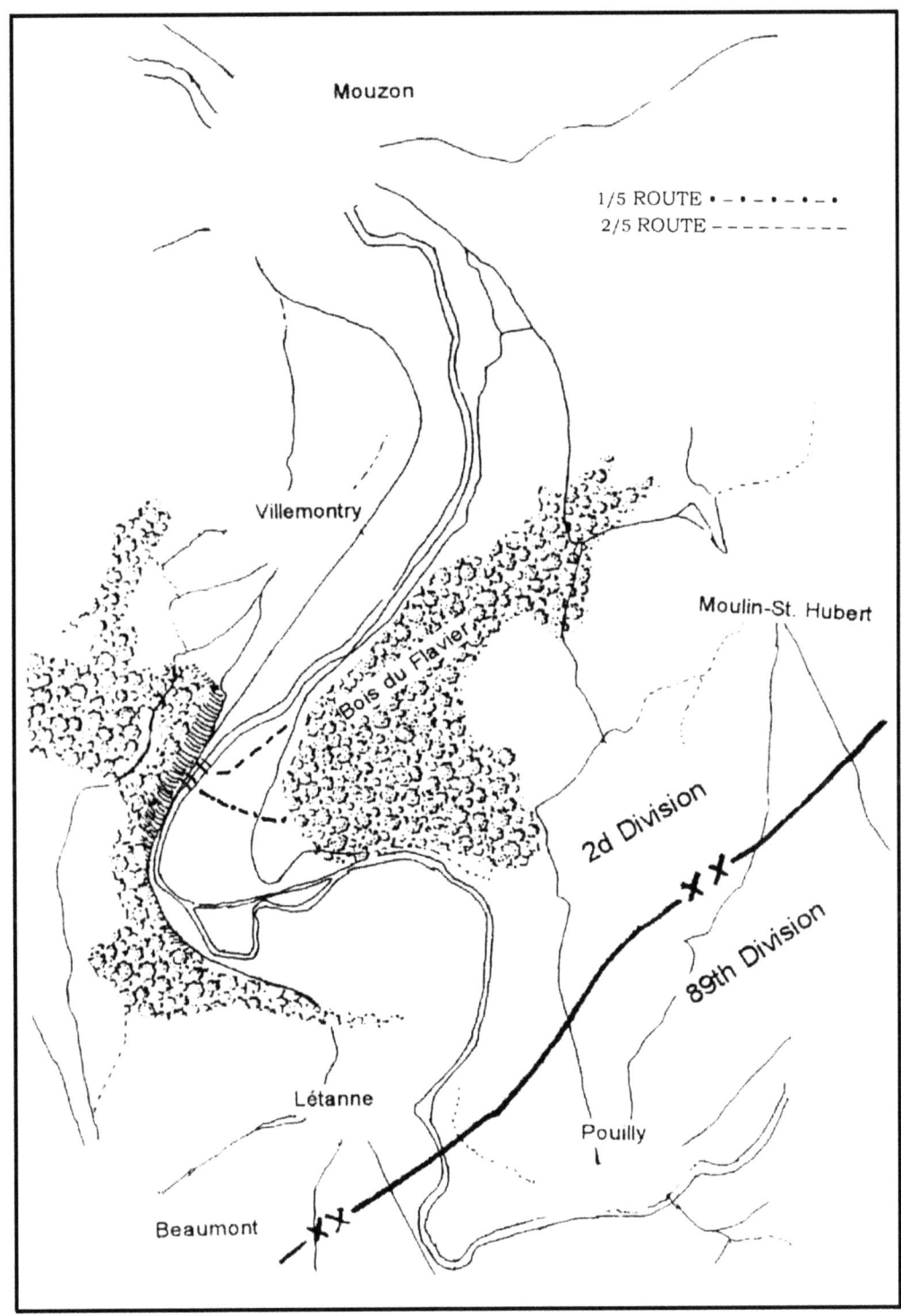

MEUSE RIVER CROSSING
10TH TO 11TH NOVEMBER

the few survivors took prone positions and blindly opened fire at their front, with no expectations of hitting anyone in the dark.

Next came Dunbeck and 2/5. The story is told that the men of 2/5, after seeing what happened to 1/5, were sensibly reluctant to cross the bridge. In fact they soon had a situation in which Marines were beginning to take off. Upon seeing that, Charley Dunbeck, another "bravest of the brave" said something to his men as he stood by the bridge. "Men, I'm going across and I expect you to go with me." And they did, taking a severe pasting as they crossed. The few that made it then moved to their left. Later, in the early morning hours of the 11th, Hanna from 2/356 brought up several companies and they too crossed, digging in with the Marines on the opposite bank.

At first the fighting was relatively severe, but it soon settled down, as the time got closer to the 11th hour the Germans were more reluctant to die. Hamilton and Dunbeck kept at it, however, and the Marines advanced their lines considerably and entered into the woods before them. At 1100 the war ended, except for a scattering of firearms throughout the area. Everyone had had enough to last them a lifetime, only, as we know, it didn't.

> *Results:* The entire campaign was a great success for Allied arms. German soldiers continued the fight, and, if they hadn't agreed to reasonable terms, which weren't lived up too, they would have continued to fight.[36] Nonetheless, they had agreed to an armistice and, temporarily, were happy to quit. Therefore the war was over.
>
> The 4th Brigade was pretty much used up during the entire period, and especially from 1 to 11 November, but that wasn't unusual. What seems to be a bit unusual (or even stupid?), was to waste so many brave men in an unnecessary crossing of the Meuse River the night before the war ended. The same thing happened to several other groups, notably the Canadians further west. Supposedly, it was to get across so the Germans couldn't claim any advantages to holding more French ground. Orders didn't originate with the 2nd Division, they came down from Marshal Foch's staff, but Maj. Gen. John A. Lejeune could have stalled it, if he had chosen to, much like Maj. George Shuler did to save the 6th Marines.

Afterword

The Allies advanced into Germany and occupied much of the western portion for a number of years. The 2nd Division was a part of that occupying force for the next eight months. Finally, it was allowed to come home. It received a late but reasonably joyous welcome for the survivors of the best division in the AEF, and possibly in the world. Editorial comment.

17

Nicaragua

The United States began a tradition of intervening in Nicaragua on 11 March 1853 when Orderly Sgt. James E. Thompson led ashore the Marine detachment aboard the *Cyane* to protect the American Steamship Company's railroad and other property. That was the rail line that crossed from east to west, carrying passengers from the Caribbean to the Pacific Ocean, where they would board ships and continue their journey.

In the latter part of 1853, Mr. Borland, the American minister to Nicaragua, was assaulted and kept a prisoner overnight while in San Juan del Sur. It wasn't until 9 July 1854 that the *Cyane* returned, whereupon Capt. Hollins demanded retribution and apologies for the treatment of the minister. He went so far as to threaten to bombard the town. A lack of response brought Sgt. Thompson and his Marines back into town on the 12th. They and the few sailors who went ashore with them managed to find and destroy some powder, muskets and three field pieces. With still no proper response to his demands, on the morning of the 13th Hollins prepared his starboard battery to fire the town. Beginning at 0900, they fired steadily until about 1330, when all the ship's ammunition was expended. Hollins sent the Marines and sailors back ashore at 1530. They returned to their ship at 1930 having accomplished their mission: the complete destruction of the town. Later, on the 17th, another force went ashore and destroyed the last of the powder, then located at nearby Punta Arenas. Captain Hollins then sailed away. Nicaragua's minister to the U.S. tried to obtain reparations but was rebuffed by the U.S. secretary of state.

In 1894 foreign-owned property was at risk around Bluefields and U.S. naval forces were in the area, prepared to intervene. A force of Marines and Bluejackets was assembled and led ashore by 1st Lt. Franklin J. Moses at 1800 on 6 July and remained ashore to protect property and lives until 7 August. Again, in 1896, a few Marines and Bluejackets, led ashore by Lt. Albert W. Dodd, assisted by 1st Sgt. Frederick W. M. Poppe, landed at 1400 on 2 May and returned on the 4th.

At 1600 on 4 February 1898, the American consul, Charles Holman, had the American flag raised with the union down, which meant "Help!" Marines and sailors were landed to protect lives and property and returned aboard ship the following day when the Nicaraguan military commander declared he and his men would provide the necessary protection.

A minor disturbance in February 1898 brought more sailors and Marines ashore at Bluefields on the 24th but they returned aboard on the 28th.

Date: 22 February to 4 September 1910.
Location: East and west coasts of Nicaragua.
Involved: Nicaraguan rebels and troops versus U.S. Marines.

Situation: Nicaragua was almost always in a state of insurrection. When the citizens were unhappy when "their guy" was not elected (or perhaps did receive the popular vote but wasn't allowed to take office), they frequently rose in revolt against the group which had assumed control. Usually, in the latter 19th and early 20th century, it was the dictator Jose Santos Zelaya who caused most of the upset. When two Americans were executed for revolutionary activities, the U.S. State Department made moves to intervene.

A detachment of Marines from the *Buffalo* landed at Corinto, Nicaragua, on 22 February 1910 to obtain information on conditions in that town. Captain John A. Hughes with a detachment of Marines was sent into town at 2000 to learn exactly what was going on. He returned later, at near midnight, having completed his mission.

Two ships, the *Paducah* and *Dubuque*, arrived at Bluefields in April to look after American lives and property during a rebellion. Commander Harold K. Hines, CO of the *Dubuque*, led Marines and seamen ashore from both ships on 19 May, but soon realized that his command was not sufficient to deter the local rebels led by General Larra. On the 27th the *Dubuque* sailed for Colon, Panama, to transport a battalion of Marines stationed there to Bluefields. Major Smedley D. Butler and his command of six officers and 200 enlisted Marines arrived at their destination and on 31 May he landed with half his command. The other half was temporarily transferred to the *Paducah*, and then they landed on the same date. During this period ashore, Butler decided he didn't need the Bluejackets with him and sent them back to their ships. Butler and his command remained ashore in Nicaragua until the 4th of September, when they returned to Panama City aboard the *Tacoma*.

Date: 3 and 4 October 1912.
Location: Western Nicaragua, especially La Barranca — Coyotepe Hills.
Involved: 1st Provisional Regiment of Marines and Nicaraguan "rebels."
Situation: Trouble in Nicaragua between rebels and federal forces brought in American Marines to protect American lives and property. Strife between the national government and the leader of the Liberals, Benjamin Zeledon, had forced the U.S. to intervene. As usual, unpaid foreign loans required payments to be collected to avoid foreign intervention and in order to protect the custom house and incoming duties, the U.S. felt compelled to take control and collect them.

Conditions in Nicaragua worsened and, at the request of the State Department, MGC Biddle ordered Brig. Gen. Joseph Pendleton to assemble a two-battalion force to support Maj. Smedley D. Butler, who with his battalion was already in Nicaragua. This would become the 1st Provisional Regiment. On 27 August 1912 Pendleton and 750 Marines were on their way south from Philadelphia.

The 424 Marines of the Butler's 3rd Battalion, with occasional Bluejacket support from U.S. ships off the west coast, had already opened the railroad running north to south. There had been some fighting along the line when rebels in a small town through which the train passed opened up and wounded five of his men. Three more were missing. The rebels, however, appear to have suffered severe losses from the Marines' accurate return fire, a number, according to a *Marine Corps Gazette* article in 1921, totaling 68 killed and 60 wounded. By mid–September, Butler's command had taken several towns and cities, including Granada when Butler and his 424 Marines talked the minister of war, Luis Mena, into it on 22 September. However, rebels led by Zeledon, numbering over 800, were still holding a strong position atop several hills nearby. These hills were named Barranca and Coyotepe and were joined by a saddle. Consequently, when the rebels refused to surrender, both hills had to be taken.

On 2 October government forces had joined Pendleton's Marines and both were making preparations to assault positions on the hilltops. Most of the rebel strength was on top of Coyotepe, in what the rebels considered an impregnable position. The Marines had three battalions of infantry, an artillery battalion led by Capt. John C. Beaumont, and eight Benet-Mercie 30-caliber machine guns. Additionally, they were supported by a battalion of Bluejackets from the *California*. The term "battalion" was somewhat of an exaggeration, as might be the word "company."[1]

Waiting a brief time for an expected rebel surrender, Pendleton finally realized that it wasn't going to happen. There was nothing else to do, so he gave the order: Go up the hill and get them. At 0515 on 4 October Butler and the government troops were to link up and advance. On their right was the 1st Battalion led by Maj. William McKelvey, and farther to the right were two companies of the Bluejackets led by Lt. Comdr. George W. Steele, Jr. Butler, McKelvey and Steele went up the hill but their allies, the Nicaraguan troops, were nowhere to be seen. Gaining the top and driving the surviving rebels off Coyotepe, the Marines and Bluejackets then aimed toward La Barranca, somewhat lower in height. After they turned their guns upon it, the rebels soon were put to flight. Zeledon made a personal effort to flee but his angered men turned on him and he was killed as he attempted to escape. Twenty-seven rebels were killed and nine captured. The Americans suffered the loss of four Marines and three sailors while eight sailors and Marines were wounded. It had actually taken the Americans 37 minutes to climb and take the most fearsome position in Latin America.

Instead of supporting the Americans, the national forces had taken the city of Masaya and set about burning, killing and raping everyone and anyone, until they were satiated. Nearby León wisely surrendered to Lt. Col. Charles Long and his Marines. The Marines soon left Nicaragua in January 1913 but a legation guard remained behind. Marines would return in 1927, with a vengeance.

> *Results:* Marines moved in and quickly settled disputes along the railroad's main line and later successfully assaulted the rebel positions on the twin hills and soon defeated all rebel actions. Nicaragua was once again peaceful.

—⚞—

Date: 1 August 1925 to 3 January 1933.
Location: Nicaragua, mostly in the north and west but also in the east in the early period.
Involved: U.S. Marines, 2nd Brigade, versus various rebel factions; later, after the Treaty of Tipitapa, mainly Sandino's guerrillas.
Situation: The two main Nicaraguan political parties, the Liberals and the Conservatives, were unable to function in the same country. The U.S. Marine guard at the Managua legation was withdrawn on 1 August 1925 and sailed for the U.S. three days later. Trouble between the various political factions began almost immediately. American citizens held large portions of land and

other properties and they began having difficulty from marauding bands. A cry for help was issued.

Captain John W. Wainwright of the *Cleveland* arrived at Bluefields on 6 May 1926 and on the 7th landed his Marine detachment led by 1st Lt. Charles S. Finch. Additionally, a segment of his Bluejackets led overall by Lt. Comdr. Spencer S. Lewis was landed, all of whom remained ashore until 5 June.

The following August, on the 27th, a large segment of Bluejackets and Marines from the *Galveston* was ordered ashore at Bluefields for the same reason. The Marines were led by Capt. Joseph W. Knighton and the naval party consisted of six naval officers and 132 Bluejackets. On 11 September, two officers and 103 Marines, under Capt. John W. Thomason, Jr., from aboard the *Rochester*, landed at Bluefields. They boarded the steamer *Dictator* and sailed about, then returned to shore. Two days later they again went aboard the *Dictator* and did much the same and then returned aboard the *Rochester*.

The next group of Marines and Bluejackets to land was from the *Denver*, when the captain ordered them to land at Corinto on the west coast on 10 October to protect American lives and property. When the naval detachment withdrew to the *Denver*, a dozen Marines under 1st Lt. Henry T. Nicholas remained ashore until 13 November to patrol the district.

More Marines from the *Rochester* landed at Bluefields on 31 October, where they relieved the detachment from the *Galveston* which had landed back in August. However, Thomason and the larger portion went to El Bluff, while the smaller group, led by 2nd Lt. Kenneth B. Chappell, went to Bluefields. Thomason and Chappell's Marines were relieved by Marines and Bluejackets from the *Denver* on 30 November. *Rochester*'s Marines were dropped off at the entrance to the Rio Grande in the north of eastern Nicaragua on 23 December and on the same day another detachment, from the *Cleveland*, landed at nearby Bragman's Bluff. Late this year it was decided that foreigners as well as American citizens were in need of protection. Consequently they too could come to Marine units when threatened.[2]

During the early months of 1927 more Marines and Bluejackets were landed on both coasts while those from the *Cleveland*, *Denver*, and *Rochester* were still ashore. But the going became rather heavy, and on 10 January, the 2nd Bn., 5th Marines, with supporting elements and commanded by Lt. Col. James J. Meade, landed at Bluefields. There was constant activity as Marine detachments from various ships continued to land forces on the east and west coast. On 8 August, 19 Marines from the 51st Co., of the 2nd Bn., 5th Marines, led by 1st Lt. Charles Connette, moved north by ship to Puerto Cabezas. In late February the next major organization that arrived in Nicaragua was Marine Observation Squadron One, led by Maj. Ross E. Rowell and accompanied by a Marine rifle company. Next came the 2nd Brigade headquarters with Brig. Gen. Logan Feland, and the balance of the 5th Marines, which landed at Corinto on 7 March.

The opposing factions became somewhat concerned by the influx of so much U.S. military power and on 7 May began serious negotiations to settle their disputes. It was desired (by the U.S. State Dept.) to have more Marines to help in the overall settlement. So the 11th Marines (then an infantry formation) and Observation Squadron 4, all under the command of Col. Randolph C. Berkeley, arrived as part of the 2nd Brigade. Matters seemed to be coming to a desirable conclusion by the middle of 1927, and Marine units were being withdrawn. By the last of September just two battalions of the 5th Marines and one aviation squadron remained in Nicaragua.

Meanwhile, back in November 1926, the U.S. had recognized Adolfo Diaz, the president selected by the Liberal Congress, a man most Nicaraguans could tolerate. His presidency lasted until another election in 1928. Doctor Juan B. Sacasa, the vice president, was not selected to be his successor, and he and some followers rose in revolt. There were still problems with rebels and now a rather confused situation became even more so. The situation didn't improve much, even after the "good offices" of the U.S. were required to settle a new treaty known as Tipitapa. It was settled between the warring factions and included American supervision of the 1928 elections. A barely solved situation became worse when a rebel refused to accept the U.S. settlement.

However, like many things that happened in Nicaragua, there was one sore loser, and that was Sandino, a first-class rabble-rouser. He refused to accept the American-brokered peace treaty and began to collect other disaffected persons until he had accumulated a substantial body with which to cause trouble. His name, or pseudonym or nom de guerre, was "General" Augusto Sandino. Though a very poor general, in the ensuing guerrilla campaign he lost all the battles, but not the war. When it became clear that there would be some serious fighting in Nicaragua, Brig. Gen. Logan Feland and two battalions of the 11th Marines, together with a squadron of aviation, arrived before the end of January 1928.

The first main attack by Sandino was on the Marine and Guardia garrison at Ocotal on 16 July. His 500-man force was pitted against the 38 enlisted Marines and their three officers, led by Capt. Gilbert D. Hatfield. Additionally, Capt. Grover C. Darnall, GN, and two officers (probably USMC sergeants or corporals) and 48 enlisted Nicaraguan men from the 1st Guardia Nacional Company were on duty there.[3] Ninety-three men in all, and all located in the city hall.

For some time before this date, Sandino and Hatfield had been exchanging letters. The Nicaraguan's letters were vitriolic and Hatfield's replies insulting. Sandino would always end his with sentences like "Your obedient servant who wishes to put you in a handsome tomb with flowers." It appears that Sandino thought this was a serious exchange, and Hatfield obviously was having fun at Sandino's expense.

Early on the morning of the 16th, Sandino's men began infiltrating the town. They had two machine guns, well-placed on buildings and covering with interlocking fire the main portion of the town, including the city hall. They also had a sufficient stock of dynamite to enable them to break into defended buildings. A Marine sentry had observed movement early that morning and had opened fire, thereby voiding any serious opportunity for the rebels to take the defenders by surprise.

First Lieutenant Thomas G. Bruce, GN, brought his Browning machine gun out into the street and, though unprotected, by superior shooting quickly silenced at least one of Sandino's guns. At 0300 the rebels launched a severe attack but the defenders were ready for them. With aimed rifle fire, machine guns, and BARs, the attack was beaten back with heavy losses. Later that morning Ross Rowell and some of his squadron came over and machine gunned the rebels while dropping bombs on their defensive positions. Nevertheless, the fighting went on for hours, with the planes returning several times to base for ammunition and fuel. As the planes attacked, Hatfield's command advanced, proceeding to take the rebels in flank. Finally, the rebels got the word and it was all over. Sandino's ineffectual tactics caused the loss of numerous rebels, estimated as possibly 300, and he foolishly would attempt several more efforts like this one.

On the night of 19 September Sandino tried another attack upon a Marine position at Telpaneca, against a Marine force of 20 Marines and 25 Guardia. The Marines on sentry were sloppy and the rebels got in close. Fortunately for them they had erected a barricade and when the rebels fired into their windows, they had few visible targets. The Marines beat back three waves, and when the daylight came the attackers went. A number of attacks upon Marine patrols caused huge losses to the rebels. Sandino still hadn't learned that he couldn't fight well-trained military forces in a stand-up battle, but eventually he would and then he became dangerous.

Sandinista rebels caught a long train of Marines and Guardia in a well-prepared ambush along the Jicaro River, and if the Marines hadn't been professionals they might have suffered enormous casualties. These types of attacks were happening to the Marines of the 2nd Brigade, until the Guardia finally came of age and began to take over the constant patrolling themselves.

The balance of the fighting in Nicaragua was mainly contests between small formations of rebels and Marine-led Guardia, though on earlier occasions, regular Marines were heavily engaged. The last engagement between the Sandinistas and the Guardia took place on 31 December 1932. Captain Lewis Puller, GN, led the final one that included Marines. He also had seven enlisted Marine assistants, all lieutenants in the Guardia, one of whom was "Iron Man" Bill Lee. The date was 26 December 1932 and it was listed as the 508th patrol. By that time almost all the other patrols were led by Nicaraguan members of the Guardia. This was the final intervention in which Marines would interfere with local governments, anywhere, at anytime. Except in a major war.

Results: The U.S. Marines were finally phased out of Nicaragua in January 1933 when the Guardia, a recently formed police/militia unit, was ready to fully assume the role the Marines had filled, that of guardians of the peace.

18

World War II

Wake Island

Date: 8 December to 23 December 1941 (Wake time)
Location: Wake Island, Pacific Ocean
Involved: Japanese naval forces versus a detachment of the 1st Marine Defense Bn. and Marine Fighting Squadron 211, a small group of Navy personnel and an even smaller group of U.S. Army radio personnel, plus numerous civilian construction workers, some of whom volunteered to fight.
Situation: Not long after attacking the USN and USA bases in the Hawaiian Islands, that same day Japan launched an air attack upon Wake Island that was a disaster for the Marines. Fighting Squadron 211 had 12 planes, of which eight were on the ground and four on patrol. Enemy bombing aircraft came over in the midst of a tropical storm and caught the entire base off-base. All planes were for all intents destroyed, leaving just the four planes then in the air on patrol duty. Gasoline tanks went up, as did many of the newly constructed buildings.

For a few months work had been in progress to develop island defenses, but generally in a haphazard manner. Admiral Husband E. Kimmel had prophesied in April 1941 that when the Japanese attacked the U.S., they wouldn't take on Wake Island early in the war because it would leave their fleet open to the U.S. Navy's fleet based at Pearl Harbor. He was partly right — they didn't start with Wake, they started on Pearl instead. Most of the development had been restricted to what the civilian workers had been hired for, the construction of air facilities and housing for civilian air personnel. Additionally, the powers that be finally decided to build up the aerial forces in the Philippines, instead of the British as the U.S. had been doing. B-17 bombers were being flown across the Pacific with frequent stops along the way for refueling, Wake being the last on their trip.

In August a detachment of five officers and 173 Marines from the 1st Defense Battalion landed on Wake to begin work on defenses for a full battalion of approximately 1,000 officers and men. This had nothing to do with the civilian or Air Force needs — it was to defend the island stuck out in the far western Pacific all by itself. Major James P. S. Devereux arrived to assume command of the Marines ashore and temporarily the island. More Marines from the 1st Defense Bn. arrived in November, but just another 250 or so. Many of their weapons,

5-inch for coast defense and some 3-inch aerial defense weapons, had arrived and it took some time to place them in permanent locations on the three islands of the Wake group. On 4 December, a small detachment from VMF-211 arrived from the carrier *Enterprise* and things began to look up. Nevertheless, the planes were brand-new to the squadron and no one had really a chance to even examine them, let alone try them out.

At this late date, the island defenses were incomplete. Instead of a Marine defense battalion totaling 43 officers and 939 enlisted Marines, the garrison had 15 officers and 373 men. Most of the battalion was spread around at various other isolated posts in the three-island atoll. Because the garrison was so short of manpower, the six 5-inch seacoast guns, twelve 3-inch AAA guns, and machine guns plus searchlights were never completely manned. Tools and repair parts for the guns were practically nonexistent. The radar units were never delivered, but were still in crates at Pearl Harbor.

Only the crews of the 5-inch seacoast batteries were at or near authorized strengths. But they were short of ammunition, replacement parts, and tools. Peale Island's development was probably in the best shape, though none of the guns had been completely protected with sandbags. Wake Island emplacements were next, with Wilkes Island in the worst shape.

Grumman F4F-3s were new planes to the men of the squadron, most never having even seen the model before. They had no armor, their tanks were not self-sealing, and their bomb racks didn't match the bombs available. Fuling had to be done with hand pumps and the width of the airstrip allowed but one plane to surface at a time. In later years Maj. James

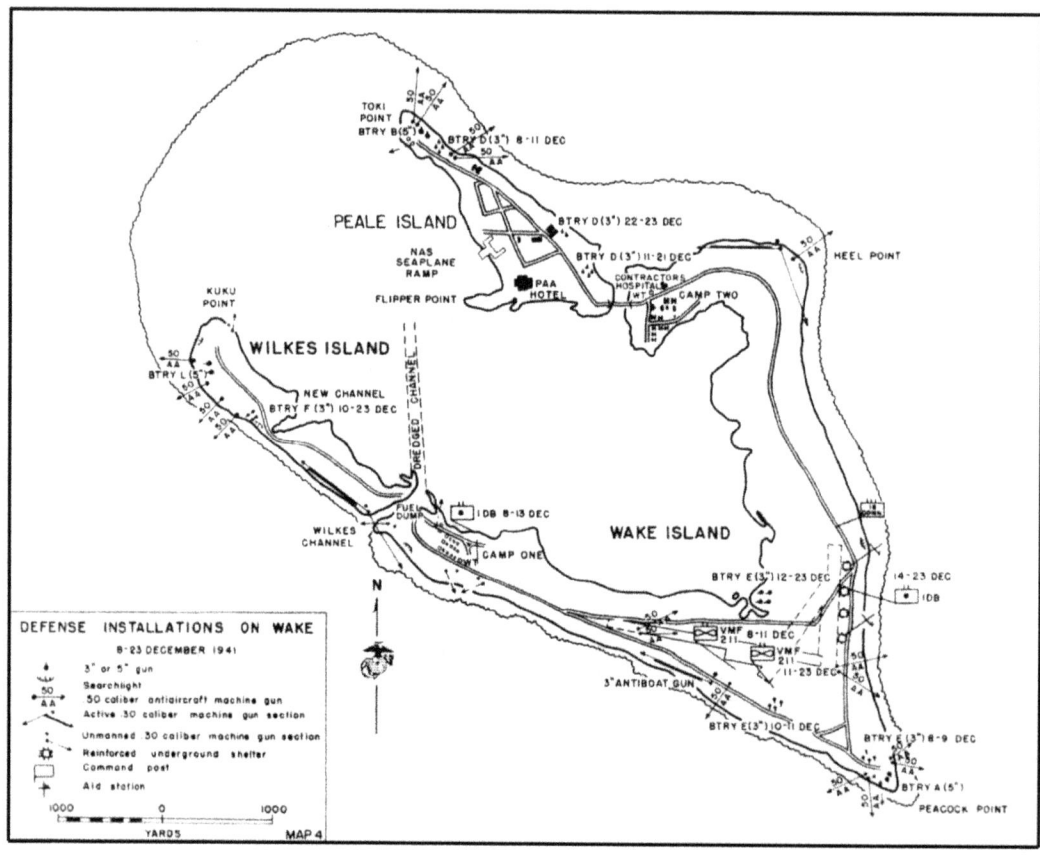

Devereux, then running for Congress, remarked, "They sent us garbage trucks when we needed radar." However, even if he had had radar, he had no one trained to operate the units. Last but not least, the U.S. Naval Air Station had 10 officers and 58 enlisted men, all without arms. The U.S. Army Air Corps had one officer and four enlisted men, none with arms.

This then was the state of the defense situation at Wake Island. These few Marines, ground and air, would have to face a goodly portion of the Japanese fleet, an overpowering number of fighting planes, and eventually an invasion force of about 10,000 soldiers. Devereux tried, in the short time he still had, to get the gunners trained to respond to the "Call to Arms" he knew would be coming very soon. Another thing Devereux originated was the creation of phony ground weapons so the enemy would waste its bombs and ammunition destroying wood.

On 8 December (Wake time) four planes were in the air scouting the northeast when over 30 enemy bombing planes came in on the island from the south and through a rain squall, destroying seven of the eight planes on the ground. The eighth plane was damaged a few minutes later. The following day during another air attack, the Marine planes then in the air managed to hit 14 of the enemy's bombers; one was shot down by two flyers of VMF 211, 1st Lt. David D. Kliewer and Tech. Sgt. William J. Hamilton, and another by AAA fire. Later more planes were shot down by VMF-211 as they lost part of their small number of planes almost on a daily basis. During the first raid, most of the islands' storage tanks of fuel had been destroyed. Somehow, pumping the limited gas by hand, the ground crews of the squadron were able to get the few planes back in the air and the pilots worked wonders with the little resources they had.

In a later report Maj. Paul A. Putnam criticized the later attacks made by the Japanese air fleets. "The original raid was tactically well conceived and skillfully executed, but thereafter their tactics were stupid." He went on to state that they came in at the same altitude and hour each day, and the attack pattern never varied. Even though the Marine flyers caught them each day, they never varied their timetable or pattern.

On 11 December the Japanese tried a full-fledged landing on the island. Their warships fired upon Wake and destroyed numerous facilities, including the few remaining gasoline storage tanks. This was going to hurt the VMF-211 and also any B-17s that might be flying on to the Philippines. In this action, Devereux had his seacoast gunners hold their fire until the enemy fleet got in close and was actually attempting to land troops, when they blasted them. The cruiser *Yubari* was badly hit several times but managed to avoid sinking. But the Marines did sink several vessels, two destroyers — the *Hayate* being the first Japanese ship sunk in the war — and possibly a submarine. Numerous Japanese troops were killed or wounded aboard their transports or in landing craft. It frightened the enemy that the defenders would be so strong after the daily pasting they had taken for a week.

There were more air attacks nearly every day after, to soften up the defenders. Finally on the 23rd the enemy closed and managed to land a large number of infantry. The Marines whose guns or planes had been lost were now fighting back as infantry. Though the defenders fought back with great spirit, and many Japanese paid the price, the enemy managed to land enough men, many more than the defending force, with even more waiting to land, that Cmdr. Winfield Scott Cunningham, island commander, declared the issue was "in doubt." The issue was never in doubt. From the beginning the overpowering enemy had the situation "well in hand." Cunningham rightly decided to surrender the island so as to preserve the lives of his command and the many civilian workers on Wake.[1]

Results: Eventually, after 16 days of trying, Japan's air, naval, and 10,000-person landing force overwhelmed the modest Marine garrison of about 400 men. The island was surrendered on the 23rd by the commanding officer, Cmdr. W. S. Cunningham, USN, as the Japanese naval landing force was occupying each of the three islets. Although it remained in the control of the Japanese, it was never of appreciable value during the war.

Siege of Corregidor

Date: 29 April to 5 May 1942
Location: Manila Bay
Involved: Japanese army and naval forces versus the U.S. Army, 4th Marines, a few sailors.
Situation: Imperial Japanese Forces had driven the U.S. Army down the Bataan Peninsula and finally, after months of suffering malnutrition, the badly depleted force surrendered to the Japanese. However, the minuscule force on the island of Corregidor now had to face the entire Japanese army and navy without reinforcements.

When the two-battalion 4th Marines finally evacuated Shanghai, China, on 27–28 November, they were ordered to the Philippine Islands, arriving at Olongapo on Subic Bay on 1 December. When war came, at Gen. Douglas MacArthur's request, the senior Navy officer, Adm. Thomas C. Hart, assigned the regiment to him. Initially MacArthur tried to make them his personal guard unit, which Hart refused to sanction.

When Col. Samuel Howard reported to Hart at Navy Headquarters in Manila on Christmas eve, he was advised that he and his regiment had been transferred to the Army for "such tactical control and employment as he [MacArthur] may desire in the defense of Luzon." Hart added that MacArthur had requested the transfer of the "powerful, veteran 4th Marines" to his command. Hart also said that he should visit MacArthur for deployment instructions, but added the codicil that disbursement of the 4th Marines remained solely under Howard's jurisdiction. In other words, no splitting the regiment up. Howard was also made aware that Lt. Col. John P. Adams, 1st Separate Battalion, of approximately 400 officers and men, was to be incorporated within the 4th Marines as the 3rd Battalion, as soon as they could move away from Cavite. This was Hart's "swan song." He and his ships were moving south to Java to join most of his ships already there or on their way. His fleet would soon be destroyed.

Howard next met with MacArthur, who, in his usual fashion, was profuse with words of praise regarding the Marines and their great capabilities.[2] Howard was directed to Mac's chief of staff, Maj. Gen. Richard K. Sutherland, who admitted that the enemy were doing a through job on the U.S. Army on Luzon. He described how the American-Filipino troops were falling back all over the place and Manila was being evacuated, telling him that Mac was going to transfer his headquarters to Corregidor. With that, Sutherland ordered Howard to Corregidor to man the beach defenses—the latter, however, came back with the suggestion that the Marines would be deployed more advantageously as infantry on Bataan proper. Howard told him that his reconnaissance of the peninsula indicated that the defense of landing beaches from Bagac Bay to Mariveles was a better assignment, but Sutherland insisted that they go to Corregidor instead. The best-trained fighting men in the Philippines were relegated to defending an undefendable island, certainly not the best way to utilize Marines.[3]

Commander Francis J. Bridget, USN, a grounded naval aviator, was assigned duty with the 4th Marines. His command consisted of grounded aviation personnel or shipless sailors Hart had no need of. Bridget and his "troops" were sent to support the Army units still on Bataan by defending the western tip of the peninsula. Bridget was awarded two USMC artillery batteries headed up by 1st Lt. William F. Hogaboom with Battery A, and 1st Lt. Willard C. Holdredge with Battery C. This disparate group defended the Longoskawayan Point from 14 January until the entire unit was recalled to Corregidor. In the meantime, since the sailors, including Bridget, were lacking ground-fighting techniques, Col. William T. Clement was assigned to back them up.[4]

After the U.S. Army surrendered on Bataan, the Japanese began preparing for the destruction of the Americans on Corregidor. Their heavy artillery moved to Mariveles and other points on the peninsula opposite Corregidor and began a heavy pounding of the island. Finally, on the morning of 5 May 1942, the landings began.

Meanwhile, over a period of several months, the 4th Marine Regiment, composed originally of two battalions, was increased by a third (McAdams from Cavite), then a fourth, composed of six men, the remnants of the few Marines on Bataan which had managed to escape. Then 166 more were added as a reserve battalion, making a total of 1,440 Marines. This, however, was just a beginning. Sailors supplemented those five battalions with another 841 men. Then the U.S. Army added another 615 men. The remnants of the Philippine army, navy, air force, constabulary, and scouts added another 951 fighting men, making a grand total on 1 May of 3,891 "Marines" in five battalions with 19 companies, Company A through Company T. The physical condition of the starving soldiers from the U.S. Army was deplorable, and an influx of beri-beri was catastrophic. Many of the sailors, mostly petty officers of the highest pay-grades, had basically a very limited training in ground soldiering, and no time or place was available to educate them.

Finally the axe fell. After an intense artillery barrage fired from the south shore of Bataan, the Japanese landed between Cavalry and North Point late on the evening of 5 May 1942. After falling back slowly, the defenders managed to withstand the aggressive assaults along the line at Infantry Point from 0230 until 0930. Hand-to-hand fighting continued for many hours. At about 1000 the Marines, plus their Army and Navy comrades of the expanded 4th Marines, were forced to fall back to a line at Artillery Point. At 1130 Maj. Francis H. Williams reported to Col. Samuel Howard that his men were exhausted from fighting so many continuous hours, that they could no longer hold. He was told that Maj. Gen. Jonathon M. Wainwright, island CO since MacArthur left, had decided to capitulate at noon that day.

One band of Marines, led by Sgt. Milton A. Englin, defended the entrance to Malinta Tunnel, the location of Army headquarters, and refused to surrender until threatened with court martial "when we get back to the states." So as not to surrender it, the 4th Marines burnt their flag. Colonel Howard cried when that happened and to his executive officer, Col. Donald Curtis, he blurted out, "My God ... and I had to be the first Marine officer ever to surrender a regiment."[5]

The losses for the Marines and their comrades were 89 dead and 167 wounded in action. The total prisoners for the regiment, including soldiers and sailors in the 4th Bn., were 1,487, of which 474 died in captivity. The enemy's losses on Corregidor are not known, but prisoners of war remembered burning hundreds of bodies taken from the ground and the surrounding sea.

> *Results:* The 4th Marines were the designated defenders of the island but were unable to control the situation. They were under direct orders of the senior members of the USA, but it probably wouldn't have made any difference even if they had been in control of their destiny. When the enemy landed, the Marines, supported by Navy and Army personnel, fought a desperate action, but the result was a foregone conclusion.

Midway Island

Date: 4 and 5 June 1942
Location: Midway Island, Pacific Ocean.
Involved: U.S. naval forces, 3rd Marine Defense Bn., and Marine Air Group 22 versus Japanese naval forces.
Situation: Following the Doolittle bombing raid upon Japan, Japanese leaders realized that they must keep American air forces from being able to fly over the home islands. This required taking the closest American base, Midway Island, and keeping that as their extreme line of defense.

Japanese naval forces had been defeated in the Battle of the Coral Sea and Adm. Isoroku Yamamoto, commander in chief of the Japanese Combined Fleet, decided to draw out the sad remains of the U.S. Pacific Fleet for final destruction. He had been erroneously informed and believed that the U.S. Navy's carriers had been destroyed at the Coral Sea. That was a major mistake because the IJN was not expecting to be attacked by carrier planes, only by a pitiful force of sadly out-of-date Marine planes based at Midway. Those planes, the Brewster "Buffalo," were a death crate for Marine pilots, as we shall see.

Yamamoto divided his attacking fleet into five major groups. Planes from one carrier force would attack Dutch Harbor in Alaska and another would land troops on several islands in the Aleutian chain. Vice Admiral Chuichi Nagumo's fleet, including their four biggest fleet carriers, *Akagi*, *Kaga*, *Hiryu*, and *Soryu*, would go after Midway. Hopefully, the pitiful balance of the U.S. fleet at Pearl Harbor would come racing to its doom in order to protect the Aleutian chain and then head to Midway. Yamamoto and his main battle fleet would then go for the kill of the entire U.S. Pacific Fleet. Besides his carriers, his huge fleet included seven battleships and three light cruisers. They planned to sink the U.S. fleet on 5 June.

Because the USN had cracked the Japanese code, they had an inkling of what was going on and were in fact proactive. Admiral Chester Nimitz believed that Midway was the real target and his fleet was based about 300 miles northeast, where it was in the process of refueling. The enemy's submarines were posted closer to Midway and had no idea the Americans were out in force. None of Nimitz's ships had been seen. It would be Yamamoto and company that would be surprised.

The U.S. Marines' part in the coming fight was mainly the 3rd and 6th Defense Bns., backed up by two companies of 2nd Raider Bn., and a few tanks on Midway Island. Their major part in the battle was in defending the island against air attacks, though they would have been important if the Japanese had made a landing. Colonel Harold D. Shannon, a hero of World War I, commanded the Marine ground forces and Lt. Col. Ira E. Kimes was CO of MAG-22 air defenders of the island.[6] This included Maj. Floyd B. Parks' VMF-221 in Brewster Buffalo fighters, "a perfect dud in combat," and Maj. Lofton R. Henderson with VMSB-241 flying Vindicator, partially fabric-covered, and a few SBD dive bombers.[7] The former two were already badly out of date, though the latter was a much better plane. An addition of seven relatively new Grumman F4F-3 fighters was helpful.

At dawn on 4 June 1942, Japanese bombers, screened by Zeros, were heading toward Midway when they were intercepted by a flight of 12 Brewsters of VMF-221. In planes not fit for the scrap heap, the Marines valiantly attacked their superiors, and 9 of the 12 were shot down, with some losses of bombers to the enemy. In the second wave, 6 of 13 Marine fighters went down, but it wasn't a complete loss. Overall, 32 enemy bombers were destroyed.

Fifteen minutes later, the remaining Japanese planes hit Midway. Now down to 40 planes, they came in and plastered the positions on both islands and destroyed numerous structures. Marine anti-aircraft batteries brought down ten more of the bombers, which a Japanese pilot later said was "vicious fire."

Meanwhile, the Marine dive bombers hit the Japanese fleet carriers and battleships about 150 miles northwest of Midway. VMSB-241 divided into two attacking units. One of 16 SBD-2s led by Maj. Lofton Henderson and the second of 11 SB2U-3s, led by Maj. Benjamin W. Norris climbed to 9,000 feet to locate the enemy carriers. When they did, the carriers were under attack from the TBFs and B-26s. As the Marines went down to join in they lost eight planes over *Akagi* when they were set upon by a flight of Zeros flying cover. Henderson was shot down, as were all but eight Marine planes. Norris' group came upon *Haruna* and tried to inflict pain but were unable to do so and lost three planes. The few Marine planes that survived this beating made it back to Midway. Of the Brewsters that went up only ten returned. It wasn't a good day for Marine aviation.

The next morning Capt. Richard E. Fleming, leading a flight of SB2U Vindicators, dove his hit plane into the turret of one of the Japanese cruisers and earned a Medal of Honor.

On the islands, the various bomber attacks had caused much damage and the Marine air and ground force had suffered 48 killed and 39 wounded. MAG-22 had destroyed a total of 43 enemy planes, and the defense battalions had shot down another ten. But, it was the rest of the naval force which broke the back of the Japanese fleet. Their planes and ships accounted for practically the entire enemy carrier force, along with 300 fighter planes and pilots. Japan also lost a heavy cruiser, but the loss of all four carriers was something from which they were never able to recover.

> *Results:* Though the Americans suffered severe losses to their aircraft, the survivors managed to destroy Japan's aircraft carriers, kill hundreds of Japanese pilots, and drive the surviving ships away. Thereafter, Marines defending the island were no longer at risk of a landing by the large invasion force. The involvement of Marines in this total operation was not limited to ground operations; the main contact with the enemy was in the air and it was a disaster. For the U.S. it truly was, however, the turning point of the Pacific war.

Guadalcanal

Date: 7 August 1942 to 9 February 1943.

Location: Solomon Islands, including Guadalcanal, Gavutu, Tanambogo, and Tulagi Islands.

Involved: Japanese army and navy versus the 1st Marine Division (1st MarDiv.), the 2nd Marines, 1st Raider Bn., 1st Parachute Bn., 2nd Raider Bn., U.S. Navy, U.S. Army Americal Division and 25th Infantry Division, Allied air force and eventually, the 2nd MarDiv.

Situation: It was discovered, and confirmed by aerial photos,[8] that the Japanese army was building an airfield on the recently captured island of Guadalcanal, Solomon Islands. This airfield, when complete, would give the enemy complete control, naval and air, over the approaches to both New Zealand and Australia. The U.S. couldn't allow that to happen since most of its plans for regaining the Pacific areas already taken by Japan were based upon using both nations as bases. Therefore, recovering Guadalcanal was of the utmost importance.

Admiral Nimitz, commander in chief of the Pacific Ocean Area (CinCPOA), selected the 1st MarDiv. (less the 7th Marines) to be the instrument of re-conquest, and its CG, Maj. Gen. Alexander A. Vandegrift, was handed his orders. His plan was to divide his force: Brig. Gen. William H. Rupertus, his assistant division commander (ADC), would lead Task Force Yoke in landing in the Florida Group (Florida, Gavutu, Tanambogo, and Tulagi) with the best-trained forces. He would also have attached the 2nd Marine Regiment from the 2nd MarDiv.

On 7 August 1942, after a preliminary bombardment, Task Groups Yoke (Florida area) and X-Ray (Guadalcanal) of the 1st MarDiv. landed. Yoke included the 1st Raider Bn. (Lt. Col. Merritt A. Edson, MoH); 1st Parachute Bn. (Maj. Robert H. Williams, Navy Cross); 2nd Marines (Col. John M. Arthur) and 2/5 (Lt. Col. Harold E. Rosecrans, Silver Star); all with reinforcing units attached. Edson commanded on Tulagi, and Williams the Gavutu-Tanambogo landing. Across Sealark Channel, the 1st Marines (Col. Clifton B. Cates) and the 5th Marines (Col. Leroy P. Hunt), less 2/5, landed on Guadalcanal near Lunga Point. The 2nd Marines (2nd MarDiv.) had been included in the task force and waited aboard ships as landing force reserve. They were then landed on various parts of Florida Island to successfully cover the flank of the landings on the other three islands.

The Marines on Florida, Tulagi, Gavutu, and Tanambogo got their bellies full of fighting, for that was where most of the enemy soldiers were located. Meanwhile, Marines of the 1st (Lt. Col. William E. Maxwell) and 3rd Bns. (Lt. Col. Frederick C. Biebush), 5th Marines, landed unopposed on Guadalcanal. They, and the 1st Marines that followed them ashore, quickly moved inland and by the end of the day had taken possession of an incomplete air field. The enemy on the island was estimated as being composed of about 1,000 laboring Koreans and another 1,000 Japanese soldiers. Vandegrift ordered the occupation of the air field and the establishment of a defensive line along the Lunga River.

In the meantime, Edson and his 1st Raider Bn., plus 2/5, had met no opposition and then pushed southeast, parallel to the ridge that runs the length of the island. That night they halted at a heavily fortified ravine where the spine ends. The Raiders bivouacked the first night. Shortly after darkness settled in, the enemy came filtering through the Marine's lines, penetrating deep, and were soon killing sleeping Marines. The Raiders, however, fought back and soon had the Japanese on the run. The next morning, 8 August, the Marines outflanked the enemy around the ravine and by mid-afternoon the island was secured. Marines learned quickly, always be alert or die; the enemy was always on duty.

Major Williams and his Parachute Bn. had a difficult time landing because of damage caused by the naval bombardment. Their first wave landed without encountering enemy fire, but the second was clobbered as it crossed the damaged jetties and endured fire from nearby Tanambogo, 500 yards away. The Japanese on Gavutu were mainly in caves so the Marines had to go up and dig them out. Dig them out they did, suffering many casualties. The Parachute Bn. fought all night. The next morning Lt. Col. Robert G. Hunt (Silver Star) with 3/2 came up to support them and help mop up. On 8 August 3/2, supported by two tanks from the 2nd Tank Bn. (Maj. Alexander B. Swenceski), managed to successfully take most of Tanambogo. But first it absorbed a nighttime assault with their knives and bayonets, having received the same treatment as Williams' men. However, the Japanese were unable to drive off the Marines, who had come to stay.

The Marines were successful, but the U.S. Navy was badly hurt the night of 8-9 August when five cruisers, four American and one Australian, plus several destroyers, fell victim to an Imperial Japanese Navy (IJN) fleet off Savo Island. These were the U.S. warships set to protect the land forces from an enemy naval bombardment. After the attack RA Richmond K. Turner withdrew the mostly unloaded transports, effectively leaving the 1st MarDiv. with but 4 units of fire and a 37-day supply of food. There was also no air support because RA Frank J. Fletcher had already withdrawn the carriers. The 1st MarDiv. and its supporting units were effectively all alone with minimal supplies. On 12 August the Marines were reduced to two meals a day. Although the enlisted men had no idea of the USN's defeat at Savo, they soon wondered why IJN submarines were able to stroll into the area and shell the ground positions, seemingly at ease. Enemy planes also worked their will and Marine defenses were just deep foxholes. It was a very unpleasant period for the men of the 1st Mar-Div., but they held.

On Guadalcanal, Maj. Gen. Vandegrift had established a defensive arc. From the east flank on the Ilu River, to the west on what later became known as Edson's Ridge, about two miles from the coast. In between were periodic strong points in ridges and ravines. This was the best that could be arranged under the circumstances, given the lack of personnel and matériel. This same perimeter was what the Marines defended until American naval superiority was established in November. The enemy continued landing troops on Guadalcanal and would launch four major assaults against the Marine lines, one each month.

The first, on 21 August, erroneously called the Battle of the Tenaru, was really against the Ilu River line. Marine patrols soon discovered a large party of Japanese troops ashore on 19 August and defenses were strengthened along the Tenaru River and between it and the Ilu River. It was also learned that the enemy, about 1,000 strong, were located east of the Tenaru. The west bank of the Ilu was held by 2/1 (Lt. Col. Edwin A. Pollack, Navy Cross) and the enemy commander decided to take the Marines out. On the evening of 20 August flares went up and firing began against the Marines defenses. At 0310 the enemy started across the sand bar in a tightly packed formation and were slaughtered. Some few survived and got into the Marines' positions but a reserve company counterattacked and drove them out. Then artillery and mortars began exchanging fire and by morning when 1/1 (Lt. Col. Lenard B. Cresswell, Navy Cross) crossed the Ilu and flanked the Japanese the end was in sight. At 1700 the fight was over. More than 900 of the enemy lay scattered about the river. It was a perfect example of a Japanese officer's stupidity and severe lack of flexibility and maneuvering skills. There would be many more examples before the war terminated.

On 20 August, the forward echelon of Marine Aircraft Group 23 (19 4F4s of VMF-223 and 12 SBD-3s of VMSB-232) arrived at Henderson Field. Two days later, five P-400s from the USAAF 67th Fighter Squadron landed at Henderson. And on the 24th 11 Navy dive bombers also landed there. This was the beginning of the later famed "Cactus Air Force." Planes would continue to arrive during August, nine more P-400s, plus VMF-221 and 231 on the 30th.

The next example of Japanese-style ground warfare, a more famous account than all the others, was between 12 and 14 September when the Japanese attempted to retake the important ridge just southwest of the all-important Henderson Field. The high ground was defended by Edson and his Raiders and the remnants of the 1st Parachute Bn. Fighting had been going on all day, with air attacks on the ridge as well as shelling from Japanese destroyers. It wasn't until 1830, however, that the main ground attack began. The enemy went straight for the main part of the defensive line, driving a hole in the line 250 yards wide. The Parachute Battalion retaliated, soon filling that gap and losing 40 percent of its manpower in so doing. Edson was forced to withdraw a short distance in order to keep his lines intact.

The next night 2,000 enemy tried once again. As they came forward near Edson's lines, they yelled "gas attack" in hopes that the 300 Marines would fold up. They didn't, but during the fighting Edson was down to but 60 men to hold one section of the ridge. Yet they continued to hold. All the while enemy ships were firing into the ridge indiscriminately, causing heavy casualties even amongst their own men. Major Kenneth D. Bailey (Silver Star), now CO of Company C, 1st Raider Bn., took its place as a reserve battalion between the line and Henderson Field. They were severely threatened on the right flank where the Japanese had penetrated the front line. He and his men repulsed this attack and while the main line of Marines was withdrawing, managed to cover their pullback. Despite a severe head wound, Bailey continued fighting hand-to-hand for over ten hours. Bailey's skill, indomitable courage, and fighting spirit held his men together. He was a posthumous recipient of a Medal of Honor. His "boss," Col. Merritt A. "Red Mike" Edson, in command of the Raider Bn. and attached Para. Bn., was also awarded a Medal of Honor for his defense of the ridge that now bears his name.

Pressure continued most of that night until about 0500 the following morning, 14 September, when it began to slow down and then ceased. The ridge had held; it was to be known thereafter as "Edson's Ridge" for the stalwart leader who did so much to defend it. It has been recognized as the key position on Guadalcanal.

On the night of 12-13 September the enemy tried once again to take out the Marines at the Ilu, the eastern flank, but 3/1 (Lt. Col. William N. McKelvy, Jr., Navy Cross) drove them off with bayonets. The following day, 14 September, the Japanese also tried the defenses on the west flank, but 3/5 (Lt. Col. Frederick C. Biebush) managed to repulse that attack with minimal trouble. The Japanese were getting a bit frustrated. Yet they continued to send their men in attacks in small units, not waiting for reinforcements. Lieutenant General Haruyoshi Hyakutake, who was at Rabaul, was sent to command on Guadalcanal.

Finally, on 18 September, the orphan 7th Marines (Lt. Col. Amor LeR. Sims, Silver Star) arrived and was immediately pressed into service. Another welcome arrival, earlier in the month, was Brig. Gen. Roy S. Geiger with the command echelon of his 1st Marine Air

Wing. However, the badly shot-up 1st Para. Bn. departed for Espiritu Santo. Between 23 and 27 September a Marine effort to cross the Matanikau upstream was repulsed by the enemy. The defeat was shared by 1/7 (Lt. Col. Lewis B. Puller), 2/5 (Lt. Col. Walker A. Reeves), and the 1st Raider Bn. (Lt. Col. Samuel B. Griffith, II). Puller's battalion landed in a shore-to-shore operation and was quickly isolated behind the enemy's lines and forced to withdraw. This would be the only defeat suffered by the 1st MarDiv. during their Guadalcanal engagement.

In the meantime the newly arrived Marine, Navy, and Army flyers were busy. By the end of September they had dropped 171 Japanese planes. Captain Joe Foss and Majs. Bob Galer and John Smith were each awarded the Medal of Honor for their part. Another MoH was awarded posthumously to Coast Guard coxswain Douglas Munro for his part in retrieving Puller's Marines from their isolation at the Matanikau.

The Marines, who for weeks had been mainly on the defensive, were now bringing the war to the enemy. Between 7 and 9 October the 5th Marines (Col. Merritt A. Edson) went after the Japanese at the mouth of the Matanikau.[9] While they were so engaged, the 7th Marines, supported by 3/2, crossed the river inland and attacked the Matanikau village and the Point Cruz area. They managed to take the east bank of the river, from which the Marines would not be dislodged. This was now their east flank and they set back Lt. Gen. Hyakutake's plan for a forthcoming drive. Major Leonard K. Davis and his VMF-121 arrived on the 9th to join Cactus.

On the night of 12 October the lack of USN heavy ships nearby caused numerous Marine casualties when a IJN fleet consisting of two battleships, a cruiser, and eight destroyers made it into Sealark Channel. For over one hour the IJN pounded the shore positions of the 1st MarDiv., the worst bombardment the Marines suffered during the entire war. Not only the men but the irreplaceable planes were very badly hurt. The following night, the one remaining plane spotted a fleet of enemy transports bound for Guadalcanal. Two nights later, a few repaired Marine planes managed to get at the transports, sinking three ships, but only after most of the troops had been landed ashore. However, more planes were flying in and were absolutely essential to the continuance of the fight for Guadalcanal.

On the 13th transports arrived with the very welcome reinforcements from the U.S. Army Americal Division's 164th Infantry, led by Col. Bryant E. Moore, USA. They were at once blended into the defensive perimeter, now increased to five sectors. The Matanikau River sector was the most likely entry for Japanese forces and consequently was the place of greatest manpower. The night of the 14th witnessed a huge and successful raid by enemy air against the "Cactus Air Force" with the ultimate destruction or damaging of 42, or about half, of the 90-plane air force. On the 15th, Cactus SBDs battered an IJN transport landing at Tassafaronga, forcing the ships to scatter up Sealark Channel, but not until 80 percent of the troops and supplies were safely ashore. These would provide about 20,000 men of the IJA for future operations.

General Hyakutake had planned to attack and recover Henderson Field and, as part of this program, had sent a large force inland through the jungles. He decided not to await their positioning before making a poorly coordinated attack upon a Marine position on the Matanikau bridgehead. At about 1700 on 23 October, Japanese troops, supported by ten medium tanks and preparatory mortar and artillery fire, moved rapidly across the river and attacked positions held by 3/1 and 3/7 (Lt. Col. Edwin J. Farrell). The supporting 11th Marines (Col. Pedro del Valle), with ten batteries of 105 mm guns, sent death and destruction into the narrowly packed IJA, wiping out an estimated two battalions. Those few enemy soldiers that got into the Marines' defensive positions were eliminated by Marine rifle, bayonet, mortar and machine-gun fire.

The 5,600 IJA men of the 2nd Division (Lt. Gen. Masao Maruyama) moving through the jungle were well equipped with artillery and supporting troops. Vandegrift now had five defensive sectors around Henderson Field. They included (clockwise from Kukum) the 3rd Defense Bn. (Col. Robert H. Pepper) holding 7,100 yards that straddled the Lunga River, in the sector one; the 164th Infantry holding 6,600 yards from the beach inland along the Ilu River to a point near the east slope of Bloody Ridge; in sector three two battalions, 1/7 and 2/7 (Lt. Col. Herman H. Hanneken, Silver Star), on a 2,500-yard front from Bloody Ridge west to the Lunga River; and the First Marines (Cates), less 3/1, holding 3,500 yards west from Lunga to the inland flank of sector one. Even with reinforcements, Hyakutake had his work cut out for him. On 23 October another Japanese attack was launched against the Matanikau with several tanks leading. It was repelled with the loss of one tank. The following day another attempt was made with the same results.

On 24 October repeated IJA assaults against the southern defensive positions, defended by 1/7 (Puller, Navy Cross) and 2/164 (Lt. Col. Arthur C. Timboe) and 3/164 (Lt. Col. Robert K. Hall), were repelled each time. The following day, during a IJN shelling of the 3rd Defense Bn.'s positions, enemy bombers attacked Henderson Field. Meanwhile, an attack against 1/164 (Lt. Col. Frank Richards) on the south flank of the Lunga River was repulsed, as was another attack upon 2/7 south of Hill 67. That latter attack was partially successful and elements of the 5th Marines helped 2/7 drive the IJA out of their positions.[10] The IJA had had enough exercise for the moment and were withdrawn into the jungle. Marine patrol activity continued, as did sea action in the general area.

The 5th Marines, with 1/5 (Maj. William K. Enright) and 3/5 (Maj. Robert O. Bowen) leading, advanced and overcame enemy resistance over 2 and 3 November. On 4 November the 164th Infantry moved to aid the 7th Marines around Koli Point. Meanwhile, more troops landed, including the 8th Marines (Col. Richard H. Jeschke), 1st Bn., 147th Infantry (attached to the Americal Div.), a provisional battalion of the 246th FA (Lt. Col. Alexander R. Sewall), Americal Div., Carlson's Raiders and Seabees to build another airfield. Upon landing, the 2nd Raider Bn. (Lt. Col. Evans Carlson, Navy Cross, Silver Star) was ordered by Vandegrift to march overland toward Koli Point and intercept any enemy forces escaping eastward from the envelopment of the 7th Marines and 164th Infantry. The 7th Marines, attacking eastward on 6 November, crossed the Nalimbiu River and moved along the coast, pushing back IJA forces. The next day Brig. Gen. Louis E. Woods replaced Brig. Gen. Roy S. Geiger in command of Guadalcanal air operations.

Moving eastward on 8 November, 1/7 and 2/7, plus the 164th Infantry, planned to surround IJA forces on Koli Point. Over the following four or five days both American units would attack Japanese troops at Gavaga Creek, but by 12 November the enemy had managed to escape the entrapment. On the 10th and 11th Col. Arthur's 2nd Marines (less 3/2), supported by the 8th Marines and the 164th Infantry (less 2/164), pushed west from Point Cruz toward Kokumbona, but the attack was called off by Vandegrift. He had information that Hyakutake and Adm. Yamamoto were planning a severe strike against him and he wanted all available hands under his direct control and near Henderson Field.

For the next few days the action was mainly naval when on 12 November an IJN force intent on destroying Henderson Field was driven back by Adm. Halsey's naval force. Losses for the USN were heavier than for the enemy but air support from Cactus was the factor that led to the "victory." On the 12th the 182nd Infantry (Col. Daniel W. Hogan) less 3/182 (Maj. Charles L. Marshall), the 245th FA Bn. (Lt. Col. Elisha K. Kane), and assorted engineer and medical units arrived at Guadalcanal and unloaded. On 14 November the USN scored a victory when it defeated a transport force with the IJA 38th Division headed for Guadalcanal. Seven of the eleven transports went down, drowning most of the division's strength. The following day, the remaining transports went aground on Tassafaronga. They and their troops were literally destroyed by the 3rd Defense Bn., the 244th Coast Artillery Bn., USA, plus assistance from the air and a USN destroyer. The few Japanese that escaped into the jungles would join the others already starving on Guadalcanal.

There were no more serious encounters while the 1st MarDiv. remained on the island. Brigadier General Edmund B. Sebree, USA, was taking over more responsibility for the operations on Guadalcanal, and the Army units, supported by the 8th Marines, were relieving the exhausted 1st MarDiv. On 9 December 1942 command passed from Maj. Gen. Vandegrift to Maj. Gen. Alexander M. Patch, USA, and the 1st MarDiv. began loading up, bound for Australia, however, units of the 2nd MarDiv. would remain. Meanwhile, Maj. Gen. Vandegrift was awarded a Medal of Honor for the entire period he successfully commanded on Guadalcanal.

Air support on Guadalcanal during the seven-month period included Army, Navy, and Marine Air units, most of which was compiled into a force known as "Cactus Air." However, the various Marine units involved included the Detachment Headquarters (HQ) of the 1st Marine Air Wing (MAW) which served as ComAirGuadal; Forward Echelon, 2nd MAW; advanced detachments of MAG-25, MAG-14, and 23; and following subordinate units Marine Fighting Squadrons (VMF) 112, 121, 122, 123, 124, 212, 223, 224; Marine Scout–Bombing Squadron (VMSB) 131, 132, 141, 142, 144, 232, 233, 234; Utility Squadron 152, 253; Photographic Squadron 154; and Observation Squadron 251. Most of the above were eventually a part of the "Cactus Air Force."

In addition, carrier air support was provided by *Enterprise* Air Group Ten, including Bombing Squadron 6 and *Enterprise* Flight 300; *Saratoga* Scouting Squadron 3 and Fighting Squadron 5; *Wasp* Bombing Squadron 71; and U.S. Army 67th Fighter Squadron from the 58th Fighter Group.

When the 1st MarDiv. left the island, the 2nd Marines, 8th Marines and elements of the 10th Marines remained behind, including much of the Americal Division. Colonel Arthur's 2nd Marines had been on the island since 7 August and by now were well worn out. The 3rd Bn., 8th Marines had arrived first in September, followed by the rest of the regiment on 9 November. They too had been pressed hard and were tired.

Only the 6th Marines, led by Col. Gilder D. Jackson, were missing. They were briefly in New Zealand, but they too arrived on the Canal on 4 January 1943. It was planned that when the 6th arrived, the 2nd and 8th Marines would head back to New Zealand. That became impossible when the new island commander, Maj. Gen. Alexander M. Patch, USA, wanted all three Marine regiments for a planned attack. Essentially, the 2nd MarDiv. was finally together.

Patch's plan was to push toward Cape Esperance with the 25th InfDiv. on the left, parts of Americal in the middle and the 2nd MarDiv. on the right flank. The acting commanding general of the 2nd MarDiv. was now Brig. Gen. Alphonse De Carre. He decided to relieve the well-worn 2nd Marines with the 6th Marines for the forthcoming attack. Patch had planned to launch the assault on 10 January with the two Marine regiments (now 6th and 8th) holding on the beach and the 25th moving forward in a northeasterly direction.

By the night of 12 January the 25th had attained its objective and the next morning the Marines launched their attack. On 15 January 3/6 (Maj. William A. Kengla, Silver Star) relieved the 8th Marines on the beach. Major Raymond L. Murray (Silver Star) and 2/6 took the center while Maj. Russell Lloyd (Silver Star) with 1/6 was inland. The latter failed to dig in and that night were battered by the enemy's 8-inch guns. Company A lost six dead and 11 wounded in 30 seconds.

The long-suffering 2nd Marines were finally allowed to retire to a reserve position on the 14th of January and soon after began boarding ships for that ride to New Zealand. By the 18th the Marines' front had been narrowed and they had reached their target. The 8th were relieved by the 182nd Inf. On the 16th the 8th Marines had been moved into division reserve and on 31 January the 8th began to move to civilization (New Zealand).

It took a while, but eventually the young, untried men of the 6th Marines became veterans. They served very well with their Army comrades for the balance of the war on Guadalcanal, which terminated when Patch declared the island secured on 9 February 1943. The next day the 6th Marines marched from Cape Esperance to the camp from which the 2nd and 8th Marines had recently vacated. From 10 to 19 February the regiment was assigned as coast defense. On that latter date the 6th Marines loaded up and finally all Marines were gone. The Marines were finished with that blasted island.

The total human losses for the Americans were, for the length of time involved, quite modest. The Marines suffered 1,152 dead and 2,799 wounded and 55 listed as missing. Their air support allowed for 55 dead and 127 wounded, with 85 missing. The Army losses were, in comparison, even more modest at 446 dead and 1,910 wounded. Japanese losses were estimated at 24,000 dead, 1,000 prisoners and air losses of 600 planes and pilots.

Naval losses were extreme. The Allies and the Japanese each lost 24 ships, with over 126,000 tons for the Allies and 135,000 for Japan. In capital ships the United States was the great loser.

Results: When the 1st MarDiv. retired from its conquest, the island was nearly secured, but the Army and 2nd MarDiv. would continue fighting until finally driving off the remnants of Japanese forces. The end date listed is 9 February 1943, but it was made possible by the 1st MarDiv. with the attached 2nd Marines and later the 8th Marines, which had fought the enemy to a standstill for months, often with minimal food and ammunition, and usually without naval or even air support. It earned the Presidential Unit Citation, five men earned the Medal of Honor, well over 115 were awarded the Navy Cross and numerous more were awarded the Silver Star. In so doing it paid heavily in men and material. The 1st MarDiv. had over 4,100 casualties, plus 5,600 cases of malaria. By November 1942 the division was literally "out of business." The U.S. Navy's losses in ships and manpower were extensive. It was a difficult campaign, but in the Pacific the United States was now on the road to complete victory.

Central Solomons

RUSSELL CAMPAIGN

Date: 21 February 1943 to 20 June 1943.
Location: Russell Islands' two main islands, Pavuvu and Banika (30 miles northeast of Guadalcanal).

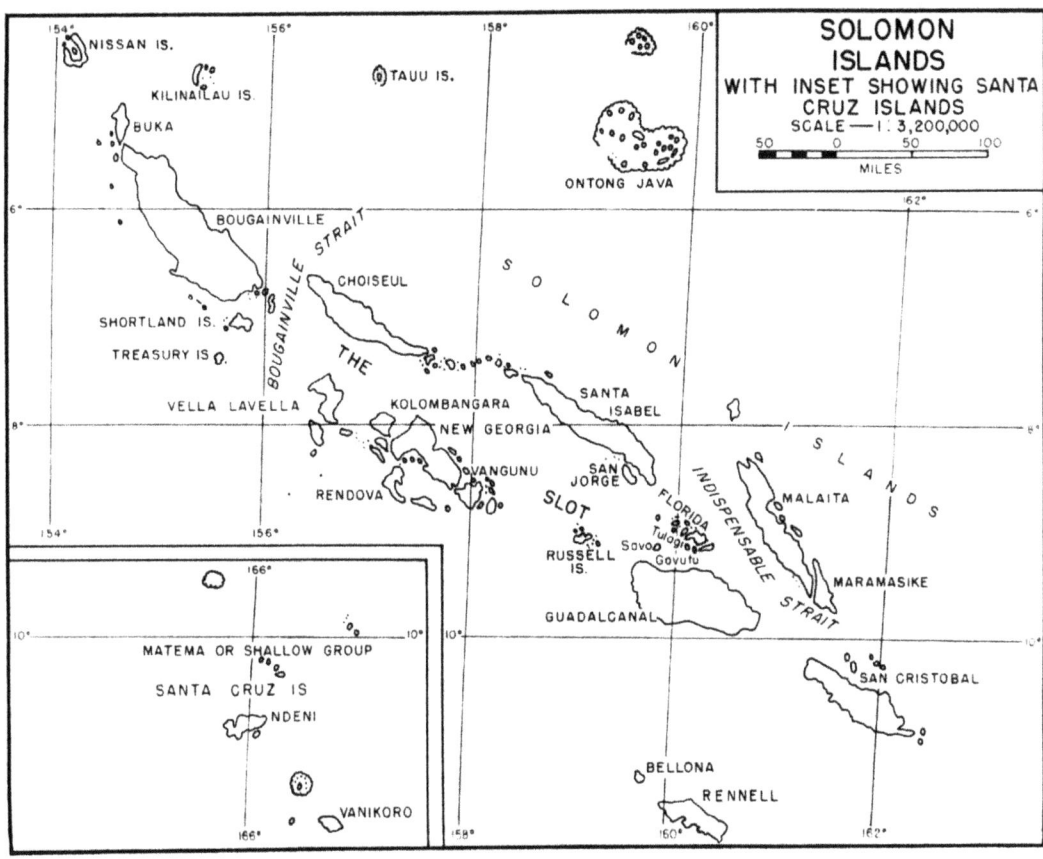

Involved: Japanese military forces versus the 43rd U.S. National Guard Division (less one combat team), 3rd Marine Raiders, 10th Defense Bn., 11th Defense Bn. (a detachment), Marine Air Group-21.

Situation: The Japanese military, defeated on Guadalcanal, made a decision to strengthen the balance of the Solomons, the Bismarcks and New Guinea and occupy the Russell Islands as a near station to supplement Guadalcanal. Admiral Halsey and his advisors saw the potential problems inherent in that happening and planned to occupy the two main islands, Pavuvu and Banika.

On 10 February 1943 Halsey's subordinates, RA Richmond K. Turner and Lt. Gen. Millard F. Harmon, USA, were directed to come up with plans for the operation. Harmon selected the 43rd NG Div. (Maj. Gen. John H. Hester) and Turner added the 3rd Marine Raider Bn. (Lt. Col. Harry B. Liversedge), the 10th Defense Bn. (Col. Robert E. Blake, Silver Star), and a detachment from the 11th Defense Bn. (Maj. Joseph L. Winecoff) and MAG-21 (Lt. Col. Raymond E. Hopper), plus a few Army and Navy units as reinforcements. Hester and the 43rd were to land on the southernmost island of the group (Banika) and Liversedge and the 3rd RB on the northernmost (Pavuvu).

Hester and the 43rd landed on Banika on 21 February and found no Japanese. Liversedge and his units landed on Pavuvu and found the same situation. Regardless, the Americans set to work immediately and began developing airfields, a radar station and a patrol torpedo boat base. Within a week Turner had 9,000 men on the two islands, including the

35th Naval Construction Bn. Though the enemy seemed not to have immediately realized what was taking place, by 6 March they had begun air attacks. Those were to continue almost every day and night for the following four months. By 15 April, however, American planes were flying out of the airfields on both Banika and Pavuvu.

> *Results:* The U.S. military captured another site from which American air could attack Rabaul and the Russells became a major Allied forward operating base and staging area.

New Georgia Campaign

Date: 20 June 1943 to 16 October 1943

Location: New Georgia (180 miles northeast of Guadalcanal). Marines were involved in three landings: at Segi-Viru, at Rendova-Munda, and at Rice Anchorage-Enogai. The main landings, a U.S. Army project, were to take the Munda airfield. Marines would support that effort.

Involved: Japanese forces totaling about 4,500, half army and half naval versus the U.S. Army 43rd NG Div., 1st and 4th Bn. of 1st Marine Raider Regt. (Liversedge, Navy Cross), 9th Defense Bn. (Lt. Col. William J. Scheyer), 2nd Marine Air Wing (Maj. Gen. Francis P. Mulcahy). Several other smaller USMC units participated for a very brief period at the end of the campaign.

Situation: This was part of the planning that Adm. Halsey, Adm. Turner, and Lt. Gen. Harmon, all under pressure from Gen. Douglas MacArthur, had decided for the next operation. It was mainly to knock out the troublesome airfield at Munda at the southern edge of the island of New Georgia. It was conceived as a primarily USA show with input from small but fast-moving USMC units, most of which were from the 1st Marine Raider Regiment.

A British district officer, Capt. Donald G. Kennedy, leading a small detachment of native followers, had been harassing the Japanese. Kennedy's operation saved many downed Allied air personnel and had launched numerous attacks upon Japanese outposts, killing many more than his own small numbers. So much so, that the Japanese decided to put a stop to it and moved a regiment into the area in which he had been operating. This was in eastern New Georgia.

To protect Kennedy and preserve his valuable coast-watching activities, the 4th RB (less two companies) under the command of Lt. Col. Michael S. Currin (Silver Star) landed at Segi, in western New Georgia on 21 June. As soon as a USA unit relieved him, Currin and his battalion set out for the Japanese-held Viru Harbor. Their 11-mile march through a dense jungle with constant harassment from Japanese patrols took four days. When they were near, Currin divided his command into two units and stormed two points, one at Tetemara and the other at Tombi at the entrance of Viru Harbor. This action was costly, costing 28 Marine casualties, but the enemy lost 61 killed and another 100 wounded. By the afternoon of 1 July 1943, U.S. vessels were unloading in Viru Harbor.

Meanwhile, on 30 June the next move was against the island of Rendova. This was just south of New Georgia and about 8 miles from the Munda airfield. The limited part played by Marines was that of the 9th Def. Bn. led by Lt. Col. William J. Scheyer. Its part was to make the airfield untenable for the enemy planes, which it did extremely well. Many enemy planes were destroyed. Besides their usual anti-aircraft units the Marines also were equipped with two batteries of 155mm "Long Toms" to shell the airfield and support the

Army's advance on Munda itself. A detachment of the 11th Def. Bn. also participated and by 5 August the airfield was taken.

Next on the Army's agenda was what became the most arduous Marine campaign on New Georgia—the landing at Rice Anchorage and the taking of Enogai Inlet and then Bairoko. On 5 July Col. Harry B. Liversedge, CO of the 1st Marine Raider Regt., with two USA battalions (Cos. A and D, 103rd Inf.) attached, landed at Rice on northwest New Georgia to prevent Japanese landings from reinforcing Munda. His mission was to take Rice Anchorage then capture Enogai and Bairoko. First to land was Lt. Col. Samuel B. Griffith, III, with the 1st RB at night. It was raining and their job was to cut through the jungle and take Enogai. It was a tough task but the raiders did it.

Griffith and his men attacked Enogai on 9 July and then on the following morning hit them again, this time taking the objective. In so doing they killed 350 Japanese and captured four 140mm guns which had harassed U.S. destroyers and PT Boats in the Kula Gulf. Marine losses, however, were not skimpy, the dead numbered 54 and the wounded 91.

Bairoko, on Dragons Peninsula, was Liversedge's next target, and it was a tough one. His command included the 1st and 4th RBs plus the 3rd Bn., 148th Inf. (Lt. Col. Delbert E. Schultz), but did not include any weapons larger than the 60mm mortar. The had no flamethrowers to counter the enemy coconut log and coral bunkers, or the 81mm mortars they might have. The Marines made it to Bairoko on 20 July and spent most of their time there trying to make it past the well-defended line mounting heavy automatic weapons supported by 90mm mortars. Every attempt was met with an ever-mounting level of casualties and no break in the line. Soldiers began coming up to provide supplies and then to reinforce the Marines. Nothing worked. There were numerous reasons this attempt was a failure and by 22 July, Liversedge had made the decision, after 236 casualties, to withdraw to Enogai. Ultimately, the Japanese evacuated the position and the USA occupied it without opposition.

The last participation by Marines in this very difficult operation was by the 4th Def. Bn. (Col. Harold S. Fassett) when on 15 August it and a USA landing force, supported by VMF-123 and VMF-124, landed on Vella Lavella. Later, Maj. Gen. Robert B. McClure, USA, commented: "Marine defense battalions, a very superior organization indeed." They had shot down 42 Japanese planes during 12 enemy raids.

Most of the air support for the entire operation was provided by the 2nd Marine Air Wing, commanded by Brig. Gen. Francis P. Mulcahy. The subunits involved (at different periods) included HQ of the 1st MAW; MAG-14, -21 and -25; VMF 121, 122, 123, 124, 213, 214, 217, 221 and 223; MAG-23; VMSB-131, 132, 133, 141, 232, 233, 234, 235, 241, 243 and 244; VMSB (Torpedo) 142, 144, and 243.

Results: This entire operation, code-named TOENAILS, gave Gen. MacArthur his flank protection as he maneuvered up the chain toward the Philippines. Air attacks from Japanese-held Rabaul was MacArthur's main problem and gaining airfields within range gave the USA/USN an opportunity to reduce that threat. The part played by small Marine units provided the USA with vital support, since most of the units were veterans of previous encounters. The campaign quickly spelled out that those Marine units were underweaponed. It would not be very long before that was corrected, when all were eventually merged into regimental size.

Bougainville

Date: 1 November 1943 to 28 December 1943.
Location: Bougainville in the northern Solomon Islands.
Involved: Japanese army and naval forces versus the 1st Marine Amphibious Corps (IMAC), including the 3rd Marine Division and ancillary Corps troops.
Situation: After the 3rd MarDiv. was trained and considered ready for a combat role, it moved to the nearest appropriate spot for the planned invasion of the island of Bougainville. In October a decision was made by IMAC that D-day would be on 1 November at Cape Torokina, located at the north end of the Empress of Augusta Bay on the west coast of Bougainville. Enemy forces on the island were estimated to have been at least 45,000, perhaps as many as 70,000 troops. This was the equivalent of three Marine divisions.

Following Maj. Gen. Barrett's death, Lt. Gen. Vandegrift re-assumed command of IMAC until 9 November and was then replaced by Maj. Gen. Roy S. Geiger.[11] IMAC would include, in addition to the 3rd MarDiv., the 1st Marine Parachute Regt (Lt. Col. Robert H. Williams), the 2nd Marine Raider Regt. (Lt. Col. Alan Shapley), and the 37th InfDiv. (Maj. Gen. Robert S. Beightler, USA) in reserve.

D-day, 1 November 1943, dawned bright and clear. The 9th Marines landed farthest from the cape on five beaches on the left and on the right, the 3rd Marines nearer Cape Torokina on six beaches. Layout for the two regiments was from left to right on Red beaches, Col. Edward A. Craig's 9th Marines with 1/9 (Lt. Col. Jaime Sabater), 2/9 (Lt. Col. Robert E. Cushman), and 3/9 (Lt. Col. Walter Asmuth, Jr.). Then on Blue beaches Col. George W. McHenry's (Navy Cross, Silver Star) 3rd Marines with 3/3 (Lt. Col. Ralph M. King), and 2/3 (Lt. Col. Hector de Zayas, Silver Star), and on Blue 1, at Cape Torokina, 1/3 (Maj. Leonard M. Mason, Navy Cross). To 1/3's left was the Buretoni Mission, which was the target of Lt. Col. Alan Shapley's 2nd Raiders, landing on beach Green 2. The 3rd Raiders (Lt. Col. Fred D. Bean, Navy Cross) were scheduled to take the island of Puruata, located about a thousand yards off the cape. H-hour was 0715. After a brief but vigorous bombardment, the landing party made for shore. At 0726 the first waves of Marines hit the beach.

On the right, 1/3, led by "Spike" Mason, had its work cut out for it. Cape Torokina was heavily defended, with an estimated 300 Japanese soldiers dug in, with log and sand bunkers, and they would fight to the death. One enemy 75mm gun sited on the cape destroyed 14 boats and caused enormous casualties. But that was taken out by Sgt. Robert A. Owens, a native of South Carolina, who unhesitatingly charged the bunker with four comrades and entered through the firing port, driving the crew out the rear door. Though wounded, he survived and earned a Medal of Honor.

In the meantime, Japanese carrier aircraft made every effort to inflict heavy casualties on the landing force. Nonetheless, they were instead destroyed by Marine air and the hail of anti-aircraft fire from the converging ships. Successive flights were beaten off and 26 enemy planes were shot down. On 1/3's beach one of the boats hit contained a legend of the Corps, Gunner Milton C "Slug" Marvin and his unloading party. When several of his men were killed or wounded, Slug decided to form them into a marauding patrol and they made their way into the jungle. In the course of that period, Marvin and company managed to knock out seven pillboxes while killing many Japanese. His reward: a Silver Star.[12]

It was one of the first occasions in the Pacific war when the enemy met the invasion force at the beach. The enemy was well dug in and each emplacement had to be taken apart by groups of Marines. Early on, Mason was wounded and instead of taking advice to slow his battalion down he exhorted his replacement, Maj. John P. Brody (Silver Star), "to get the hell in there and fight." It was later reported as "the bloodiest beach of the entire Solomons campaign."

One by one 1/3 knocked out the pillboxes and after three hours at least 270 of the enemy defenders were prone, permanently. By the end of the day, the Marines were on their objectives, 600 to 1,000 yards inland. The invasion force quickly learned that they had inadequate maps. There was an impenetrable swamp just beyond the landing site which, of course, no one had planned for. With just one passageway up Mission Trail, it made forward movement near impossible and it would be several days before that hazard was overcome. Later, the 3rd MarDiv.'s CG, Maj. Gen. "Hal" Turnage (Navy Cross), commented, "Never had men in the Marines ever had to fight and maintain themselves over such difficult terrain as was encountered on Bougainville."

On 2 November, the 3rd RB had taken Puruata Island and soon it became the supply "dump" for the invasion force. That fact was soon discovered by the ever-watchful Japanese and it quickly became a major target of their air attacks. Supplies and gasoline blew sky-high on a daily basis. But there was no other place available in Marine territory that was suitable, so the dump remained and losses continued for days to come. At the end of the second day, the perimeter was about 1,200 yards in depth, but now at the swamp. The use of amtracs solved some of that difficulty and by the following day, 3 November, the depth had been pushed back another 300 yards. Not very far, but at least Cape Torokina was just about cleaned out of Japanese defenders.

Seabees began building roads through the swampy areas on 3 November and even began to build a fighter strip. Twenty-one days later Marine fighter planes began landing on it.[13] On 4 November hard-hit 1/3 was relieved by a battalion of the 9th Marines and went into division reserve. Rain continued without abatement. This was a period when malaria and dysentery were more of an enemy than the Japanese. Because of it, combat activity was at a minimum for the 4th, 5th, and the 6th of November.

On 6 November, more American ships arrived, bringing the 1st Bn., 21st Marines, more Seabees, advance units from the 148th Infantry, USA, and some members of the 3rd Def. Bn. On 7 November the Japanese played the Marine's game. They landed a force estimated at about 500 bodies (accurate word, as it later turned out) between the Laruma River and the nearby Koromokina Lagoon. The latter was about 100 yards west of the river of the same name. Marine defenses had 3/9 just across that river as the western perimeter of the division line. Company K, 3/9, was located on the western end and his mortars were ordered by Lt. Col. Asmuth to attack the interlopers. He also requested help from the 12th Marines (Col. John B. Wilson) to resist the onslaught. Two platoons of Co. K, however, were not available, both then being on patrol. One platoon ran into a large body of the enemy as it was making its run and though it held its own, the platoon was forced to retire away from the fighting. It would be another day and a half before it could rejoin 3/9. Another patrol was also right in the middle of the enemy force on the beach and they had a knockdown fight. Eventually it made its way back to 3/9 by boat.

At 1330 1/3 (Brody), which had been in reserve, was sent forward to relieve 3/9 at the front. Companies B and C were rushed along the beach into a counterattack. No more than 30 yards separated the two enemy forces and a fierce fight raged for hours through a dense jungle undergrowth against severe machine-gun fire. Breaking through the enemy lines, a squad led by Sgt. Herbert J. Thomas, of Columbus, Ohio, fought with grenades and rifles and destroyed the crews of two guns. He was killed while smothering a grenade and earned a Medal of Honor.

That night enemy infiltrators broke through to the 3rd Medical Bn.'s headquarters and attempted to halt the life-saving going on within. However, cooks, bakers, and stretcher-bearers provided a line and stopped them from interfering with Cmdr. Robert R. Callaway and his staff in their operations. Meanwhile, Maj. Brody's 1/3 kept close to the enemy to their front. Insults were continually exchanged between the forces. The Japanese shouted "Moline you die" and Capt. Gordon Warner (Navy Cross), fluent in Japanese, gave back better, including inciting the Japanese to "charge" so Marine rifles and machine guns could slaughter them.

Turnage realized he would need reinforcements and on 6 November had sent in the 21st Marines, led by Lt. Col. Ernest W. Fry, Jr.'s, 1/21. Fry, senior man at the scene, was now in direct command. On the 8th, Marine artillery and mortars slammed into the area, 300 yards wide and 600 deep. When Fry's two advance companies went in they found nothing but desolation. As they advanced forward the Marines passed over about 250 Japanese lying prostrate. In the meantime, on 7 November, the Japanese 23rd Infantry had arrived before the 2nd Raiders at the Buretoni Catholic Mission and provided the latter and 9th Marines with some action.

General Turnage had decided that it was imperative to take and hold the junction of Piva and Numa-Numa Trails lying a few hundred yards east of Piva village. He ordered Col. Edward A. Craig of the 9th Marines to do the job. Craig assigned the job to Lt. Col. Alan B. Shapley, CO of the 2nd Raider Regt., who had Beans and the 3rd RB lead the actual attack. In addition, Beans would have some of the 9th Marines to aid his gang. The Japanese didn't wait for the Marines. Instead, on the 8th they launched their own attack. It appeared that they would overrun the trail block. Two PFCs with a BAR held their position with one, Henry Gurke, being killed while smothering a grenade. For that he was awarded a posthumous Medal of Honor. Donald G. Probst held on and he was awarded a Silver Star. The post held, the line held, and the enemy were driven back. The fighting continued for two days until finally the enemy could take no more and what was left of them retired. Later count showed 550 enemy dead, with losses of 19 dead and 32 wounded Marines. The 9th Marines sent in more men and aggressively held the positions fought over, thereby ensuring the maintenance of ground paid for. The Battle of Piva Trail was another victory for the 3rd MarDiv. Yet the victories were not yet driving the Japanese out of the area, let alone from the island. They were still fighting for every inch of ground.

On 9 November the Army's 37th InfDiv. had begun landing its troops and numerous supplies. Marines lacking nearly everything managed to openly pilfer (steal) them. The Army was angry, and it was not a good time for either service.

On 11 November IMAC issued an attack order for the Army (left) and Marine (right) units ashore. Army-Marine artillery would provide support, under IMAC control, and Marine air would provide close support. The first objective was the junction of the Numa-Numa and East-West Trails. On 13 November Co. E of 2/21 led off the attack beginning at 0800. But, at 1100, it was ambushed by a sizeable enemy force concealed in the coconut palm grove near the trail junction. Lieutenant Colonel Eustace R. Smoak, CO, 2/21, sent his executive officer, Maj. Glenn Fissell (Silver Star) with some 12th Marine artillery observers to find out what was happening. It was bad and Fissell was killed. Smoak moved his battalion closer, through the enemy, and fed his companies into the fight. Smoak ordered Co. F forward to cover a withdrawal by Co. E, which was accomplished, but Co. F disappeared and 2/21 was in a very bad state. Smoak decided that the lateness of the hour and darkness would force him to wait until the following day. With that, 2/21 went into perimeter defense.

The next day, 14 November, tanks were brought up and the division artillery registered all around Smoak's 2/21. According to sources he also called in 18 Marine torpedo bombers (?) and his disorganized riflemen were ordered to go forward once again.[14] H-hour was set for 1155 after a 20-minute artillery preparation, followed by a rolling barrage. The Marines were met by a heavy enemy response. Rifles, machine guns, and mortars began to decimate the advancing Marines. The tanks lost their directions and began firing into and running down the Marines, costing several "friendly" casualties. Captain Sidney J. Altman, "skipper" of Co. E, 2/21, earned himself a Silver Star when he jumped aboard the turret of the lead tank and redirected the tank commander, who in turn managed to reorient the rest. Within a few hours the Marine attack was successful. Enemy resistance was overcome, the remnants retired, and a perimeter defense was established for the night.

On 14 November the balance of the 21st Marines came in and relieved the 9th Marines on the front lines. The 129th Infantry, USA, also landed and took up a position in the center of the perimeter. However, the newcomers were not quite ready for frontline duty just yet. They inadvertently allowed Japanese patrols to come down the nearby Numa-Numa Trail, which caused trouble in the rear areas for Army and Marines. Company F of 2/3, just then ingesting some hot stew in their helmets, were rushed to the breach and, to say the least, were very angry with the 129th Infantry. Insults were part of the exchange, none of which hurt the Japanese one little bit but certainly didn't help the U.S. forces.

Dry ground was discovered and Turnage ordered his troops to move forward rapidly and take it for the development of landing fields. The offensive began on 19 November when all troops were pushed beyond the Piva River to established strong positions. It wasn't easy. The enemy was ready and made life very difficult for those trying to advance. Yet 2/3 found high ground and 2nd Lt. Steve Cibik (Silver Star) and his Co. F platoon climbed the 400-foot edifice and occupied it. It gave the Marines a valuable piece of real estate from which they could view much of the surrounding countryside, especially where the offensive was to take place. The advance continued and Cibik and his men managed to hold the height despite being continually attacked. The Japanese had been using the same place to spy on the Marines every day, but should also have remained there at night. They didn't, the Marines did, and the enemy couldn't retake it.

Thanksgiving Day, 24 November, saw more Marine casualties when the Japanese replied to a 20-minute Marine artillery fire, causing many more dead and wounded amongst the 3rd Marines. One company waiting to move forward lost 100 of its 190 men while waiting for H-hour. Nonetheless, at 0900 the 3rd Marines moved forward. Enemy mortar shells really gave the Marines in the open a horrible reception. But Marines using flamethrowers and dropping grenades into the apertures helped slowly take the bunkers.

The swamp was waist-deep in some places, making that route even more difficult as the mortar shells dropped in on the advancing Marines. The explosions tore huge Banyan tree limbs free and sent them down upon the Marines, killing or wounding many. Meanwhile, steady Japanese sniper fire was also coming from the same trees.

Company L, led by Capt. John Kovacs (Silver Star), was practically wiped out by sniper fire, including the "skipper" and all the other officers. Yet the handful of survivors continued forward. The back of the Japanese defense was broken, especially when the rest of 2/3 plunged far ahead by 1,100 yards, deep into enemy-held territory. Late in the day the cooks managed to get bits and pieces of turkey up to the men on the line, because, after all, it was Thanksgiving Day.

The next day the Japanese launched a major assault against the lines of the 3rd Marines. When it was broken up the battle known as Piva Forks was over. The 23rd Japanese Infantry was eliminated; over 1,100 enemy dead were counted. The 3rd Marines were barely in better shape, with only 150 men in 1/3 still on their feet. The regiment had paid a high price and was relieved by the 9th Marines.

On the right, the 21st Marines were sent in to help the 1st Marine Parachute Regt., which had gotten into a bit of difficulty. They had stormed a wooded hill and failed. Over the next few days they continued trying, but were cut to pieces in the process.[15] The 21st Marines came up and tried their luck. They too were stopped at first but after five days went up again and took what is known as "Helzapoppin" Ridge, the regiment's first victory.

During December the Marines and Army units kept going forward, creating new landing fields as they took additional territory. As the Army units began relieving the 3rd MarDiv. on 23 December, Hill 600a, near "Hellzapoppin," fell to Marines and the main part of the campaign was concluded successfully. On 24 December the 3rd Marines were withdrawn from Bougainville. As they arrived on the beach a violent earthquake startled them and one Marine yelled, "Let's get the Hell outta here before anything else happens." The rest of the Marines of the 3rd MarDiv. were relieved by incoming Army units and all were returned to their beloved encampment on Guadalcanal. The 3rd Def. Bn. (Lt. Col. Edward H. Forney) remained to support the Army.

Air support for the Bougainville operation included the Forward Echelon of the MAG-24. Elements of other units over the entire period included VMTB 134, 232 and 233; VMSB 23, 143, 234, 235, 243 and 244; VMF 211, 212, 214, 215, 216, 218, 221, 222 and 223; and Night Fighter Squadron (VMNF) 531. For the initial period, the air CG was Maj. Gen. Nathan F. Twining, USA, until 20 November when Maj. Gen. Ralph J. Mitchell, USMC, assumed command.[16] During the Cape Torokina battle, a number of ground personnel from the various air units were converted to ground support troops to aid in the defense of the Cape Torokina perimeter until the end of March 1944.

Losses were rather minimal, compared to other assaults by Marines during the Pacific war. The 3rd MarDiv. lost 295 killed and 1,022 wounded. Within the subordinate units the Corps troops had 6 killed, 31 wounded; 1st Parachute Regt. 45 killed, 121 wounded; 2nd Raider Regt. 64 killed, 204 wounded; and 3rd Def. Bn. 13 killed and 40 wounded, or a combined total of 423 killed and 1,418 wounded. Japanese losses were estimated at 2,458 killed and 25 taken prisoner.

> *Results:* Though the Bougainville campaign was a success and Rabaul was being surrounded, it was obvious that in the planning stages, little effort was made to select an assault location which would allow the attackers to spread out. More than likely, no one paid much attention to the huge swamp lying directly opposite the landing beaches. Since getting off the beaches was next to impossible without extraordinary losses in men and material, the Marines had to pay the price for this lack of foresight.[17]

18. World War II

Tarawa

Date: 20 November to 24 November 1943.
Location: Betio Island in the Tarawa atoll in the Gilbert Islands.
Involved: Japanese army and naval forces (Special Naval Landing Force) versus the 5th Amphibious Corps (VAC), including the 2nd Marine Division.
Situation: The island of Betio had an airfield which the IJN was using to inflict pain upon the U.S. supply lines in the South Pacific. U.S. naval air attacks continued against various islands in the atoll, with Betio, obviously being built up, gaining the most attention. This went on for weeks and then literally months.

United States Navy planes from the Southern Carrier Group bombed Betio on 18 November and on the 19th, Cruiser Division 5 walloped the island with its main batteries. Another air and naval bombardment on 20 November silenced the main IJN batteries. It was presumed by the Navy senior officers, that this would be sufficient to make the landing easy. They were very wrong.

That day, 20 November, the 2nd MarDiv. (reinforced) landed on Red Beaches 1, 2, and 3. Leading forces were 2/8 (Maj. Henry P. Crowe, Navy Cross), 2/2 (Lt. Col. Herbert R. Amey, KIA that day, Silver Star), and 3/2 (Maj. John F. Schoettel), supported by 1/2 (Maj. Wood B. Kyle, Silver Star) and 3/8 (Maj. Robert H. Ruud) in reserve. Colonel David M. Shoup, CO of the 2nd Marines (MoH), was designated assault commander and the 6th Marines (Col. Maurice C. Holmes) constituted Corps Reserve. The Navy was convinced

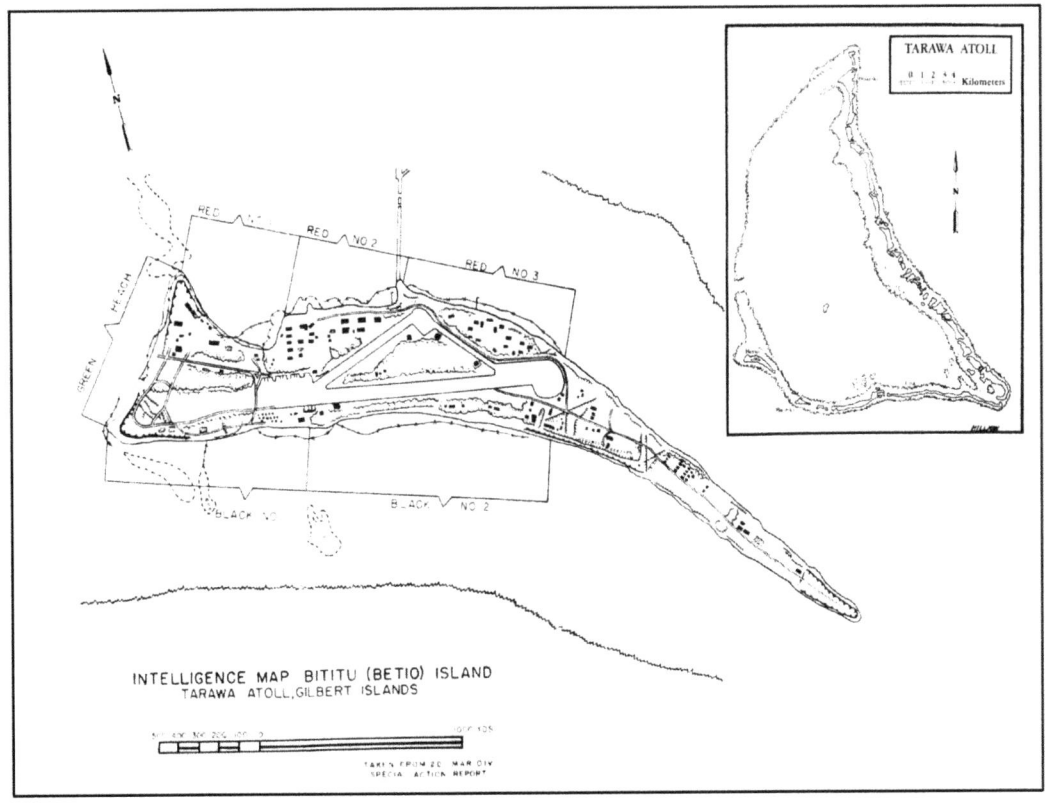

INTELLIGENCE MAP BITITU (BETIO) ISLAND
TARAWA ATOLL, GILBERT ISLANDS

that they had literally "wiped out" the enemy on the island and the Marines would just "walk in and take it." Wrong. How very wrong they were. This landing would be possibly the most fouled-up and bloodiest of all the Pacific amphibious operations, but the 2nd MarDiv., through its personnel, would overcome all the handicaps and win out over the most tenacious defense the Japanese would mount in the World War II island campaign. Bravery was not extraordinary, in fact it was most common. From all reports, it appears that just about every Marine and Navy Corpsman on Tarawa were heroes.

After the third wave, Amey and his command, 2/2, moved out in their LCMs. Upon reaching the reef, Amey found that his LCM would not cross it and he secured the use of two LVTs. Transferring to the LVTs, they headed in to Beach 2. About 200 yards out barbed wire stopped them. They went over the side and began treading water as they approached the beach. Machine-gun fire from the right nailed several of them, including Amey, and the other Marines swam to the protective lee of the abandoned boat. An observer, Lt. Col. Walter I. Jordan, assumed command until Maj. Howard J. Rice (Silver Star), Amey's executive officer, could make contact.[18]

A platoon of Scout Snipers (1st Lt. William D. Hawkins) from the 2nd Marines was the advance party and the first Marines to land. Their job was to secure the long pier jutting out from the north side of Betio before the rest of the 2nd MarDiv. arrived on the scene. Their fight was fearsome, but they successfully made it to the beach after destroying many of the enemy along the way. Hawkins was the first to disembark and unhesitatingly moved forward along the pier under intense fire. Leading his troops to support those Marines already ashore and desperately trying to establish a beachhead, he was dangerously exposed and ultimately mortally wounded. He was posthumously awarded a Medal of Honor, one of three for the landing force.

In the meantime, as the main landing force was approaching the island, the personnel carriers were forced to go over coral reefs. Only the tracked vehicles could make it, and the other boats had to drop the Marines offshore, into the deep water, sometimes as far as 1,000 yards from the beach. Consequently, the enemy had an easy time of it, picking off those Marines who waded in with their weapons held overhead to keep them dry. After that abuse the survivors came upon the barbed wire in the water, which they had to climb over. It was a very bad time for the Marines and their losses were dreadful.

The first unit to reach shore was 3/2 when its tractors climbed up on Red Beach 1 at 0910. The first three waves were hit hard by machine-gun fire and anti-boat guns, which damaged most of the tractors. Company I leaped out of the LVTs and over the log seawall and began advancing inland. A strong Japanese position, located between Beaches 1 and 2, raked 3/2, and Co. K lost heavily before it could reach the log barricade. Both I and K companies lost half their men in two hours. Company L (Maj. Michael P. Ryan, Navy Cross) and the mortar platoon came in as far as their boats would take them, about 500 yards from the beach. Then everyone got out and walked, or rather treaded water. They lost 35 percent of the company in the water.

The next battalion to reach the shore was 2/8, Maj. Henry P. "Jim" Crowe, at 0197 on Red 3, located just east of the troublesome pier. Companies E and F were first, with a part of G following. Two of the tractors, with troops aboard, made it through the seawall and as far as the airfield main strip. The 500-plus men suffered 25 casualties, a record low for the day, mainly because they were well-protected by their armored carriers, but losses to the officers was serious. Company F lost five of its six officers coming on the beach, its left flank along the pier. Company E landed to their right.

One of the reasons there was some success on D-day was the impact of individuals, like "Jim" Crowe and "Mike" Ryan of 3/2. Crowe was the first battalion commander to reach shore. Braving intense machine-gun and shell fire, constantly with his men at the most violent points of fighting, he organized the establishment of a beachhead and directed the elimination of hostile snipers and gun crews from along the seawall and inland of the beachhead. Without rest and at great personal risk, he maintained continuous aggressive pressure against heavily reinforced enemy emplacements. Major Crowe was personally largely responsible for winning and maintaining the beachhead at Tarawa. His citation for the Navy Cross read, "For extraordinary heroism, the greatest of personal and unflinching valor, great military skill, inspirational and outstanding leadership, and ceaseless energy."

During the first day, all the news was bad. All the news that could be reported, that is the Marine's TBY radio sets were inefficient when running at full speed, but now most were waterlogged and wouldn't work at all. Kyle's Combat Team Two was ordered by Shoup to provide support for 2/2 and when Ruud's 3/8 was released to Shoup he had them come ashore on Beach 3.

That night many Marines were scattered around behind the seawall and a few were on the beaches. Having lost direction during the day, many were unattached to their units. They would be lost to the effectiveness of organization until pulled together on D-day plus one, 21 November. They would also be in serious difficulties if the Japanese launched attacks that night.

Major Michael P. Ryan, of Company L, had assumed command of 3/2 when his battalion commander, Maj. John F. Schoettel, failed to reach shore. As senior officer Maj. Ryan immediately began his task of collecting the badly disorganized and isolated survivors of three battalions. He organized and directed critical operations of these elements throughout the battle, leading assaults on enemy positions, retaining initiative in his sector, and clearing his isolated beachhead, into which reinforcements could be moved. He would then be able to report to Shoup, at 1450, that several hundred of his Marines and two tanks had pushed 500 yards beyond Red Beach 1. That greatly pleased Shoup, it being one of the first positive messages he had received. There weren't many more that day.

Aside from a couple of tanks, Ryan's men, with just infantry weapons, had overrun many Japanese pillboxes. They had no flamethrowers or demolitions, just grenades that would usually put the "hard places" out of action only temporarily. Ryan later acknowledged that he expected the enemy still hidden in the bunkers to counterattack after dark. Fortunately they didn't. Ryan, like Crowe, was accorded recognition as another Marine who held the beachhead together those first few troublesome hours.

There were several other men who made a great impact on D-day and the days following. From Atlanta, GA, came 1st Lt. Alexander Bonnyman, Jr., with 2/8, an older man who, when war came, had volunteered for service with the Marines. When he arrived ashore the Marines were pinned down at the end of Betio Pier by a heavy concentration of artillery and machine gun fire. Taking the initiative, Bonnyman organized and led the men along that long pier and then assumed command of several flamethrower and demolition men. He began directing the destruction of several installations before the end of D-day. On the following day he, alone, crawled forward toward the entrance of a massive blockhouse where he placed demolitions. However, not entirely successful in his first attempt, he then organized an assault upon that same position, having munitions placed at both entrances while he took to its roof. The ensuing blast had killed 50 Japanese inside the blockhouse and driven out at least 100, who were instantly cut down by the waiting Marines. Bonnyman was on the top of the structure when he was assaulted by a large body of the enemy which charged his position. He killed three more before succumbing to mortal wounds received as he made his last stand.[19]

Another Marine, SSgt. William J. Bordelon, a San Antonio, Texas, native with the 18th Marines, landed early on D-day with the assault waves. He and just three others in his boat survived the violent enemy fire. Once ashore, putting together demolition charges, Bordelon personally took out two pillboxes and, while assaulting a third, was hit by machine-gun fire and the charge exploded in his hands. Though he was badly wounded, he grabbed a rifle and began furnishing cover fire for men going over the seawall. When another demolitions man was hit, he rescued the man, ignoring his own serious condition. Then, still refusing first-aid for his own wounds, he made another demolitions charge and single-handedly charged another Japanese machine-gun position. He was caught in a cross fire of several machine guns and killed instantly. For his courage and initiative he too was awarded a Medal of Honor.

Replacements for the U.S. Marines ashore were badly needed, as were reinforcements. When night closed down, the active assaults on D-Day had ceased, but the shooting continued. A beachhead had been established, however, against determined resistance, and even though it wasn't always apparent, the Americans were on Betio to stay. In fact, Shoup sent a positive message to command offshore: "Casualties many; Percentage of dead not known; Combat efficiency: We are winning."

Colonel Elmer E. Hall, CO of the 8th Marines, received his orders at about 0715 to land 1/8 on 21 November. He and his men had been afloat at the line of departure throughout the previous night. Several times, in official histories, the suggestion is made that the communications of Maj. Gen. Julian Smith, the division CG, "failed again." Those in command seemed to mistakenly believe that Hall had received orders to land late on 20 November but he hadn't. Major Lawrence C. Hays, Jr., (Silver Star), and 1/8 came ashore at Red Beach 2 to reinforce the landing force. Division headquarters had incorrectly assumed that 1/8 and 1/10, with pack howitzers, had been ashore on 20 November, but the units had spent 20 hours on the landing craft waiting for the word. Fog of war, as it is called, and seasickness no one mentioned.

Hays and his men were subjected to much of the same as their buddies had received the day before. Regardless, by 1400, 1/8 was ashore and had established themselves. By the end of the day, though they had not advanced very far, 1/8 had destroyed numbers of the enemy located in numerous defensive positions. Jim Crowe and 2/8 were unable to move far the second day. All the same, in the morning Mike Ryan brought his men from Red Beach 1 south to conquer Green Beach and the entire west end of the island.

In the meantime at 1740 Brig. Gen. Leo D. Hermle was sent orders, by Julian Smith, to assume command over all Marines ashore. However, there followed some contention between he and Col. Shoup, who had not received the order. As far as he was concerned he still commanded ashore. Hermle was senior and ADC, but Shoup upheld his previous orders. With him Shoup had Lt. Col. Evans F. Carlson as an observer. Luckily, since the radios weren't working well, Carlson was Shoup's efficient liaison officer with Division.

Holland Smith released the 6th Marines to Julian Smith at 1525 that day, which was helpful, because they were badly needed ashore. Major William K. Jones (Silver Star) then led 1/6 ashore onto Green Beach, on the east side of Betio. They were to be followed by 2/6 (Lt. Col. Raymond L. Murray, Silver Star) as support, but Murray's orders were changed to instead land on Blue Beaches 1 and 2 on Bairiki Island "immediately." It seems that some of the enemy were deserting to another island adjacent to Betio and 2/6 was to stop that flow and contain them on Betio. The atoll was nearly all connecting land to Buariki Village at the extreme northern end. Jones found Green Beach secured by Ryan and his crowd. Therefore, upon arrival at 1855, he set up defensive positions for the night. Murray landed on Bairiki at 1655 with minimum resistance and by nightfall had secured that island.

At 0700 on 22 November, D-day plus two, 1/8 moved westward and met strong enemy fortifications. Three light tanks from the 2nd Tank Bn. (Lt. Col. Alexander B. Swenceski, Silver Star) were unable to deliver the knockout punch required and withdrew. By evening Companies A, B, and C of 1/8 had so severely weakened those enemy positions that the enemy was completely cut off. The airfield was taken by 1/2 and 2/2 and they then moved to the south coast, splitting the enemy forces on the island. Major Kenneth F. McLeod (Silver Star), with 3/6, landed on Green Beach and headed eastward. Jones' 1/6 advanced along the south coast to secure that side of the island and then attacked east toward the airfield. Shoup was still commanding ashore until late on D-Day 2, when the CG Maj. Gen. Julian Smith came ashore and relieved him of the burden.[20] Shoup would be awarded a Medal of Honor for his command of all action on the island, plus his courage and intrepid behavior.

The night of 22-23 November, 1/6 repelled three enemy counterattacks, and on the 23rd, 3/6, in four hours' fighting, secured the southeast tip of Betio. Major General Julian C. Smith then declared that all organized resistance on Betio had ceased. However, some Japanese from the eastern tail didn't hear the news and were killed while counterattacking the 6th Marines during the night of 23-24 November. The next night, the 2nd and 8th Marines were transported to their new base camp at Kamuela, Hawaii, while the 2nd Defense Bn. arrived from Samoa to defend Betio. Smith ordered the ADC, Brig. Gen. Leo D. Hermle, to send the 6th Marines around the atoll to wipe out any pockets of Japanese resistance, and by the 27th all was clear. On 4 December Maj. Gen. Smith turned over the island to Capt. Jackson R. Tate, USN. The 2nd MarDiv. was finished with Tarawa and Tarawa nearly finished the 2nd MarDiv.[21]

> *Results:* The total time for the invasion and final conquest of Tarawa was 76 hours. During that period the 2nd Division suffered 3,080 casualties, of which 989 were killed. Arguably, these were proportionately the most serious losses for the Marines during the entire war. Most of the casualties were created as they tried to make the shore. The available landing craft, for the most part, was not capable of crossing the reef, which left the Marines a long walk to get to the beach. The enemy were able to concentrate their fire — artillery, mortars, machine guns, and rifles — on the defenseless men as they made their way to shore. It also appears that no genuine air support was available during the landing. The USN planners had not taken into account the tides and water depth.
>
> The Japanese were well-prepared, and the pre-invasion pounding by the naval guns was terribly inadequate, as was the equipment to land the landing force. Later, after some discussion, it was determined by the powers that be, that Tarawa was totally unnecessary. Tell that to the Marines.

New Britain

Date: 26 December 1943 to 4 May 1944.[22]
Location: Bismarck Archipelago, especially Cape Gloucester.
Involved: Japanese army and naval forces versus the 1st MarDiv. (reinforced).
Situation: In July 1943, MacArthur's headquarters sent initial orders to Maj. Gen. William H. Rupertus, CG, 1st MarDiv., to prepare to aid the 6th Army in his campaigns in the Japanese-occupied Bismarck Archipelago. This placed the Marines directly before his planned advanced to the Philippines. The Japanese airfield at Cape Gloucester on New Britain was to be their immediate target. In late August 1943 the division engineers departed first to prepare camps, and in late September the rest of the division sailed for different locations in New Guinea. This was followed by several reconnaissance efforts by the Alamo Scouts, a conglomerate organization of soldiers, Marines and a few sailors. After some rather haphazard plans were put forward and objections stated, the 1st MarDiv. received 6th Army Field Order No. 5, which directed the entire 1st MarDiv. to land at Cape Gloucester, located on the western end of the island of New Britain. That is, roughly 75 miles east of New Guinea across the Vitiaz Strait.

By the evening of 24 December 1943 the invasion flotilla was loaded and had rendezvoused at Buna Harbor. It probably isn't necessary to add that the men were quite solemn at this time. They had, after all, been out of action for over a year and this long period of inactivity had sapped all desire for more jungle warfare. Landings would be made on decent beaches, but they weren't any deeper than a few hundred yards. Then they had to traverse inland on what has euphemistically been called "damp flats."[23] This island would be the wettest the U.S. troops would ever have to serve upon. Weather conditions would actually be worse than those on Guadalcanal. Marines would suffer incessant rain, pounding them the entire period they were at Cape Gloucester. BACKHANDER, the code-name of this operation, would take all the resilience and fortitude the Marines could muster.

A naval bombardment, attacks by the 5th Army Air Force, and Marine Fighter Squadrons 214, 216, 222, 223, and 321 aided in the landing of the 7th Marines, also known as "Combat Team C" (Col. Julian N. Frisbie, Navy Cross), of the 1st MarDiv. on the morning of 26 December 1943. Lt. Col. William R. Williams led 3/7, which landed at Yellow 1 at 0746, and 1/7 (Lt. Col. John E. Weber, Navy Cross and Silver Star) landed two minutes later on Yellow 2. Elements of 3/7 ran into a modest firefight, which didn't impede them or last very long. On the right, Target Hill (Hill 450), aka Sankokuyama, was soon taken, which established a sound and reliable flank position for the landing. Soon, Yellow Beach 1 and 2, located on the north side of the cape, were secured and the 7th Marines and two battalions of the 1st Marines, aka Combat Team B (Col. William J. Whaling), landed, turned right and headed across the swamps for the airfield.

At the opposite (southern) side of the cape, 2/1 (Lt. Col. James M. Masters, Sr.) landed at Green Beach. Its part of the operation was known as STONEFACE. Their task was mainly defensive, to block a trail and hold it against elements of Japanese Infantry that would be rushing to defend the airfield. On the southeastern end of New Britain, Maj. Gen. Iwao Matsuda ordered his 141st Infantry and 51st Reconnaissance Regiment to join their colleagues at Cape Gloucester to defend the airfield.

Temporarily, the enemy reaction was mainly an aerial counterattack which badly damaged some of the USN ships offshore, but their own losses from AAA fire precluded any further raids in strength.

The first moves made by the division were partly southeast toward Hill 660 (aka Manjuyama), an important feature of the southern defense perimeter, and partly westward toward the airfield. But the Japanese weren't just sitting on their hands while the Marines were busy. They reacted with numerous small attacks upon the perimeter as the 1st Marine's assault forces, beginning on 27 December, advanced on the defenders at the airfield.

Initially, the plan had been an advance of a 500-yard front, but the left flank in the damp flats was unable to keep up with those units nearer the beach. Whaling then reformed them into a column of companies on the road. The attack was led by 3/1 (Lt. Col. Joseph F. Hankins, Navy Cross) with Co. I in the advance. They were supported by a platoon of medium tanks from Co. D, 1st Tank Bn. (Lt. Col. Charles G. Meints). On the 28th the advance was delayed to allow two additional platoons of medium tanks to be brought up over the badly chewed-up road. Company I maintained the lead, followed in order by Co. K and Co. L. As the ground became firmer, Co. A of 1/1 (Lt. Col. Walker A. Reaves, Silver Star) assumed a place at the left as flank guard. At 1215 the Marines ran into their first major opposition. With that, Capt. Carl E. Conron, Jr., (Navy Cross) of Co. I deployed his unit wide to the left and brought up tanks to pound enemy emplacements.

Japanese positions were strong but primarily designed to ward off a seaborne attack. They fought hard and withstood a severe pounding by the tank assaults and artillery of the 11th Marines. Meanwhile, that same afternoon, Co. A had moved about 500 yards further inland to the left of the 3rd Bn. and eventually ran into a reinforced company-sized defensive system with interlocking fire from log bunkers. Running out of ammunition, Co. A commenced withdrawal toward the beach at 1545. The next morning the Marines learned that the enemy had departed, leaving behind 41 dead. Marine losses totaled 8 dead and 16 wounded.

Company K remained to the left when Co. A retired. With three tanks they managed to destroy a 75mm gun, but discovered they were actually fighting against a dozen bunkers. Enemy fire was directed toward the tanks, but the guns were poorly placed, most facing toward the sea before they were repositioned. The fight was difficult for the exposed Marines but the combination of infantry and tanks working together roughed up the enemy. By 1700 the 1st Marines, less 2/1, were digging in around the entire perimeter of the defense positions and another 200 yards beyond. In the course of the fighting, though the losses of 3/1 were 9 dead and another 36 wounded, the enemy losses totaled 266 dead in 300 square yards. The locality was quickly named "Hell's Point," but soon after renamed after Co. K's dead captain, Joseph E. Terzi (Navy Cross).

Combat Team A (5th Marines, Col. John T. Selden) up till now had been taking and occupying several offshore islands. At Rupertus' request, they were released for service at Cape Gloucester. On 29 December portions of 1/5 (Maj. William H. Barba) and 2/5 (Lt. Col. Lewis W. Walt, Navy Cross) each landed at Yellow Beaches while other parts of Combat Team A landed at Blue Beach. By force of circumstances, 3/5 (Lt. Col. David S. McDougal) was in a craft that had difficulty retracting from the beach and didn't initially participate in the action.

It was decided that the 1st Marines would continue forward on the beach road with 1/1 (Reaves) leading while the 5th Marines would make a wide sweep on the left flank to cut off an enemy withdrawal. Lew Walt's 2/5 led off in a column of companies at 1500 with

Co. F in the assault position. By 1925 2/5 was at the center of Airstrip no. 2. At the same time, Barba and 1/5 were supposed to be following 2/5, however, they were having difficulties advancing over the terrain. Although both battalions sent out patrols trying to make contact, they were unsuccessful and Barba decided to establish his own perimeter defense where he stood.

With support from the 11th FA, and with tanks leading, the 1st Marines bolted through to the eastern edge of Airstrip 2, arriving at 1755. They commenced to set up a defensive perimeter at once. Three/1 was following and Hankins was directed to proceed forward to the west and make contact with 2/5. So far, the Japanese defense had been desultory and the terrain was being taken at less cost than the Marines anticipated. That day's gains had cost one dead and two wounded Marines from the leading 1/1.

The next morning, 30 December, Marines who believed that the enemy had disappeared from the area found themselves the object of their serious attention. Japanese shells came dropping in on them as they assembled about the airstrips. The fire was coming from the foothills of Mt. Talawe, aptly named by the Marines "Razorback Ridge," which rose about 1,500 feet above the airfield. Trying to make contact with Barba and 1/5, a scouting patrol from Co. F, 2/5, which was in reserve back at the eastern edge of Airstrip 2, had run into a detachment of the enemy in its defense area and retired after an exchange of shots. Nonetheless, the fighting was just beginning. Japanese were on-site in company strength and it wasn't long before they enemy came charging down at them, screaming the usual epithets. Repulsed, they fled back to their holes but their mortars and a lone 75mm field piece continued shelling the Marines. Knocking out numerous bunkers, the Marines continued their attack until 1130, when fighting ceased.

Meanwhile, on the morning of 30 December, the "lost" 1/5 moved forward in a column of companies and promptly ran into a Japanese defensive position. Companies A and B were successful in a firefight but it cost them 6 dead and 12 wounded Marines. Arriving at the position between 3/1 and 2/5, the now-bloodied 1/5 took up positions at 1800. Generally speaking, the Marines had occupied all Japanese positions within the perimeter and Airfields 1 and 2 were both considered secured on 31 December 1943. Rupertus proudly sent the CG, 6th U.S. Army, Lt. Gen. Walter Krueger, a radio message: "First Marine Division presents to you an early New Year's gift the complete airdrome of Cape Gloucester."

Meanwhile, 2/1, which had landed on D-day at Green Beach, opposite the Cape Gloucester tip, was doing fine. Because of the rugged, jungle terrain, Battery H, 11th Marines, personnel had been unable to emplace its 75mm pack-howitzers, so they became infantry. On the morning of 30 December things changed. The enemy began their attack at 0155 under cover of extreme darkness and a tropical rainstorm at a place in Co. G's terrain to be known as "Coffin Corner."

Supported by mortar, machine-gun and small arms fire, the Japanese attack developed to a great intensity. Marine return fire then was followed by an assault by elements of Co. G and an improvised platoon from H/11. One of the latter, GySgt. Guiseppe Guilano, Jr., cradled a light machine gun in his arms, firing from the hips where most needed. He was a minor casualty when they taped his arms to heal the burns. He was rightly awarded a Navy Cross. At the approach of dawn the fire slackened and patrols found 89 enemy dead, six of whom were officers, and they brought in five prisoners. Marine losses were six killed and 17 wounded. A Japanese officer later wandered in and surrendered, after which he described his comrades as being from two companies of about 116 officers and men.

Brigadier General Lemuel C. Shepherd, ADC, spent the first two days ashore at the division command post. He soon received orders from the CG to strike southeast with Combat Team C, the 7th Marines, and clear the enemy from the Borgen Bay area. In the meantime, the 7th Marines defended the beachhead from continual attacks by the IJA's 2/53 and 2/141, which the Marines effectively put out of action. With that success, CT C, reinforced by 3/5, began preparing for the eastward shift. The important terrain to cover included Hill 660 lying close to Borgen Bay, 2,000 yards away.

Thrusting eastward on 2 January 1944 were 2/7 (Lt. Col. Odell M. Conoley, Silver Star) and 3/7 (Lt. Col. William R. Williams), supported by 3/5 (Lt. Col. David S. McDougal), all led by Brig. Gen. Lemuel C. Shepherd. In the meantime, on 3 January, 1/7 (Lt. Col. John E. Weber) repulsed an enemy attack upon Target Hill within the Yellow Beach defensive perimeter. The following day, 3/5 and 3/7 took out 2/53 defending Suicide Creek, thereby moving their lines another half mile outward. On 11 January 3/5, now led by Lt. Col. Lewis W. Walt (replacing two COs who had been WIA and the temporary replacement Col. Lewis B. Puller), with support by Marine artillery, assaulted and took Aogiri Ridge (later known as "Walt's Ridge"), which had been tenaciously defended by 2/53 and 2/141.

During this second phase, through 16 January, the Marines suffered their heaviest casualties. The taking of Hill 660 by 3/7 (Lt. Col. Henry W. Buse, Silver Star) on the 16th was what shattered that IJA defensive line. The hill dominated all else at the eastern end of Borgen Bay. The Marine tanks, which were in the advance of the infantry, were soon bogged down in the mud and had to be left behind. It was a tough climb up the steep hill, with weapons slung, and the enemy contested every foot. The hill was taken but the IJA tried a massive counterattack to retake what was now Marine property. That failed, and with it the entire Japanese defense of that part of New Britain. Essentially, the Marines had taken the airfields and Borgen Bay, and had won. During the next few months all action would be in other areas of the island. On 10 February operations in western New Britain was declared ended. Army and Marine patrols met at Gilnit on the Itni River, effectively ending any aggressive enemy action in western New Britain.

It became evident, however, that the only route that could be used by escaping IJA forces heading eastward would be along the northern part of the island. Therefore, several landings by Marines were made along that line to intercept and defeat any groups found. This went on for many weeks. On 23 February Lt. Gen. Yashushi Sakai received orders to get his 17th Division back to Rabaul. Most of his men began making tracks to join him at his headquarters but were still two weeks from Talasea on the Willaumez Peninsula.

The Marines had already formulated a plan to upset any effort to save the remnants and on 6 March the 5th Marines (Col. Oliver P. Smith), reinforced, landed at the Volupai Plantation on the west side of the Willaumez Peninsula. This was the narrowest part of the peninsula, only 2 miles wide, and in a few days they had crossed the neck and taken Garua Harbor, Talesea town and the Garua Island and plantation. Company K of 1/5 was down to the village of Garili by 11 March. The advance continued and in addition to cleaning up stragglers, the 5th Marines continued their move southward along the eastern side of the peninsula. They were at Kilu on 16 March and, after a fight with a contesting company from the IJA, continued their advance. Weeks of fighting by patrols was ended on 9 April when Marines caught Maj. Shinjuro Komori and three of his men in an ambush, killing three and wounding one. That effectively ended the 1st MarDiv.'s part in the New Britain campaign. On 11 April, after being relieved by units of the 185th Infantry, 40th Division, the Marines began their withdrawal from what was perceived as essentially a U.S. Army type of action, ill-suited for the amphibious-trained Marines. Marine losses have been calculated at 1,400 killed and wounded and the Japanese killed and wounded are estimated to have been at least 3,900.

As Heinl wrote, "The New Britain campaign ... was, for example, the only Marine amphibious operation in World War II not supported by naval or Marine aviation."

Results: As Maj. Gen. Rupertus told Lt. Gen. Krueger, "Happy New Year, the airfield is yours." They also made sure the Japanese would not be able to provide the new USA occupants with real difficulties. For all intents and purposes, the Japanese were driven from New Britain. The few remaining would only provide modest difficulties for the USA. Another well-done job by the 1st Marine Division in a terrain suitable only for mosquitoes.

Marshall Campaign

Date: 31 January to 24 February 1944.
Location: Marshall Islands, including Kwajalein Atoll, Majuro Atoll, and Eniwetok Atoll.
Involved: Japanese army and navy versus the 5th Amphibious Corps (VAC), including 4th MarDiv. (Maj. Gen. Harry Schmidt), 7th InfDiv. (Maj. Gen. Charles H. Corlett, USA), and attached troops.
Situation: Before World War I, the Marshall Islands had been German territory which Japan, as a member of the Allied nations, occupied in 1914. The "islands" were really small rocks jutting out of the ocean. They were usually classified as atolls, with just the westernmost part being of interest to the U.S. high command. The distance between each was considerable. It was about 250 miles between Majuro on the east to Kwajalein, located nearly in the center of the group. There were eight primary atolls with but two of interest, Kwajalein and, farthest west, Eniwetok. All ground operations were to be under the control of V Amphibious Corps (Maj. Gen. Holland McT. Smith).

The entire atoll consisted of about 85 islands extending 65 miles in length and 18 miles across, at its widest. Kwajalein Island, which lies at the far eastern southern tip, was to be the first attacked. That landing was to be effected by the venerable 7th InfDiv., a veteran of the Attu campaign and well-versed in amphibious landings as taught by the Marine Corps.

Forty miles almost directly north are the dual islands, Roi–Namur. That was the 4th MarDiv.'s target. The division was part of the Northern Landing Force (Maj. Gen. Harry Schmidt). This is the one we will concentrate upon. Roi on the left was 1,200 by 1,250 yards at its widest, Namur on the right was 800 by 900 yards. Roi had an airfield, one of the finest in that part of the Pacific. Namur was primarily covered with pillboxes and other man-made defensive structures. A decision had been made to land the 23rd Marines (Col. Louis Jones) on Roi and the 24th Marines (Col. Franklin A. Hart) on Namur. Both islands were well-defended and this first operation of the 4th MarDiv. would be quite costly in manpower.

Two days before D-day, the *Tennessee*, *Maryland*, and *Colorado*, along with five cruisers and 19 destroyers, shelled both islands nonstop for 24 hours. They were aided by aircraft

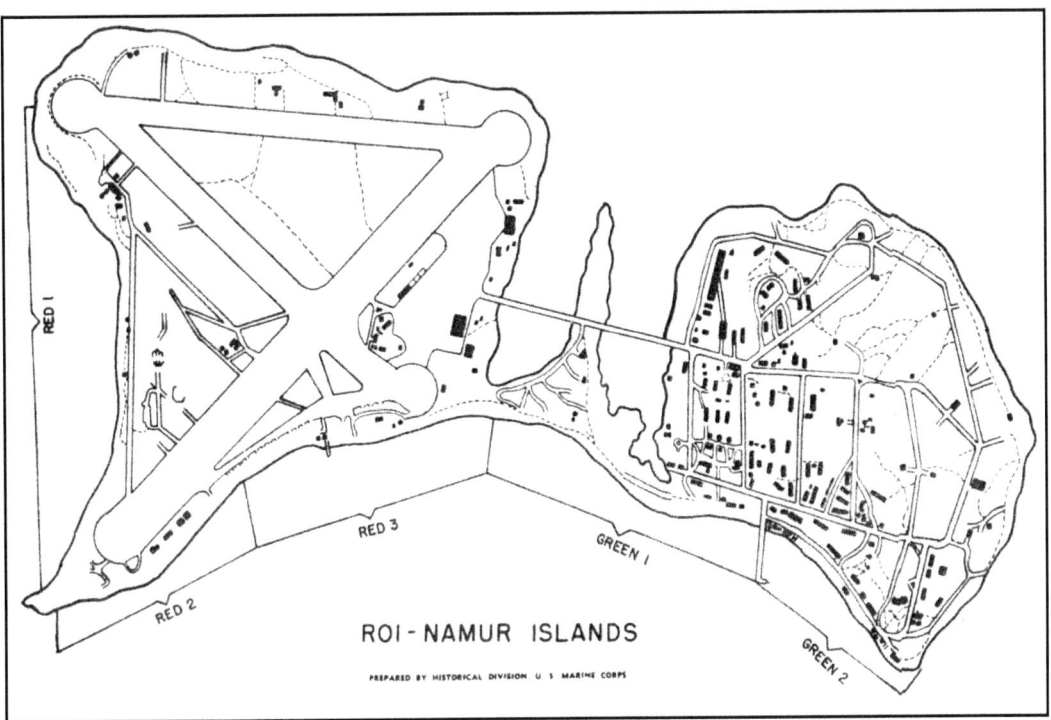

ROI - NAMUR ISLANDS

flying from the Fast Carrier Task Force, which continued to paste Roi and Namur as the landing boats were launched. It was also planned to take two smaller nearby islands to land most of the pack howitzers for ground operational support. The seizure of Ennuebing fell to the division's Scout Company. Mellu, somewhat larger and further away, was the target of 1/25 (Lt. Col. Clarence J. O'Donnell). Both were secured by noontime on D-day, 1 February 1944. Three other islands, lying on the opposite eastern string of the atoll, were taken when 2/25 (Lt. Col. Lewis C. Hudson, Jr.) and 3/25 (Lt. Col. Justis M. Chambers) landed on Ennugarret, Ennumennet, and Ennubrr. Phase two of the operation, the landing on Roi and Namur, from the lagoon side, was now ready for initiation.

H-hour was set at 1000, but the actual landing time was delayed until 1100 to enable the assault regiments to boat up. There were enough for the 23rd Marines (Col. Louis R. Jones) but of the required 110 amtracs only 62 were really available for the 24th (Col. Franklin A. Hart). Naval gunfire and aerial attack once again preceded the landing. The first landings began and the 23rd Marines found that most of the occupants of Roi had fled to Namur for protection. It seemed, at that time, to be too good to be true. Marines already landed proceeded without major mishap. One Marine of the 23rd, PFC Richard B. Anderson from Tacoma, WA, began to toss a live grenade but it slipped down into the shell hole and his buddies looked aghast. Without hesitation, Anderson flung his body on the grenade and absorbed the blast, saving the lives of his comrades. His selfless act brought him a posthumous Medal of Honor.

In barely more than a quarter of an hour the original Phase-line 1 was reached. When Col. Jones had the good news relayed back to Maj. Gen. Schmidt, he ordered the regiment to halt and reorganize. During the intervening time, two tanks and two supporting companies had moved forward and had to be recalled.

Franklin Hart's 24th Marines going onto Namur did not have life quite as easy. The strongest defenses were already established on that island and the heavy vegetation provided splendid cover. Lieutenant Colonel Francis H. Brink's 2/24 had landed on Green Beach 2, the right, and then managed to move forward at least 200 yards. Lieutenant Colonel Austin B. Brunelli's (Silver Star) 3/24 was to their left and had one hell of a time. The fire from undamaged pillboxes hit many Marines and effectively slowed down the battalion. It wasn't until 1400 that the main body reached Phase-line 1. At that point they awaited the arrival of tanks to soften up the defenses.

On the right 2/24 ran into what has been remembered vividly by many veterans of that campaign, both Navy and Marines.[24] Marines had arrived at a large blockhouse which, unbeknownst to them, housed torpedoes and aerial bombs. Something caused the explosion which set off an enormous cloud and killed some Marines and concussed others as they fell to the ground. Metal fragments and concrete caught many before they were under cover. One officer described the scene as "an ink blackness spread over the island so that the hand could not be seen in front of the face." Debris continued to fall, including much steel and concrete, and many Marines without protection also fell. Those in nearby boats also suffered from flying debris. During the following half-hour two more explosions went off and expanded the list of casualties. That battalion suffered more than half its total island casualties at this time.

With tanks in support, 3/24 began to push ahead at 1630. A reserve officer from Worcester, MA, 1st Lt. John V. Power, was badly wounded in the stomach while engaged in knocking out pillboxes. To everyone's amazement, Power held his wound with one hand and charged forward, emptying his carbine into the narrow slot on one door. His effort doomed the occupants because his platoon continued his work and finished off the pillbox while others pulled Power to a shell hole, where he died a few moments later. He was awarded a posthumous Medal of Honor.

A tank commanded by Capt. James L. Denig (Silver Star) was the victim of five Japanese, one of whom tossed a grenade through an aperture which set off a gasoline fire when it exploded. BAR man Cpl. Howard E. Smith bravely ran onto the tank, pulled Denig out, then hauled out Cpl. Bill Taylor and finally Cpl. Ben Smith, dragging all to relative safety. Smith unsuccessfully tried to reach an already dead fourth man. He was awarded a Navy Cross for his courage.

Sergeant Frank A. Tucker, using "Kentucky windage," pulled a Sgt. York on a trench full of Japanese soldiers, about 75 in all. Getting into a position looking directly down the trench, he killed 38 of the enemy. His helmet, canteen and binoculars each took a bullet but he had no scratches himself. His reward was a Navy Cross. This island battle was a series of individual fights, with many heroes.

At 1700 Brink's 2/24 began moving again, but found the going difficult in the well-defended, very extensive rubble. After moving about 300 yards the battalion called it a night. Whereas 3/24 was within a couple of hundred yards of the northern shore, but found it had to angle its right flank back to connect with 2/24.

The 23rd Marines on Roi, though moving rapidly ahead, found many Japanese popping up behind them. Though the Japanese position was hopeless, no one had told them and with those tactics they continued to cause heavy Marine casualties. Nonetheless, flamethrowers and demolitions men managed to make it more than obvious that they were finished. As a result the suicidal enemy began blowing themselves up with their own grenades. At 1800, just six hours after landing, the island of Roi was declared secured.

Yet a few Japanese nestled against the northern shore planned and executed a banzai attack against 3/24. Companies I and L received the brunt and the Marines' line was compelled to fall back a short distance to a more secure position. Pharmacist's Mate Second Class James V. Kirby of Pontiac, MI, along with numerous wounded Marines he had gathered together, were caught between the lines. That night he and his charges sat out the fighting going on all around them and as the Marines came forward again, additional wounded men were dragged into his hole for care. One of those men was a private from Anoka, MN, Richard K. Sorenson, who had sat on a Japanese grenade to protect his fellow Marines. Kirby managed to make his way to Sorenson and was able to stop the bleeding and save Sorenson's life by tying up a severed artery. The former was awarded a Bronze Star and Sorenson was the recipient of a Medal of Honor.

Lieutenant Colonel Aquilla J. Dyess and 1/24 were still in support as the day ended. On the morning of 2 February they and the remnants of 2/24 were given the task of cleaning up the enemy remnants on Namur. Placing himself between the enemy and his battalion to point out objectives and avenues of approach, Dyess led a charge against the defending force. Concentrated enemy machine-gun fire eventually brought him down as he was standing upon a parapet of an anti-tank gun site. He was posthumously awarded a Medal of Honor.

Marines continued going forward, sweeping northward so effectively that they were able to declare Namur secured by 1215 of 2 February 1944. In two days a brand-new, untried Marine division had overwhelmed a well-fortified island, occupied for many years. Like many Marines in World War II, they were officially listed as reserves, yet they would always be in the forefront of Marine assaults in the Pacific War.

The 20th Marines (Engineers), commanded by Col. Lucius W. Burnham, arrived and began the massive job of restoring the islands, especially the airfield. Also landing was the 15th Def. Bn. (Lt. Col. Francis B. Loomis, Jr.), which was to take up the task of clearing up the die-hard Japanese who hadn't already died, and to remain to protect the island against further Japanese attacks.

Meanwhile, in the south the praiseworthy 7th InfDiv. had landed on Kawajalein Island and by 1330 on 4 February that island was also secured. That division then continued to take various smaller islands within the atoll until finalization of their campaign on 7 February.

Next was the operation at Eniwetok Atoll, in which Tactical Group 1, including the 22nd Marines (Col. John Walker, Navy Cross), till then held in reserve, and two battalions of the 106th U.S. Infantry grouped under the command of Brig. Gen. Thomas E. Watson were involved. They were to take three principal islands: Engebi, Eniwetok, and Parry. Engebi, considered the strongest held, was for the 22nd Marines, and the 106th Infantry was to take the other two. Afterward the 10th Def. Bn. (Lt. Col. Wallace O. Thompson) would then take over those islands. For both major units, the 22nd and 106th, this would be their first combat enterprise. Watson had 10,376 officers and men, of which 5,820 were Marines.

On 17 February the Navy and AAF planes began bombing the islands, then VAC Reconnaissance Company was landed on two unoccupied islands off Engebi. With that protection Army and Marine light artillery went in and began shelling Engebi, even after dark, making life unpleasant for the 1,200 Japanese defenders. The next morning the 22nd Marines, supported by medium tanks from the 2nd Separate Tank Co. (Capt. Harry Calcutt), were landed on Engebi's lagoon shore by the USA 708th Amphibian Tank Bn. The two battalions of Marines (1/22 and 2/22) landed and went directly across the island; by

1450 the island was declared secure. Nevertheless, a great deal of clean-up was necessary afterward, even into the wee hours.

With about 2,200 enemy on Eniwetok and Parry, the 106th's two battalions, supported by 3/22, had a tough time. They landed on 19 February and the contest was decidedly difficult. According to a Marine Corps "official history," 3/22 bore the heaviest fighting. Watson was displeased at the "slowness" of the operation on Eniwetok Island and decided to instead send in the 22nd Marines on Parry Island. Pack Howitzers were landed on a small island north of Parry and began bombarding the latter. In order to give the combat-weary 22nd a reserve, Watson had a 500-man infantry force developed from the 10th Def. Bn.

At 0900 on 22 February, the 22nd Marines landed on Parry. Though the fighting was tough, the Marines went straight through and by evening all but a 400-yard tip of Parry had been taken. That tip was taken next morning and the island was really secure. The entire operation cost the Marines and Army 254 dead and 555 wounded. Within a few days the 22nd Marines were on their way to join the rest of the 4th MarDiv. back "home" on Maui Island.

Marine air in the Marshall campaign included the 4th MAW (deployed as 4th Marine Base Defense Aircraft Wing, re-designated on 10 November 1944) and subunits included MAG-13, -15, -21, -22, and -31; VMF 111, 113, 224, 311, 441, and 442; VMSB (Torpedo) 151 and 155; VMSB 231 and 245; VMFN (Night Fighters) 532, 534, and 541; VMB 613; and Air Warning Squadron 1.

> *Results:* The assault on the Marshalls proved that the U.S. Navy and Marine Corps had well learned its lessons at Tarawa. This operation was professional in every aspect and the modest personnel losses suffered, in comparison, by the Marines and Army showed how much had been learned. These islands had been held by Japan for about 30 years and had been well-prepared for defense. Obviously, the heavy USN bombardment that slammed them had not been given serious thought in their pre-planning stage. And, like most of the other islands defended in the Pacific, the Japanese had anticipated an easier time destroying a landing force before it could successfully conquer.

Saipan

> *Date:* 15 June 1944 to 1 August 1944.
> *Location:* Saipan Island, northernmost in the Marianas Group.
> *Involved:* Japanese army and navy versus the U.S. Marines, Army, and Navy.
> *Situation:* Saipan lay less than 1,500 miles south of Japan proper and taking it would place B-29s within bombing range. All the islands of the Mariana chain, except Guam, had been in Japanese possession for many years and taking them would prove costly. There were an estimated 30,000 Japanese soldiers on Saipan, of which a third were Special Naval Landing Force (Marines). As all Marines were well aware, they would tenaciously fight to the death, taking many Americans with them. Additionally, the perils to health were many. In the sea were sharks and barracudas. There were reefs, razor-sharp coral, sea snakes and giant clams which could grab a man in their

"jaws." Ashore, presuming the Marines would bypass all the other hazards, would be snakes, giant lizards, dysentery, dengue fever, typhus, leprosy, filariasis, and typhoid. In other words, who wanted it anyway? The U.S. Army Air Force, that's who.

In the planning stages for the forthcoming attack upon the Mariana Islands, Saipan was selected to be the first target and Tinian the second. In addition to the 2nd MarDiv. (Maj. Gen. Thomas E. Watson), the 4th MarDiv. (Maj. Gen. Harry Schmidt) and the U.S. Army's 27th Infantry Division (Maj. Gen. Ralph C. Smith) would tackle this large, well-populated, well-defended island. In addition, the high command was well aware that the landing might be very punishing. So the 3rd MarDiv. (Maj. Gen. Allen H. Turnage), included in the planned landing on Guam, waited offshore for a stretch of days until its was obvious his men wouldn't be needed on Saipan. This entire divisional group formed V Amphibious Corps (VAC), led by Lt. Gen. Holland McT. Smith.

Saipan had thousands of civilians, many of whom were native Japanese, and numerous roads, schools, caves, and mountains. It probably wouldn't be as terrible as Tarawa, but it would not be easy.

On 11 June the entire Task Force 56, led by VA Richmond Kelly Turner, would set sail from Eniwetok for its target, Saipan. It and VA Marc Mitscher's Task Force 58 would arrive at Saipan for the invasion on D-day, 15 June. On that date, at 0542, six battleships and cruisers of the fleet opened fire with their big guns. The firing continued until the first amtracs made the beaches at 0843. Both Marine divisions went in on the western beaches, south of the large town of Garapan. The 2nd MarDiv. landed on the left, on Red and Green Beaches and the 4th MarDiv. to their right landed on Blue and Yellow Beaches. The 27th InfDiv. remained aboard ships as the support group for the Marines.

Both divisions were quickly engaged in heavy fighting. As usual, the operational plan had broken the advance up the island into daily objectives, O-1, 2, 3, and so forth. Anticipating the worst, Holland Smith made the decision to not wait long before committing his reserve, the 27th InfDiv., except for the 106th Infantry (Col. Russell C. Ayres), which would remain aboard ships as Corps reserve. It too would be made available for immediate commitment if, as expected, it would be necessary.

The 2nd MarDiv. landed two battalions of two regiments abreast, on the far left was 2/6 (Lt. Col. Raymond L. Murray, Navy Cross, wounded that day), and the 3/6 (Lt. Col. John W. Easley, wounded that day) was on the right, both on Red Beach. To their right on Green Beach 1 was 3/8 (Lt. Col. John C. Miller, wounded that day) and then 2/8 (Lt. Col. Henry P. Crowe, also wounded that day). For some reason both latter battalions landed on the same beach. Officially it was caused because the currents were very strong and it was expected that the boats would move to the left as they went in. The enemy's anti-boat gun positions lining that beach, undoubtedly also helped the navy coxswains to make their decision where to land.

The 8th Marines (Col. Clarence H. Wallace) had a tough fight securing its beach, as did the 6th (Col. James P. Riseley). In fact, as soon as it could organize ashore, 2/8 began a move southwards toward Afetna Point. The 2nd Marines (Col. Walter J. Stuart) landed later as support for the 6th.

The 4th MarDiv. landed on the southwest coast, from the town of Charon Kanoa down to Agingan Point. Order of battle for the 4th MarDiv. was 2/23 (Lt. Col. Edward J. Dillon) and 3/23 (Lt. Col. John J. Cosgrove) landing on Blue Beaches 1 and 2; on Yellow Beaches 1 and 2 were 1/25 (Lt. Col. Hollis U. Mustain) and 2/25 (Lt. Col. Lewis C. Hudson, Jr.). Meanwhile, Col. Franklin Hart's 24th Marines would stage a diversionary demonstration north of Garapan, then revert to division reserve.

The 4th MarDiv. was ably supported by the U.S. Army's 534th and 773rd Amphibian Tractor Bns., which placed 4,000 Marines ashore within 20 minutes. Another good unit, the U.S. Army's 708th Armored Amphibian Tractor Bn., with 75mm guns aboard, pounded the enemy-fortified ridgeline running about a mile inland. When the Marines landed they came under intense artillery and mortar fire from weapons well placed. It had been planned that the armored vehicles would continue to carry their human cargo to the ridgeline, but due to organizational and communication error, they stopped at the beach and there unloaded their cargo.

The plan to drive inland and take Mount Fina Susa only partially succeeded. Vehicles pushed ahead but over swampy ground, and the attendant enemy gunfire made their travail much worse than had been expected. Located to their direct front, Susupe Swamp hurt the 23rd Marines badly, slowing down all their movements and leaving them stuck on the artillery-targeted beach. A mortar platoon of 3/23 did move forward and set up near Mt. Fina Susa. With good observation plus concentrated fire, they gave the Japanese artillery and mortars on the mountain almost as good as they were taking. Late that afternoon the Marines were ordered to retire but the mortar men stayed behind to cover their withdrawal. When it was their turn to fall back their tubes were too hot to handle; no vehicles were nearby to assist, so they had to leave their guns behind.

Lieutenant Colonel Ralph Haas and 1/23 had landed behind 3/23 and that night occupied the town of Charan Kanoa, which was a constant target of Japanese artillery fire all through the night. The Marine casualties mounted as the town was being destroyed around them. So too was the pier which the Marines anticipated utilizing for unloading incoming supplies. The enemy use of artillery was frightfully effective and it soon became apparent that, contrary to previous experience, the Japanese were trying to defeat the Americans on the beach. That night at 2000 the enemy launched a serious counterattack where the two Marine divisions joined. They generally drove quite deep into the 2nd MarDiv.'s lines before concerted action stopped and threw them back.

Holland Smith quickly recognized that this was going to be another long and costly battle. Therefore, on D-day plus one, 16 June, the 27th InfDiv. was landed, but continued in Corps reserve, with the 165th Infantry landing on the right flank of the 4th MarDiv. This was so it would be in position to move southward with the 4th MarDiv. on the 17th to clean up the enemy that were expected to retreat in that direction.

By the end of the second day the beachhead was well-controlled. The 2nd and 4th MarDivs. had gained a depth of 1,500 yards with a frontage of 10,000 yards. It was tough going, but they were there to stay. That night, 16-17 June, the Japanese launched a night attack once again against the 2nd MarDiv., supported by three or more companies of tanks. The 2nd and 6th Marines were ready for them. Both regiments bore the brunt of the assault but 1/6 (Lt. Col. William K. Jones, Navy Cross) was most affected. The attack was stalled by 0700 on the 17th, primarily from fire by five heavy tanks from Company B, 2nd Tank Battalion (Maj. Charles W. McCoy). They had broken the back of the enemy armor, setting 30 enemy tanks ablaze or scattering them about the area.

The 2nd Division made plans to attack on the morning of the 17th, following a 90-

minute artillery and naval gunfire preparation. The 6th Marines were on the left and the 8th Marines on their right. The 2nd Marines would constitute their support. However, Gen. Holland Smith, at Northern Troops and Landing Force (NTLF), decided to alter the plans for 2nd MarDiv.'s advance. Poor communication resulted in the divisions' regiments moving forward at 0730 as originally planned. The fact that the 6th Marines, plus the attached 2/2 (Lt. Col. Richard C. Nutting, Silver Star), were able to advance as scheduled, just one hour after stopping the Japanese attack, was a tribute to excellent training. The CO of 1/8, Lt. Col. Lawrence C. Hays, Jr., with Lt. Col. Guy E. Tannyhill's 1/29, division reserve (but attached to the 8th Marines), had a more difficult time of it. Before them lay the marshy area surrounding Lake Susupe, and while the men were sinking waist deep in the muck the area was replete with enemy snipers. Tannyhill and his men were up against a hill containing a series of enemy defensive positions. South of that, directly on the 29th's right flank, lay a coconut grove infested with Japanese. By mid-afternoon no advance had been made and they were stymied. Tannyhill had been wounded, and up came Lt. Col. Rathvon M. Tompkins as his replacement. He soon spotted four Marine tanks of McCoy's battalion and began to direct them. With this base of fire, 1/29 was soon up and at em' once again. They quickly pushed to the top of the hill and after a quick mop-up, dug in for the night. Tompkins would pick up a Navy Cross for this day's work.

Stuart's 2nd Marines advanced in a column of battalions, regulating its advance on the 6th Marines to its right. By 1800 3/2 reached just a thousand yards south of Garapan's outskirts. There it dug in. All day the 1st (Col. Presley M. Rixey), 2nd (Lt. Col. George H. E. Shell), and 4th Bns. (Lt. Col. Kenneth A. Jorgensen) of the 10th Artillery had been supporting the three Marine regiments. VAC's 2nd Howitzer Bn. (Lt. Col. Marvin H. Floom) commenced landing its 155s at 1500, but was detached from the 2nd MarDiv. with orders to support the 4th MarDiv.

As with so many islands in the Pacific, Japanese military had the advantages of 30 years of ownership (since 1914), the best terrain (the ridgeline), scores of well-prepared caves and dugouts, and many heavy weapons already pre-targeted. The 14th Marine Artillery (Col. Louis G. DeHaven), with 15 batteries of 75mm pack howitzers, were ashore but the enemy's accuracy immediately knocked out four batteries, creating havoc amongst the others. Accurate enemy mortar fire in the south had slowed 1/25 to just 700 yards' advancement. The bombardment on Charan Kanoa and the beaches continued all day and casualties mounted. During the 16th, PlSgt Robert H. McCard, tank commander of Company A, 4th Tank Battalion, found himself nearly out of business when enemy 77mms put his tank down. Placing all the tank's weapons upon the Japanese, they continued the unequal fight until McCard finally ordered his crew to use the escape hatch. Meanwhile, this Syracuse, NY, native exposed himself by hurling grenades at the enemy to cover the escape of his men. Seriously wounded and out of grenades, McCard then dismantled a machine gun and delivered a vigorous fire into their positions, demolishing 16 of the enemy. He was finally overcome by his wounds and gallantly gave his life for his country. Posthumously he was awarded a Medal of Honor. At the end of the day one company of the 25th Marines (Col. Merton J. Batchelder) was down to just 13 men, while overall the total casualties ashore were about 2,000 Marines.

Before dawn on the 17th, two battalions of the 165th Infantry (Col. Gerard W. Kelley) landed and moved into line to support the drive on Aslito Airfield and by mid-morning 3/165 was also safely ashore. That day word came that the enemy fleet was heading for Saipan and as a consequence, the U.S. warships congregated and headed out to intercept them. Supply ships scattered; just when the ammo and food was most necessary, it was gone. At the end of the day the 165th Inf. was close to Aslito Airfield.

On the night of 17-18 June small groups of Japanese soldiers, usually no more than a squad, probed the lines to locate a spot to penetrate, especially along the 2nd MarDiv. front. It was raining and observation was poor. At midnight the enemy launched an attack where the 6th and 8th Marines joined. Though they made a small impression, they were soon driven out and the lines were restored. At 0430, the Japanese tried to go the Marines one better. They were going to attempt an amphibious landing behind the 2nd MarDiv.'s line, but they were spotted just north of Garapan and 4/10 opened up on them. Additionally, the remaining U.S. vessels in that area around Mutcho Point also saw the 35 or so enemy barges and blasted them, doing the most damage. At least 13 of the barges, and their passengers, were destroyed, ending any chance of a successful landing.

Mount Tapochau, lying in the center of the island, was by far the best location for observation, but it was still held by the enemy. By 18 June the hard-driving 25th Marines had managed to get to a point where they could see Magicienne Bay on the east coast. Counter-battery fire, air support, and the digging out of so many enemy artillery positions by the grunts had well-nigh eliminated that vicious weapon. The Japanese had no air or sea support, and most if not all of their inadequate tanks had already been disposed of. In other words, the enemy was still playing the game but on nerve only. The Americans had cut the island and taken most of the southern portion. They were now in a position to turn northward and take the balance of it.

On the 18th at about 1000 the 165th Infantry took Aslito Air Field and on 22 June the airfield would become operational for fighter aircraft. That day the NTLF issued orders for the three divisions to launch an attack. The Marines to go at 1000 and the 27th at 1200. The 2nd MarDiv. was the pivot of the entire line and since it was a bit farther forward than its cohorts it moved very little on the 18th. The 4th MarDiv. made up for the lack of activity in the 2nd MarDiv. with both the 24th and 25th Marines making headway, though the 23rd Marines met great opposition.

The night of 18-19 June was relatively quiet. The NTLF Operational Order for 19 June instructed the three divisions to "complete missions assigned." Progress beyond Aslito Airfield was good but the 27th InfDiv. was having more difficulty advancing as the enemy reduced their lines and concentrated their firepower. It would be many more days before the entire Nafutan Point was taken. Meanwhile in the northeast, the 4th MarDiv.'s progress up Magicienne Bay ground to a halt on the 19th. Lieutenant Colonel John J. Cosgrove was wounded on the 19th while directing 3/23 in its attack and he too was awarded a Navy Cross. His replacement was his executive officer, Maj. Paul S. Treitel.

Lieutenant Colonel Justice Chambers' 3/25 made the attack with a company commanded by Capt. James Headley leading. They ran into a nest of six machine guns that tore into the company and wounded Headley twice, though not seriously. Of his 100 Marines, 51 became casualties, and it was all they could do to withdraw to safety, eventually getting back down the hill. Throughout the day the Marines of the 25th also suffered intensely from artillery fire.

The next morning, 20 June, Chambers, nicknamed "Jumping Joe," personally directed another assault by Headley and his men. Up the hill they went, in a "Hell-bent-for-leather" charge. The enemy machine guns were knocked out by grenades, the flamethrowers burned Japanese in caves, and bayonets caught those trying to escape. After an hour and a half, Headley and company took Hill 500. In the meantime, Chambers, with a concussion from an exploded land mine, was taken unconscious to a field hospital. But he'd be back and would really do his stuff on Iwo Jima.

Captain Headley, from Cincinnati, OH, would be awarded a Navy Cross for his consistent courage and leadership while at Saipan. He would also pick up an Oak Leaf Cluster in lieu of a second Navy Cross on Iwo Jima. That was the kind of men who were leading Marines in the Pacific War.

The 2nd MarDiv. advanced quite a way up the island, with the 2nd, 6th, and 8th Marines in line, left to right. By the end of the day the two Marine divisions were facing northward. Before them, 2,000-plus yards for the 6th and 8th Marines, lay the highest point on the island, Mt. Tapotchau, 1,554 feet high and lying at about the geometric center of the island.

Although the 6th Marines actually took the mountain, it was a recon patrol by the 25th Marines that made it possible. Sergeant Major Gilbert L. Morton of the 25th Marines led it and reached the top on 22 June. That was almost the easy part. When they reached the summit all of a sudden they found they were surrounded by the enemy. After digging in and creating a modest defensive position, they beat off continual attacks. Morton, of New Orleans, LA, planned to withdraw under cover of darkness, however, there were too many wounded so he and his men decided to stick it out. All night the Japanese came for them but each time were beaten back. Morton managed to personally strangle two of them himself. In the morning another patrol came to their rescue, but only five Marines were still alive. Gilbert L. Morton was one of the living and was awarded a Navy Cross for his courage and leadership.

On 22 June, as the island widened eastward, the 27th was called up to fill the center and advance between the 2nd and 4th. It was imagined, at the time, that because the 27th was relatively inexperienced, being supported on both wings by divisions already bloodied would furnish them an easier time. The conception was to have all three divisions abreast, and then to move forward up the island at the same time, leaving no enemies in their rear areas. Unfortunately, the best-laid plans often go awry.

On the 23rd the 105th Infantry had still not completed the capture of Nafutan Point, while both the 106th and 165th Infantry Regiments had managed to get themselves entangled and made very slow progress to their assigned positions in the center.

When the 106th and 165th made it to their positions they advanced, but began having great difficulty taking on the hills lying before them, quickly assigning them nicknames such as "Purple Heart Ridge" and "Death Valley." This book isn't the place to describe their difficulties or the controversy between Lt. Gen. Smith and Maj. Gen. Smith. Sufficient to state, the two Marine divisions advanced while the 27th did not. Obviously, both Marine divisions were strung out and on their inner flanks were hurt quite badly by those Japanese that had not been pushed back by the 27th. After some communication, Smith relieved Smith and in so doing, created a firestorm. It is an entire story in and of itself. Ralph Smith was replaced in command of the 27th InfDiv. by the designated island commander, Maj. Gen. Sanderford Jarman, USA.

Meanwhile, the 2nd MarDiv., with the line-up as before — 2nd Marines left and 8th Marines right with the 6th in the middle — continued to advance. Though it was now mostly rubble, the 2nd had the fair-size town of Garapan lying before them. Flametree Hill, to the town's right, provided the 2nd Marines with enough difficulty to satisfy them on 24 June. The going would become more stressful and for the next few days the American advance slowed way down. However, the 4th MarDiv. branched out to the east and was headed forward, successfully taking the entire Kagman Peninsula.

The 8th Marines and 1/29 completed the capture of Mt. Tapotchau on 25 June, a major event since the promontory oversaw all of Saipan. On that date Private First Class Harold G. Epperson of Akron, Ohio, a machine gunner with 1/6, fought his post fiercely, with his emplacement receiving the full blast of the enemy attack. He is credited with successfully breaking up several attacks. A grenade fell in his hole and he, without hesitation, leaped upon it and absorbed the full blast with his body. He was a posthumous recipient of a Medal of Honor.

In the meantime, the Japanese CG sent messages to Gen. Iketa, then located on the island of Yap, that he had only about 1,100 soldiers with no artillery and but three tanks. He also added, "there is no hope for victory." The 47th Independent Mixed Brigade was commanded by a 1st lieutenant and the 70 members of the 7th Independent Engineers by a sergeant. American estimates of their troop strength were somewhat higher, but without the proof the Japanese had. Regardless of their depleted condition, they were doing their best to slow up the Americans.

On the night of 26-27 June, the remnants of the Japanese still holding Nafutan Point broke out and made a dash for Aslito Airfield and Hill 500. Upon arrival they raised hell. Nevertheless, the Japanese found the 25th Marines, a NTLF reserve unit atop Hill 500 and when the Marines recuperated from their surprise they went to work. By morning the 25th mopped up and counted about 500 enemy dead, some in American uniforms with M-1 rifles. In the north the 27th InfDiv. was now making good progress under its new commander.

The NTLF orders issued on 27 June called for a general advance by all three divisions. But it would be 30 June before some units of the 4th MarDiv. would approach that line. Fighting south of Garapan and Flametree Hill was still difficult for the 2nd MarDiv. It did, however, manage to take the site lying before the 8th Marines known as the "Four Pimples."

It was now two weeks into the campaign and all troops were exhausted. Fortunately, the night of 29-30 June was relatively quiet, which gave everyone a little bit of rest. The 2nd Marines, as the entire American line's left pivot, had been patrolling and pushing at Garapan; the 6th Marines had pushed north to come alongside; the 8th Marines had a tough row to hoe at Mt. Tapotchau but managed to come down on the north side and join the line. The 27th InfDiv. was doing well in the middle and the 4th MarDiv. had cleaned up the Kagman Peninsula and was in line in advance of the others. The entire American force was located at Objective 6, with the greatest part of the island conquered.

From 2 to 4 July the entire line moved forward and swung over toward Tanapag Harbor, at Flores Point, and the 2nd Marines took Garapan. The 4th MarDiv.'s 24th and 25th Marines were farther advanced in the north than the other two divisions and spent two days taking two hills, Hill 721 and 767, calling the latter "Fourth of July Hill."

As the days passed, the Japanese on the island began to force the island's civilians to jump off cliffs before the advancing Americans. Nonetheless, the advance continued and Marines earned awards. Private First Class Harold C. Agerholm, of the 4th Battalion, 10th Marines, from Racine, Wisconsin, was awarded a Medal of Honor on 7 July when he helped stem an enemy attack against the regiment and then made numerous personal efforts to retrieve wounded Marines. The enemy ran right into the 10th Artillery's lines, forcing many of the gunners back. They pulled out the firing locks of their guns and fought as infantry as they fell back. Agerholm evacuated approximately 45 casualties before an enemy sniper nailed him. He was awarded a posthumous Medal of Honor.

The following day, on 8 July, a 2/6 tank commander, Sgt. Grant F. Timmerman, a native of Americus, Kansas, who was way out front, used his body to block a grenade from going into his tank. He paid the extreme price for his valor and was another posthumous Medal of Honor awardee. The enemy launched several more banzai attacks on 8 July but mostly against the 4th MarDiv. positions.

The 9th of July would be the final day of this long, grueling campaign. The 4th MarDiv., with the 2nd Marines attached, reached Marpi Point, the farthest northern point on the island, killing most of the surviving Japanese soldiers. Although Saipan Island was declared secured at 1615 on that day, mopping up continued and so did casualties.

For all intents, the war on Saipan was over but had cost the three American divisions 3,225 killed, 13,061 wounded, and 326 missing. The enemy losses totaled a known 23,811 dead with 1,810 captured. Radio Tokyo proclaimed a national week of mourning for the loss of Saipan.

Marine air in the fight for this island was, as Bob Sherrod noted, "lukewarm." Most support came from carrier aircraft. Marine Observation Squadron 4 launched from the USS *Fanshaw Bay* supported the 4th MarDiv. The following supported Marines ashore: Assault Air Warning Squadron 5; Marine Utility Squadron 252, 353, and 952; VMF 114; and VMF (N) 532.[25]

All three divisions would remain on Saipan, relatively undisturbed until the 4th MarDiv. landed on Tinian Island on 24 July which was followed the next day by the 2nd MarDiv. The 27th InfDiv. would remain on Saipan.

Results: This, the first of the islands in the Mariana chain, would be the most difficult to take, but it provided the USN and USAAF a base within 1,500 miles of the main islands of Japan. Thus the war with Japan drew closer and closer to the end.

On 24 June a B-29 airbase was begun and on 24 November 100 planes left to bomb Tokyo, the first attack since Lt. Col. Jimmie Doolittle's daring raid in 1942.

Tinian

Date: 14 July to 10 August 1944.
Location: The island of Tinian, part of the Marianas, which also included Saipan, Aguijan, Rota, and Guam.
Involved: Japanese army, navy troops versus U.S. Marines (2nd and 4th MarDivs.) and Navy.
Situation: The U.S. forces had taken the island of Saipan and were determined to also have custody of Tinian, just three nautical miles south of Saipan, and, of course, eventually to recover Guam. The primary reason for the selection of Tinian, other than the fact that it lay close to Saipan, was the need of the U.S. Army Air Force for its fine airfields. Aguijan Island was very small and not much consideration was given to taking it, and after Guam, Rota would be isolated and unavailable to Japan.

As the official USMC comment made it, the invasion force "went over beaches which the Japanese had regarded as impassable for a major landing—and, in fact, mostly over the very beach at which the enemy utterly scoffed."[26]

From a slew of captured documents, the Americans were able to quickly piece together the layout of Tinian, the order of battle, fortifications, the layout of dumps, and the plan for defense. Essentially, this would be a shore-to-shore operation, utilizing small landing craft, with LSTs the principal mode of transportation. Reconnaissance patrols were sent over from Saipan in rubber boats to look around and U.S. forces were well-prepared as to what to expect. It would also be entirely a U.S. Marine operation, with the 27th InfDiv. assuming occupation duty on Saipan.

Beginning on 11 June, Task Force 58 began a systematic destruction of anything above ground useful to the defenders. A rubber boat landing by the VAC Recon Battalion on the night of 10-11 July discovered that proposed landing beaches, White 1 and 2, were lightly defended and that the rough coral at Beach 2, not more than 6 to 10 feet high, could be easily surmounted by troops. The highest point on the island was Mt. Lasso at a mere 540 feet at its peak. Elsewhere, Tinian was relatively flat with cane fields. It was decided that Regimental Combat Team (RCT) 24 (Col. Franklin A. Hart) would go ashore, in a column of battalions, on White Beach 1. RCT 25 (Col. Merton A. Batchelder) would land to their south by a few hundred yards. RCT 23 (Col. Louis H. Jones, Navy Cross) would be briefly in division reserve and not land until later, the same for the 14th Marines (Col. Louis G. DeHaven). The latter had 4 battalions of 75mm howitzers loaded in DUKWs also for a Jig-Day landing. The 2nd MarDiv. (Maj. Gen. Thomas E. Watson) was to create a diversion off Tinian Town (see 2nd MarDiv. for details).

Since 20 June artillerymen on southern Saipan had been hammering Tinian. Corps artillery fired 155 missions on 23 July and on Jig-Day Brig. Gen. Arthur M. Harper, USA, XXIV Corps Artillery CG, had 13 battalions fire a massive attack upon all known installations and approaches to White Beaches on northern Tinian.

Jig-Day (hereinafter J-Day), 24 July 1944, and H-hour at 0740, was entirely a 4th MarDiv. (Maj. Gen. Clifford B. Cates) show. The 24th Marines struck at Ushi Point, across a narrow beach, and immediately took the airfield. The 25th Marines moved onto White Beach 2 and fanned out. However, because of botched orders and equipment malfunction, 2/25 (Lt. Col. Lewis C. Hudson, Jr.), right flank of the 4th MarDiv., had great difficulty moving ashore. Landing abreast to their left was 3/25 (Lt. Col. Justice M. Chambers) and abreast of them was 2/24 (Maj. Frank E. Garretson). On White Beach 1, 2/24 was especially plagued by the enemy and at 1515, Maj. Gen. Harry Schmidt, who had replaced Holland Smith in command of NTLF, ordered a battalion of the 8th Marines ashore to assist. He wanted them ashore at 1600 but because of "transport confusion" the landing was hampered until 2000, when the battalion, 1/8, (Lt. Col. Lawrence C. Hays) logged itself as "dug in in assigned position." The balance of the 2nd MarDiv. was still floating offshore.

Meanwhile, the 23rd Marines landed at noon and during the intervening time moved supplies inland to create dumps. Tanks, half-tracks and other vehicles were unloaded. The 4th MarDiv.'s landing party CO, Lt. Col. Nelson K. Brown, aided by group beachmaster, Lt. Samuel C. Boardman, USN, was instrumental in solving any problems that day. Other than 2/25's problems, everything else on the first day was going extremely well for the 4th MarDiv. All batteries of the 14th Marines were ashore, as were the attached (2nd MarDiv.) 10th Marines' (Col. Raphael Griffin) batteries. Casualties were extremely light, with

15 killed and 150 wounded by nightfall and a gain of 4,000 yards wide and 2,000 yards deep.

That evening the 24th Marines, supported by 1/8, was seemingly prepared for whatever the night would bring forth. 1/8 occupied the northernmost part of the defensive line. The enemy launched severe attacks but were decisively defeated. At the end of the day the strip held by the Marines was between 2,000 and 3,000 yards long and 1,500 yards in depth. Not much.

On the morning of the 24th, from 0557 to 1015, the 2nd MarDiv. made a feint toward making a landing at or near Tinian Town, far to the south on the west coast. In reality, on J-Day there were many more casualties to offshore American naval forces, Navy and Marines, in that feint at Tinian Town than during the actual landing on the northwest coast. While the BB *Colorado* was engaged in shelling the shoreline, two previously undiscovered 6-inch naval guns managed, within 15 minutes, to score 22 direct hits on *Colorado* and six on its destroyer escort, the *Norman Scott*. The crews of both suffered 62 killed, of which there were 10 Marines, and 223 wounded, of which 31 were Marines, a very large portion of the Marine detachment. The local Japanese commander, Col. Kiyochi Ogata, was convinced, as he witnessed the "landing force" turn away, that he had repelled the invasion and so notified his headquarters.

The anticipated counterattack came that night, beginning at 0200 on the 25th, but the Marines were well dug-in. It was a true, well-organized and well-executed banzai that hit the perimeter at several points simultaneously. It was preceded by the usual artillery and mortar fire upon the Marine lines. Six tanks, followed by infantry, hit the center which was held by the 23rd Marines. Of the six tanks, all but one was destroyed, and that, somehow managed to escape its destiny. Nonetheless, the Japanese infantry kept coming and soon they and the Marines of 2/23 were in close hand-to-hand combat. Some of the Japanese penetrated the lines, some as deep as the artillery positions. Howitzer crews lowered the muzzles and fired point-blank, slaughtering most of the enemy, and then attacked the remnants with small arms fire. One machine gun crew piled up 250 bodies before its position. At least 350 enemy dead were counted in front of one company.

On the left, before the 24th Marines, a platoon led by Sgt. John F. Fritts, Jr., killed 150 of the enemy. By morning, overall at least 1,250 Japanese were dead, and that wasn't counting those bodies retrieved by their comrades, an estimated 700 to 800 more. It was calculated that about one fifth of the enemy's total strength on that island was gone.

Upon its arrival at the landing beaches, the 2nd MarDiv. had a relatively easy time of it. The 4th MarDiv. had pretty much cleared the northern section from Ushi Point down to around the airfield. The balance of the 8th Marines and the 2nd Marines were landed. At this time the 6th Marines were also being brought over from Saipan. By nightfall the entire division had landed on Tinian. The 2nd MarDiv. took up position to the northeast while the 4th remained in the northwest and south. The role of the 4th MarDiv. was to advance south toward Tinian Town on the west coast while the 2nd MarDiv. would advance down the east coast to Marpo Point.

Moving southward, the 4th MarDiv. had four RCTs led by tanks providing a base of fire and partial cover for the infantry. Their advance, though obstructed, was never seriously in danger of being interrupted.

On that same day the 2nd MarDiv. moved a slight distance along the northern coast and to the east, taking part of Airfield 3. Then, on 26 July the 2nd MarDiv. moved rapidly, taking the balance of the airfield and down to Asigo Point on the east coast. The 25th

Marines overran Mt. Lasso, which had been Ogata's command post and primary observation point.

The 2nd MarDiv. ran into modest difficulty on the 27th when, after an artillery preparation, the division jumped off at 0730 and was harassed by small arms fire most of the morning. But by 1345 the Marines had driven south about 4,000 yards.

As the days passed, enemy forces began to retreat southward and into caves and other natural defense locations in which the Marines were once again forced to dig them out. However, napalm made that task much easier. This campaign was the first in which the newly arrived napalm became available and that put a different slant on the problem. Now the enemy was driven out or burnt out. Mostly it was the latter. It was a terrible way to die. Japanese discipline required that each man tolerate anything rather than surrender, and napalm had to be one of the ultimate tests.

On the 28th it was the 4th MarDiv.'s turn to move forward while the 2nd MarDiv. just moved ahead a couple of hundred yards. On that date the airfield near Garguan Point was taken. On the following day, J-Day plus five, both divisions moved forward against lesser resistance although the 2nd MarDiv. ran into pockets of opposition at Masalog Point. By nightfall Tinian Town had fallen to the 4th MarDiv. and more than half of the island was now in the custody of the Americans.

On the east coast, 3/2 (Lt. Col. Walter F. Layer) moved against occasional opposition from several machine-gun positions and a 70mm howitzer. They quieted that down and drove across open fields chasing a Japanese force and driving them into caves. With the help of a napalm firing tank they killed 89 Japanese and wiped out 4 machine guns and crews. They then came under mortar fire which caused numerous casualties to the battalion, until tanks and half-tracks came up with supporting fire. But the 2nd MarDiv. reached its objective by 1830 and the Marines now held 80 percent of the island. With all possible haste the Japanese now began to seriously dig in and resist ceding each inch of ground. The Marines would have to dig them out, with the consequent casualties that always brought.

On 30 July, one group of five Marines, including Pvt. Joseph W. Ozbourn from Herrin, IL, of 1/23, 4th MarDiv., was having a difficult time of it. Their job was to clear out the remaining enemy from pillboxes hindering their final moves on the island. Ozbourn, with four others, moved forward to throw a grenade into one opening when a blast from the entrance severely wounded the three Marines. Ozbourn had the armed grenade in his hand. Unable to throw the grenade into the opening of the pillbox, he grasped it tight to his own body, absorbing the full blast and saving his four comrades. He was awarded a posthumous Medal of Honor for this courageous act.

At 0200 on the morning of 31 July, the Japanese launched a counterattack against both 1/8 and 2/8. On that date, Col Ogata mustered about a company-sized strike force and, preceded by a mortar barrage, attacked the 24th Marines. They were, however, quickly repulsed, with Ogata as one of their casualties. Resistance continued to be relatively light until 1 August. That night a banzai attack along the line especially hurt the 8th Marines, which suffered 74 casualties. Schmidt made a statement that the island was secured at 1855 that night. Unfortunately the enemy didn't seem to get the word because they continued resisting.

Down at the southern tip, between Lalo and Parpo Points, on difficult ground, the dug-in enemy awaited the Marines. Offshore, two USN battleships, one heavy and two light cruisers, plus loads of destroyers and bombing planes, shelled the hell out of the area. Both Marine divisions appeared on the scene and prepared to take those last positions from their enemy. At the southern point of the island, the 2nd MarDiv. had the worst ground to take. The grunts went in with flamethrowers and a liberal use of demolitions, with BARs covering them they were successful.

On 1 August 1944 Tinian Island was again declared secured. Some Japanese civilians and soldiers went over the cliffs, as they had on Saipan. There continued to be terrible incidents. Most were on purpose, such as civilians throwing their children off cliffs, followed by the parents and groups of civilians being blown up by explosives attached to them by Japanese military forces. But, overall, and unlike on Saipan, many civilians were saved. The Marines managed to get a prominent citizen to broadcast an appeal to the civilians and at least 13,262 were saved.

On the morning of 2 August a force of about 200 Japanese attacked 3/6 (Lt. Col. John W. Easley, Silver Star) and within two hours it suffered a loss of 119 men, including the battalion CO. Soon after, 100 of the enemy hit 2/6 (Lt. Col. Edmund B. Games), and withdrew after the loss of 30 men.

One more Marine of the 2nd MarDiv., Private First Class Robert Lee Wilson, a member of 2/6, born in Centralia, IL, on 4 August threw himself on a grenade while in the process of cleaning up the enemy. Posthumously he too was awarded a Medal of Honor.

Though Gen. Schmidt had declared the island secured, the fighting continued for many months to come. The 8th Marines were left on the island to support the new island commander, Maj. Gen. James L. Underhill, in suppressing the militant remnants of hiding Japanese. By the end of 1944 it was estimated that the Japanese had lost another 500 men while the 8th Marines suffered casualties numbering 38 killed and 125 wounded. It was over, but not quite.

The 4th MarDiv. was pulled entirely out of the Marianas, but the 2nd MarDiv. remained on Saipan. The 2nd and 6th Marines were there when 2/8 and 3/8 rejoined them on 25 October, while 1/8 remained on Tinian until after the end of the year.

At least 6,000 known enemy soldiers died on Tinian, not counting those buried by their comrades. The 4th MarDiv. losses were 290 killed and 1,515 wounded, with 24 missing. The division, because of its performance on Saipan and Tinian, was the third Marine division to be awarded the coveted Presidential Unit Citation. The total casualties for the 2nd MarDiv. on Tinian amounted to 107 killed and another 654 wounded.

By 14 August the last of the 4th MarDiv. troops boarded transports for the ride back to Maui. There they would have rest, relaxation, and exercise, with training being the main thing. It would allow the members of the division some time before getting back into harness.

Even though the island was declared "secured," fighting would continue for many months to come. Though the 2nd and 6th Marines would leave the island and take up residence on Saipan, the 8th Marines would remain on Tinian to help clean up the remaining Japanese soldiers that continued fighting. At the end of the year the entire 2nd MarDiv. left and became a part of Geiger's III Amphibious Corps, preparing for the invasion of Okinawa. Though they were scheduled for the Okinawa operation, this would be the final combat operation in which the 2nd MarDiv. participated during World War II.

Air support by Marines was limited to just one organization: a detachment from Marine Utility Squadron 252 between 24 July and 1 August 1944.

Results: The success provided air bases for the ultimate needs of the U.S. Army Air Forces in their efforts to bomb the Japanese home islands and Marine losses were modest. Several senior leaders were laudatory. Admiral Sprunace is quoted as saying "the Tinian operation was probably the most brilliantly conceived and executed amphibious operation in World War II." And Holland Smith, the perfectionist, added, "Tinian was the perfect amphibious operation in the Pacific War."

The island has been acclaimed as furnishing the U.S. Army Air Force with the airfields capable of providing the necessary location for bombing mainland Japan, just 1,200 nautical miles away. The *Enola Gay*, part of the 20th Air Force, carried the bombs for bombing Hiroshima and Nagasaki, both raids effectively ending the war.

Guam

Date: 21 July to 10 August 1944.
Location: The southernmost island of the Mariana group, Guam.
Involved: Japanese army and navy versus the U.S. Marines, Army, and Navy.
Situation: The island of Guam, the only possession the United States held in the Marianas pre-war, had been taken by the Japanese in a massive assault, by nearly 6,000 men, on 10 December 1941. Captain George J. McMillan, USN, the island commander, surrendered the island after a brief defense by the 153 Marine detachment aided by the even smaller 80-man native Chamorro garrison.

The assault code STEVEDORE was to be launched by the 3rd MarDiv. (Maj. Gen. Allen H. Turnage), the 1st Marine Provisional Brigade (Brig. Gen. Lemuel Shepherd) and the 77th InfDiv. (Maj. Gen. Andrew D. Bruce, USA), all under the command of Maj. Gen. Roy Geiger, CG Southern Landing Troops and Landing Force, re-designated III Amphibious Corps on 15 April. The entire operation was under the overall command of Lt. Gen. Holland M. Smith as CG of the Expeditionary Troops. The 1st Provisional Brigade, which would eventually become the 6th MarDiv., was activated at Pearl Harbor on 22 March 1944.

Originally, Guam, the southern half of which is all mountainous, was to have been invaded on 18 June, but the invasion date was postponed after the northern islands were taken. Marines had confidence in RA Richard L. Conolly, USN, who was Geiger's complement in the naval structure; it was a fine working relationship. The difference in dates gave Conolly the time for a more thoroughgoing heavy gunfire preparation than had happened at either Saipan or Tinian.

Working together, Geiger and Conolly and their staffs managed to bring fire to bear on the most apparent targets and eventually every known target on Guam. During the 13-day preliminary bombardment, the Navy fired 6,258 heavy shells, 3,862 8-inch shells, 2,430 6-inch shells, and 16,214 5-inch shells. The surviving senior Japanese officer, Col. Takeda, later told interrogators that all coast defense guns in the open, half in caves and on shore, and most in defensive positions, were destroyed, with an appropriate decline in the defenders spirit.

On 14 July, underwater demolition teams spent three nights reconnoitering the Asan and Agat beaches. By midnight of the last day before the landing, the Navy swimmers had destroyed 940 obstacles. The Navy men even had time to place a sign at Agat saying "Welcome Marines." Unfortunately the Japanese had no part in that welcome.

On 21 July 1944 the guns of Task Force 53 opened up to support the landing of the IIIMAC. As the Marines loaded into their landing craft, some of their ships played the "Marine's Hymn" from loudspeakers. They had already been apprised by Maj. Gen. Geiger that in their selection to retake Guam, they "have been honored." I bet there were lots of wisecracks to respond to that one.

The Guam beachhead selected for the 3rd MarDiv. was south of Agaña Bay, a mile below Agaña town, beginning at Adelup Point and continuing further south to opposite Mount Tenjo. All three regiments were to land. The 3rd Marines (Col. W. Carvel Hall, Navy Cross) were on Beaches Red 1 and 2 on the left, the 21st Marines (Col. Arthur H. Butler, Navy Cross) in the center on a narrow Beach Green and the 9th Marines (Col. Edward A. Craig, Navy Coss) on the far right on Beach Blue. Once again it was the ill-fated 3rd Marines to have the toughest front. The 3rd Bn., 3rd Marines (Lt. Col. Ralph L. Houser, Navy Cross, WIA 22 July) was before Chonito Cliff, which rose up from the beach. Next to them on their right was 2/3 (Lt. Col. Hector de Zayas, Navy Cross), located before half of what later became Bundschu Ridge, while 1/3 (Lt. Col. Henry Aplington, II) had the other half. This was where most of the toughest fighting would take place until the Marines managed to get off the beach.

One hero, PFC Luther Skaggs, Jr., from Henderson, KY, while serving as a squad leader of a mortar section of 3/3, proved that he had more than it takes. On that D-day heavy mortar fire caused Skagg's squad leader to become a casualty soon after landing. Skaggs assumed command and led his men forward at least 200 yards off the beach through intense firing. Soon they set up and began dropping shells on a nearby strategic ridge. His command defended its territory that night and when a grenade was lobbed into his hole and shattered his leg, he hurriedly put on a tourniquet and continued firing his M-1 at the enemy. With his rifle and grenades he continued to resist for over eight hours. Skaggs did all this without a complaint or excuse to leave his men during the entire period. For that he was awarded a Medal of Honor.

The 21st Marines landed 1/21 (Lt. Col. Marlowe C. Williams, Silver Star), followed by 2/21 (Lt. Col. Eustace R. Smoak) and 3/21 (Lt. Col. Wendell H. Duplantis, Silver Star), all of which pushed ahead. On their right the 9th Marines landed 3/9 (Lt. Col. Walter Asmuth, Jr.), then 1/9 (Lt. Col. Carey A. Randall) and 2/9 (Lt. Col. Robert E. Cushman, Jr.), all of whom were soon off the beach. Both the 21st and 9th Marines made dandy advances, giving the 3rd MarDiv. some substantial ground on the first day.

In the south, down below the town of Agat, the 1st Provisional Brigade (Brig. Gen. Lemuel C. Shepherd, Jr.) landed 1/22 (Lt. Col. Walfried H. Fromhold) and 2/22 (Lt. Col. Donn C. Hart) on Beaches Yellow 1 and 2, and from the 4th Marines (Lt. Col. Alan Shapley, Navy Cross), 1/4 (Maj. Bernard W. Green, Silver Star) and 2/4 (Maj. John S. Messer) on Beaches White 1 and 2. The 22nd (Col. Merlin F. Schneider, Navy Cross) moved inward, then turned northward. In went the 4th Marines, who then headed southward. By the end of the day both regiments had taken sufficient territory to ensure the future success of that southern landing. The 4th Marines was a re-creation, effective 1 February 1944, of that hard-luck unit which the Philippine Island commander Maj. Gen. Jonathon Wainwright, USA, surrendered on Corregidor in May 1942. The new 4th Marines was formed from the various disbanded Raider units. Other than a brief part at undefended Emirau Island on the 20th of March, this would be their first activity as the re-instated 4th Marines.

The next day, up north, Company A of 1/3, led by Capt. Geary R. Bundschu with exceptional bravery, took what became known as "Bundschu Ridge." In so doing, Bundschu lost his life and earned a posthumous Navy Cross. With acquisition of the ridge, the 3rd Marines managed to grab an essential piece of ground, and they continued to hold it. By the 24th the 3rd Marines were onto and holding Fonte Plateau, another tough piece of ground taken by drastic measures. In fact, with both Mt. Alutom and Mt. Tenjo, it governed the entire battlefront. Their left border and front line was now completely on the Fonte River.

Meanwhile, PFC Leonard F. Mason, of 2/3, a BAR man engaged in cleaning out hostile positions, came under fire from two enemy machine guns. Climbing out of his protected position in a gully, Mason, alone and entirely upon his own initiative, moved toward the rear of one gun's position. Wounded repeatedly by enemy rifle fire, Mason continued forward until stopped momentarily by a burst of machine-gun fire which caused him another serious wound. Nevertheless, without personal regard, he continued onward and cleaned out the hostile gun, killing five enemy personnel. Somehow making it back to his company, Mason reported his action, all the while refusing to be evacuated until he had satisfied himself that his mission was duly recorded. He died soon after from that serious wound and was posthumously awarded the Medal of Honor.

Meanwhile the 9th and 21st Marines were moving at a faster rate. Each was heading in a southeasterly direction and by 22 July, the 21st was almost upon the Radio Towers and the Masso River line. The 9th Marines had also turned right and, moving with the sea as their right flank, had taken ground almost to the Tatgua River line. Continuing to move forward, the 21st had gotten as far south as Mt. Chachao while the 9th was assaulting the Piti Navy Yard. In the south, the 305th Infantry landed between the 22nd and 4th Marines and quickly moved through them and forward, taking over the major offensive assault into Guam territory. At about 1550 on 25 July a patrol of the 9th Marines reported making contact with the 22nd Marines. The two landing groups had made slender contact, but Orote Peninsula was a remaining obstacle between them.

Later that evening the Japanese launched a serious counterattack upon the lines of the junction of the 21st Marines and 9th Marines, with others hitting the 3rd Marines. At first the attacks were sparse and scattered and it was several hours before the actual intentions of the enemy became known. It actually was a full-blown effort to drive the 3rd MarDiv. from Guam. Skipper of Company F., 2/9, Captain Louis H. Wilson, Jr., of Brandon, MS, was well aware of the enemy's tenaciousness. He and his command were fighting around Fonte Hill the afternoon of 25 July when he received a direct order to take that portion of the hill which lay before his company. Led by Wilson, Co. F went up the hill and over open terrain against horrific enemy rifle and machine-gun fire. They advanced 300 yards and successfully captured their objective. Wilson also assumed command of mixed groups of Marines plus various equipment and prepared a zone for defense for that night. Although he was wounded three times, Wilson continued his work, enabling the Marines to successfully defend that position for a good five hours under terrific attacks. When it was obvious that his command was safe, he turned it over to a subordinate and retired for medical attention.

Shortly afterward, when the enemy launched a series of violent attacks upon his men, Wilson voluntarily returned and rejoined his badly handled unit. He repeatedly exposed himself to flying lead and in one instance, ran 50 yards out front to retrieve a wounded Marine. For ten additional hours he and his men, in violent hand-to-hand combat, managed to retain their precarious hold on their real estate. Early the next morning Wilson and his command finally crushed the enemy lying before them.

A strategic slope overlooked his post and, for security's sake, it had to be taken. Wilson organized a 17-man patrol to take the slope. In so doing they guaranteed that his unit would retain the high ground, so essential for the success of this operation. For his courage, ability, leadership and conduct, he was awarded a Medal of Honor. General Wilson would later become the 26th Commandant of the Marine Corps.

About 0100 on the 26th the Japanese began making small-scale attacks all along the line. They were well-armed, equipped with large demolition charges and using the terrain to great advantage. As they rolled numerous charges down the slopes, the Marines had great difficulty escaping them. One position, on the far left of the line, had been relatively quiet until this night. Maj. Henry "Hank" Aplington's 1/3, which had been in division reserve, was brought up to maintain the far left flank position in the hills. He later recalled that "with the dark came rain and the Marines huddled under their ponchos ... around midnight there was a probing of the lines of the 21st Marines and slopping over into those of the 9th Marines. My first inkling came at about 0430 when my three companies erupted into fire and called for mortar support.... I talked to my company commanders ... and was told that there were Japanese all around them ... the Japanese had been close. Three of my dead had been killed by bayonet thrusts."

All along the line, the enemy managed to get in deep, almost to the beach and well into the gun positions of the 12th Marines. Fighting around the guns was fierce, but Marines soon drove away the bulk of the enemy. Offshore Navy gun fire was called in to flatten certain areas, especially before the 3rd Marines. Many Japanese were crushed by that fire as they fell back.

Meanwhile, at daybreak on the 26th, the 4th Marines led off the offensive on the Orote Peninsula. They were followed an hour later by the 22nd Marines. For the next three days, both regiments would be fighting desperate and determined defenders in many pockets throughout the peninsula. One of the casualties of the 4th on the 27th was Lt. Col. Samuel D. Puller (brother of "Chesty"), engineering officer of the 4th Marines.

After taking Orote, the 4th Marines were deployed south of Mt. Alifan, the high ground which extended from about Gaan Point south to nearly the southernmost point on the island. Essentially, they were to "hold the southern portion of the island," while the 77th InfDiv. joined with the 3rd MarDiv. in a drive to the north.

All night the wild attacks continued, but they were unlike the banzai attacks; these were not disorganized suicidal charges. It was later contended that empty enemy canteens smelling of Saki indicated that the Japanese, though organized, were on a wild drunken rampage. At 0400 all hell broke loose. Enemy troops were opposite the Marines' line and volleys of machine-gun and rifle fire, plus volumes of hand grenades, poured in upon the Marines. The nearly five sleepless nights the Marines had experienced were beginning to tell as morning and daylight came in. The 21st Marines were getting hit as badly, and in some places worse than the 3rd Marines. Company B of 1/21 was nearly wiped out. By morning there were only about 18 men left for duty and still the Japanese came on. The mortar platoon of 1/21 was also practically wiped out as the enemy continued their attack where the 21st and 9th Marines joined. Many Japanese had been killed but those who survived were raising hell behind the lines. Perhaps 600 of their dead were lying before and within the positions of 2/9, commanded by another future commandant, Lt. Col. Robert Cushman, also the recipient of a Navy Cross.

The fighting continued through the early portion of 26 July. Estimates made at the time claimed as many as 3,200 enemy casualties, but they still hadn't been stopped. By this date, Marines and their Army comrades fighting in the Pacific War were well aware how dangerous the enemy could be. Lines were reorganized and Marine casualties sorted out. Between 0900 and 1900 the lines were generally intact. At night there were more infiltrators but the assaults of numerous enemy seemed to have decreased.

On the morning of 27 July, orders were received for 2/9, which had been attached to the 3rd Marines, to go forward and take the military crest of the reverse slope of Fonte Plateau. As the regiment moved forward, "friendly" shells and aerial bombs fell on Company G (Capt. Francis L. Fagan, Navy Cross), disrupting its forward motion. Meanwhile, Company E (Capt. Maynard W. Smith) went forward and retook ground lost the day before. By 1500 all three companies, G, E and F, were on the plateau and digging in for the night. A banzai attack was launched and Company G stopped it. All night the enemy continued their infiltrating and harassment tactics, allowing 2/9 very little rest and no sleep.

The following day, E and F Companies advanced and reached their objective after facing modest resistance, but G had a rough time. Just one officer remained and the company's skipper had been replaced three times in two days. In the afternoon an estimated company-sized enemy attack hit F and G Companies but that was soon wiped out. Fonte Plateau was now permanently U.S. Marine. That last attack was soon found to be a last gasp. Many of the deceased were Japanese officers, some quite senior in rank; it was really a suicidal rush, and in that, they were successful. After the 3rd and 21st Marines had secured Fonte, the 9th Marines took the Mount Alutom–Mount Chachao massif and saw that the venerable 305th Infantry had taken Mount Tenjo. The Marines had worthy companions in the 77th InfDiv., and were especially comfortable with the CG of the 77th, Maj. Gen. Bruce, a fighter.

In the meantime, the 22nd Marines had driven up the coast and was assaulting the Orote Peninsula. That was where the Marines had been housed before 9 December 1941. The southern landing group, 1st Provisional Brigade and 77th InfDiv., had been making excellent progress. The Marines were very laudatory of the soldiers, calling them the 77th MarDiv. Probably, if the soldiers ever heard it said, that intended compliment went over like a lead balloon. But our story is the Marines, so we digress.

The 3rd MarDiv. soon found that the majority of remaining enemy forces was retreating up the island. The division pushed toward the enemy and between 31 July and 2 August, 1/3 and 1/9 captured Tiyan Airfield. The honor of liberating the ruins of the capital city, Agaña, fell to 3/3, which it accomplished on 31 July. Meanwhile, the 77th InfDiv. came up on the 3rd MarDiv.'s right flank and both divisions then pushed ahead, northward. The 1st Provisional Brigade remained in the south and was responsible for the cleanup of all enemy formations in that part of the island. On 3–4 August the 77th InfDiv. captured Mount Barrigada while the 3rd MarDiv. was taking Finegayan.

On the 3rd of August, in the battle for Finegayen, PFC Frank P. Witek, from Derby, CT, a BAR man with 1/9, stood up and fired at point-blank range into well-hidden Japanese positions, killing at least eight of the enemy. His act allowed the balance of his platoon to take cover. While the platoon was so engaged, Witek remained behind and safeguarded a wounded comrade. After the man was evacuated he then covered the stretcher bearers' withdrawal. After returning to his unit, he again moved forward to support tanks by throwing grenades and firing his Browning automatic rifle as he moved to within 10 yards of the enemy. His destruction of another enemy machine gun and eight more Japanese was concluded when he was struck down by Japanese rifle fire. He was posthumously awarded a Medal of Honor for gallantry and giving up his life for his comrades and his country.

Marines and Army continued to press forward. On 8 August, the 22nd Marines had reached Ritidian Point and two days later the Americans had taken almost every inch of Guam. The final day, 10 August, was spent combing the beaches and heavily wooded area on the north shore. The number of dead Japanese was estimated at 5,200 men. Briefly, from the time Turnage returned to the States in September, Brig. Gen. Alfred H. Noble assumed command of the 3rd MarDiv. He in turn was relieved one month later by Maj. Gen. Graves B. Erskine when Noble was also returned to the U.S. Colonel John B. Wilson was his ADC and Col. Robert E. Hogaboom came with Erskine as the new chief of staff and all "G" positions were changed.

From 1 to 23 October, the division was engaged in "cleaning up" the island. Contacts were widely scattered and on 24 October the last major effort began. It lasted until the 3rd of November, when its task was considered completed. From then on only small patrols would venture into the brush. This, then, began the "peaceful" occupation of Guam. Now the 3rd MarDiv. would prepare for its next engagement, another tough one.

The casualties were huge for the Marines in the 21 days of combat. The Marine losses totaled 1,567 killed and 5,308 wounded. The Army suffered substantially less, 177 dead and 662 wounded. The 1st Provisional Brigade, with the addition of the 29th Marines and service troops, soon would became the 6th MarDiv. and would participate in the assault upon Okinawa. The 3rd MarDiv. would be one of three Marine divisions assaulting the horrific island Iwo Jima in February 1945. Meanwhile they would remain on Guam, preparing for the "big fight."

Marine air support during the Guam campaign increased substantially from the recent campaigns. It included Marine Air Warning Squadron 2; VMJ 252; VMF 216, 217, 225; VMF (N) 532 and 534.

Results: After the reconquest of Guam, the United States now controlled the entire Marianas Island chain, most of which had been Japanese-owned for many years. This placed the American military forces, especially naval and air forces, that much closer to the main Japanese islands.

However, it was calculated that after 10 August, as many as 10,000 Japanese soldiers remained alive on Guam. Nonetheless, they were obviously lacking cohesion and most would be dedicated to surviving rather than assaulting any American positions. Starvation was the constant specter, and for the survivors of the 31st Japanese Army, Guam became a nightmare.

Peleliu

Date: 15 September to 15 October 1944.
Location: Peleliu Island in the Palaus group, lying east of the Philippine Islands.
Involved: Japanese army and naval personnel versus U.S. Marines, Navy, and Army.
Situation: Originally known as STALEMATE, the operation was changed to STALE-

MATE II on 7 July 1944 when revised orders were issued to all commands taking part in the assault in the Palaus Island group. The Palaus group was necessary to protect MacArthur's left flank as he and his army proceeded to retake Leyte in the Philippine Island chain. Taking Peleliu, the largest and most heavily fortified of that group, proved to be expensive protection. MacArthur was going to land at Leyte on 20 October 1944 and the Marines were required to take Peleliu beforehand. The whole operation was expected to be short. Maj. Gen. William H. Rupertus, CG, 1st MarDiv., even went so far as to tell his division officers "We're going to have some casualties, but let me assure you this is going to be a short one, a quickie. Rough but fast. We'll be through in three days. It might only take two." It turned out to be more a matter of months than days. But optimism reigned, at least among the senior officers and the joint chiefs of staff.

Preceded by carrier-based air and heavy bomber support, Task Force 32 arrived off Peleliu and began an intensive naval bombardment on 12 September 1944. This was scheduled as a 1st MarDiv. affair in anticipation of a fairly easy task. On D-day, 15 September, there were three beach assignments: White 1 and 2, upon which the 1st Marines (Col. Lewis B. Puller) were to land; Orange 1, 2, and 3, upon which two Bns. of the 5th Marines (Col. Harold D. Harris) would land; and on that right flank, the 7th Marines (Col. Herman H. Hanneken) would land. On the opposite side of the island was Purple Beach, which in a period of about ten days would become a hospital/rest home for a badly battered 1st Marine Regiment.

After a preliminary bombardment of the beaches by RA Jesse B. Oldendorf's fire support ships, at 0800 on 15 September Marines headed for the beaches in their landing craft. The LCIs and LVTs began landing on the beaches at 0832 with armored amphibians leading, troops following. The blanket of fire laid down on that island by warships, naval aviators and LCI/LVTs equipped with 4.5 rocket launchers and 4.2 mortars seemed, at the time, to be adequate. But, it didn't really make a dent on the left flank, where the enemy had created caves with armored doors, which they could easily open and shut for protection. That was where Puller's 1st Marines landed and they immediately took a shellacking, especially 3/1 (Lt. Col. Stephen V. Sabol) on White Beach 1, and most especially Co. K (Capt. George P. Hunt, Navy Cross), on the extreme left flank. Their story in the next two days was the story of the 1st MarDiv. during the coming weeks. Directly before Co. K was a hill with a cave protected by steel doors. The enemy had artillery which they fired down into the positions upon the beach. They fired then closed the doors and then opened and fired again, and again. All of 3/1 were the targets, though Co. K was at the extreme left of the line and caught most of it.

The enemy had spent much time on these islands, preparing them for war. The entire island was a veritable fortress. For the Marines, getting off the beach was very difficult, elsewhere the situation was almost as bad. Marine casualties were enormous, and the survivors suffered greatly from the 105-degree heat. The entire landing was a disaster which ultimately proved to be completely unnecessary, and, like Blanc Mont in World War I, almost forgotten — perhaps purposely — by nearly everyone for years, including the Marine Corps.

Lieutenant Colonel Robert W. Boyd (Navy Cross) and his command, 1/5, landed on Orange 1 with two rifle companies abreast while Lt. Col. Austin C. ("Shifty") Shofner and 3/5 landed on Orange 2, in the same formation. Major Gordon D. Gayle (Navy Cross) commanded 2/5, the regimental reserve, which landed at 1015 on Orange 2. Gayle's command immediately got off the beach and headed inland.

Boyd's Marines went directly to the western edge of the airfield, arriving at 0900. There they and three tanks from Lt. Col. Arthur J. Stuart's 1st Tank Bn. dug in and awaited an anticipated Japanese tank attack. Shofner and 3/5 came over the beach to Boyd's left and proceeded inland, making the Phase One line within an hour of landing. Heavy enemy fire at landing craft coming in forced those carrying 3/7 (Maj. Edward H. Hurst) to veer to their left and land Marines on Orange Beach 2, causing some confusion. It was soon righted and 3/7 managed to move to its right and begin its phase of the assault.

Late in the afternoon enemy light tanks, with soldiers aboard, rumbled toward the lines of Marines, the latter picking off the riders and the tanks swerving out of the line of fire. Marine Shermans moved up and shelled them, completely breaking up the attack. As they were retiring they were followed closely by Gayle's 2/5, which reached nearly the center of the airfield. During this fighting, an officer of 1/5, 1st Lt. Carleton R. Rouh, from Lindewood, NJ, was wounded. While being escorted to the rear an enemy grenade dropped among he and two Marines helping him. Dropping on the grenade, he absorbed the blast and saved the lives of the two other Marines. Somehow he survived and earned a Medal of Honor. Another member of 1/5, Cpl. Lewis K. Bausell, of Washington, D.C., while engaged in attacking a pillbox, saw a grenade drop within his group and he dropped upon it to save his buddies' lives. However, he lost his own and a posthumous Medal of Honor was presented to his next of kin.

By dusk, the 5th and 7th Marines had crossed the island and the latter had pushed south to close off that portion of the island to the enemy. However, the 1st Marines were still having great difficulties and were unable to get anywhere near their Phase One line, thus forestalling the 5th and 7th Marines from their planned trip northward. Within an hour of landing, all assault platoon leaders, and their platoon sergeants, were casualties. Command was now down to sergeants, when and if they were still available.

The next morning, Captain Hunt was only able to muster 78 Marines for duty, including the walking wounded. Despite that, the 1st Marines were still working over, as best they could, the worst position on the island. Their leader Col. Puller was constantly pressuring the regiment to "do more." Eventually, the regiment was near and even on what became known as "Bloody Nose Ridge." The name was given for obvious reasons. There was lots of blood all about it.

The other two regiments, 5th and 7th, were very busy but had less imposing obstacles to overcome and were able to manage the enemy much better. The 7th cleaned up the southern portion during the next few days and by the 18th were the victors. They had two Marines that earned the ultimate decoration. PFC Arthur J. Jackson, 3/7's own hero, from Cleveland, OH, boldly took the initiative when his platoon's left flank was being held up by Japanese in heavily fortified positions. Charging one, he poured fire from his BAR into the aperture and then tossed phosphorus grenades, then satchel charges. He demolished the pillbox and killed at least 35 of the enemy. He proceeded to destroy two more pillboxes and then charged other enemy positions, killing everything in his path. He eventually succeeded in demolishing 12 pillboxes and killing at least 50 Japanese soldiers. This one-man Marine Corps was appropriately awarded the nation's highest honor, a Medal of Honor.

While Jackson was killing and surviving, 2/7's PFC Charles H. Roan of Claude, TX, dropped on and absorbed a grenade and saved the life of other Marines of his squad. His posthumous award was a Medal of Honor. That same day 2/1 (Lt. Col. Russell E. Honsowetz,

Navy Cross) and 2/7 (Lt. Col. Spencer S. Berger) took Hill 210 and Company B, 1/1, managed to take Hill 205. The 5th's obligations were a bit heavier and required the best they could provide, which was most satisfactory. They continued to press the IJA backward, taking most of the planned phase lines within their assignment.

The hard-luck 1st Marines had the worst terrain to cover, rugged high ground in which the enemy was well dug in, but they continued their efforts. Elements of 2/1 managed to reach the "Five Sisters," the southern face of the final pocket of resistance, on 19 September. Company C of 1/1 crossed Horseshoe Valley and gained the summit of Hill 100 and a patrol from 2/5 reached the east coast just below Purple Beach.

Captain Everett P. Pope of Milton, MA, the skipper of Company C, 1/1, witnessed his company's disorganization and destruction and decided to do something about it. He rallied his men, and they once again attempted to assault the rock face which had defeated them so often. The machine guns, mortar, and rifle fire had reduced his command so badly it was a wonder that they could hold their place in line, let alone attack anyone. However, the remaining few made it and Pope decided to remain on this height all night with his one wounded officer and 12 men. All night they beat back attacks, resorting to hand-to-hand combat when their ammo was depleted. When daylight finally arrived he and his remaining eight Marines still held. He was ordered to withdraw, but his leadership and determination to stand against overwhelming odds earned him a Medal of Honor.

The well-worn 1st Marines were so wasted that eventually, on 21 September, the regiment was replaced by the fresh, untried 321st Infantry (Col. Robert F. Dark, USA) of the 81st InfDiv. Most Marines in a position to know were not surprised and many wondered why it took so long. General Rupertus and Col. Puller were the two notable dissenters. They were dead set against an Army unit replacing a Marine unit. But Maj. Gen. Roy S. Geiger, IIIMAC commander, fully realized that the 1st Marines were essentially wiped out, and ordered it done. The regiment had suffered a total of 1,672 casualties, of which 1/1 incurred 71 percent of its total strength. It was 56 percent for 2/1 and 55 percent for 3/1. Regimental headquarters and the weapons company were 32 percent.

The 321st Inf. would have its hands full on this extreme left flank, but the 1st Marines had absorbed the heavy punishment, and the worst was over. Company B of 1/5 concluded its mission by taking Island A and Co. F took the tiny island north of Ngabad on 23 September. It was now up to the infantry to take most of the burden on the west side of the island. A group from the 81st InfDiv., the Neal Task Force, USA, landed on the west coast, in mid-island, on 25 September, and headed north.

Meanwhile, on 25 September, another man from 2/7, PFC John D. New, of Mobile, AL, was with two other men who were directing mortar fire. Suddenly a Japanese soldier emerged from a cave and hurled a grenade toward them. New spotted the grenade and threw himself upon it, giving his life for his country and earning a posthumous Medal of Honor for his courage.

On 26 September Lt. Col. Boyd and 1/5 attacked toward the Amiangal, the northernmost hills on the island, and reached the northern tip, sealing it off. Company B secured Hill 2 and 2/5 bypassed Hill 1 and moved north. They then secured Hill 80 and reached the northwest peninsula's eastern shore, thereby sealing off the northern portion of Peleliu. On the following day, the national standard was raised over the 1st MarDiv. headquarters, symbolizing that the island was secured.

The infantry continued the fight to compress the Umurbrogal pocket until relieved by 1/7 on 29 September. Ngesebus Island, off the northern tip of Peleliu, was taken by 3/5

(Maj. John H. Gustafson, Silver Star), and Co. G of 2/5 captured the northern tip of the peninsula.

The island, or most of it, was, for all intents and purposes, entirely in the hands of the U.S. by 30 September. All except the "pocket," which was in the middle of the island, occupying an area 900 by 400 yards. That was so heavily developed and defended that the Marines and soldiers were subjected to costly attrition at its deadliest. It was mainly the 5th Marines' action, but the others assisted, as did recently landed Marine fighters from MAG 11. Sincere efforts were made to convince the very reluctant IJA to surrender, even to the extent of using captured Japanese soldiers to entice them with gifts of food, cigarettes and candy bars. None of it was very successful. Heat prostration with an accompanying near lack of water caused more agony.

As the month of October came in the rains also came; the seas became more turbulent and providing water and supplies from ships became even more difficult. On 3 October 2/7 secured "Walt's Ridge" and Co. K, 3/7, reached the summit of "Boyd Ridge." These were two points that bordered the notorious Umurbrogal pocket on the east. The fighting for the pocket continued.

One more member of 3/7, Pvt. Wesley Phelps of Neafus, KY, threw himself on a grenade on 4 October. He lost his life but was posthumously awarded a Medal of Honor. The next day, 5 October, a member of the 8th Amphibious Tractor Bn., PFC Richard E. Kraus, born in Chicago, IL, also threw himself upon a grenade to save his fellow Marines as they were trying to save wounded men. He too was posthumously awarded a Medal of Honor.

On 6 October the 5th Marines relieved the now exhausted 7th as the assault team. The 5th Marines continued doing what the 7th had been doing, but even though they were wearing the IJA down, they in turn were being worn down. Companies E and G, 2/5, attacking the pocket, captured "Baldy Ridge" on the 10th. The following day, Hill 140, located north of the "Five Brothers," a tactically important site, was secured by 2/5.

On 14 October the 321st Infantry relieved the 5th Marines and on 15 October the 81st InfDiv. (Maj. Gen. Paul J. Mueller, USA) officially relieved the 1st MarDiv. After one month, the Marine casualties numbered nearly 6,800, of which 1,300 died, plus 300 attached Navy personnel. There had been nearly 2,000 casualties on D-day alone. The 1st MarDiv. had many heroes, possibly the entire personnel, but the seven Marines that earned Medals of Honor are the standouts.

The much depleted 1st MarDiv. was removed back to Pavavu Island for rest and rebuilding. This was, however, a totally different Pavavu than the one the division had suffered on earlier. The new division CG, Maj. Gen. Pedro del Valle, had seen to it that many changes were made and that the men finally had decent facilities on which to bind their wounds and recover from possibly the bloodiest battles of the Pacific War.

Marine air support during the Peleliu campaign included MAG-11. Subordinate units were VMO 3 (supporting the 1st MarDiv.); VMF 114, 121, and 122; VMBS 134; and Marine Transport Squadron 353 and 952.

> *Results:* The reason for the reduction and capture of the Palaus group had been Gen. MacArthur's insistence upon having his right flank cleared while his forces assaulted Leyte. In fact, it was later determined that the entire operation had not been essential, and the manpower losses suffered were not only unnecessary but excessive. The attitudes of both Rupertus and Puller about the

Army relieving the battered 1st MarDiv. would appear once again in reverse when Gen. Buckner refused to utilize the 2nd MarDiv. on Okinawa. General Rupertus was deemed ill and was relieved by Maj. Gen. Pedro del Valle. Colonel Puller, who had been wounded, was returned to Pavavu, where he was operated on. Soon after he was considered to be battle weary and returned to the U.S. Overall, it was not a good experience for the officers and men of the 1st MarDiv.

The Philippine Islands

Leyte

Date: 20 October 1944 to 20 December 1944.
Location: Island of Leyte
Involved: Japanese army and naval forces versus the U.S. 6th Army, U.S. Navy 7th Fleet, and Marine Corps. The latter provided the VAC artillery which included two Marine artillery battalions and one headquarter's battery, plus the U.S. Army's 198th, 226th, and 287th Field Artillery Battalions, and, initially, several senior Marine air observers (Maj. Gen. Ralph J. Mitchell, USMC, and three members of his staff). Later at different dates the Marine air would arrived and serve notably.
Situation: The U.S. Army, under the overall command of General Douglas MacArthur, landed on the northcentral east coast of Leyte on 20 October at the Dulag and San Jose area and moved toward Tacloban City, opposite the island of Samar, in the north. Besides moving westward at least a dozen miles into the center of the island, they also moved well northwest across the island and a half-week later had taken the northwest coast of Carigara and Barugo.

Marine artillery under the command of U.S. Army 24th Corps had the unique distinction of being commanded by Brig. Gen. Thomas E. Bourke, USMC, who had been detached from VAC to serve the U.S. Army in the Philippine campaign. Marine artillery consisted of the 5th 155 Howitzer Battalion (Lt. Col. James E. Mills), the 11th 155 Howitzer Battalion (Lt. Col. Thomas S. Ivey) and Headquarters Battery (Capt. George K. Acker). Bourke also had two other USA 155mm battalions and assorted support services.

On A-day, 20 October, most of Bourke's artillery units were ashore by the end of the day. By the 21st all guns were planted to support the 7th, 96th InfDiv. and 20th Armored Group advances until 13 December. Meanwhile, the Japanese fleet tried to smash the U.S. 7th Fleet in Leyte Gulf, but, essentially, the latter destroyed what was then remaining of Japan's once-vaunted navy. Aircraft from the numerous small U.S. carriers sunk during the naval battle began looking for a new home on Leyte. Mitchell was at the Tacloban airfield. He realized that the badly shot-up airfield was such that only the ground to its right, the original sod, was ripe for landing and take off. With a pair of signal flags he brought the naval air down safely. In the south, at Dulag airfield, the Navy wasn't as successful. The ground was not as sound and eight of the 40 aircraft were destroyed.

The infantry continued its drive to secure the island of Leyte, supported by the 1,500-plus Marines in VAC. Spotter aircraft worked wonders and allowed the guns to fire in direct support. The artillery's major problem as they advanced was to locate solid ground upon which to place their guns. The island was notoriously wet, with few dry locations. Japanese air was the artillery and infantry's primary enemy. They bombed regularly, destroying much of the ammunition and other supplies lying on the ground. The 7th InfDiv. dumps were badly hit several times.

By 1 November the Marine gunners were with the 96th InfDiv. west and northwest of Dagami, about ten tough miles inland. Corps artillery continued to fire reinforcing missions for the division's artillery. The season's heavy rains found artillery close to the front lines and they too came under heavy enemy air attack, especially those battalions close to the airfields. Local perimeter defense assumed major importance for artillery as well as infantry. Infiltrating Japanese snipers made major efforts to interfere with artillery performance, mainly while the guns were firing, thereby hoping to avoid detection from defense groups.

One example of infiltration was when, on 24 October, the 226th Artillery Bn. was attacked by about 35 Japanese equipped with automatic weapons, explosive charges, magnetic mines, and of course grenades. When the action was over a part of Battery A was neutralized because one piece had been disabled. The enemy, however, left 26 dead in the battalion sector. Nighttime continued to be that period when the enemy was most active and destructive.

The fighting continued and the enemy unexpectedly brought in thousands of troops from elsewhere. Even to the extent of bringing in paratroops. One group of paratroops landed on Buri airfield, which harbored the Marines of the artillery air section. Those Marines gathered their small arms and two machine guns, one of which had been taken from a wrecked plane, and fought back. The enemy was more powerful and the Marines began to fall back. At this point 175 additional Marines from the guns were organized under the command of Capt. Eugene S. Roane, Jr., (Silver Star, 7–8 December 1944) and arrived in time to stem the attack.

That fighting continued until 10 December, with the Japanese coming out sporadically at night, lobbing grenades and disappearing when the return fire became too intense. The next day, when the XXIV Corps artillery arrived from Saipan on 11 December, the VAC artillery packed up and sailed from Leyte to Guam on 13 December. General Burke departed by air on the same day. His unit suffered according to their participation, 2 officers and 7 enlisted men killed, 3 officers and 31 enlisted men wounded, plus one Marine missing, but their part was recognized by the Army as essential to the success on Leyte.

In the meantime, kamikaze attacks had been extremely destructive to the USN. Likewise the Japanese regular air interdicted the air above Leyte and allowed the IJA to land troops from Formosa (now Taiwan) on a regular basis. The Navy under VA Thomas C. Kinkaid was impatient, as was Gen. MacArthur. Air power was badly needed and the result was a call for Marine air to come in and land on those air bases that had been taken and prepared for active service.

Marine air had been kept, by Lt. Gen. George C. Kenney, in overall command of all air services in the SWPac, pretty much out of any combat roles. At this point the pressure came down heavy and he was literally forced to bring the under-utilized Marine air into the Philippines. The first actual group to arrive in late November was the Marine Night Fighter Squadron 541 under Lt. Col. Peter D. Lambrecht. They had been trained in night intercept operations and equipped with special radar devices. Three days later Gen. Mitchell ordered Marine Aircraft Group 12 (MAG-12), commanded by Col. William A. Willis, to move four of his fighter squadrons, VMF-115, 211, 218, and 313, to Tacloban by 3 December for duty with the 5th Air Force. With service support from both the 5th AF and 7th Fleet, the move was made with minimal problems.

Conditions at the still ill-prepared airfields on Leyte delayed regular air support for some time after arrival. Weather conditions were such that monsoons and "the stories about the mud at Tacloban are still legendary." That according to Robert Sherrod in his commendable *Marine Corps Aviation in World War II*, p. 276. However, VMF (N)-541 flew its first mission in the Philippines by covering PT boats in the Surigao Strait and providing air cover over Ormoc Bay on the day of their arrival. It was on 5 December that Marine air drew its first blood when a Hellcat in southern Leyte shot down an enemy fighter. A Corsair fighter pilot also claimed its first enemy fighter that same day.

Enemy bombing was restricted to night, dusk or dawn and VMF-541 was, or should have been, having the time of their lives. A problem they faced was Army ground controller personnel using procedures very different than those the Marine controllers used. Yet, rather than close-ground support, which was what they had been trained for, the Marine air was utilized in stemming enemy reinforcements. Some losses from enemy Zeros were encountered while attacking Japanese troop ships.

At Ormoc Bay, when the Japanese and USA 77th InfDiv. landed nearly simultaneously and almost at the same spot on 7 December, things became very hot. Attacks by the Japanese on the American landing force were very destructive, especially when they utilized their kamikaze against the ships.

On 11 December, the last time the enemy attempted to reinforce Leyte, 27 Corsairs from four squadrons encountered enemy fighters in a dogfight and shot down four of them. Meanwhile several fighters from VMF-313 dive-bombed a transport, scoring two hits, and VMF-115 hit a cargo ship. Later that day, another 30 Marine planes aided by USA P-40s attacked the same convoy and added to the carnage. Marine air suffered some losses but essentially did more damage and sank several enemy ships, causing many personnel casualties.

Next day, while flying cover near Ormoc Bay, 541 came upon a huge Japanese air fleet of 33 torpedo, dive bombers, and fighters breaking up their formation. Inevitably, some of the enemy got through even though the Marines kept most of them off-balance. When the fighting ended, 541 had shot down 12 enemy aircraft with no losses to themselves. They were flying Hellcats and not the latest planes the Americans had.

By the middle of December Marine air began hitting Japanese ground targets on Leyte, as well as on Mindanao and Luzon, causing untold damage to enemy supplies. Yet they still weren't flying close support to the ground troops, which was their primary training and duty. Differences between 5th AF and Marine air procedures and guidelines made a difference in numerous encounters where both were cooperating with the other group. Army air, when attacking enemy ground during bombing runs, would ditch their bombs if attacked and fight enemy aircraft. Marines flew to their targets and essentially ignored the enemy attacking them, while dropping their bombs upon the targets. This was credited as the primary reason Marine air was more successful in obtaining results than Army air.

Marine Air Group-12, in close teamwork with the two Army fighter groups 348 and 475, and two A-20 and B-25 groups, bombed and strafed enemy concentrations at Palompon on Leyte's west coast. But then, most of the group's work consisted of attacking Japanese sites on Luzon during the balance of the month of December. Especial targets were railroad trains in transit. They and their Army comrades are credited with knocking out 79 locomotives and 456 railway cars, about half the pre-war total of locomotives and at least 25 percent of the cars. Marine air continued to utilize the near-disastrous airfields around Tacloban, making landings and take-offs dangerous, with several losses.

In less than four weeks of operations Marine fighter pilots of MAG-12 had flown a total of 264 missions, mainly in F4Us (Corsairs), in which they had destroyed 22 enemy ships and knocked down at least 40 enemy planes. Their losses were substantial: 9 pilots killed and 34 aircraft lost. Night Fighter Squadron 541 carried out 312 combat flights totaling 924 combat hours. They accounted for 27 enemy aircraft, and four sailing craft loaded with enemy personnel. For their performance 541 received Letters of Commendation from the 5th Air Force praising the squadron for making "an important contribution to the control of the air that is now assured our forces."

> *Results:* Although playing a subdued role on Leyte, Marine artillery performed at the height of its capabilities. They supported their Army comrades all through the Leyte campaign, providing the heavy artillery necessary for the USA's success in overwhelming the enemy. Though Marine air never really had the opportunity to show its prowess in close air support, it did manage to get into the war, finally, and provided the 5th Air Force with substantial support when it was badly needed in one of the U.S. Army's most important campaigns during the war in the SWPA.

Luzon

> *Date:* 6 January to July 1945.
> *Location:* Island of Luzon.
> *Involved:* Japanese army and naval forces versus the U.S. 6th Army, Navy 7th Fleet, and Marine Corps air.
> *Situation:* The war in the SWPA was decidedly placed on hold as Gen. MacArthur made his plans to return to the Philippines, as he had proclaimed he would in early 1942 when making his escape to Australia. Luzon, the island with the largest population and with Manila, the major urban area, was the most important island in the Philippine archipelago. Because of enemy strength located there, it was necessary for nearby islands to be taken first. Consequently, most of MacArthur's air support would be based on Leyte and Samar, while landings were made on Luzon.

Other than the U.S. Navy's sea support and the Marine air flying missions, it was an all–Army show. Before the scheduled infantry landings at Lingayen Gulf on 9 January 1945, the 5th AF was particularly anxious to knock out bridges at Plaridel and Calumpit, each about 25 miles north of Manila. For Marine air F4Us it was an exceeding long 350 miles each way and many of the planes had to sidestep to the island of Mindoro to refuel.

On 6 January 5th AF sent 23 A-20s and 15 F4Us of MAG-12 against the Calumpit bridges and a larger force of AF fighters and bombers against those at Plaridel. Both raids destroyed or badly damaged the highway and railroad bridges. The following day 40 5th AF and 7 planes from MAG-12 went after both bridges to eliminate what remained of each, and on the 8th 31 F4Us and 8 P-38s went again. Finally all bridges were finished and landings on the 9th could proceed successfully.

MAG-12 flew 306 missions during those Lingayen landings and during the following period as the U.S. Army landed and made its way across the island. In the meantime, MAG-14 (Col. Zebulon C. Hopkins) flew another 150 missions, destroying rolling stock, motor transport, harbor installations, and enemy airfields. Meanwhile an airfield was constructed at Mangalden and two more Marine groups, MAG-24 (Col. Lyle H. Meyer) and MAG-32 (Col. Clayton C. Jerome) arrived, expecting to provide the infantry with close air support. For some reason the 5th AF didn't or wouldn't recognize the Marine skills and didn't utilized them in that fashion, but as the saying goes, "things change." In January their dive-bombers worked wonders even though they were still flying the old SBDs which everyone else had side-lined years before. One interesting, but unfortunate, incident was when an F4U strafing Japanese trucks was shot down by Japanese riflemen on 22 January.

In February most of the attacks on Luzon were by the Marine SBDs. Each of the two other Marine groups continued flying missions but in different directions. MAG-12 was assigned sites as far south as Mindanao, 320 miles from its base at Tanauan back on Leyte Island, and the closer Cebu and Negros islands, barely 200 miles away. In the month of February MAG-12 flew 1,848 sorties, of which about 85 percent were combat related.

On 27 January the U.S. Army's 1st Cavalry Division arrived on Luzon and, apparently being a favorite of MacArthur, it was given an operational order that not only provided that division with a reputation but utilized the SBDs in close air support. He told them, "Go to Manila. Go around the Nips, bounce off the Nips, but go to Manila."

To sustain this 100-mile dash the 308th Bombardment Wing alerted the seven Marine squadrons on Luzon to provide a screen of nine planes over the 1st CavDiv., "from dawn to dusk." This would be the first time Marine air would perform as trained, to fly close air support. The ground would call in air strikes, and Marine air would go in and bomb. Then ground would tell them where and when they went off, if they did. As can be expected, the division had little if any chance to reconnoiter the ground beforehand.

On 1 February off they went, with limited vehicles, carried out over primitive roads and in a complete blackout. Despite enemy interference, their mobility paid off and the column was never long delayed. They followed orders: avoid costly delays, bypass the enemy. In three days the 1st Cav. was on the outskirts of Manila. Though Marine air was never needed in close support they were a continual cover for the infantry column, providing aerial protection from "dawn to dusk." For the entire three days they searched an area 30 miles to the column's left for any major attacks.

When the Army entered Manila, its real fighting began and the Marines' air was helpless to intervene. The fighting within the city required street-to-street actions, resulting in the city not being entirely relieved until 1 March. Army Maj. Gen. Verne D. Mudge, CG 1st CavDiv., said, "On our drive to Manila, I depended solely on the Marines to protect my left flank against possible Japanese counter-attack. The job that they turned in speaks for itself. I can say without reservation that the Marine dive bombers are one of the most flexible outfits that I have seen in this war." The balance of his statement is more laudatory but lengthy. General William C. Chase, the brigade commander that led the charge south, was equally praiseworthy, saying, "[I] had never seen such able, close and accurate air support as the Marine flyers were giving [me]."

Most of the work of the SBDs was in the Shimbu sector, east of Manila. They were, however, also busy in the central Kimbu sector, which had about 30,000 Japanese soldiers defending Clark Field and Fort Stotsenburg. Next came an even more dangerous assignment. It was to provide close air support to bands of Filipino guerrillas who were everywhere battering Japanese formations, especially in the mountainous region of northern Luzon, where there were another 140,000 Japanese.

With numerous Marine ALP (Air Liaison Parties) now available, several were assigned to the north and the first mission awaiting them was the elimination of the Japanese entrenched on a ridge just east of enemy-held San Fernando. That port was about 50 miles north of Lingayen Gulf in La Union province. Several air strikes by Army planes helped, but as soon as they left the area, the Japanese counterattacked the guerrillas and recovered lost territory. When Marine air came in with napalm on 28 February, that finally did it. It broke the back of the enemy defenses and the guerrillas took the ground.

Between 1 and 31 March, 186 missions were flown in support of guerrilla missions in northern Luzon. Numerous ALPs and Marine air were strewn around the island, making defense by Japanese forces nearly impossible. Everywhere, guerrillas were successful. In the mountains northeast of Manila, about 80,000 Japanese soldiers were holed up in caves and pillboxes. In the south to southeast another 50,000 defended the so-called Shimbu line which threatened not only the city but the reservoir which was its mainstay. Marine ALP officers were everywhere trying to convince Army senior officers, including CGs of divisions, of the skill of Marine flyers in providing close support. One CG, Maj. Gen. Edwin D. Patrick of the 6th InfDiv., was most difficult and hard to convince. He feared a lack of accuracy which would cause his command numerous casualties, and nothing said by Marine officers would convince him otherwise. "He was polite but absolutely firm" in his denial. It wasn't until he witnessed the accuracy of support called in by Maj. Gen. Mudge for his 1st CavDiv. on 8 February that he changed his mind. Then on 24 February, when the 6th InfDiv. was to advance, Patrick called in Marine air, which surpassed his anticipated results. Even then, one of his regimental commanders, a Col. James E. Rees of the 1st Inf. Regt., refused to call in close support because of the damage and casualties resulting from a USAAF bombing run of B-25s earlier in February.

On the 28th it became necessary for Rees to call in support and he too became convinced when a platoon-sized body of his men, who were trapped in a ravine, were saved by close Marine support. During the balance of the Army's campaign on Luzon the Marine air groups included support for the 6th, 25th, 37th, 38th, 40th, and 43rd InfDivs., as well as the 1st CavDiv. and the 11th Airborne Div.

During the time MAGs 24 and 32 flew support missions on Luzon, they had flown a total of 8,842 combat missions, fired over one and a half million rounds of .30 and .50 caliber ammunition and dropped 19,167 bombs. General Walter Krueger, CG 6th Army, had this to say: "In the crucial stages of the Luzon campaign ... this support was of such high order that I personally take great pleasure in expressing to ever officer and enlisted man ... my appreciation and official commendation for their splendid work ... [ending with] outstanding leadership, initiative, aggressiveness and high courage in keeping with the finest traditions of the Marine Corps."

Meanwhile, Marine air was greatly involved in the fighting in the southern Philippines. MAGs 24 and 32 were shunted south after the Luzon campaign, along with MAGs 12 and 14, which had been flying from Leyte and Samar. Guerrilla operations were active on the islands of Negros, Cebu, Panay, Bohol, Palawan, and other islands in the Sulu Archipelago. There were more than 102,000 Japanese military forces in the south and a prevailing attitude that perhaps the Americans would bypass those islands as they had so many others in the South Pacific area. Except for a few Australian recon aircraft, Maj. Gen. Ralph Mitchell of the 1st Marine Air Wing controlled all aircraft in the area. The plans developed for the recovery of the southern Philippines were known as the VICTOR Missions. VICTOR I was for Panay on 18 March 1945. VICTOR II was for Cebu, Negros, and Bohol on 25 March 1945. VICTOR III was Palawan on 28 February 1945. VICTOR IV was Zamboanga and the Sulu Archipelago on 10 March 1945. Finally, VICTOR V was Mindanao on 17 April 1945.

As usual, the Marines participated to their ultimate ability and, in fact, on 29 March a ceremony was held on Moret field on Zamboanga honoring Col. Clayton C. Jerome and his command. They received a plaque from Maj. Gen. Jens Doe, CG of the 41st InfDiv. The plaque requires a brief description: it stood six feet four inches in height, and was trimmed with captured Japanese naval signal flags, a Japanese light machine gun, and an enemy battle flag, written upon it were the various islands on which the Marine air had supported the 41st InfDiv.

The success of Marine aviation in the Philippines was not without cost; 58 officers and 42 enlisted men of the aviation units were killed in action. Forty-six officers and 81 enlisted were wounded, while another 22 officers and 28 Marines died in operational accidents or were missing.

Results: Because it finally had a real opportunity, Marine air proved its exceptional capability to provide the ground forces with close aerial support. This was, in fact, the longest extent of its participation in ground support fighting during the war. The total time that Marine air was on duty in the Philippines was from 10 October 1944 to 20 July 1945.

Iwo Jima

Date: 19 February to 18 April 1945.
Location: Iwo Jima, an island in the Volcano-Bonin Island group.
Involved: Japanese army and navy troops versus U.S. Marines and Navy.
Situation: If captured, this island, with two developed airfields and an undeveloped third, would provide a place, not only for a fighter base but also for a convenient stop-off for hurt bombers coming back from raids on the Japanese home islands. The B-29s were very expensive, and attaining Iwo Jima was considered worth whatever lives would be expended.

Its main feature, with little value, was a dead volcanic mountain at its southernmost tip, Suribachi. However, that mountain had to be taken soon after landing, otherwise the landing force would be subjected to direct observation and destruction by enemy artillery.

As the CG of VAC, Maj. Gen. Harry Schmidt was directly responsible for training and preparation of all units placed under his command for the Iwo Jima operation. Both the 4th (Maj. Gen. Clifton B. Cates) and 5th MarDivs. (Maj. Gen. Keller E. Rockey) carried out amphibious exercises in the Hawaiian Islands, utilizing new equipment and concepts. The 3rd MarDiv. (Maj. Gen. Graves B. Erskine) trained for their part of the operation, stressing their delayed landing and movement between the two other divisions as all advanced northward.

Following the Hawaiian Island exercises, in late December the 4th and 5th began assembling and moving aboard transports, but the 3rd MarDiv. didn't move until January. In the meantime, as early as June 1944, carrier aircraft were engaged in air strikes upon the island, with regular strikes after August 1944. On 8 December B-24s on the 7th Air Force began their bombing raids, continuing for 74 days, and were aided by Marine B-25s of VMB-612.

When the 3rd MarDiv. was aboard ships, the 21st Marines were ordered to move out ahead and provide the 4th and 5th MarDivs. with an immediate reserve. The rest of the 3rd MarDiv. would be a temporary floating reserve until called upon to land.

On 19 February RA Harry Hill's Task Force 53 arrived off Iwo and was joined by RA William H. P. Blandy's Amphibious Support Force. The Gunfire and Covering force under RA Betram J. Rodgers opened fire at 0640 and the pre–H-hour bombardment began. Gun crews of the *North Carolina, Washington, New York,* and *Texas,* plus two ancients, the *Arkansas* and a Pearl Harbor relic, the *Nevada,* added their voices to the din. The island is eight square miles in area, and it would be an unpleasant eight square miles for the men of the three divisions.

D-day for the 4th and 5th MarDivs., was on 19 February 1945. The plan developed was for the two divisions to land abreast on 3,500 yards of beach: the 4th on Beaches Yellow 1 and 2 were for 1/23 (Lt. Col. Ralph Haas) and 2/23 (Maj. Robert H. Davidson, Silver Star), while 1/25 (Lt. Col. Hollis U. Mustain, Navy Cross) and 3/25 (Lt. Col. Justice M. Chambers) would land on Blue 2. This was on the right, and after landing the division would turn right and head north along the eastern shore. Division Reserve would be the 24th Marines (Col. Walter I. Jordan).

The 5th MarDiv. would land on Beaches Green and Red. The 28th Marines (Col. Harry B. Liversedge, Navy Cross) were slated to land at the southern end, right below 556-foot Suribachi, and then they were to move upward and take it. The 27th Marines (Col. Thomas A. Wornham, Navy Cross) would land to their right and go directly across the island's southernmost narrow waist to the west coast and then drive northward. After the 28th Marines took Suribachi, the division would turn right and head north along the west shoreline. The 26th Marines would be held in reserve, but not for long.

Marines of the 4th and 5th MarDivs. began their movement from ship to shore. At H-hour, actually one minute before 0900, the first wave of the 27th Marines landed on Beach Red. At exactly H-hour men of 1/28 (Lt. Col. Jackson B. Butterfield, Silver Star) were onto Beach Green. Minutes later, when the Japanese had recovered from the awful pasting the island had received, they began firing upon the landing beaches. Every inch of the beach was sited and the enemy artillery didn't waste any shells; each scored hits and caused numerous Marine casualties. On the beaches, the Marines were moving as rapidly as they could in the shifting volcanic sand, but to little avail. Being unable to move rapidly, they were taking terrible punishment.

One of those that died on the beach that day was "Manila John" Basilone, a MoH man from Guadalcanal. In the forefront of the assault at all times, he pushed forward with dauntless courage and iron determination until, moving upon the edge of the airfield, he fell, instantly killed by a bursting mortar shell. He was awarded a posthumous Navy Cross for this day's work.

At 1035 1st Lt. Frank J. Wright, PFC Remo A. Bechelli, and PFC Lee H. Zuck, all from Co. B, 1/28, reached the opposite shore, effectively cutting Suribachi off from the rest of the island. They and their comrades from Co. B had a devil of a time keeping it. In fact Wright lost four of his officers and many of his men along the way. Wright later received a Navy Cross. The battalion was badly extended across the island, with one flank in the air. It was in no position to help 2/28 (Lt. Col. Chandler W. Johnson, Navy Cross) with its job of taking the mountain. At 1245, 3/28 (Lt. Col. Charles E. Shepard), released from its division reserve status, landed and was soon taking heavy losses.

Lieutenant Colonel William R. "Rip" Collins (Silver Star) and his 5th Tank Battalion landed and began to advance while cleaning up bypassed positions behind 1/28. But almost as soon as they landed, five tanks crossed land mines and were knocked out just beyond the beach. Halftracks and Weasels were hit hard coming ashore, before their heavy weapons could be utilized.

At 1430, 5th MarDiv. ADC Brig. Gen. Leo D. Hermle was the first general officer ashore on Iwo, bringing a headquarters reconnaissance party and setting up an advance Division CP. Hermle went forward to his frontline units around Motoyama Airfield No. 1 just to see what was happening. Hermle would earn a Navy Cross for the first week ashore.[27]

Late that afternoon the 26th Marines (Col. Chester B. Graham) were also called in. Upon arrival they faced worse attrition from enemy fire than either the 27th or 28th regiments. The Japanese had succeeded in intensifying the conflagration on the beach. Some elements of the 13th Marines (Col. James D. Waller) managed to get ashore with their 75mm pack howitzers, plus a few 105mm howitzers, and move into position. According to the records, Sgt. Joe L. Pipes, commanding a 105mm howitzer, was the first artillery piece to land on Iwo and within minutes of arrival began firing upon Suribachi. As the other guns began firing they were soon on the receiving end of counter-battery fire and several of the guns were lost.

Meanwhile, many wounded Marines from both divisions were making their way back to the beaches, but there was no cover to protect them from enemy fire. The chaplains and doctors were doing their best, but many wounded died from the constant exposure to enemy fire and were given the last rites on the beach, even as they waited for boats to take them off.

Initially the leadership, Navy and Marine, thought the landing would be smooth and the fight equally so. The sea was relatively calm, visibility was excellent, there were waves of B-29s overhead to drop blockbusters and napalm, and there were a record number of heavy warships to blast the island. As the 4th Division history proclaimed, "From all directions, from every type of weapon, molten steel rained on the island." The only trouble was that the enemy had umbrellas and raincoats: their many holes in the earth.

Before H-hour at 0900 the 4th MarDiv. boats were nearing a landing and it seemed unopposed since no return fire was coming from Iwo Jima. When the tractors began landing on their beaches, however, all hell broke loose. Japanese artillery pieces were well-registered and the shells landed on the tractors as they arrived. A few of them went down in the water, as did a few planes strafing the ground near the beaches. The Marines landed exactly at 0900 and found they were ankle-deep in volcanic ash which was not deep enough to dig into but greatly impeded forward movement. Nonetheless, for some reason most of the division's assault landing force, in the first hour, made it ashore with little trouble. Even the valuable support services, medical aid and a contingent of Seabees, made it in the first hour or so.

At 1000, the honeymoon was terminated, as were many Americans, exposed as they were to everything the enemy had planned for them. Big Japanese guns were depressed, as were little guns, machine guns, and mortars, and the lack of cover became disastrous for the Marines. It appeared, to those taking it, as though the Navy's big guns and the enemy's big guns were dueling, with the Marines between them. Later the Marines counted over 50 pillboxes in 500 yards of beach, plus two huge blockhouses, numerous tank traps and scores of rifle pits. Fortunately the USN shelling had destroyed many, which was undoubtedly the only reason the Marines could get ashore and remain there.

By noon the Marine assault companies of both divisions were driving hard despite the volcanic ash and they made it to Motoyama Airfield No. 1. The airfield zone had been divided between the 27th Marines on the left and the 23rd Marines on the right. Both had lost many officers and men. Many platoons were now commanded by sergeants, and numerous corpsmen were killed off or wounded, leaving the hundreds of wounded Marines without any chance for repairs. One field music (Marine terminology for a musician), Sgt. Darrell S. Cole, begged for a post with a line company. Cole made three trips forward with grenades to a pillbox, dropping them into a slot and putting the pillbox out of action. On his way back a sniper cut him down. His parents received his Navy Cross.

There were no rear areas on Iwo. All tanks were ashore by 1300, as were two battalions of artillery, which were able to fire later that afternoon. By 1600 3/25 reported 50 percent casualties and an hour later more than a thousand wounded 4th MarDiv. men had been transported to ships. When the order came to "dig in" the lines were inland by 500 yards. This was not very far for a successful landing and it left the Marines little defense capability or room to fall back, should that become necessary.

During the night there was no expected counterattack but the enemy continued firing their artillery. The 1/23 CP was wiped out almost entirely from heavy artillery fire, including its CO, Lt. Col. Ralph Haas. On 20 February, the 23rd Marines (Col. Walter W. Wensinger, Navy Cross) captured the balance of Airfield No.1. This allowed the 25th Marines to move ahead but they took enormous casualties in so doing. So much so that the reserve 24th Marines (Jordan) were landed to try to keep the movement continuing ahead. This was an entirely different kind of fight that the enemy was fighting. No great banzai charges with numerous casualties to the Japanese. They were fighting from down deep and causing the Marines to come and dig them out and the price was very high. By the end of the second day Marine casualties in both divisions reached over 2,000.

Suribachi was one gigantic observation post which served the Japanese well. It was the considered opinion that the enemy never considered that the mountain could be taken. The Japanese could see all over the island and a mere phone call to the artillery would plunge a shell into the mass of targeted Marines. It could only be taken from the land side and that was where all the remaining heavy stuff was located. Unfortunately for the Japanese, the 28th Marines weren't privy to their philosophy. So 1/28 went fighting up the hill on 20 February, but it wouldn't be until the 23rd when the first flag was raised in victory.

At night the bypassed enemy came out looking for Marines to kill. They packed their bodies with grenades or used demolition charges to explode amidst any group of Marines they could happen upon. They did manage to hurt a number of Marines that way. One platoon led by 1st Lt. Harold H. Stirling met one such group at dawn on the 20th and slaughtered at least 50 Japanese, with the loss of two Marines killed and several wounded. There were many individual encounters. Private Leo Jez, a Marine from Chicago, earned a Silver Star when he took an enemy's sword, cutting the man's head off. One Marine was in the process of bayoneting a Japanese soldier in his rear as the latter ran but a BAR man caught him before he was bayoneted to death. Marine witnesses laughed aloud at the incongruity or humor of the situation. Another situation which the Marines also found funny was when a Japanese soldier ran into a Marine mortar section yelling "cease firing." "Who the hell are you?" asked a Marine, and the enemy took off with bullets whizzing after him. When engineers placed a charge in a cave, a soldier walked out carrying the charge in his arms. They shot him down, then returned the charge to its rightful place.

Lieutenant Colonel Johnson and 2/28 were on the left, Lt. Col. Shepard and 3/28 were in the center, and Butterfield's well-worn 1/28 was on the far right. Before the Marines jumped off that morning, once more the ships offshore and planes overhead bombarded the mountain. Once again up the 28th went, burning out defenders, blasting with grenades and satchel charges those in caves or blockhouses, and struggling with the enemy in hand-to-hand combat. Other Marines followed the leading companies and took out the bypassed hard spots. It was slow but the only way to do it, and the 28th did it. The 28th Marines' executive officer, Lt. Col. Robert H. Williams (Silver Star), a former paratrooper, obeyed Liversedge's command to establish the CP practically in the front lines. Williams then wisecracked that "it's a hell of a good way to make your battalions move faster."

Four days after the Marine landing, Suribachi still hadn't been taken. Digging out the enemy, sealing up their caves and pillboxes, and killing them were slow and painful. On 23 February the climb began again in earnest. A patrol of 40 men led by 1st Lt. Harold G. Schrier from Co. E went up with a small flag which he had been instructed to place on top of the volcano. Schrier would received a Navy Cross for today. Behind him was PlSgt Ernest I. Thomas (Navy Cross) and the rest of the patrol. As the flag was being implanted a Japanese soldier raced out of hiding and made an effort to hurl a grenade. He was slain and most of the patrol went down into the crater to attend to other enemy soldiers down there. This was the first flag planted on top of Suribachi, and a cheer went up from the Marines down below. That raising was photographed by SSgt Lou Lowry, who went with the patrol. However, as most of us know, a few hours later another much larger flag was purposely sent up with a crew of men to install it. That was the subject of a most famous photograph which has generally thrilled Americans ever since. Nearly everyone has forgotten the first picture, except the men that planted it. Too bad.

At this point, with the taking of Suribachi, many of the members of the 28th Marines assumed, or wished, their job was finished. It wasn't. Three days after the foregoing events, the regiment was back in the war.

During the period from 19 to 22 February, no matter what obstacles were encountered, Lt. Col. Justice M. "Jumping Joe" Chambers (Medal of Honor), CO of 3/25, was the main instrument keeping his battalion moving. Soon after landing he found his men stymied and stopped. By personal leadership from the front, he managed to get them moving against fierce machine-gun and rifle fire from the cliffs ahead. In eight hours of savage fighting he led his men upward and eventually took the ridge, forcing the enemy to give way. This freed up the regiment and it began moving forward once again. On 22 February, while directing the fire of a rocket platoon, he was seriously wounded and evacuated under heavy enemy fire.

Bad seas also created problems. Small boats with supplies overturned, as did several with one battalion of howitzers, losing seven of twelve guns. Japanese artillery still had the beach well-covered and on day three, 21 February, the beach was so littered with wreckage that few boat lanes were open to moving traffic. Combat efficiency for the 4th MarDiv. was calculated at 68 percent. Regardless, Capt. Joseph J. McCarthy (Medal of Honor), the "skipper" of Co. G, 2/24, decided to open up the way before Motoyama Airfield No. 2. Acting on his own to break the determined enemy resistance before the airfield, he pulled together a demolitions crew, flamethrower personnel, and a picked rifle squad. He then led the way across 75 yards of fire-swept ground, charging a heavily fortified pillbox on the ridge to his front. McCarthy hurled grenades into the emplacement while directing the operations of his small group in destroying the hostile position. Joe killed several individuals and then rallied his men. With him in the lead, they launched a furious attack upon the other positions remaining on the ridge. An inspiring and indomitable fighter, McCarthy was mainly responsible for capturing the ridge.

On 20 February, morning orders had been issued to the 3rd MarDiv. for the 21st Marines (Col. Hartnoll J. Withers, Silver Star) to prepare to land. The situation was confused and they circled around for six hours in their LCVPs in the rain and rough water, until their travail was terminated. On the next afternoon, 21 February at 1345, they landed in a drizzling rain. On D-day plus three, in line alongside the 24th Marines and attached to the 4th MarDiv., they moved forward with the 26th Marines (Col. John R. Lanigan, Navy Cross) of the 5th MarDiv. on their left. The regiment advanced into the "jaws of Hell" at 0815. In relieving the battered 23rd Marines, the 24th was stunned by the firestorm of artillery and mortar shells, as well as the machine-gun and rifle fire they absorbed.

On the left, the 21st Marines had landed on the 22 February; on his right Lt. Col. Lowell E. English with 2/21 and Lt. Col. Marlow C. Williams with 1/21 endeavored to advance but it was considered impossible. The 21st was nearly surrounded and could see nothing but sand dunes in all directions. Skippers took heavy punishment. Company F's was killed, G's had his leg blown off, the replacement for F was badly wounded and Col. Williams was hit. His replacement, Maj. Clay M. Murray, was also wounded that same day. Major Robert H. Houser, formerly CO of Weapons Co., and a Navy Cross on Guam, was Murray's replacement, and he somehow managed to survive.

Meanwhile, both the 9th Marines (Col. Howard N. Kenyon, Navy Cross) and 3rd Marines (Col. James A. Stuart) anxiously awaited their opportunity to land. The latter regiment was in Expeditionary Reserve and would not land on Iwo Jima. Maj. George A. Percy, temporarily CO of 2/21, had become involved in a ferocious firefight early on 23 February and was unable to advance until 0935. Percy was another Marine who would earn a Navy Cross on Iwo Jima for his perseverance during the entire campaign. Percy and his men required a second artillery preparation and both battalions had companies that managed to get to the southwest approaches of Airfield No. 2. Houser and 1/21 did advance at 0730, but heavy enemy fire eventually forced them to fall back and lines were consolidated for the night at the southern edge of the field.

One of the great moments on the 23rd was when Cpl. Herschel W. Williams (Medal of Honor), born in Quiet Dell, WV, now a demolition sergeant with 1/21, went forward to clear obstructions. Those were mainly pillboxes with devastating machine-gun fire, causing numerous casualties to Marines. He burned the defenders with his flamethrower using their air vents or other openings, continuing in several periods and killing numerous of the enemy.

Houser's 1st Battalion was relieved by 3/21 (Lt. Col. Wendell H. Duplantis, Silver Star) on the morning of 24 February. At 0915 they advanced. Because of the excellent work of 1/21, that advance made it somewhat easier for 3/21 and they took approximately another

600 yards that day. However, 2/21 was unable to keep pace when they ran into severe mortar and artillery fire. After noon they went forward once again but the severity of 2/21's losses caused them to hold up for the balance of that day.

Regardless of the unfortunate situation delaying 2/21, that afternoon 3/21 again went forward, even without the support of tanks, which had not arrived on time. It managed to get two companies, I and K, across the center of the airfield. Company K's skipper, Capt. Rodney L. Heinze, was wounded, and four minutes later Capt. Clayton S. Rockmore of Co. I was killed. Company K's exec., Capt. Daniel A. Marshall, assumed command and 1st Lt. Raoul Archambault brought in Co. I, and the attack continued. Though K took most of Hill 199 and the northern edge of the airstrip, "friendly" artillery fire, however, inadvertently dropped in on them and drove them from their conquest. When the shelling ceased, back up the hill they went. This time the enemy drove them from their conquest. Because their flanking units did not keep abreast, K and I both were taking enfilade fire.

At 1350 Co. I went forward once again and the Marines went at the Japanese with everything they had. Hand-to-hand combat was ferocious in that severe hacking and screaming melee that was over in a few short minutes. Fifty enemy soldiers were counted dead. By 1820 the battalion, with severe losses, now held the ground and was ordered to "hold at all costs." Archambault was awarded a Navy Cross. Colonel Withers requested relief for his battered regiment and the following day, 25 February, the 9th Marines were called up. Upon relief, the 21st went into reserve.

Division headquarters had landed and now the 3rd MarDiv. assumed control of the center of the line and the two other Marine divisions, the 4th on the right and the 5th on the left, were now able to compress their lines. This was just as well since both had already suffered severe losses. That morning of 25 February found the 9th with orders to advance at 0730. On the right was 1/9 (Lt. Col. Carey Randall) and 2/9 (Lt. Col. Robert E. Cushman) was to the left. After artillery preparation the regiment began its advance. Cushman's men met the most resistance and were taken in front and left flank by strong enemy fire, making little progress.

Tanks of the 3rd Tank Battalion (Maj. Holly H. Evans, Silver Star) had been called in to support 1/9 and drew heavy mortar fire and massive artillery shelling, resulting in many casualties to 1/9 and the tanks. Nine were knocked out before they managed to destroy enemy installations, including three heavy guns. Motoyama Airfield No. 2 lay directly in the path of the 9th Marines and it was heavily defended. Its flat terrain provided marvelous fields of fire for machine guns, anti-tank guns, and other enemy flat trajectory weapons. This high ground lying before the Marines went across the entire island and gave the enemy undisputed observation of all ground the Marines then occupied. It was necessary that the Marines advance their front soon, otherwise their losses would become uncontrollable. It was decided that all available artillery must be focused upon those positions to provide the cover necessary.

On 23 February the 24th Marines fought a bloody battle for Charlie–Dog Ridge and on 24 February they captured it after some of the toughest fighting on the island. They and the 21st Marines drove into, and on the 25th captured, Motoyama Airfield No. 2. The 25th Marines were still moving, slowly, on the east coast toward Tachiiwa Point. One of the island's chief strong points (Hill 382) was directly in the path of the 24th Marines. After Mt. Suribachi it was the second-highest point on the island and was loaded with natural and man-made crevices 15 to 50 feet deep. It was the backbone and nerve center for the northern portion of the island's defense. There were three other difficult points within the sector of the 4th MarDiv.: they were branded "Turkey Knob," "Amphitheater," and Minami Village. Because each was interdependent with the others, all three would have to be assaulted at the same time.

On 26 February, to the 23rd Marines went the task of Hill 382; to the 25th Marines went Turkey Knob and the Amphitheater. The defensive positions included four tanks buried up to their turrets, at least 20 pillboxes, several 75mm anti-aircraft guns with muzzles depressed to fire horizontally, and many machine guns, both light and heavy.

Major James S. Scales and 3/23 went up the hill and after a knock-down day-long fight, two companies took the high ground. One of their men, PFC Douglas T. Jacobson (Medal of Honor) of Rochester, NY, wiped out a 20mm AA gun and crew with his newly acquired bazooka, then went to the summit of Hill 382 and used his weapon with accuracy. He destroyed two machine-gun positions, then attacked a large blockhouse, killing off the occupants. Then he went after another pillbox, killing more Japanese before destroying the site with an explosive. Next he wiped out six more positions, killing off all ten occupants. Volunteering for a nearby company, he knocked out another pillbox, then destroyed an enemy tank and another blockhouse. All in all, he is credited with knocking out at least 16 positions and killing approximately 75 of the enemy.

The fighting going north was tough for the 26th and 27th Marines. They advanced in a two-battalion formation, 1/26 (Lt. Col. Daniel C. Pollock) on the left and 3/27, led by Lt. Col. Donn J. Robertson, on the right. Robertson and Pollock would both earn a Navy Cross for these first few days on the island. Robertson's battalion ran into stout resistance, finding upwards of 135 pillboxes in their sector. Both battalions, however, with tanks from the 5th Tank Bn., moved ahead and together overran the Motoyama Airfield No. 1. One of the first groups to cross the airfield was Capt. John K. Hogan's company, known far and wide as "Hogan's Goats."[28] A platoon of tanks from Co. A (1st Lt. John J. Stemkoski, Silver Star) probed deep; at least 1,000 yards up the beach. There they quickly silenced numerous machine guns, an ammunition dump, and generally shot the hell out of the Japanese.

One thing that the troops had been finding were mounds of sand with phony fire ports. These appeared in photos as real pillboxes and had received much attention from artillery and naval gunfire. The Marines also found numerous dummy tanks, most constructed of wood, all of which had also drawn extensive shell fire.

The skipper of Co. C, 1/26, Capt. Robert H. Dunlap (Medal of Honor) of Galesburg, IL, fought his Co. C hard. Nothing seemed to slow them down. A key terrain feature facing the western beaches was a steep, cave-pocked cliff out of which poured a stream of accurate fire. At the face of this cliff Dunlap led Co. C upward. Moving up as far as they could physically go, Dunlap decided to leave his force and personally moved ahead another 200 yards. There he observed what the enemy was doing, and also located their gun positions. With that data he returned to his own lines and relayed the information gained to supporting artillery. They in turn passed the coordinates to naval gunfire. Placing himself in an exposed vantage point where he could observe the results, and working without respite for two days and two nights, he skillfully directed the bombardment.

The 27th Marines had swamped the Japanese in the so-called battle of the "Boat Basin," where the enemy's primary water supply was located. But eventually they ran into one of the most important defensive positions on the island, Hill 362. Basically, the enemy's defensive lines ran across the island from there to Hill 382, where the 4th MarDiv. would be so badly bloodied. VAC headquarters had a pattern which remained the same: each morning at 0800 Marine artillery and naval gunfire laid down a barrage into the enemy lines which lasted until 0830. By the clock, the enemy then came out of their deepest blockhouses and dugouts to re-occupy their defensive positions and waited for the unfortified Marines to once again assault them. It never failed, and it never changed. VAC was doing what the Japanese were criticized for doing, never changing their pattern.

By D-day plus seven (26 February), and after suffering heavy casualties, the 26th Marines had managed a day's rest before going back into action. The 3rd MarDiv. had been having a difficult time in its sector. It had not yet taken the bluff to their left, the one which made the advance of the 26th Marines nearly impossible. On 27 February, GySgt. William G. Walsh (Medal of Honor), a native of Roxbury, MA, led an assault platoon from Co. G, 3/27, against the enemy stronghold. Up they went, despite being repeatedly driven back. The fire from the enemy made any advance seemingly impossible, but Walsh went and his men followed. Their losses were horrendous but they followed their sergeant. The few survivors finally made it to the top. The 27th Marines, badly hurt but not yet out of the game, was relieved by the 28th Marines.

Tactics as outlined by VAC didn't change, it was still a general advance straight against the well-dug-in enemy. Consequently, casualties among the Marines of all three divisions continued to mount. Hill 362, with all its caves and pillboxes, in twisted terrain, was just as bad as Suribachi, a fact which the 28th learned to its regret. Each seemed to have many entrances and probably each could have held a battalion. As efforts were made to seal one opening, the Japanese continued to come out of others and fire at those attempting to close one. Digging them out was a never-ending job, and costly in manpower. While trying to cross open ground in front of a cave, Co. F of 2/28, Capt. Arthur H. Naylor, Jr., CO (Silver Star), lost 94 men in an hour. Naylor set up his CP only 25 yards from the opening and established a 24-hour guard at the mouth. However, that didn't trouble the Japanese, who hurled grenades directly into Naylor's CP.

The worst times were when the Marines advanced past the enemy and as they pushed ahead the enemy came out of their digs, fired upon them and threw grenades from behind. Mounted upon trucks, hundreds of rockets were rained on the reverse of each slope, which happened to be just as well-fortified as the forward slope. Finally, on 1 March the 5th MarDiv. took Hill 362. Paying that bill included the loss of Lt. Col. Tom M. Trotti, 3/26, killed in action by a mortar burst on 22 February, and Lt. Col. Chandler W. Johnson, 2/28, killed in action on 2 March as he was returning to his CP from a forward observation post. Johnson was awarded a Navy Cross for his exploits during the period from 19 February until his death.

But by now the numbers of Marines were so depleted that they were forced to retire and the enemy then went up the hill and reclaimed it. Once more the 23rd Marines went up and again were forced to retire and once again the Japanese regained the hill. The Marines' casualties taking the height didn't allow them to hold it, and every night the positions were reversed.

A battalion of the 24th Marines tried the Amphitheater and also caught hell. The 25th Marines caught the same treatment at Turkey Knob, from all sides. Day after day for four days, each regiment received the same handling. On 1 March Wensinger's badly handled 23rd Marines were relieved by Lt. Col. Richard Rothwell (Silver Star) and 2/24. This battalion succeeded in scaling Hill 382 but no fewer than six company commanders became casualties during the four days of battle. Capt. Walter Ridlon and Co. F, plus the remnants of Co. E, were credited with the hill's capture. Ridlon earned a Navy Cross for the period 19 February to 16 March 1945. Sergeant James Beddingfield and a squad of Marines came up from behind and surprised the eight remaining enemy still on the hill. "They never had a chance," said Beddingfield, "they couldn't get their gun wheeled around before we had them." Consequently, Turkey Knob and the Amphitheater became untenable for the Japanese. In 13 days of fighting the 4th MarDiv. had suffered 6,591 casualties and, though some replacements had arrived, the combat efficiency was rated at only 50 percent.

Only three of the 12th Marines' (Lt. Col. Raymond F. Crist) batteries were ashore on 25 February. However, artillery from the 4th and 5th MarDivs. and naval gunfire ably supported the 3rd MarDiv. At 1400 the 9th Marines were in a comparative stalemate. A large gap had developed in their center and it was decided that Cushman's badly hurt 2/9 was unable to keep up the pace. Lieutenant Colonel Harold C. Boehm's 3/9 was called up to replace them and immediately pushed ahead and effected a junction with the 26th Marines on the left.

Boehm's battalion got plastered, hit hard on the front and left flank. Casualties rapidly mounted as the companies moved swiftly to take the high ground to their front. By 1700 the assault companies had lost both skippers and a high percentage of officers and noncoms. The battalion was quickly becoming disorganized, lines were wavering and the ground taken was being lost. Company K on the right had lost five officers and most NCOs. Captain Joseph T. McFadden, S-3 (Silver Star), was ordered to take command of K and reorganize it. Lieutenant Raymond A. Overpeck (Silver Star), senior officer remaining of Co. I, was issued similar orders. Preparations were made for the anticipated counterthrusts that night.

The next morning, 26 February, 1/9 and 2/9 jumped off after an artillery preparation, but the sheet of fire they ran into stopped them from making but modest gains. Boehm's 3/9 was in no shape to continue and was ordered to be pulled back. They went into regimental reserve and occupied a defensive position. Boehm would also earn a Navy Cross for his courage and skills on Iwo Jima. The assault battalions were unable to make any headway, even though several Marine bombers made four close support sorties before their positions.

That night a BAR man, Arkansas native Private Wilson D. Watson (Medal of Honor) of 2/9, having been halted with his squad before some heavily defended caves and pillboxes, boldly rushed one of them. Watson fired his weapon into the aperture and threw in a grenade, then ran to the rear of the box to wait for the exiting enemy. He slaughtered many shooting from the hip. Standing fearlessly erect and all the while firing, Watson managed to hold the hill for 15 minutes. He killed at least 60 Japanese before his comrades came up to join him.

Kenyon's 9th Marines had had their work cut out for them during the previous few days. While the 12th poured in the artillery the regiment continued making an effort to break through the well-dug-in enemy. Cushman's 2/9 was on the left and Randall's 1/9 was on the right. The former reached the north end of the airfield and stopped long enough to catch its collective breath while reorganizing. Boehm's 3/9 pushed through them and advanced a modest distance before it was stopped by massive mortar and artillery fire.

So far, in comparison, the regiment had a relatively easy time of it. From here on the going got really tough. Lying before them was at least 100 feet of rough tumbled boulders to climb. Nothing affected the Japanese atop that hill: not artillery, not gunfire from the ships, not even planes. Once again, it was a job for the infantry to dig 'em out.

This time 3/9 shone brightly. Up that rugged mass they climbed, and while fiercely engaged in hand-to-hand combat Col. Walter S. Campbell's 3rd Engineer Bn. helped the infantry with their flamethrowers. The next morning the 21st Marines were back and during the day pushed 500 yards forward through what was left of the pillboxes covering the approaches to the incomplete Motoyama Airfield No. 3.

The fighting was slow during the following week and the Marines were unable to make but modest gains daily. Lt. Col. Lowell E. English, CO, 2/21, was wounded on 2 March and his exec., Maj. George A. Percy, again assumed command. Though the USMC artillery poured in 45,000 rounds upon the Japanese in a few hundred square yards on the sixth, Marines could barely make another hundred yards' advance that day. It was, and would continue to be, rugged going for all three divisions on Iwo. In many ways it was more like the desperate attempts on the Western Front in World War I than a battle in the more mobile World War II. Advances were reckoned in yards.

The following day, 7 March, at 0500, the 9th and 21st jumped the Japanese. They surprised the enemy and gained a valuable several hundred yards of strong positions that had been holding up the division. Company B of the 9th was nearly wiped out taking one rocky position. For a day and a half Co. F was isolated from the rest of the 9th Marines and when it was relieved by tanks, only 22 Marines remained. The enemy nearly wiped out the headquarters of the 9th Marines with land mines and aerial bombs that night.

On 6 March, Co. G of the 21st was the first Marine unit to spot the far northern end of the island. However, it wasn't until the following day that Percy and 2/21 were on the rocks overlooking the northern coast. The following day Co. A sent a 28-man platoon down the cliff to the seashore, cutting the enemy positions in half. The platoon sent a can of sea water back to Gen. Erskine with the message, "Forward for approval, not for consumption." As an example of the losses, Co. A, 1/21, had on that final day only three Marines left of the original landing force. The rest of the men came from two replacement drafts.

By the 6th of March the ground action and terrain was such that the 5th MarDiv.'s intelligence officer decided that the artillery of the 13th Marines was no longer effective; it had become a "grunt's war." The Japanese had finally given up the center of the island and were now in residence at the northwest corner. This was even worse territory to fight over and the enemy continued to make the Marines pay heavily for every inch of ground they gained. It was there and would stay because the situation required it, but it was no longer an effective fighting division.

Casualties were close to 100 percent in some units. So many officers and noncoms had become casualties that privates were leading in their stead. One company had had six different skippers since D-day. One first sergeant related later that he had landed with 17 sergeants and none were left. A few hours later he too was evacuated with a wounded leg. Cooks, bakers, and candlestick makers were now part of the infantry teams, as were company clerks. And because each was a Marine, he was also a rifleman.

General Kuribayashi, the island CG, was still alive and the defense went on. The Marines continued to "dig 'em out." Blasting caves, knocking out bunkers, locating and destroying mortar positions, and the same for OPs. Nights were cold — it was late winter in the north Pacific. The front changed and the 25th Marines was now the pivot. They continued holding the enemy's southern flank while the rest of the 4th MarDiv. tried to clean up the northern edges. But it was still the same old story. After a half-hour preparatory artillery barrage, the 23rd went forward and barely eked out a 100-yard gain. The 24th

Marines attacked in conjunction but fared no better. One platoon of the 23rd was ambushed and only one man survived uninjured.

On the night of 8-9 March the Japanese tried the only organized counterattack of the entire campaign. After an artillery, mortar and machine-gun barrage at 2200 they began trying to infiltrate the Marines' lines. That continued all night, all along the lines. Some got through to the OPs. Some with land mines strapped to their chests charged into a group of Marines. Others blew themselves up with grenades as they witness their comrade's failures. The next morning 784 enemy bodies were counted all along the front, but the lines had held.

This northwest pocket was nicknamed "Death Valley" by the Marines. The ratio of living to the dead climbed rapidly, especially the dead to wounded. Because the Marines grabbed every bit of cover they could find, many caught the big one in his head. Consequently, Corpsmen had less to do, since more Marines died than survived. The enemy was still dug in and waiting for the advancing Marines to come into their sights. At such close quarters, the heavy stuff, on both sides, was useless. No close air support, no heavy naval guns or even ground artillery was used. Even mortars were of little help.

Tanks moved up and fired directly into the cave mouths. Gasoline was dumped into the caves to burn the Japanese out. Rockets were fired directly into caves. Explosives were also tried. Flamethrowing tanks burned the defenders in their holes and caves but still the enemy fought back, piling up Marine bodies.

The 27th Marines were in a bad way but Col. Wornham managed to scrape together enough remaining men to form a provisional battalion. One of his men, PlSgt. Joseph R. Julian (Medal of Honor), from Sturbridge, MA, was another one-man Marine expeditionary force. On 9 March Julian and his men faced a determined enemy effort to slow down and defeat his battalion's advance. The terrific mortar and machine gun barrage forced Julian to place his men in defensive positions, but he continued forward in a one-man assault. Against the nearest pillbox he hurled both phosphorus and regular grenades, killing two and driving the other five enemy out of the emplacement before quickly taking those five out.

Obtaining more explosives, with another Marine he went forward and took out two more emplacements. Then unassisted, he took a bazooka and, firing four rounds, ended the last remaining pillbox but was mortally wounded by a burst of enemy fire.

The fighting continued. The gorge before them was littered with enemy caves and the dead bodies of Marines and their foe. The audacity and bravery of men on both sides were exemplary or discouraging, depending upon one's point of view. Out of the 200-plus men of one Marine company, only 100 remained after attempts to take the gorge. As one captain said, "it was easier to go into the gorge than climb out." The enemy targets were the wounded Marines. Whenever anyone tried to save one, he and the potential savior were usually hit numerous times.

The fighting went on. On 14 March two more Marines earned the highest honor their nation could bestow. Private George Phillips of Rich Hill, MO, while a member of 2/28, courageously pulled an enemy grenade to himself to save the lives of his comrades. Another, Pvt. Franklin E. Sigler (Medal of Honor), born in Little Falls, NJ, with 2/26, voluntarily took command of his rifle squad when his leader became a casualty. Fearlessly leading the squad against an enemy machine gun emplacement, he managed to throw numerous grenades, annihilating the entire crew. From the heights above many more Japanese guns opened up on him and his men so he courageously scaled the heights, surprising the enemy with his one-man assault. Though severely wounded, he crawled back to his squad and continued to direct their operations. Sigler went out to drag in wounded Marines, carrying in three; it wasn't until he was ordered to the rear for medical attention that he finally stopped.

Another Marine who earned the Navy Cross was Lt. Col. Austin R. Brunelli, CO of 1/24, for extraordinary heroism in action against the enemy as commander of a Marine infantry battalion from 8 to 16 March 1945. Brunelli, whose regular duties were as regimental executive officer, had been painfully wounded and evacuated 20 February, but returned on 21 February. On 9 March he was ordered to assume command of 1/24, which had suffered heavy casualties and was disorganized. Upon assuming command from Maj. Paul S. Treitel, he made a personal reconnaissance of his entire front lines, and reorganized his badly depleted units into two rifle companies. By his heroic conduct he restored the fighting spirit of his men and was able to resume the attack in coordination with units on his flanks. Under his fearless and inspiring leadership the battalion made substantial gains against the determined resistance of the enemy. This advance of his battalion eliminated a salient, and thereafter the general advance continued daily until the resistance of the enemy was completely overcome.

Throughout the action Lt. Col. Brunelli repeatedly exposed himself, with utter disregard for his own personal safety, to strong enemy fire in order to direct and encourage the men of his battalion. His conduct throughout was in keeping with the highest traditions of the United States Naval Service and he was awarded a Navy Cross.

On 10 March the Marines' final push began. Later that day patrols from the 4th MarDiv. reached the northeast shore and on 11 March the division had managed to reach the ocean. In the meantime, some Japanese had been bypassed, but the 25th Marines crushed the group the following day. On 16 March the entire island was considered secured by VAC headquarters.

But the campaign was not yet over. The entire island was loaded with Japanese still within caves and it was now time to mop them up. With all the firing the island was nearly as dangerous to life and limb as before being "secured." As soon as the 3rd MarDiv.'s area was cleared they then helped the 4th and 5th MarDivs. with their areas.[29] The final fighting occurred around Kitano point.

It wasn't until 26 March that the final battle for Iwo Jima was fought. On that morning a last charge by the Japanese ended their defense of the island. It was also the final Medal of Honor awarded during the campaign for the 5th MarDiv. Most of the remaining Japanese were members of the medical corps; one was a doctor (dedicated to saving lives) and others were medicos. Many carried M1s or grenades taken from dead Marines. The 5th Pioneer Battalion, led by Maj. Robert Riddell, had a big hand in stopping this last desperate sortie. Their casualties numbered nine dead and 40 wounded.

One outstanding individual from that group, 1st Lt. Harry L. Martin (Medal of Honor), from Bucyrus, OH, instantly organized a firing line and succeeded in repulsing an attack upon his small group. Sustaining two severe wounds, he worked his way through the enemy, killing many as he went forward. Arriving at the place where his men were surrounded, he directed them back to their lines. Meanwhile a few of the enemy had taken possession of a machine gun which Martin, with just his pistol, charged, killing in the group. He called to his men to follow him. They charged into the strong enemy formation with Martin leading and he fearlessly killed as many as he could before he was felled by a grenade.

Marine air units serving the Marines on Iwo included VMO 1, 4 (supported the 3rd and 4th MarDivs.), and 5 (supported the 3rd and 5th MarDivs.); VMJ 252, 353, and 952; VMSB 612. The following flights were all from carriers: USS *Bennington*, VMF 112 and 123; from *Essex*, VMF 124 and 213; from *Wasp*, VMF 216 and 217; from *Bunker Hill*, VMF 221 and 451.

Essentially, the fighting on Iwo had ceased, though over the next few months scores of individuals and a few groups of Japanese would attack Americans and be killed in so doing. On 4 March, while the fighting was going on, the first crippled B-29 had landed on Airfield No. 1. The Air Force had already landed and established a repair base for returning damaged B-29s, of which at least 40 had been saved. Incidentally, more Medals of Honor were awarded at Iwo Jima than at any previous or later battles for Marines. The 3rd MarDiv. earned three, the 4th seven and the fighting 5th 14, plus three more for attached "docs."

The cost to the 5th MarDiv. was severe. Nearly 2,500 Marines of the 5th MarDiv. or attached Corpsmen were buried on the island and another 6,218 had been wounded, with most removed offshore.

The 4th MarDiv.'s total casualties numbered 9,090, of which 1,731 had been killed. Of the 22,000 Japanese killed on the island, 8,982 were counted in the 4th MarDiv.'s sector. Perhaps another 1,000 had been sealed up in cave closings, uncounted for obvious reasons. The division's captured POWs numbered just 44.

Manpower losses in the two-regiment 3rd MarDiv. were somewhat lighter than in the other two divisions: 5,569 total, of which 1,131 were killed in action.

The few surviving old-timers from each division, those with 27 months overseas or three campaigns, were sent home. Some replacements arrived, but most went to the 1st and 6th MarDivs. for the forthcoming wear and tear on Okinawa, which got first claim.

This was the final call for two of the three divisions. The 3rd MarDiv. would be on Guam when the war ended in August 1945. The 3rd Marines were utilized to patrol Guam and in so doing found and killed a few Japanese stragglers. But it wasn't until the peace was signed that another 500 Japanese came forward, but even then many more remained in the boonies for years to come.

The 4th MarDiv. returned to Maui, where it was disbanded later that fall. For some reason the 5th MarDiv. was selected to make a landing at Kyushu, Japan, and on 22 September the 26th Marines landed first. The division remained there until December, when they were returned to San Diego and disbanded.

> *Results:* Controversies over assigning to the Marines the conquest of Iwo Jima haven't gone away in more than 60 years. The U.S. Army Air Force generals wanted it, in fact, they demanded it. So the joint chiefs assigned it and the Marines went ahead and took it. But at what a cost in humans, both Marines and the enemy, though the latter weren't given much humane thought at the time. However, another, somewhat lesser complaint was the late entry of the 3rd MarDiv. to combat.
>
> Later, Adm. Turner and Gen. Holland Smith both defended their decision not to land the 3rd Marines earlier, though the VAC CG (Maj. Gen. Harry Smith) and staff greatly disagreed. The latter insisted that there was plenty of room on the island for another regiment, though the former maintained that wasn't possible. At any rate, the first two divisions, 4th and 5th, had a tough row to hoe, as their losses proclaim.

The justification for taking the island, that being the need for an air field close enough to the home islands for emergency landings, continued to be maintained by the USAAF long after the war. Numbers such as more than 29,000 airmen saved have been bandied about. Perhaps those figures are authentic, but upwards of 20,000 Marines and perhaps as many as another 30,000 Japanese paid the price.

The lack of initiative and change by VAC headquarters seems to indicate either questionable leadership decisions or staff failures, or perhaps both.

Okinawa

Date: 1 April to 22 June 1945.

Location: Okinawa and the surrounding smaller islands of the Ryukyus chain. Considered by Japan as home islands.

Involved: Japanese army and navy versus the 10th U.S. Army, including the following divisions: 7th InfDiv. and 96th InfDiv.; and XXIV Corps: 2nd MarDiv. (LFR), 27th InfDiv. (AR), 77th InfDiv. (AR); and III Marine Amphibious Corps: 1st MarDiv. and 6th MarDiv.

Situation: ICEBERG was the operational title given this final amphibious assault in the Pacific War. Three divisions of Marines were to participate, the 1st (Maj. Gen. Pedro del Valle), and the newly created 6th MarDiv. (Maj. Gen. Lemuel C. Shepherd, Jr.), which, as a division, would be going into its premier landing. They would be part of the Marine IIIMAC (Lt. Gen. Roy S. Geiger). The 2nd MarDiv. (Maj. Gen. Thomas E. Watson) was part of the initial overall plan, but was not brought ashore to solve a severe problem in the southern portion of the island. Elements of that division would, however, be engaged in a feint on L-day and suffer the first casualties of the operation.

This was a joint effort and the IIIMAC was part of the 10th Army. Twenty-fourth Corps (Maj. Gen. John R. Hodge, USA) was the second half of the 10th Army (Lt. Gen. Simon B. Buckner, Jr., USA) and also included the 7th InfDiv. (Maj. Gen. Archibald V. Arnold, USA) and the 96th InfDiv. (Maj. Gen. James L. Bradley, USA). Two other divisions plus the 2nd MarDiv. (Landing Force Reserve) were part of the XXIV Corps, the 27th (Maj. Gen. George W. Griner, Jr., USA) and 77th InfDiv. (Maj. Gen. Andrew D. Bruce, USA). The latter had been actively cleaning out small pockets of Japanese troops on various islands in the Ryukyu chain while the former had served on Saipan with the 2nd and 4th MarDivs. Planners were well aware that the most trouble would be encountered in the southern portion of the island, and, presumably, took that into account. Unfortunately it seldom appeared that way to the infantry who would bear most of the burden for the first weeks.

Tenth Army landed four divisions on L-day, 1 April 1945, and much to their collective surprise, against token resistance. Due to the importance of the island, the Japanese Imperial High Command had assigned the competent Lt. Gen. Mitsuru Ushijima to defend the island. His forces, the 32nd Army, included many independent artillery, mortar, AAA, AT, and machine-gun groups, nine infantry and three artillery battalions, and the 44th Independent Mixed Brigade consisting of approximately 5,000 infantry. Additionally, the 24th InfDiv. arrived followed by the 62nd InfDiv. There was also a modest tank force known as the "27th Tank Regiment," but which was actually a force of about 750 men in companies of one light and one medium tank, with very modest ancillary support services. American calculations credit Ushijima with having about 100,000 fighting men, which included 67,000 Japanese army troops, 23,000 local militia and at least 9,000 naval forces.

The real strength assigned to the island defense would seem to have been the air services. The 8th Air Division (Army) included 190 bombers and fighters plus 250 kamikaze, and the 6th Air Army (Army) had 180 fighters and bombers, 45 recon, and 300 kamikaze aircraft to attack American transports. It also had 60 fighters, 30 bombers and 100 kamikaze to attack carriers and captured airfields. Another 445 planes were for combat air patrols. The navy added four air fleets, totaling another 1,350 fighting planes. And if that wasn't sufficient they had 1,300 training planes which volunteers could and would fly into ships on the seas and ground positions if it seemed feasible.

Generally, on land the Japanese defense force seemed quite modest for the job assigned to them unless the American estimate was reasonably accurate. Gen Ushijima had his work cut out for him, but he did it well.

The actual landing of the 10th Army consisted of both MarDivs. north of the Bishi Gawa (River) and the 7th and 96th InfDivs. south of that line. In order from north to south they were the 6th MarDiv. (Beaches Green 1 and 2, Red 1, 2, and 3), the 1st MarDiv. (Blue 1 and 2, Yellow 1, 2, and 3), 7th InfDiv. (Purple 1 and 2, Orange 1 and 2) and lastly the 96th InfDiv. (White 1, 2, and 3, Brown 1, 2, 3, and 4).

At 0630 6th MarDiv. troops in APAs transferred to landing craft and began moving shoreward, as did LCMs with tanks. Two battalions of the 22nd Marines, the 2nd (Lt. Col. Horatio L. Woodhouse, Jr., Silver Star) and 3rd (Lt. Col. Malcolm "O" Donohoo, Silver Star), were landed at Green Beaches 1 and 2 with 1/22 (Maj. Thomas J. Myers, Navy Cross) in support, while 1/4 (Maj. Bernard W. Green) and 3/4 (Lt. Col. Bruno A. Hochmuth) of the 4th Marines were landed at Red Beaches 1, 2, and 3, with 2/4 (Lt. Col. Reynolds H. Hayden) in Division reserve. Their first target was the Yontan airfield and the numerous small villages lying north of it. The landing was relatively unhampered and tanks were among the earliest elements ashore. This lack of machine-gun, mortar and artillery fire surprised everyone, but it was an extremely welcome change.

The accelerated pace of the assault on the left flank, however, soon caused the 22nd Marines (Col. Merlin F. Schneider) to become overextended. Because 2/22 was forced to move toward their left, their right soon separated from 3/22. This caused Schneider to quickly call in the reserve, 1/22, from offshore. By 1000 the 22nd had moved rapidly inland but its left flank was considered dangerously thin. Gen. Shepherd requested that IIIMAC release a battalion of the 29th Marines not yet landed, for his employment.

Meanwhile, the 4th Marines (Col. Alan Shapley) were moving forward, meeting minimal resistance, and soon tied up with the 7th Marines (Col. Edward W. Snedeker, Navy Cross) from the 1st MarDiv. on their right. Before noon they had taken Yontan field and by 1300 they had crossed the field and secured their objective to the east of it. Nonetheless, in so doing, they managed to create a wide gap between themselves and the 22nd Marines to their left. Rapid progress was the name of the game and both regiments took advantage of their potential, soon passing their first-day objectives and moving toward the next. Objectives which were accorded three days were taken on day one. One Japanese aviator landed on Yontan, apparently not realizing that the Marines were in possession of the field. After he got out of the Zero he realized what he'd done and pulled his pistol from his holster. He was dead before he hit the ground. Equipment was being landed and the engineers were already building roads. By the evening of the first day, Col. Victor Bleasdale's 29th Marines, in Corps reserve, was already ashore and took up the 6th MarDiv.'s left flank. Nevertheless, word was that the army divisions were having a tough time in the south, a harbinger of things to come.

The next day, 2 April, the 6th MarDiv. began the move northward. Except for occasional flourishes and isolated combative groups of enemy soldiers, the division encountered no trouble and was three days ahead of anticipated schedule. By 3 April the 22nd and 4th Marines had crossed the mid-island watershed and worked down into the foothills on the opposite slope. Each regiment had met scattered elements of enemy soldiers but nothing substantial to hold them up.

On 4 April they reached the East China Sea and a point which planners had expected would take at least two weeks. They were now in a rolling grassy land with few trees and still running into scattered Japanese soldiers, but nothing to hinder their forward motion. Within five days they were on the L plus 15 objective. IIIMAC was busy modifying plans to take advantage of this rapid forward movement.

Shortly after landing, the 1st MarDiv. was able to drive across the island south of the Yonton Air Field. The USA divisions would be severely tested as they headed southeast, for that is where the IJA had decided to defend Okinawa.

The 1st MarDiv. reached the easternmost coast by 3 April with minimal resistance. Actually, the 1st MarDiv.'s recon company made it to the east coast on 2 April. Del Valle and his staff were perplexed. This was totally unexpected, yet highly welcomed by everyone in the division. By the 4th they held all of that mid-portion of the island. This state of affairs went on for two weeks, during which time souvenir-happy Marines collected anything not nailed down. This included livestock such as goats and even horses. Here, at the beginning of their fourth major landing, the division was living the life of Riley, yet, during this early period, the division usually lacked immediate artillery support. Prime gun movers were not available ashore to move the guns for several days. Fortunately, the guns were seldom required, but all that would change.

The 4th Marines were on the right going up the isthmus and the 22nd was on the left, with, until 6 April, the 29th in support. The 6th MarDiv. was on its way. On that date 3/29 (Lt. Col. Erma A. Wright), accompanied by tanks, passed through the 22nd Marines. The Division Reconnaissance Company (Maj. Anthony Walker, Silver Star), with accompanying tanks, moved into Mobutu Peninsula and ran into what seemed like all the Japanese on Okinawa. The company had quite a few sharp actions and their reports indicated that this was probably where the 6th MarDiv. could expect to find what they were looking for: the Japanese army. However, regardless of appearances, it was only a relatively small portion, though they would engage the division for a few days.

Patrols from the 29th Marines were the first to enter the peninsula and between 7 and 9 April ran into few of the enemy. The night of 9 April, 3/29's bivouac was hit by artillery and mortar fire, killing and injuring at least 10 percent of the battalion. On 10 April Col. Bleasdale sent out more patrols and found the enemy had retreated into numerous well-hidden caves. The next day, 11 April, Bleasdale's men had taken the wreck of the village Manna, a mile northeast of the peninsula's dominating mountain peak, Yaetake, which was located near the southerly coast of Mobotu. The enemy was well-placed on the 700-foot rise and was engaged in shooting into Marine formations as they gathered around it. The 29th Marines made several attempts to move up the height, to no avail. The enemy was too strong for anything but a massive and serious effort. Gen. Shepherd decided he needed his tried-and-true 4th Marines to go up and take the mountain.

Shapley's men started up and soon ran into well-placed troops in the wild terrain and engaged in hand-to-hand fight all the way up. The Japanese machine guns and mortars were efficiently situated and the Marines found themselves caught by their fire no matter where they were. The enemy was so fluid in their defense that they could fire and then withdraw. So well-located were all the other guns that going after them in the brush was considered tantamount to suicide. As one Marine lieutenant told a Marine combat correspondent, "it was just one damned ambush after another."

Regardless of their losses, the 4th Marines and 3/29 continued on. Artillery support from the 15th Marines helped a great deal. They knocked out several artillery emplacements while the Marines were going on different trails in attempts to get behind obvious enemy locations. Col. Victor F. Bleasdale was relieved of command of the 29th Marines on 14 April and was replaced by Col. William J. Whaling. The latter, already with two Legion of Merit awards, would also be awarded a Navy Cross on Okinawa.

A scout from the 15th Marines, PFC Harold Gosalves, a native of Alameda, CA, bravely faced the enemy artillery and machine guns to aid his Forward Observation Team to direct well-placed artillery fire. With an officer and another Marine, on 15 April Gonsalves went up again despite a slashing barrage of enemy mortar and rifle fire. As they reached the front, a grenade fell among them and Gonsalves dived on the deadly missile. He gave his life for his comrades, earning a posthumous Medal of Honor. Another loss that day was Maj. Bernard W. Green, CO of 1/4, who was killed by a Japanese Nambu while he was in his observation post.

Caves were being sealed up, with their occupants forever in residence. On 16 April, 1/4 (Lt. Col. Fred D. Beans), supported by 3/29 (Lt. Col. Erma A. Wright), finally made it to the hills surrounding Yaetake. The enemy had no new positions to fall back upon and the Marines got even for the punishment already taken. They used every weapon they owned, including BARs, and the Japanese were mowed down by the dozens. A native of Glasgow, KY, Corporal Richard E. Bush, a squad leader with 1/4, with indomitable courage rallied his men and led them forward through the slashing fury of the enemy's still formidable artillery and machine-gun fire. He continued leading until seriously wounded. It was then that a grenade was tossed into the midst of his group. Without hesitation, Bush grabbed the live grenade and pulled it to him, absorbing the full blast with his own body. He managed to survive this terrible calamity and was awarded a Medal of Honor for his bravery.

The next day, the attack was resumed. In this final assault some Marine companies lost upwards of half their men. It was mainly hand-to-hand combat and, later, banzai raids by the already disorganized Japanese. This latter mode of fighting was fine with the Marines. That way they could more easily kill off the Japanese while suffering fewer casualties themselves. The Japanese soldiers on Moboto died in the hundreds, making Mt. Yaetake a major grave site. As Col. Shapley later said, "It was as difficult as I can conceive an operation to be. They had all the advantages of terrain ... an uphill fight all the way."

While the fighting on Mobotu continued, 1/22 and 3/22 had managed to continue the advance northward. In the meantime, Lt. Col. Horatio C. Woodhouse and his 2/22, still relatively bloodless by 12 April, was way up ahead and took the farthest point on the island,

Hedo Misaki. Nonetheless, it was still a fight until at least 28 April when Marines caught the balance of Col. Takehiko Udo's force, 123 men, and destroyed them near the village of Kawada, on the east coast. The northern end of Okinawa was considered secured.

The division had a few days to catch their collective breath. The 1st MarDiv., which had been in Army Reserve, except for the 11th Marines, and not yet involved in the drive south, was ordered on 4 May to the southern fighting line to replace the 27th InfDiv. in line. In the meantime, the 11th Marines had been supporting the drive of the USA units. In the 6th MarDiv. everyone from Gen. Shepherd to the line private knew the 6th MarDiv. would be next.

But what of the enemy? Where was he? Why had he not defended the beaches or at least this central part of the island? The IJA had made its defensive plans and didn't share them with the American command. It was its decision to select its own ground and it was found to be formidable as the XXIV Corps made its way southeast. The ground south of the airfields became rough and that continued down to Shuri, about 10 miles below the Kadena Air Field. There are two horrific ridges in between and, in getting through, the XXIV Corps had their work cut out for them. They ran into the Machinato Line on 4 April and, temporarily, were effectively stopped "dead in the water."

On 6 April the IJN launched a suicide mission led by the super battleship *Yamoto* (largest warship on earth) with just enough fuel to get to where the invasion fleet was anchored. Rear Admiral Raymond Spruance was informed and prepared to receive the monster before it reached its target. On 7 April USN fleet aircraft destroyed *Yamoto* and its accompanying light cruiser. Also on 7 April came the first of the "Divine Wind" (kamikaze) suicide aerial attacks against Allied shipping. To the sailors aboard anchored ships, they were horrendous, and each attack created havoc even though their ultimate value has historically been minimized. Meanwhile ashore, the XXIV Corps was running into violent opposition and the casualties mounted precipitously.

Buckner called in the as yet unengaged 27th InfDiv. on 9 April to assist the badly used 96th and 7th InfDivs. He also took the 11th Marines from the 1st MarDiv. and placed them in line with the 7th and 96th Artillery Regiments. The 10th Army's new formation had the 27th on the western flank, the 96th in the center and the 7th still on the far eastern flank. The slugfest went on. Gen. Buckner decided to utilize the 1st MarDiv. by incorporating it into the XXIV Corps, but in small units, not as a complete division. It seemed evident that Buckner didn't want too many identifiable Marine units involved. On 27 April he decided to parcel out the balance of the 1st MarDiv., leaving Maj. Gen. Geiger with a one-division (6th MarDiv.) corps.

However, the advance of the understrength 27th InfDiv. soon stalled, and on 1 May Buckner placed them in the rear areas as garrison troops. He substituted the united 1st MarDiv. in its place in line on the western flank and they continued the battle from there. Giving up lives was immediate for the 1st MarDiv. On 2 May a Marine from Cleveland, OH, 3/1's PFC William A. Foster, with a comrade, was engaged in tossing grenades at the enemy. When one landed in their hole he quickly absorbed it, gave his grenades to his buddy and yelled "Make 'em count." This brought a posthumous Medal of Honor. This was followed on 4 May by the heroism of a Greenville, TN, Marine, Sgt. Elbert L. Kinser of Company I, 3/1, who also absorbed a live grenade and "gallantly gave his life for his country." His award for this courageous action was a Medal of Honor.

On 3 May the IJA made an amphibious landing in substantial force behind the 1st

MarDiv. but was defeated and literally destroyed by 5 May. In the meantime, the unused 2nd MarDiv. was shipped back to Saipan. Army management had decided that two Marine divisions ashore were enough.

After a week of slugging it out, Gen. Geiger was ordered to assume command of the 1st MarDiv. zone and to bring the 6th MarDiv. into line on their right along the coast. With that the IIIMAC was brought into action and assumed positions on the western flank of the 10th Army. That was accomplished by 7 May and there were now four divisions on line, two of which were Marines. The Army XXIV Corps remained on the eastern flank, and both corps pressed southeastward.

Three Medals of Honor were awarded for actions by 1st MarDiv. Marines on 7 May 1945. Chicago's Cpl. John P. Fardy, of 1/1, tossed himself on a grenade, thereby giving up his own life that his comrades might live. Over in 2/1, Wisner, NE's own Pvt. Dale M. Hansen, took the initiative when he took a rocket launcher and attacked several hostile pillboxes. When his weapon was destroyed by enemy fire he then grabbed an M1 and continued his one-man assault. Jumping into a hole with six Japanese, he killed four with his rifle and when it jammed beat the other two off with his rifle butt. Falling back to his comrades, he grabbed more grenades and another rifle, then ventured forth once more. Hansen destroyed a mortar position and annihilated eight more of the enemy. He was heavily responsible for the success of the division on that front that day. His reward was a Medal of Honor, which he richly deserved. The third went to a member of 1/5. A flamethrower man from Oklahoma named PFC Albert E. Schwab. Schwab, seemingly without fear, advanced straight at the enemy under a hail of bullets, and quickly demolished a machine gun. Suddenly another machine gun opened up, killing and wounding several Marines. Schwab went forward and though low on fuel and severely wounded by the gun, attacked and destroyed the second gun. This enabled his company to advance and his reward was a Medal of Honor.

Shortly after dark on 9 May the engineers provided the 22nd Marines with a footbridge across the Asa Kawa River. On 10 May, Co. K, followed closely by Co. I, of 3/22, started crossing the bridge. Company A of 1/22 began wading across the river and at 0530 two human Japanese "demolition charges" rushed the footbridge, destroying the south end. The engineers repaired the bridge and more suicide bombers blew up the repairs. The officers and men of the 22nd, not to be hindered by the Asa Kawa inlet, pushed south, keeping pace with the 1st MarDiv. The major problem was trying to bring the wounded back across the ruined bridge.

While going south that day, the 22nd Marines took very heavy losses trying to take Charlie Hill, located between the rivers Asa and Asato. It fell to Capt. Warren F. Lloyd's (Silver Star) Co. C to take the hill. The enemy was so well entrenched in the limestone that though tanks were called up, they too were finding advancement near impossible. One platoon had seven men left of the original 65, another had but 12.

For Co. C, the second day seemed worse. When the Marines killed Japanese soldiers in one cave opening they would draw fire from another. That continued all day and on 10 May they calculated advance in inches. Regardless, at the end of the day, Company C clung to the ridge. Two men, Cpl. Victor Goslin (Navy Cross) from Ashland, ME, and Pvt. George Campbell of Philadelphia held off a banzai attack with grenades and rifle fire. In the morning the tanks came up once again, as did flamethrower tanks to pour in fire upon the inhabitants of pillboxes and tombs, which were used extensively by the Japanese soldiers on Okinawa. The assault upon Charlie Hill lasted most of the day and by the end of the day there was no more firing from it. The next morning Co. C counted its losses: 35 killed and 68 wounded of the original 256. Examination of the terrain, especially the interior of the caves, spoke volumes. The whole area was a labyrinth of winding corridors and rooms of varied sizes, including those used as field hospitals and ammo dumps. The weapons were many and included field pieces mounted on railroad tracks that run out of cave openings and, after firing, run back in.

Meanwhile 3/22 had been moving by the sea onto a ridge above the Asato River. From there they could look down upon the main city of Naha. Along the interior lines, the 4th Marines had been keeping pace with the 5th Marines, then pushed ahead. The center of the U.S. advance was now concave with the ends pushed ahead. The Americans were coming close to a town located quite close to Naha, Shuri, a place that would get much attention in the next few weeks. Part of the important Naha–Shuri–Yonaburu Line had been broken by the 22nd Marines and the enemy was well aware they would have to make a strong stand in the sloping hill northeast of Naha. The Marines named it "Sugar Loaf" for some reason, but taking it would be less than sweet. Arguably, this would be the site of the bloodiest of the Okinawa battles.

On 11 May 10th Army opened an all-out attack upon Shuri's inner defenses and 2/5 eliminated the last pocket of resistance in the Awache Pocket. Then on 12 May it was the turn of the 7th Marines (Snedeker) to lead the 1st MarDiv. and for about a week they suffered heavy casualties while taking Dakeshi Ridge and trying to take Wana Ridge.

On the night of the 12th Lt. Col. Woodhouse ordered the CO of Co. G, 2/22, 1st Lt. Dale W. Bair, who earned a Navy Cross that night, to take 11 tanks and assail the hill. The tanks went roaring up the hill and the Japanese, assuming this was a major attack, began to fall back. When they realized the attack was only company-size they returned to their superb positions and the company was in rough territory. Company G was raked by a withering fire; Bair was wounded three times but continued the fight. Cradling a machine gun in his bleeding arms, he tried to reach the crest but failed. The drivers of the amtracs which came up to haul off the wounded Marines were all dead. Only a heavy artillery barrage allowed Co. G to free itself to withdraw.

Sugar Loaf was the apex of three hills in a triangle, and Woodhouse and his staff realized where the focal point was located. Their Marines had been driving between two hills and taking heavy fire from each. After Woodhouse advised Gen. Shepherd of their findings, the plans were changed from a frontal attack to a more strategic assault. On 14 May Companies E and F worked all day upon the two outer hills, west and east of Sugar Loaf. Time after time each company was driven back, leaving dead and dying Marines on the slopes.

Between 14 and 17 May, a Marine corporal from East St. Louis, IL, James L. Day, fought a gallant battle against tremendous odds. He led his squad to a critical position forward of the front lines of Sugar Loaf amid intense mortar and artillery fire. They were quickly assailed by at least 40 of the enemy. Day was outstanding during the fight, encouraging his men, hurling grenades, and directing his squad's deadly fire. Despite the loss of half his men he continued his fight, and when reinforced by six men he then attacked the enemy. Faced with three sizable night assaults and the loss of five additional Marines, Day continued his valiant leadership and helped four wounded to safety in the rear, all while under intense enemy fire. Assisted by a wounded Marine, Day then held his position that night with a light machine gun, halting another attack. His weapon destroyed, and receiving wounds from phosphorous and fragmentation grenades, he managed to reorganize his position in time to halt a fifth attack. Three times the enemy closed upon him and yet he continued to kill them off. The following day the Japanese continued their numerous swarming attacks upon his exposed position. Seventy of the enemy were counted dead before his position. The following day, wounded and exhausted, he continued his defense and killed off at least 30 more of the enemy. It was considered, many years later, that Cpl. Day had contributed greatly to the success of American arms on Okinawa. He was finally presented a Medal of Honor at the White House on 20 January 1998. By then Major General, James L. Day had already been awarded a Navy Distinguished Service Medal (probably in Vietnam), three Silver Stars, one in Korea, two in Vietnam, and a Bronze Star with a combat "V."

Major Henry A. Courtney, Jr., of Duluth, MN, executive officer of 2/22, already wounded on 9 May, was now ordered to hold for the night in a static defense behind Sugar Loaf. He weighed the advantages of holding or counterattacking during the night of 14-15 May. Deciding for the latter, he received permission to begin. Courtney explained his plan to his remaining subordinates and then began a one-man attack up the slope. He was blasting caves with grenades and neutralizing enemy machine guns as he went, and his men got up and followed him. Soon, requiring more grenades, he waited for a LVT loaded with them and an additional 26 more men. They started up again with Courtney leading by example, up front. Throwing grenades into caves, blasting everyone in his way, he finally made the crest. There he came upon large numbers of Japanese forming up to attack. He and his followers went right for them, killing many and driving the balance into caves. He had his men dig in and had begun aiding the wounded when a mortar round blast caught him in the open, killing him and ending his rush to glory. He was another posthumous recipient of the Medal of Honor. On the 15th Maj. Thomas J. Myers, CO of 1/22, and his runner, PFC Guido Conti, from Freeport, PA, died when a mortar round exploded in Myers' CP. Major Earl J. Cook replaced Myers in command of the battalion.

One of Courtney's men, Cpl. Donald "Rusty" Golar, from San Francisco, CA, was another hero. In fact he was a self-proclaimed "glory hunter." His buddies added, "keep your eye on that redhead." In the early hours of 15 May Rusty gave the Marines something to watch. He had a "personal" light machine gun which he'd used effectively on Guam and now set up on this ridge for use on Sugar Loaf. He emptied his belts into the enemy and when they fired upon him from the flanking hill he switched to face the newcomers. Out of ammo, Rusty also found that only he and two other Marines of his group had survived and that ammo carriers coming up the hill had all been knocked off. He then began firing his pistol until it too ran dry. Rusty then stood up and hurled his machine gun at the enemy. Next he gathered up all the grenades he could pry from the downed Marines and began hurling them at the enemy. The grenades ran out and he found a BAR. Up on his feet, he began firing until that weapon jammed. Undaunted but now weaponless, Rusty got Don Kelly, one of the survivors, to help him carry some of the wounded. As Rusty carried one man a sniper caught him. He carefully put his burden down and rolled over dead. His award for heroics was a Silver Star.

Private Harry "the Beast" Kizirian, from Providence, RI, earned a Navy Cross on Sugar Loaf. Three times wounded, but scorning evacuation, he continued to help other casualties down to safety. Then he led several rifle squads in assaults against Japanese strong points. With a BAR and later a machine gun, he personally eliminated three dozen of the enemy. The battle continued all night with the so-called "Double Deuce" (22nd Marines) at the forefront of the fight for Sugar Loaf. Eleven times 2/22 had gone up that hill, and each time had been driven back. Their casualties numbered in the hundreds and the battalion was no longer in any shape to keep going. It wasn't just privates and corporals taking the deep six, any Marine up front was putting his life on the line, including battalion commanders.

After this great effort, 2/22 was relieved by elements of the 29th Marines and 3/22. The 22nd's colonel, Merlin F. Schneider, was relieved in command of the 22nd Marines by Col. Harold C. Roberts.[30] Lieutenant Colonel Donohoo, CO, 3/22, was also wounded on 16 May. For the next several days the 29th tried and failed, as had 2/22. Seven times the 29th went up the hill and seven times they were driven back, with heavy losses. On the 18th one more assault was launched and they finally made it, staying permanently. The enemy had been driven off Sugar Loaf and the wise-guy Marines were sarcastically calling for "PX supplies" to be shipped up to them.

On the morning of the 19th tanks were able to go over the saddle between Sugar Loaf and Half-Moon Hills and caught Japanese swarming out of their caves on the reverse slopes. Turning their guns on the exposed enemy, the tanks slew scores. The 29th Marines were relieved by the 4th Marines.

On 20 May the Japanese launched a counterattack in the vicinity of Crescent Hill, southeast of Sugar Loaf. They ran into the tough 4th Marines, not a shattered 22nd or 29th, and they didn't make it. That night, after a powerful artillery and mortar barrage, 500 or more Japanese attempted to infiltrate the lines. Colonel Shapley called in counter-artillery which kept more of the enemy from coming up. As the Aussies might say, the 4th Marines "gave 'em what for." In the morning nearly 500 bodies were counted lying before the lines of the 4th Marines. All in all, the Japanese had lost two infantry battalions, torn apart a third, and knocked out an antitank battalion, a service company and 300 Japanese sailors, sometimes called Marines. Individual Marines performed outstanding deeds, with many dying in the process. The vaunted Naha–Shuri–Yonaburu Line, however, had been busted wide open.

By 22 May the 4th and 22nd Marines were sending patrols across the Asato River down into the outskirts of Naha. In the meantime there had been persistent rain for eight days and most roads on the island were now impassable. On 23 May there was an end to their waiting. Across the footbridges built across the Asato by the engineers went two battalions of the 4th Marines into Naha. Down from Shuri Heights came the Japanese and furious fighting ensued in and around the city. Much of it was hand-to-hand. The 4th Marines took heavy casualties, but they convinced the Japanese command to withdraw to a new defensive line beyond the Oroku Peninsula.

The fighting in and around Naha continued for days. During the course of it many men were casualties, including such notables as Lt. Col. Horatio C. Woodhouse, CO of 2/22, who was killed in action on 30 May. Meanwhile, the kamikazes, both suicide planes and suicide boats from Okinawa, were lambasting the offshore fleet, sending many into the deep and many more scattering away from the island. Those that supplied the 10th Army would be sorely missed.

Snedeker and his 7th Marines were relieved on line by the 1st Marines (Col. Arthur T. Mason) on 19 May. In nine days the 7th had suffered 1,250 casualties. At the same time, on the coast the 6th MarDiv. was also pressing forward in the region of Sugar Loaf Hill, which they took on 18 May. The entire IIIMAC had run into stiffening resistance on 14 May and it became apparent that they had struck the IJA's main line of resistance. Unlike up north, this was truly a slugging match and the conquest of the island was not coming easy. The 1st MarDiv. was still trying to take the Wana Ridge and its draw and that conquest would occupy most of the balance of May.

On 29 May 1/5 (Lt. Col. Charles W. Shelburne, Navy Cross) was finally able to take Shuri Ridge and soon after captured Shuri Castle. This forced the 32nd Japanese Army to vacate the Shuri Line, which had been holding up the Americans for most of the month. The enemy fell back to the Kiyamu Peninsula at the southernmost edge of the island, thereby escaping the flanking drives of both the IIIMAC and the XXIV Corps. In a combined operation, the 1st MarDiv. and the 77th InfDiv. took the entire Shuri Line on 31 May.

On 1 June the IIIMAC launched a coordinated drive by both Marine divisions and secured the high ground overlooking the new enemy defensive positions in the Kokuba Gawa Valley. The XXIV Corps changed its direction to attack the main enemy defensive positions in the southern sector of the island. The IIIMAC boundary was narrowed as it shifted to the west and the 1st MarDiv. was made responsible for cutting off the Oroku Peninsula and for the capture of the most southerly portion of the island. The 6th MarDiv. eventually fought the peninsula, capturing it on or about 13 June.

Though it was expected that the taking of Oroku would be bloody, the 6th MarDiv. found, to its collective delight, that the Japanese had decided not to defend it or the airfield. On 4 June by noon the airfield belonged to the 4th Marines but the rest of the five-day fight for the balance of the peninsula was not easy. The 22nd Marines crossed the Kokuba from the east, the 29th Marines pushed from the west and the 4th Marines from the south. Though the Japanese were in a box, they fought an efficient and tenacious defense. Under each hill were numerous rooms, sometimes of three or even more floors, and each was home for hundreds of Japanese — 600 was estimated in one case — and each had to be taken. Systematically, with the 15th Marines providing primary support, the 6th MarDiv. went in and dug them out, eliminating the pocket.

On 7 June one Marine from Altoona, FL, Pvt. Robert M. McTureous, Jr., a rifleman in 3/29, became a notable. He went to the aid of stretcher bearers caught in a slashing machine-gun fire as they were attempting to evacuate wounded. Filling his pockets with grenades, he charged the cave openings from which the fire emanated. His furious one-man assault diverted most of the fire from the bearers to himself. Replenishing his stock of grenades, he dauntlessly returned several times to continue his work. While silencing a large number of the hostile guns he was badly wounded. Crawling over 200 yards, he finally reached his own lines before receiving aid. He had effectively disorganized the enemy by neutralizing their fire, saving the lives of many Marines. His reward was a well-deserved Medal of Honor.

The 2nd Bn., 7th Marines (Lt. Col. Spencer S. Berger, Silver Star), continuing southward, captured Itoman, a large town on the coast. Meanwhile 1/7 (Lt. Col. John J. Gormley, Silver Star) took Tera, lying about 1,000 yards to the east. Both were taken over the night of 11-12 June. Continuing forward, the 7th Marines encountered another strongly held position on Kunishi Ridge. Not only was the enemy well-ensconced on that coral outgrowth, but the ground leading to it was a broad valley containing rice paddies, and providing little cover.

The initial assault was costly and ineffective and Col. Snedeker had called it off on the afternoon of 11 June. He had made an aerial reconnaissance and decided the ridge was too strong to attack in daylight hours, choosing instead to attack it at night. During the 13th the entire division was engaged in preparation for the assault upon Kunishi planned for the early morning of the 14th.

The assault went off and included the 1st Marines as well as the 7th Marines. The fighting was intense and it was nearly a full week before the Marines had taken the last strong point leading south on Okinawa. Among other innovations during this battle, tanks were commonly utilized to bring the many wounded back off the ridge. The 1st MarDiv. casualties for the period were 1,150 and there was still more fighting to the south. In the meantime, the 8th Marines, 2nd MarDiv. (Col. Clarence R. Wallace) arrived and were attached to the 1st MarDiv. The 8th had already made several successful landings on small islands lying off Okinawa's western coast.

On 14 June Oroku's end was near and the enemy fell to form. Huge numbers of Japanese fell dead in many banzai attacks. More died by their own hand when American interpreters tried talking them in. Nevertheless, a few Japanese did surrender, along with numerous Korean labor troops. But this was only the end of part two of the fight for Okinawa.

Also on the 14th, a leader of a machine gun squad attached to Company C, 1/1, Cpl. Louis J. Hauge, Jr., from Ada, MN, boldly took the initiative when his company's left flank was pinned down by a heavy machine-gun and mortar attack, suffering severe casualties. While his guns concentrated on the enemy guns, Hauge launched a personal attack with grenades. Though suffering from several wounds, he single-handedly knocked out one gun and then went for the second. With grenades he managed to wipe out the second gun before falling to a severe density of enemy fire. His enterprise and courage enabled his company to advance and successfully attain their objective. He suffered the ultimate sacrifice and the reward was a posthumous Medal of Honor.

For a few days after Oroku the men of the 6th MarDiv. had a chance to sleep and eat and write letters home telling their folks, "I'm fine." But on 17 June the 6th MarDiv. was on the move once again. Elements were sent to relieve right flank units of the 1st MarDiv. Major Earl J. Cook (Silver Star), CO of 1/22, was wounded while leading his battalion on 18 June. His replacement was Weapons Company's CO, Lt. Col. Gavin C. Humphrey. Colonel Roberts was killed while trying to get aid to a surrounded captain and his company. On the 19th the 4th Marines took Kiyamu and on the 22nd both the 4th and 29th Marines continued to mop up the remnants. By this date the Marines were actually taking in prisoners and their stockade of POWs was soon loaded.

Meanwhile, much pressure was still being exerted upon Buckner to bring in the 2nd MarDiv. to deploy at the tip end of the island and take the IJA in the rear. For some reason he continued to refuse everyone, including RA Richmond K. Turner, who wanted rapid movement in the ground movement in order to move his ships away from their kamikaze-targeted positions just offshore. One correspondent wrote, complaining that "our tactics were ultra-conservative. Instead of an end-run, we persisted in frontal attacks." The enemy air attacks had been creating havoc, especially upon the smaller vessels. Instead of Buckner using the 2nd MarDiv. as recommended, the two corps continued pounding the defense lines, straight forward, much like World War I, with the resulting casualties.

On 18 June Lt. Gen. Simon B. Buckner was killed while observing the progress of the 8th Marines' first attack on the island. The senior officer on the island, Maj. Gen. Roy S. Geiger, CG IIIMAC, assumed command of and directed the final combat operations of the 10th Army. That was the first and only time a Marine general commanded an army. On 21 June the 1st MarDiv. captured Hill 81 while the 29th Marines, 6th MarDiv., took the southernmost part of the islands. The following day, 22 June, was proclaimed as the formal termination of the Okinawan campaign.

However, the two Marine divisions and the 7th and 97th InfDivs. were ordered to mop up any holdouts in the northern parts of the island, allowing ten days for the completion of that action. Their sweep began on 25 June. In the meantime, on 23 June Lt. Gen. Joseph W. Stilwell, USA, arrived from the United States and formally relieved Maj. Gen. Roy S. Geiger in command of the 10th Army. It was a remarkably rapid replacement and it certainly didn't allow Geiger much time to command a U.S. Army.

On 21 June the island was declared secured. After 82 days the 10th Army could finally look forward to a modest rest. Calculations began and the total loss to the Japanese was estimated to be over 131,000 (which included men sealed in caves, civilians caught in the cross fire, and another nearly 11,000 troops which had surrendered).

American losses in the 10th Army were calculated at about 38,000, plus an additional 26,200 non-battle casualties. (The latter figure must include offshore naval casualties, which were heavy.) The Army received 12,300 replacements and the Marines 11,200. The 6th MarDiv. had managed, in its "very first battle," to capture two-thirds of the land mass of the island, including Naha, its capital city, and several airfields, and had eliminated about 20,000 enemy soldiers. However, great victories do not fall into one's lap. That division paid a price: over 8,300 casualties, of whom 1,622 were killed, 6,689 wounded and 15 missing.

As usual, the 1st MarDiv. was badly handled; they suffered almost as badly as their enemy. Dead, 1,115, wounded, 6745, and missing, 41, a total of 7,901.

Marine aviation was greatly supplemented by USAAF and USN carrier air during the entire period. However, there was more Marine air on this most important island than at any other period, except perhaps for the hodgepodge support at Guadalcanal. Following is a listing of the units which spent time serving the 10th Army between 1 April and 30 June 1945.

All shore-based aviation, Marine and Army, was subordinate to Tactical Air Force, 10th Army, with Hdqs. 2nd MAW doubling as its headquarters. All units served at various periods. Marine units included: MAG-14, 22, and 43. MAG-31 was from both CVEs *Breton* and *Sitkoh Bay* and MAG-33 was from both CVEs *White Plains* and *Hollandia*.

The following squadrons served: VMF 113, 212, 222, 223, 224, 311, 312, 314, 322, 323, 422, and 441; VMF (N) 533, 542, and 543; VMBS (T) 131. Additional service units included MAW 1, 6, 8, and 11; VMO 2, 3, 6, and 7. MOS 2 supported the 2nd MarDiv., 3 the 1st MarDiv., 6 the 6th MarDiv., and 11 IIIMAC Artillery.

The following carrier base air units also participated. During assault and occupation of Okinawa: Marine Carrier Group 1 CVE-106 *Block Island*; incl. VMBS (T) 233 and VMF 511. MCG 2 CVE-107 *Gilbert Islands*; incl. VMBS (T) 143 and VMF 512. In attacks launched by the 3rd and 5th Fleets in support of the assault on Okinawa: VMF 112 and 123, *Bennington*; VMF 124 and 213, *Essex*; VMF 214 and 452, *Franklin*; VMF 216 and 217, *Wasp*; VMF 221 and 451, *Bunker Hill*.

> *Results:* This assault, basically the final combat action of both the U.S. Marines and U.S. Army in the Pacific War, was a success and established a forward base close to the home islands. In fact Japan considered Okinawa as part of its home islands. It brought U.S. military forces to a place where they had as close a jump-off spot for the physical invasion of the mainland as was possible. The Japanese naval forces and much of its air forces were destroyed, so little if any counter-action could be brought against any further development and build-up.
>
> Of course, at the time, no one knew that this was the final assault, so the capture was an essential step toward final victory. For the most part the U.S. Army forces involved, except for one division, kept up with their Marine comrades during the entire affair and suffered comparable losses during the three months of fighting. For some reason, which is still not clear after all these years, the 10th Army CG refused to utilize a Marine division of over

20,000 battle-experienced men in a well-prepared Navy- and Marine-proposed landing on the southern tip of the island. He had sense enough to relieve a less than active U.S. Army division, so he showed sufficient ability and capability as a leader. The Marines may be paranoid but they believed, and I think rightly so, that the USA wanted few Marines in the fight.

Notes

Chapter 1

1. There were so many, it is difficult to include most in this limited space. But these engagements helped to keep the new nation at sea for an extended period; otherwise Britain might have swept the Americans off the ocean.

2. According to the Navy Historical Center, Navy Yard, Washington, D.C., the date of establishment by the Continental Congress was 13 October 1775. After which two ships were ordered for the Continental Navy, with appropriate crews, including Marines. Those, then, were the first historically recognizable Continental Marines. There seems to be some confusion in that record. The Continental Congress was waiting in October for a plan of action to be presented by the Rhode Island delegation to the Naval Committee. The plan was finally presented and accepted in mid–December 1775. Congress then ordered 13 frigates to be purchased or built.

3. This was not unlike Marine John M. Gamble's commanding warships at sea in 1814. Gamble still retains the honor of being the first Marine to command a U.S. Navy ship at war.

4. Most of them were by now French descendants of Irish men and women who had settled in France nearly 100 years before. Some few, especially the officers, were still of Irish birth. In fact, three of them, Eugene Robert MacCarthy, Edward Stack, and James Gerald Ó'Kelly, were directly commissioned as Continental Marines by Benjamin Franklin, the American minister to France. They served notably under Jones during the entire period.

Chapter 2

1. The previous organization was officially titled the Continental Marines, which was unofficially disbanded on 26 April 1784, when the last Continental Marine is known to have served.

2. On the 12th of September, the secretary of the Navy issued orders that enlisted Marines be given the following items of clothing "as require": 1 coat, 1 hat, 1 vest, 2 pairs of woolen and 2 pairs of linen overalls, 4 shirts, 4 pairs of shoes, 1 stock of black leather and clasp, and 1 blanket.

3. That number is accurate as far as I can tell, though there may have been more.

4. The Marine Band played for the first New Year's reception ever held at the president's house in Washington (not yet the White House).

5. This was the end result of the Louisiana Purchase, which the Congress approved on 20 October.

6. He will find in September 1811, to his dismay, that he was misled and re-instate the boycott.

7. During this year the British declared King George III insane and he was replaced by his son, George IV. That was something the people of the U.S. had been wise to 35 years earlier. Matters between the U.S. and the French and Great Britain were becoming more testy each day. In the coming year the U.S. would be engaged in another major conflict with Great Britain, of which France approved.

Chapter 3

1. Also spelled polacca; a ship found in the Mediterranean with square (or lateen) sails.

2. The only other U.S. ship surrendered to an enemy was the *Retaliation* in the Quasi-War with France; Bainbridge also then commanded. Bainbridge was also captain of the *George Washington* in September 1800, when he was "forced" to accede to the demand of the Dey of Algiers that he carry goods and personnel to Constantinople, *flying the Algerian flag from top-mast*. That is another story.

3. Meanwhile, on 1 April, Captain Franklin Wharton was named the new lieutenant colonel commandant following Burrows' resignation on 7 March.

4. I have been unable to determine what happened to the wounded Pvt. David Thomas.

5. A very disillusioned and obviously disappointed O' Bannon decided to leave the Corps soon after — in my opinion, a great loss.

6. The manpower strength of the Marines Corps was 8 officers and 680 enlisted Marines.

Chapter 4

1. This is a fair example of the battles during this war. The following descriptions, when entered, will be less detailed.
2. A member of one of the great Navy families, and grandfather of the Marine hero of the same name.
3. Years later, urged by naval officers, a law was passed that prohibited this from ever happening again. Gamble's story is very adventuresome, extensive, and well worth reading.
4. This unintentional destruction was the excuse used for the British destruction of our new capitol, Washington, D.C., in late August 1814.
5. However, their campaign would turn sour in a few weeks. Poor planning reversed most of the gains attained. On 11 June, Smith would write to the commandant complaining that all his stores, extra weapons, money, records and clothing for his Marines were lost in the fires inadvertently set by order of the Navy commanding officer. He requested everything for the 26 men still fit for duty
6. A distance of about 4,000 miles from Chile.
7. Identified in the *Encyclopedia of Military History*, revised edition, as the "incompetent political Major General," p. 800.
8. As can be seen in the map, the British went for the center of the U.S. defense, which was where the Marines were located.

Chapter 5

1. The Marine Corps has ignored Gale ever since, even his previous admittedly distinguished military career.
2. If you can imagine it, Porter was court-martialed for "overstepping his authority." His sentence was six months' suspension. For a time he was in charge of the Mexican navy. He initially refused to return to the U.S. naval service afterward, but President Andrew Jackson appointed him consul general to Algiers and then charge d'affaires in Turkey.
3. According to legend, Henderson left one elderly senior sergeant alone and in command at headquarters.
4. After being defeated the Creeks willingly joined U.S. forces, and, mainly led by Marine officers, helped fight the Seminoles.
5. I believe this was the first time a U.S. Marine officer would command a U.S. Army formation.
6. The war would continue intermittently until 1842, when the last of the Seminoles departed for Indian Territory in what is now Oklahoma. The Marines, however, were involved in a very limited fashion in the later stages of the fighting. At the war's expiration in 1842, Marine losses totaled 61, while Army losses were 1,466.
7. Related by a member of Hudson's crew who had knowledge of the circumstances.

Chapter 6

1. In fact, in his General Order no. 80, Scott's *thank you* included "a detachment of Marines, under Captain Edson — which formed the line of investment and prosecuted the siege to its happy conclusion."
2. He may not have had losses but, according to official records, Alvin Edson died on 15 July 1847, obviously while engaged in landings, or perhaps he was part of the Watson's battalion.
3. Scott had approximately 12,000 men, while Santa Anna had about 32,000 located around their capital and especially dwelling in its approaches.
4. Some participants would later accuse the Marines of "skulking in the ditch" until the fighting was over.
5. McCawley was to later become commandant and Henderson (wounded) was the current commandant's son. Terrett, a superb Marine, would go south in 1861.
6. The Marines killed at Chapultepec, besides Twiggs, included Cpl. Hugh Graham and Pvts. Anthony A. Egbert, Andrew McLaughlin, John Herbert, Matthew Banks, and Thomas Kelly, all at the gate of Mexico City. Wounded at the gates were Pvts. Seebeck and Milburn. Wounded at Chapultepec were 2nd Lt. Charles A. Henderson (Co. F); Sgts. John Roach (Co. B), J. Curren, G. Tansill, and W. J. Wilson (all Co. D); Pvts. Hugh Rooney, Martin Fogg, John McGihen, P. Phoenix, and S. Williamson (all Co. B); Briggs and Connor (Co. C); Thomas Quinn (Co. D); Thomas Smith and E. Stevens (Co. E); E. Cooper, James Linns and Musician Macdonald (Co. F).
7. This was a time when the Mexican government was in great turmoil, not because of the war with the U.S., but between the various participants, including of course, Santa Anna, who was a serious threat to good government.
8. Harris was the future commandant of the Corps during the Civil War.
9. The unusual "ap" was his correct name.
10. These men, known more commonly as "Osos," which meant grizzly bears, were in a state of revolt against the Mexican government when Fremont arrived. They developed a flag with a grizzly upon it and their revolt was called "The Bear Flag Revolt." They decided that Fremont was a professional military man and elected to follow him.
11. He later became commandant, 10 June 1864.

12. Castro had been actively trying to overthrow the Mexico governor and his government since 1842. The rebels' identity was altered to a Spanish spelling.

13. Stockton had established three sections of California. Fremont to govern the upper third, Stockton the middle portion and Gillespie the bottom third. An Indian uprising in the northern section caused Stockton to move his forces there to support Fremont. In between was nothing until Los Angeles. The American forces were too spread out for the territory they wanted to control and conquer.

14. This officer would ruin Gillespie's later career by charging him, unfairly, with theft of ship's funds.

15. Kearney had traveled across the country.

16. It was a victory for the Americans because they held the field, but of what advantage was the field, especially considering the losses? Gillespie was awarded a brevet promotion to major.

17. A razee was a warship on which the upper deck had been eliminated.

18. This appears to have been the final act in the War with Mexico.

Chapter 7

1. Includes three border states with divided loyalties.

2. Participation of the Corps in this war was extremely limited. Their numbers were small, and, unfortunately, martial skills among the senior officers were very limited. There had been too many nonactive years since the last conflict. Additionally, few of them would show any serious interest in fighting the war. Rather, most just wanted to live long enough to retire.

3. Edelin had with him 1st Lt. Adam N. Baker and 66 enlisted men. Captain Jabez C. Rich had 35 men available on the receiving ship *Pennsylvania* and Capt. Matthew R. Kintzing, with 2nd Lt. Charles Heywood, had 44 men on the *Cumberland*. Rich, born in Maine, deserted from the *Pennsylvania* and accepted a commission as a captain in the Marine Corps of Virginia on 20 April 1861.

4. Senior officers agreed that the enlisted men were not ready for this initial exercise, most having less than three months service, with modest, if any, training. Brevet Maj. Zeilen was CO of Co. A; Capt. James H. Jones, Co. B; 1st Lt. Alan Ramsay, Co. C; and 2nd Lt. William H. Carter, Co. D.

5. This battalion had been created from the "cream" of the enlisted Marine population per orders from Secretary Welles. It was drawn from most posts and ships in the northeast.

6. This nearly generated a war with Great Britain, but the Southerners were eventually released, cooling the tension.

7. Sullivan says, "It is unclear what role the Marines ... played during the Battle for Roanoke Island."

8. Marines weren't involved in this battle, which decided that ironclads couldn't fatally damage ironclads.

9. The mayor and city council of St. Augustine wrote to Flag Officer, soon to be RA, Samuel F. Du Pont, commanding the fleet off Florida, "heart-felt gratification and satisfaction at the polite and urbane course of Maj. Isaac T. Doughty and officers of the United States Marines since their arrival in, and occupancy of the city, and of the good conduct and discipline of the troops under their command ... our appreciation be conveyed to Major Doughty and his command."

10. Comments by the naval commanders of the fleet and ships were laudatory of the Marine participation. Comdr. John DeCamp, of the *Iroquois*, later wrote, "The Marines behaved with spirit and gallantry, which we may always expect in well-drilled Americans."

11. These detachments were small, probably a dozen enlisted men, more or less.

12. An agreement with the local government had been reached that the Marines would not raise the national flag in its place.

13. Naval Records, Part II-101.

14. By the spring of 1864 a total of 158 officers and men manned the station and ships of that flotilla.

15. I believe this was the only time a Marine unit was captured during the war, and perhaps at any time, until World War II.

16. Generally these riots were started by recent immigrants, especially the Irish, who were forced to serve because, unlike the rich, they didn't have the money to buy their way out of the draft. They believed it was unfair, which it was.

17. Soon to become commandant.

18. An ill Zeilen was allowed to return home. He was temporarily replaced by Capt. Edward McD. Reynolds, who was soon replaced by his father, Lt. Col. John G. Reynolds.

19. A future commandant.

20. Harris had been a less than efficient commandant. He wasn't missed, except, perhaps, by his family.

21. Naval Records, IV-72.

22. During this period, the captains of the *Hartford* and *Brooklyn* commended the performances of their Marine detachments and especially noted Capt's Charles Heywood of the former and George P. Houston of the latter.

23. United States Marine Corps casualties in the Civil War amounted to 551, including those who were killed in action, died of wounds, were lost at sea, died of disease, and were wounded in action. These losses were minimal compared to those of the Army and Navy.

Chapter 8

1. Chinese engineers refused to drive the train, so a Marine private who had been a railroader, along with a sailor who had been a coal heaver, operated the train very successfully.
2. After the relief, Myers said, "I never expected to leave the place alive [but] made up my mind to die just about as hard as I could."
3. Daly became a legend of the Corps when he earned another MoH in Haiti and a DSC and Navy Cross in France during World War I. He was also recommended for another MoH, which Pershing refused to grant.
4. Until 1915, Navy and Marine officers, unlike their Army complements, were not entitled to a Medal of Honor.
5. The 15th Infantry, stationed at Tientsin, occasionally provided backup for the legation guard, as they performed the same function in reverse. That is, until the 15th Infantry was withdrawn in the late 1930s and a detachment of Marines replaced them until 8 December 1941.

Chapter 9

1. Roosevelt was actively pushing Panama rebels to secede from Colombia, even to the point of sending Marines to interfere.
2. A Marine battalion would remain in Panama, usually at Camp Elliott and with an average strength of 15 officers and about 400 enlisted Marines. During the period of harassing Nicaragua, 1910–1912, Marines based at Camp Elliott, often led by Maj. Smedley D. Butler, would embark from Panama City aboard ship, land at Corinto or thereabouts and stifle any upset, then return to Camp Elliott.

Chapter 10

1. Biddle eventually became major general commandant of the Marine Corps.
2. The flag and the letter of Admiral Dewey are now displayed with many other flags of historic interest at the Naval Academy.
3. He would become commandant following John Lejeune.
4. Reports at that time claimed they were mutilated, but it now appears they both happened to have suffered from mortal bullet wounds to their heads, which caused appalling mutilation.
5. Named after Cmdr. Bowman H. McCalla, long associated with the Marines. See also the Boxer Rebellion and the landing at Panama in 1885.
6. The officers of the *Dolphin* later said they couldn't see and therefore could not understand the first message; consequently the second was sent.
7. A Naval Appropriation Act provided for the additional enlistment of 43 lieutenants, 80 corporals, and 350 privates, a total of 473 men for permanent service. This brought the Marine Corps up to its authorized strength of 3,073 men for service during the Spanish-American War. The rank of the commandant was also raised to brigadier-general.

Chapter 11

1. Later commandant.
2. One source says it was the 19th Infantry.
3. Hemp was a major cash product of the islands.
4. In 1934 both were finally decorated with the medal by President Roosevelt. Bearss was long retired, and Porter was just about to be.
5. Several tomes tell the entire story: Joseph L. Schott, *The Ordeal of Samar*; G. B. Clark, *Hiram Iddings Bearss, World War I Hero*; John H. Clifford, *History of the Pioneer Marine Battalion at Guam, L.I., 1899 and the Campaign in Samar, P.I., 1901*. They are well worth a read to learn what fools humans can be, even the best of them.

Chapter 13

1. The reason for USN uniforms: There was an agreement with Mexico that orderlies could only be naval personnel. Butler wasn't included in the uniform changes. He would have a fascinating job ahead of him.
2. That seems far-fetched, but something was brewing for Butler to have become a spy and traveled that far inland to Mexico City before the trouble began in April.
3. These Marines were part of the Advanced Base system then being organized and trained. This was the precursor of what much later became the Fleet Marine Force utilized during World War II.
4. This situation later became a great embarrassment for Russell and the Marine Corps. It has been related that a lone Mexican horseman came to the barricades at El Tejar and proclaimed that he was with a brigade of the Mexican army and demanded the surrender of the Marine Battalion Russell requested immediate help from Col. Lejeune at Vera Cruz or "I will be forced to surrender." Lejeune and his men rapidly went to his aid and found that the lone horseman had vanished and there were no others. Russell had a difficult time living this incident down. Even when he was up for the post of commandant, several senior officers, including Butler but not Lejeune, testified against him.

Chapter 15

1. In 1821 the country declared its independence as the Dominican Republic, but as late as 1929 U.S.

State Department officials still referred to it as "Santo Domingo."
  2. Hiram's group's travel problems had been just as high-risk as Pendleton's. They had to fight their entire way to Navarette while protecting and maintaining the rail lines; tracks and rolling stock as well as the essential supplies and ammunition. They had arrived on the 3rd of July. Read the biography of Hiram Bearss for details.

Chapter 16

  1. At this time, it was the largest tactical unit ever fielded by the U.S. Marine Corps.
  2. U.S. Marine Corps, *History of the Second Battalion, 5th Regiment, U.S. Marines, Jun. 1st 1917–Jan. 1st 1919.* Reprint (Foster, RI: Brass Hat, 1980), p. 5.
  3. Warren R. Jackson, *His Time in Hell: A Texas Marine in France* (Novato, CA: Presidio Press, 2001), p. 40.
  4. It appears that Adams was being punished because his battalion, especially the 74th Co., had been badly gassed in its reserve quarters. Nevertheless, he did wonderful work with the new assignment.
  5. Like the 45th, the 84th had been the victim of an innovative tactical plan developed by the German army to attempt to overcome the stagnation of trench warfare. An interesting study, *Stormtroop Tactics: Innovation in the German Army, 1914–1918*, by Bruce Gudmundsson (New York: Praeger, 1989), is worth a look.
  6. The word Boche was French and meant "square-head." It was in common use then, although is considered derogatory today. I'm sure counter-names for the French in German were equally common.
  7. The Marines held those engineers in high esteem, much as they did the later war's SeaBees.
  8. The 4th Brigade suffered a total of approximately 12,000 casualties while in France. Since the brigade total was 8,469 men and officers, that figure meant a casualty total of 150 percent of the Marine totals in France.
  9. It was, in my opinion, the key to the entire battlefield. Far beyond the woods and centered in the middle of the field, when taken, it outflanked the enemy on two sides. Of course, the enemy outflanked it on three sides.
  10. Wise has been criticized for his personality and leadership ability, but he and his command, in my opinion, were the first to actually take and retain possession of much of the wood until relieved. What he accomplished at Les Mares Farm has not received the acclaim it deserves. Later in the war he went on to command an Army regiment and then an Army brigade, both with great success.
  11. Unknown sender—from *Records of the Second Division*, vol. 7.
  12. This was possibly because he was always in trouble, like Jackie Kelly of the 6th Marines.
  13. Lieutenant General Robert Lee Bullard, *American Soldiers Also Fought* (New York: Longmans, Green, 1936).
  14. *The Real War, 1914–1918* (Boston: Little, Brown, 1963), p. 417.
  15. Other than the two divisions at this place, the bulk were further south and included at various times the 3rd and 4th Divisions of regulars, and the 26th, 28th, 32nd, and 42nd, all National Guard Divisions.
  16. He was relieved by Pershing soon after and transferred to successfully command a debilitated supply system.
  17. *Report of Operations, Second Division*, vol. 5, n.p.
  18. Later reported in *Fix Bayonets*, by John W. Thomason, Jr., as "stamping the Maxims flat."
  19. Keyser was an intelligent observer, but must not have noticed that the slowness of the French tanks was causing direct artillery hits on the nearby troops.
  20. From all that confusion I am not able to determine just who Fay was serving at that time.
  21. According to the authority on this battle, James H. Hallas in *Squandered Victory, the American First Army at St. Mihiel*, the division's total casualties, for all days, were a modest 1,563 dead and wounded.
  22. Hiram went on to earn a Distinguished Service Cross in October, and then, as a colonel of Marines, to command the 52nd Brigade.
  23. I've been there, and advancing upward without any armor protection must have been horrible for an infantryman.
  24. The French and German divisions usually totaled no more than 10,000 men, whereas the AEF divisions were closer to 20,000 men in each. Sometimes, before they too were shot to pieces, nearer 30,000.
  25. I have been unable, in the division records, to find the orders changing the attack date from 2 to 3 October.
  26. During the war, reconnaissance was not a strong point of the Marine brigade. What happened at Bois de Belleau on 6 June 1918, because of the lack thereof, is a case in point.
  27. Once the battle started, the commanding officer of all the machine gun battalions, AEF, had little control over his command now that his companies were dispersed among the line battalions. His was, more or less, an administrative function during combat.
  28. See Elton Mackin, *Suddenly We Didn't Want to Die*, p. 188.
  29. Like all later-arriving divisions, the 36th did not have its artillery with it. This was a prerequisite the British insisted upon when they finally provided transport ships for the AEF. They and the French wanted infantry to assault German lines, and support

services were not necessary, they said. Presumably they both would supply the negative services when required, which was always.

30. G.B. Clark, *Devil Dogs, Fighting Marines of World War I*, pp. 330–31.

31. That was the nickname given to the 2nd Division by Pershing's headquarters, and probably some other divisions.

32. Pershing and his cronies had made the decision to move and grab the major city of Sedan before the French army could get there. Taking Sedan was extremely important to France because it had lost that city to the Germans in 1870. In order to be first, the 1st Division had to cross the fronts of several American divisions, throwing them into confusion and upsetting all time tables. It didn't happen, even though orders signed by George Marshall in Gen. Liggett's name stated "boundaries will not be considered binding." It was messy, but the division was recalled in time.

33. At least there is now a farm at that point, and in a personal sighting a few years ago, it appeared as though it would have been there in November 1918.

34. Shuler was a man. He was never promoted to any position of consequence following the war.

35. 3/5 was assigned to Maj. Shuler as support for his Mouzon crossing.

36. Germany had agreed to accept the 14 points put forward by President Wilson, which the other two Allies, France and Britain, ignored after the German surrender. See World War II.

Chapter 17

1. In those times, a force of 100 men was considered huge, and frequently was labeled a "battalion."

2. This was the usual effort to keep other foreign troops from landing in Latin America.

3. The Guardia Nacional ("GN") was a Marine trained and led state police force.

Chapter 18

1. Neither he, nor anyone else, had any knowledge of the savagery the POWs would endure after surrender. The number of both military and civilian personnel put to death by the Japanese on Wake and elsewhere was astounding.

2. He was until after he had managed to leave the Philippines, but then he changed his attitude, refusing to include the 4th Marines in his recommendations for unit citations, "The Marines received too many citations in World War I." When Wainwright assumed command, he corrected that "oversight."

3. One unit that had been assigned to the 4th Marines was heavily composed of sailors from sunken ships or grounded air personnel.

4. Clement had been Hart's fleet Marine officer until he was reassigned to MacArthur's headquarters at Manila. Then Mac assigned him to the 4th Marines on Corregidor. Clement was an extra colonel and would be one of the last Americans off the island by submarine. He would be recalled to Washington to advise the MGC Holcomb on Marine fighting abilities during the current war. Eventually he would be a fighting brigadier general (6th Mar. Div.) then retire a lieutenant general.

5. In fact, as far as I have been able to determine, the only time Marines had ever surrendered was when forced to in the Civil War when a Confederate cruiser captured a civilian ship with Marines aboard (see Civil War).

6. Shannon was a captain in command of the 75th Co., 1st Bn., 6th Marines, who was gassed at Verdun and distinguished himself at Belleau Wood on the 4th of June, earning a Silver Star and Croix de Guerre with Palm. Henderson was remembered by having the flying field at Guadalcanal named after him.

7. Col. Gregory Boyington, *Baa Baa, Black Sheep* (Blue Ridge Summit, PA: TAB Books, 1958), p. 55.

8. In a USA B-17 on 17 July by then Lt. Col. Merrill B. Twining, USMC, assistant operations officer, 1st MarDiv.

9. Edson had been promoted up and Col. LeRoy Hunt had been relieved. Lt. Col. Samuel Griffith was now in command of the remnants of the 1st Raider Bn.

10. It was during this period that two notable Marines earned Medals of Honor, each for maintaining their machine gun positions, Sgt. John Basilone and Plt. Sgt. Mitchell Paige.

11. Major General Charles Barrett, then the CG of IMAC, fell to his death at his headquarters shortly after returning from a meeting with Adm. Halsey about the planned landing at Bougainville. It was billed as an accident.

12. Marvin was a well-known old-timer who had earned a reputation in China and elsewhere as a tough guy.

13. Marine close-air support was an outstanding weapon in this campaign. It solved many problems the infantry were finding almost impossible to overcome. Third MarDiv. air officer, Lt. Col. John T. L. D. Gabbert, has been given the credit for outstanding planning beforehand, which made it successful. It would also work extremely well in the future.

14. That is what the records state. A typo? Perhaps they meant dive bombers?

15. The Parachute and Raider Marines were badly under-armed for sustained combat. My records all indicate that the heaviest weapon they packed was

a 60mm mortar. Otherwise, rifles and light machine guns were their main arsenal.

16. Nathan Twining was the brother of then Lt. Col. Merrill B. Twining, USMC.

17. It has been considered one reason why Maj. Gen. Barrett may very well have committed suicide. He may have realized that the plan adopted by his superiors (read Halsey et al.) would cost excessive losses. Barrett was a well-known humanist.

18. Jordan was from the newly organized 4th Marine Division.

19. Later, his young daughter was given the Medal of Honor that her father was awarded for his courage and leadership.

20. Official records maintained that the reason Hermle didn't assume command from Shoup was because of a complete failure to communicate with Smith afloat and Shoup ashore. The latter retained command ashore until Smith arrived.

21. Air support, according to available data, was provided by carrier air, none of which can I identify.

22. The date indicates the leaving of the last unit of the 1st MarDiv. The 12th Def. Bn. remained behind.

23. Damp flats on the maps really meant a jungle swamp, or as one Marine said, "damp up to your neck."

24. Many years after the event I was asked by a USN veteran if I'd been there "when the island blew-up." He, aboard ship, remembered it vividly.

25. Have no further data.

26. Shaw, et al., *History of U.S. Marine Corps Operations in World War II, Central Pacific Drive*, vol. 3, p. 387.

27. Hermle had already been awarded a Distinguished Service Cross, Navy Distinguished Service Medal, two Silver Star citations, the French Legion of Honor and the Croix de Guerre with Palm in France while serving with the 6th Marines in 1918.

28. Odorous (stinks like), named after a fictitious Irishman.

29. Their division front was much narrower for much of the campaign, but then they only had three infantry regiments ashore.

30. Roberts, while a Pharm. Mate 3rd Class, had served with the 5th Marines at Belleau Wood and was awarded a Navy Cross for bringing in wounded Marines on the night of 7 June 1918.

Bibliography

The following are listed according to period, though many are useful for later periods as well. That is especially true where the book relates to an individual who was active during more than one period. At the end are the general histories, which cover many periods. The following books are just a selection. Many more books and original sources have been utilized in the writing of the present work over many years.

Late Eighteenth Century

U.S. Government Publications

Naval Documents Related to the Quasi-War between the United States and France, February 1797 to December 1801. 8 volumes. Washington, D.C.: Government Printing Office, 1935–1938.

Smith, Charles R. *Marines in the Revolution. A History of the Continental Marines in the American Revolution, 1775–1783.* Washington, D.C.: History and Museums Division, Headquarters, U.S. Marine Corps, 1975.

Selected Books

Commager, Henry S., and Richard B. Morris. *The Spirit of '76. The story of the American Revolution as Told by Participants.* 2 volumes. Indianapolis, IN: Bobbs-Merrill, 1958.

Johnston, Henry P. *The Yorktown Campaign and the Surrender of Cornwallis, 1781.* New York: Harper & Brothers, 1881.

Stone, Edward M. *Our French Allies, ... in the Great War of the American Revolution, from 1778 to 1782.* Providence: Providence Press, 1884.

Early Nineteenth Century

U.S. Government Publications

Davis, Doris S., comp. *Levi Twiggs, 1834–1850.* Quantico: Marine Corps Museum, Manuscript Register Series, no. 5, 1967 (?).

Davis, Doris S., and Jack B. Hilliard. *Samuel Miller, 1814–1856.* Quantico: Marine Corps Museum, Manuscript Register Series, no. 3, 1967 (?).

Memorial of William H. Freeman, Brevet Lieutenant Colonel and Major United States Marine Corps, June 30 1834. Washington, D.C.: 24th Congress, House of Representatives, February 15, 1836. (A second, dated February 23, 1836,concerns naval regulations over the Marine Corps.)

Letter from the Secretary of the Navy Transmitting a Report of the Number of Non-commissioned Officers and Privates of the Marine Corps, and Where Stationed. Washington, D.C.: Gales & Seaton, 1824. (Mainly a fiscal report including the locations and stations of members of the Corps, from Lt. Col. C. Archibald Henderson.)

Letter from the Secretary of the Navy Transmitting Documents, etc. Washington, D.C.: William A. Davis, 1816. (Concerns personnel level of 1,000 men in USMC.)

Nalty, Bernard C. *The Barrier Forts. A Battle, a Monument, and a Mythical Marine.* Washington, D.C.: Historical Branch, G-3 Division, Headquarters, U.S. Marine Corps, 1961.

Register of the Navy and Marine Corps. Washington, D.C.: William A. Davis, 1814.

Santelli, Gabrielle M. Neufeld, and Charles R. Smith, eds. *Marines in the Mexican War.* Washington, D.C.: History and Museums Division, Headquarters, U.S. Marine Corps, 1991.

Selected Books

Bauer, K. Jack. *The Mexican War, 1846–1848.* New York: Macmillan, 1974.

———. *Surfboats and Horse Marines. U.S. Naval Operations in the Mexican War, 1846–48.* Annapolis, MD: United States Naval Institute, 1969.

Bowen, A. *The Naval Monument, ... of All the Battles Fought between the Navies of the United States and*

Great Britain during the Late War; and an Account of the War with Algiers, etc. Boston: George Clark, 1842.

Brewer, Lucy. *The Female Marine; or, Adventures of Miss Lucy Brewer.* New York: Da Capo, 1966.

Buker, George E. *Swamp Sailors. Riverine Warfare in the Everglades, 1835–1842.* Gainesville: University of Florida Press, 1975.

Mahon, John K. *History of the Second Seminole War.* Gainesville: University of Florida Press, 1967.

Marti, Werner H. *Messenger of Destiny, the California Adventures, 1846–1847, of Archibald H. Gillespie, U.S. Marine Corps.* San Francisco: John Howell Books, 1960.

McSherry, Richard. *El Puchero; or, a Mixed Dish from Mexico, General Scott's Campaign, etc.* Philadelphia: Lippincott, Grambo, 1850.

Messages of the President of the United States: The Mexican War. Washington, D.C.: Wendell and Van Benthuysen, 1848.

Smith, Justin H. *The War with Mexico.* 2 volumes. New York: Macmillan, 1919.

Toner, Raymond J. *Gamble of the Marines.* Chicago: Albert Whitman, 1963.

Tucker, Glenn. *Dawn like Thunder. The Barbary Wars and the Birth of the U.S. Navy.* Indianapolis, IN: Bobbs-Merrill, 1963.

Late Nineteenth Century

U.S. Government Publications

Bartlett, Merrill L. *George Barnett, 1859–1930, a register of his personal papers.* Washington, D.C.: History and Museums Division, Headquarters, U.S. Marine Corps, 1980.

_____. *John Archer Lejeune, 1869–1942, a register of his personal papers.* Washington, D.C.: History and Museums Division, Headquarters, U.S. Marine Corps, 1988.

Coker, C. F. W., comp. *Henry Clay Cochrane, 1841–1947.* Quantico: Marine Corps Museum, Manuscript Register Series, no. 1, 1968.

Court Martial of Capt. E. M. Reynolds, USMC, 1867. Washington, D.C.: Senate, 40th Congress, 1867.

Davis, Doris S., comp. *John Lloyd Broome, 1849–1898.* Quantico: Marine Corps Museum, Manuscript Register Series, no. 6, 1967(?).

_____, comp. *McLane Tilton, 1861–1914.* Quantico: Marine Corps Museum, Manuscript Register Series, no. 2, 1967(?).

Dudley, William S. *Going South: U.S. Navy Officer Resignations & Dismissals on the Eve of the Civil War.* Washington, D.C.: Naval Historical Foundation, 1981.

Gordon, Martin K., comp. *Louis McCarty Little, 1878–1960.* Quantico: Marine Corps Museum, Manuscript Register Series, no. 7, 1971.

Jones, James P., and Edward F. Keuchel. *Civil War Marine: A Diary of the Red River Expedition, 1864.* Washington, D.C.: History and Museums Division, Headquarters, U.S. Marine Corps, 1975.

Nalty, Bernard C. *United States Marines at Harper's Ferry and in the Civil War.* Washington, D.C.: History and Museums Division, Headquarters, U.S. Marine Corps, 1983.

Proceedings of a Marine General Court Martial, for the Trial of Lieut. Col. John Geo. Reynolds, U.S. Marine Corps. Washington, D.C.: Henry Polkinhorn, 1862.

Shulimson, Jack, Wanda J. Renfrow, David E. Kelly, and Evelyn A. Englander. *Marines in the Spanish-American War, 1895–1899, Anthology and Annotated Bibliography.* Washington, D.C.: History and Museums Division, Headquarters, U.S. Marine Corps, 1998.

Smith, C. Carter, Jr. *Two Naval Journals: 1864. The Journal of John C. O'Connell, CSN, and the Journal of Pvt. Charles Brother, USMC, on the U.S.S. Hartford at the Battle of Mobile Bay.* Birmingham, AL: Southern University Press, 1969.

Tyson, Carolyn A. comp. *The Journal of Frank Keeler, 1898.* Quantico: Marine Corps Museum, Manuscript Register Series, Letters Series, 1967(?).

Selected Books

Clark, George B. *The Landing at Panama, April 1885.* Pike, NH: Brass Hat, 1992.

Clifford, John H. *History of the First Battalion of the U.S. Marines.* Portsmouth, NH, 1930. Reprint. Pike, NH: Brass Hat, 1998.

Dixon, Joe C., ed. *The American Military and the Far East.* Washington, D.C.: U.S. Government Printing Office, 1980.

Goode, W. A. M. *With Sampson through the War.* New York: Doubleday & McClure, 1899.

Report of the Chief of the Bureau of Navigation. *Naval Operations of the War with Spain.* Washington, D.C.: Government Printing Office, 1898.

Sargent, Nathan. *Admiral Dewey and the Manila Campaign.* Washington, D.C.: Naval Historical Foundation, 1947.

Shulimson, Jack. *The Marine Corps' Search for a Mission, 1880–1890.* Lawrence: University of Kansas Press, 1993.

Sullivan, David M. *The United States Marine Corps in the Civil War.* 4 volumes. Shippensburg, PA: White Mane Publishing, 1997–2000.

Early Twentieth Century

U.S. Government Publications

Davis, Doris, comp. *George C. Reid, 1898–1960.* Quantico: Marine Corps Museum, Manuscript Register Series, no. 4, 1967(?).

MacPherson, R. T. *John H. Russell, Jr., a register of his personal papers*. Washington, D.C.: History and Museums Division, Headquarters, U.S. Marine Corps, 1987.

Selected Books

Adams, Lewis H. *The Adventures of a United States Marine*. New York: Vantage Press, 1979.

Adams, William L. *Exploits and Adventures of a Soldier Ashore and Afloat*. Philadelphia: J.B. Lippincott, 1911. (Adams was both a Marine and soldier.)

Clark, George B. *Treading Softly, U.S. Marines in China, 1819–1949*. Westport, CT: Praeger, 2001.

———. *The United States Marines in the Boxer Rebellion (or the China Relief Expedition)*. Pike, NH: Brass Hat, 2002.

Clifford, John H. *History of the Pioneer Marine Battalion at Guam, L.I., 1899, and the Campaign in Samar, P.I., 1901*. Pike, NH: Brass Hat, 1998.

Jodon, James K. *My Four Years in the Marines*. New York: Vantage, 1970.

Linn, Brian McAllister. *The Philippine War, 1899–1902*. Lawrence: University Press of Kansas, 2000.

MacDonald, Claude. *The Siege of the Peking Embassy, 1900*. London: Stationary Office, 2000.

Miller, Stuart C. *"Benevolent Assimilation." The American Conquest of the Philippines, 1899–1903*. New Haven, CT: Yale University Press, 1982.

Noble, Dennis L. *The Eagle and the Dragon: The United States Military in China, 1901–1937*. New York: Greenwood, 1990.

Quirk, Robert E. *An Affair of Honor: Woodrow Wilson and the Occupation of Vera Cruz*. New York: W.W. Norton, 1967.

Schott, Joseph L. *The Ordeal of Samar*. Indianapolis, IN: Bobbs-Merrill, 1964.

World War I

U.S. Government Publications

American Battle Monuments Commission. *American Armies and Battlefields in Europe*. Washington, D.C.: U.S. Government Printing Office, 1938.

American Battle Monument Commission. *2d Division Summary of Operations in the World War*. Washington, D.C.: U.S. Government Printing Office, 1944.

Annual Reports of the Navy Department for the Fiscal Year 1920. Washington, D.C.: U.S. Government Printing Office, 1921.

Annual Report of the Secretary of War, 1919. Washington, D.C.: U.S. Government Printing Office, 1919.

Blanc Mont (Meuse-Argonne-Champagne). Monograph no. 9. Reprint. Pike, NH: Brass Hat, 1994.

The Genesis of the American First Army. Washington, D.C.: Historical Section, 1938.

Navy Yearbook 1920 and 1921. Washington, D.C.: U.S. Government Printing Office, 1922.

The Navy Book of Distinguished Service. Washington, D.C.: Fassett, 1921.

Order of Battle of the United States Land Forces in the World War. Reprint. Volumes 1 and 2 of 5 volumes. Washington, D.C.: U.S. Government Printing Office, 1988.

Pershing, John J. *Final Report of Gen. John J. Pershing*. Washington, D.C.: U.S. Government Printing Office, 1920.

Report of the First Army, American Expeditionary Force, Organization and Operations. Fort Leavenworth, KS, 1923.

Smith, Gibson B. *Thomas Holcomb, 1879–1965, Register of His Personal Papers*. Washington, D.C.: History and Museums Division, Headquarters, U.S. Marine Corps, 1988.

Strott, George. *The Medical Department of the United States Navy with the Army and Marine Corps in France in World War I*. Washington, D.C.: U.S. Navy, 1947.

United States Army in the World War, 1917–1919. Volumes. 1, 3, 4 and various other volumes. Washington, D.C.: Historical Division, 1948.

U.S. Army, Records of the Second Division (Regular). 9 volumes. Washington, D.C.: Army War College, 1927.

U.S. Navy, Annual Report of the Secretary of the Navy for the Fiscal Year 1918. Washington, D.C.: 1918. (Corrected to 18 October 1919.)

Wood, Charles A. *Clifton Bledsoe Cates, 1893–1970, a Register of His Personal Papers*. Washington, D.C.: History and Museums Division, Headquarters, U.S. Marine Corps, 1985.

Personal Papers and Unpublished Memoirs

Barnett, George. "Soldier and Sailor Too." N.p., n.d. (1923?).

Bellamy, David. "Personal Diary, 23 October 1917–22 August 1919. N.p., n.d.

Draucker, James H. "Telling It Like It Was. N.p., n.d.

Jackson, Warren. "Experiences of a Texas Soldier." N.p., 1930.

Moore, William E. Personal letters to his mother, 31 March–15 February, 1919. N.p.

Paris, Gus. "Hold Every Inch of Ground." Owensboro, KY: n.d. (Unpublished biography of Logan Feland.)

Official and Semi-official Unit Histories

Akers, Herbert H. *History of the Third Battalion, Sixth Regiment, U.S. Marines*. Hillsdale, MI: Akers, MacRitchie and Hurlburt, 1919.

Burton, Allan. *A History of the Second Regiment of Engineers, United States Army, from Its Organi-*

zation in Mexico, 1916, to Its Watch on the Rhine, 1919. Cologne: M. DuMont Shauberg, 1919.
Clark, George B. *The Marine Brigade at Blanc Mont.* Pike, NH: Brass Hat, 1994.
_____. *Their Time in Hell: The 4th Marine Brigade at Belleau Wood.* Pike, NH: Brass Hat, 1996.
_____, ed. *A Brief History of the Sixth Regiment U.S. Marine Corps, July 1917–December 1918.* Reprint. Pike, NH: Brass Hat, 1992.
_____, ed. *History of the Fifth Regiment Marines (May 1917–December 31, 1918).* Reprint. Pike, NH: Brass Hat, 1995.
_____, ed. *The History of the Third Battalion 5th Marines, 1917–1918.* Pike, NH: Brass Hat, 1995.
Curtis, Thomas J., and Lothar R. Long. *History of the Sixth Machine Gun Battalion.* Reprint. Pike, NH: Brass Hat, 1992.
Donaldson, G. H., and W. Jenkins. *Seventy-eighth Company, Sixth Marines, Second Division Army of Occupation.* Reprint. Pike, NH: Brass Hat, 1994.
Field, Harry B., and Henry G. James. *Over the Top with the 18th Company, 5th Regiment, U.S. Marines, a History.* Rodenbach, Germany [1919?].
James, Henry G. *see* Field, Harry B.
Jones, William K. *A Brief History of the 6th Marines.* Washington, D.C.: Headquarters, U.S. Marine Corps, 1987.
Long, Lothar R. *see* Curtis, Thomas J.
Macgillivray, George C., and George B. Clark, eds. *A History of the 80th Company, Sixth Marines.* Reprint. Pike, NH: Brass Hat, 1991.
Mitchell, William A. *The Official History of the Second Engineers in the World War, 1916–1919.* Regimental Headquarters, San Antonio, 1920.
Money, Willard I. *History of the 96th Company, 2d Battalion, Sixth Regiment, United States Marine Corps.* Washington, D.C.: Headquarters, U.S. Marine Corps, 1967.
The Ninth U.S. Infantry in the World War. N.p., n.d. (Germany, 1919?).
Owen, Peter F. *To the Limit of Endurance: A Battalion of Marines (2/6) in the Great War.* College Station: Texas A & M University Press, 2007.
Second Division Association. *Commendations of Second Division, American Expeditionary Forces, 1917–1919.* Cologne, Germany, 1919.
Second Division Memorial Day, June 2nd, 1919, 75th Company, 6th Regiment U.S. Marines. Reprint. Pike, NH: Brass Hat, 1995.
74th Company, 6th Regiment, Second Division, A.E.F. Reprint. Pike, NH: Brass Hat, 1994.
Spaulding, Oliver L., and John W. Wright. *The Second Division: American Expeditionary Force in France, 1917–1919.* New York: Hillman Press, 1937.
Strott, George G. *History of Medical Personnel of the United States Navy, Sixth Regiment Marine Corps, American Expeditionary Forces in World War 1917–1918.* Reprint. Pike, NH: Brass Hat, 1995.
Thomason, John W., Jr. *The United States Army Second Division Northwest of Chateau Thierry in World War I.* Edited by George B. Clark. Jefferson, NC: McFarland, 2006.
U.S. Army. *The 3rd Battalion, 17th F.A. in 1918.* Coblenz, Germany, n.d.
_____. *Twenty-third Machine Gun Co., Twenty-third Inf., Second Division Army of Occupation 1917–1919.* N.p., (1919?).
U.S. Marine Corps. *History of the First Battalion, 5th Regiment, U.S. Marines. 1919.* Reprint. Foster, RI: Brass Hat, 1980.
_____. *History of the Second Battalion, Fifth Marines.* Quantico: Marine Barracks, 1938.
_____. *History of the Second Battalion, 5th Regiment, U.S. Marines.* Reprint. Foster, RI: Brass Hat, 1980.
_____, *History of the Sixth Regiment, U.S. Marines.* Tientsjn, China, 1928.
_____, *History of the Third Battalion, Sixth Marines.* N.p., n.d.
Vandoren, Lucien H. *A Brief History of the Second Battalion, Sixth Regiment, U.S. Marine Corps, during the Period June 1st to August 10th, 1918.* Reprint. Pike, NH: Brass Hat, 1995.

SELECTED BOOKS

Americans Defending Democracy: Our Soldiers' Own Stories. New York: World's War Stories, 1919.
Andriot, Captain R. *Belleau Wood and the American Army.* Trans. by W. B. Fitts. Washington, D.C.: Belleau Wood Memorial Association, n.d.
Asprey, Robert B. *At Belleau Wood.* New York: Putnam's, 1965.
Boyd, Thomas. *Points of Honor.* New York: Scribner's, 1925. (Short stories by a Marine participant.)
_____. *Through the Wheat.* New York: Scribner's, 1923. (Fiction by a Marine participant.)
Brannen, Carl Andrew. *Over There: A Marine in the Great War.* Edited by Rolfe L. Hillman, Jr., and Peter F. Owen, with an afterword by J. P. Brannen. College Station: Texas A & M University Press, 1996.
Carter, William A. *The Tale of a Devil Dog.* Washington, D.C.: Canteen, 1920.
Cates, General Clifton B. See Money, Willard.
Catlin, Albertus W. *With the Help of God and a Few Marines.* New York: Doubleday, 1919.
Chitty, Fred F. *see* Leonard, John W.
Clark, George B. *Citations and Awards to Members of the 4th Marine Brigade.* Pike, NH: Brass Hat, 1992.
_____. *Decorated Marines of the Fourth Brigade in World War I.* Jefferson, NC: McFarland, 2007.
_____. *Devil Dogs, Fighting Marines of World War One.* Novato, CA: Presidio, 1999.
_____. *A List of Officers of the 4th Marine Brigade.* Pike, NH: Brass Hat, 1993.
_____. *Major Awards to U.S. Marines in World War One.* Reprint. Pike, NH: Brass Hat, 1992.

_____. *Retreat, Hell! We Just Got Here!* Pike, NH: Brass Hat, 1992.

Collins, Harry, with David Fisher and George B. Clark. *The War Diary of Corporal Harry Collins.* Reprint. Pike, NH: Brass Hat, 1996.

Cooke, Colonel Elliot D. *"We Can Take It, We Attack": Americans vs. Germans.* 1936. Reprint, 2 volumes in one. Pike, NH: Brass Hat, 1992.

Cowing, Kemper F., and Courtney R. Cooper. *"Dear Folks at Home—" The Glorious Story of the United States Marines in France as Told by Their Letters from the Battlefield.* Boston: Houghton Mifflin, 1919.

Daniels, Josephus. *The Cabinet Diaries of Josephus Daniels, 1913–1921.* Lincoln: University of Nebraska Press, 1963.

De Chambrun, Jacques Aldebert de Pinton, Comte de, and Captain De Marenches. *The American Army in the European Conflict.* New York: Macmillan, 1919.

DeMario, Joseph. *Fifty Years to Erase.* New York: Carleton, 1971.

Derby, Richard. *"Wade in, Sanitary!" The Story of a Division Surgeon in France.* New York: Putnam's, 1919.

Emmons, Roger M. *First Marine Aviation Force, 1917–1918.* Pike, NH: Brass Hat, 1994. (He also wrote many other items of great detail.)

Gibbons, Floyd. *And They Thought We Wouldn't Fight.* New York: George H. Doran, 1918.

Gordon, George V. *Leathernecks and Doughboys.* 1927. Reprint. Pike, NH: Brass Hat, 1996.

Gulberg, Martin G. *A War Diary.* 1927. Reprint. Pike, NH: Brass Hat, 1989.

Hamilton, Craig, and Louise Corbin. *Echoes from Over There.* New York: Soldier's Publishing, 1919.

Harbord, James G. *The American Army in France, 1917–1918.* Boston: Little, Brown, 1936.

_____. *Leaves from a War Diary.* New York: Dodd, Mead, 1925.

Hemrick, Levi. *Once a Marine.* New York: Carlton, 1968.

Hewitt, Linda L. *Women Marines in World War I.* Washington, D.C.: Headquarters, U.S. Marine Corps, 1974.

Kean, Robert W. *Dear Marraine, 1917–1919.* N.p., private printing, 1976.

Kennedy, David M. *Over Here: The First World War and American Society.* New York: Oxford University Press, 1980.

Lejeune, John A. *Reminiscences of a Marine.* Philadelphia: Dorrance, 1930.

Leonard, John W., and Fred E. Chitty. *The Story of the United States Marines, 1740–1919.* N.p., n.d. (1919?).

Liggett, Hunter. *AEF Ten Years Ago in France.* New York: Dodd, Mead, 1928.

Ludendorff, Erich von. *Ludendorff's Own Story.* Volume 2. New York: Harper Bros., 1919.

Mackin, Elton E. *Suddenly We Didn't Want to Die.* Edited by George B. Clark. Novato, CA: Presidio, 1993.

March, William [pseud.]. *Company K.* New York: Harrison Smith and Robert Haas, 1933. (Highly accurate fiction by a former Marine participant.)

McClellan, Edwin N. *The United States Marine Corps in the World War.* Washington, D.C.: U.S. Government Printing Office, 1920.

McEntee, Girard L. *Military History of the World War.* New York: Scribner's, 1937.

Michelin Company. *The Americans in the Great War: Illustrated Guides to the Battlefields.* 3 volumes. France, 1920.

Millett, Allan R. *In Many a Strife: General Gerald C. Thomas and the U.S. Marine Corps, 1917–1956.* Annapolis, MD: U.S. Naval Institute Press, 1993.

Morgan, Daniel E. *When the World Went Mad.* 1931. Reprint. Pike, NH: Brass Hat, 1992.

New York Life Insurance Company. *War Stories: Being a Brief Record of the Service in the Great War of Soldiers-Sailors-Marines Who Went from the Home Office of the New York Life Insurance Company.* New York, 1920.

Otto, Ernst. *The Battle at Blanc Mont.* Annapolis, MD: U.S. Naval Institute Press, 1930.

Pattullo, George. *Hellwood.* Philadelphia: Curtis, 1918. (About Belleau Wood.)

_____. *Horrors of Moonlight.* New York, private printing, 1939. (About Belleau Wood; see Rendinell, Joseph E.)

Pershing, John J. *My Experiences in the World War.* 2 volumes. New York: E. A. Stokes, 1931.

Poague, Walter S. *Diary and Letters of a Marine Aviator.* N.p., n.d., private printing.

Ranlett, Louis Felix. *Let's Go! The Story of A. S. No. 2448602.* Boston: Houghton Mifflin, 1927.

Rendinell, Joseph E., and George Pattullo. *One Man's War: The Diary of a Leatherneck.* New York: Sears, 1928.

Russell, James C., and William E. Moore. *The United States Navy in the World War.* Washington, D.C.: Pictorial Bureau, 1921.

Scanlon, William T. *God Have Mercy on Us!* Boston: Houghton Mifflin, 1929. (Highly accurate fiction by a Marine participant.)

Sellers, James McBrayer. *World War I Memoirs of Lieutenant Colonel James McBrayer Sellers, USMC.* Pike, NH: Brass Hat, 1997.

Smythe, Donald. *Pershing, General of the Armies.* Bloomington: Indiana University Press, 1986.

Stallings, Laurence. *The Doughboys.* New York: Harper, 1963. (Marine participant.)

Stringer, Harry R., ed. *Heroes All!* Washington, D.C.: Fassett, 1919.

Thomason, John W., Jr. *Fix Bayonets!* New York: Scribner's, 1925.

Tucker, Spencer C. *The European Powers in the First World War: An Encyclopedia.* New York: Garland, 1996.

Vandegrift, Alexander A., and Robert B. Asprey. *Once a Marine.* New York: W.W. Norton, 1964.
Vandiver, Frank E. *Blackjack: The Life and Times of John J. Pershing.* Volume 2. College Station: Texas A & M University Press, 1977.
Venzon, Anne Cipriano, ed. *The United States in the First World War, an Encyclopedia.* New York: Garland, 1995.
Westover, Wendell. *Suicide Battalions.* New York: Putnam's, 1929.
Where the Marines Fought in France. Chicago: Park and Antrim, n.d. (1919?)
Wise, Frederic M., and Meigs O. Frost. *A Marine Tells It to You.* New York: J. H. Sears, 1929.

Interventions Between the World Wars

U.S. Government Publications

Fuller, Stephen M., and Graham A. Cosmas. *Marines in the Dominican Republic, 1916–1924.* Washington, D.C.: History and Museums Division, Headquarters, U.S. Marine Corps, 1974.
Gordon, Martin, comp. *Joseph Henry Pendleton, 1860–1942, Register of His Personal Papers.* Washington, D.C.: History and Museums Division, Headquarters, U.S. Marine Corps, 1975.

Selected Books

Brown, F. C., John E. Lelle, and Roger J. Sullivan. *The 4th Marines and Soochow Creek, the Legend and the Medal.* Bennington, VT: International Graphics, 1980.
Butler, Smedley D. *American Marines in China* (bound with) *Chinese American Relations.* Pike, NH: Brass Hat, 1992.
Calder, Bruce J. *The Impact of Intervention. The Dominican Republic during the U.S. Occupation of 1916–1924.* Austin: University of Texas, 1984.
Cummins, Lejeune. *Quijote on a Burro, Sandino and the Marines: A Study in the Formulation of Foreign Policy.* Mexico: private printing, 1958.
Hopkins, J. A. H., and Melinda Alexander. *Machine-Gun Diplomacy.* New York: Lewis Copeland, 1928.
Langley, Lester D. *The Banana Wars: An Inner History of American Empire, 1900–1934.* Lexington: University Press of Kentucky, 1983.
Macaulay, Neill. *The Sandino Affair.* Chicago: Quadrangle, 1967.
McCrocklin, James H. *Garde D'Haiti, 1915–1934. Twenty Years of Organization and Training by the United States Marine Corps.* Annapolis, MD: United States Naval Institute, 1956.
Munro, Dana G. *The United States and the Caribbean Republics, 1921–1933.* Princeton, NJ: Princeton University Press, 1974.
Musicant, Ivan. *The Banana Wars: A History of United States Military Intervention in Latin America from the Spanish-American War to the Invasion of Panama.* New York: Macmillan, 1990.
Schmidt, Hans. *The United States Occupation of Haiti, 1915–1934.* New Brunswick, NJ: Rutgers University Press, 1971.
Wirkus, Faustin. *The White King of La Gonave.* Garden City, NY: Doubleday, Doran, 1931.

World War II

U.S. Government Publications

Annual Reports of the Navy Department for the Fiscal Years 1940–1950. Washington, D.C.: U.S. Government Printing Office.
Bailey, Major Alfred Dunlop, USMC (Retired). *Alligators, Buffaloes, and Bushmasters: The History of the Development of the LVT through World War II.* Washington, D.C.: History and Museums Division, Headquarters, U.S. Marine Corps, 1986.
Bartley, Whitman S. *Iwo Jima: Amphibious Epic.* Washington, D.C.: Historical Branch, G-3 Division, Headquarters, U.S. Marine Corps, 1954.
Boggs, Charles W., Jr. *Marine Aviation in the Philippines.* Washington, D.C.: Historical Division, Headquarters, U.S. Marine Corps, 1951.
Clifford, Lieutenant Colonel Kenneth J., USMCR, ed. *The United States Marines in Iceland, 1941–1942.* Washington, D.C.: Historical Division, Headquarters, U.S. Marine Corps, 1970.
Condit, Kenneth W., and Edwin T. Turnbladh. *Hold High the Torch: A History of the 4th Marines.* Washington, D.C.: Historical Branch, G-3 Division, Headquarters, U.S. Marine Corps, 1960.
Gordon, Martin, comp. *Wilburt Scott Brown, 1900–1968.* Quantico: Marine Corps Museum, Manuscript Register Series, no. 8, 1973.
Heinl, Robert D., and John A. Crown. *The Marshalls: Increasing the Tempo.* Washington, D.C.: Historical Branch, G-3 Division, Headquarters, U.S. Marine Corps, 1954.
History of U.S. Marine Corps Operations in World War II. 5 volumes. Washington, D.C.: U.S. Government Printing Office, n. d. (circa 1958–1968).
Hoffman, Carl W. *Saipan: The Beginning of the End.* Washington, D.C.: Historical Division, Headquarters, U.S. Marine Corps, 1950.
_____. *The Seizure of Tinian.* Washington, D.C.: Historical Division, Headquarters, U.S. Marine Corps, 1951.
Hough, Frank O. *The Assault on Peleliu.* Washington, D.C.: Historical Division, Headquarters, U.S. Marine Corps, 1950.
_____, and John A. Crown. *The Campaign on New Britain.* Washington, D.C.: Historical Branch, Headquarters, U.S. Marine Corps, 1952.
Lodge, O. R. *The Recapture of Guam.* Washington,

D.C.: Historical Branch, G-3 Division, Headquarters, U.S. Marine Corps, 1954.
[McCahill, William]. *The Marine Corps Reserve: A History*. Washington, D.C.: Division of Reserve, Headquarters, U.S. Marine Corps, 1966.
Nichols, Charles S., Jr., and Henry I. Shaw, Jr. *Okinawa: Victory in the Pacific*. Washington, D.C.: Historical Branch, G-3 Division, Headquarters, U.S. Marine Corps, 1955.
Rentz, John N. *Bougainville and the Northern Solomons*. Washington, D.C.: Historical Section, Division of Public Information, Headquarters, U.S. Marine Corps, 1948.
_____. *Marines in the Central Solomons*. Washington, D.C.: Historical Branch, Headquarters, U.S. Marine Corps, 1952.
Shaw, Henry I., Jr. *The United States Marines in the Occupation of Japan*. Washington, D.C.: Historical Branch, G-3 Division, Headquarters, U.S. Marine Corps, 1962 edition.
Stockman, James R. *The Battle for Tarawa*. Washington, D.C.: Historical Section, Division of Public Information, Headquarters, U.S. Marine Corps, 1947.
U.S. Marine Corps World War II Monograph series (by publishing date).
Zimmerman, John L. *The Guadalcanal Campaign*. Washington, D.C.: Historical Division, Headquarters, U.S. Marine Corps, 1949.

SELECTED BOOKS

Alexander, Joseph H. *Edson's Raiders: The 1st Marine Raider Battalion in World War II*. Annapolis, MD: United States Naval Institute Press, 2001.
_____. *Utmost Savagery: The Three Days of Tarawa*. Annapolis, MD: United States Naval Institute Press, 1995.
Asprey, Robert B. *Once a Marine: The Memoirs of General A. A. Vandegrift, U.S.M.C*. New York: W. W. Norton, 1964.
Aurthur, Robert A., Kenneth Cohlmia, and Robert T. Vance. *The Third Marine Division*. Washington, D.C.: Infantry Journal Press, 1948.
Brown, Ronald J. *A Few Good Men: The Fighting Fifth Marines; A History of the USMC's Most Decorated Regiment*. Novato, CA: Presidio, 2001.
Burrus, L. D. *The Ninth Marines: A Brief History of the Ninth Marine Regiment*. Washington, D.C.: Infantry Journal Press, 1946.
Cass, Bevan G. *History of the Sixth Marine Division*. Washington, D.C.: Infantry Journal Press, 1948.
Clark, George B. *The Six Marine Divisions in the Pacific*. Jefferson, NC: McFarland, 2006.
_____. *Table of Organization of USMC Units and Associated USA Units in the Great Pacific War, 1941–1945*. Pike, NH: Brass Hat, 2003.
_____. *United States Marine Corps Generals of World War II*. Jefferson, NC: McFarland, 2008.

Clifford, Kenneth J. *Amphibious Warfare Development in Britain and America from 1920–1940*. Laurens, NY: Englewood, 1983.
Conner, Howard M. *The Spearhead: The World War II History of the 5th Marine Division*. Washington, D.C.: Infantry Journal Press, 1950.
Croziat, Victor J. *Across the Reef: The Amphibious Tracked Vehicle at War*. London: Arms and Armour, 1989.
Curley, W. J. P., Jr. *Letters from the Pacific, 1943–1946*. N.p.: private printing, 1959.
Del Valle, Pedro A. *Semper Fidelis, an Autobiography*. Hawthorne, CA: Christian Book Club of America, 1976.
FitzPatrick, Tom. *A Character That Inspired: Major General Charles D. Barrett, USMC*. Fairfax, VA: private printing, 2003.
Hallas, James H. *The Devil's Anvil: The Assault on Peleliu*. Westport, CT: Praeger, 1994.
_____. *Killing Ground on Okinawa: The Battle for Sugar Loaf Hill*. Westport, CT: Praeger, 1996.
Hoffman, Jon T. *Chesty: The Story of Lieutenant General Lewis B. Puller, USMC*. New York: Random House, 2001.
_____. *Once a Legend: "Red Mike" Edson of the Marine Raiders*. Novato, CA: Presidio, 1994.
Hough, Frank O. *The Island War: The United States Marine Corps in the Pacific*. Philadelphia: J.B. Lippincott, 1947.
Hunt, George P. *Coral Comes High*. New York: Harper and Brothers, 1946
Isely, Jeter A., and Philip A. Crowl. *The U.S. Marines and Amphibious War: Its Theory and Its Practice in the Pacific*. Princeton, NJ: Princeton University Press, 1951.
Johnson, Richard S., Jr. *Letters of 2nd Lt. Richard S. Johnson, Jr., U.S. Marine Corps*. Columbia, SC: private printing, 1969.
Johnston, Richard W. *Follow Me! The Story of the Second Marine Division in World War II*. New York: Random House, 1948.
Leahy, Edward. *In the Islands*. Tucson, AZ: Hat's Off Books, 2002.
Letcher, John Seymour. *One Marine's Story*. Verona, VA: McClure, 1970.
Matthews, Allen R. *The Assault*. New York: Simon & Schuster, 1947.
McMillan, George. *The Old Breed: A History of the First Marine Division in World War II*. Washington, D.C.: Infantry Journal Press, 1949.
Miller, Thomas G., Jr. *The Cactus Air Force*. New York: Harper & Row, 1969.
Millett, Allan R. *In Many a Strife: General Gerald C. Thomas and the U.S. Marine Corps, 1917–1956*. Annapolis, MD: United States Naval Institute Press, 1993.
Paul, Doris A. *The Navajo Code Talkers*. Bryn Mawr, PA: Dorrance, 1973.
Proehl, Carl W., ed. *The Fourth Marine Division in*

World War II. Washington, D.C.: Infantry Journal Press, 1946.
Sherrod, Robert. *History of Marine Corps Aviation in World War II.* Washington, D.C.: Combat Forces Press, 1952.
Smith, Holland M. *Coral and Brass.* New York: Scribner's, 1949.
Twining, Merrill B., and Neil Carey. *No Bended Knee.* Novato, CA: Presidio, 1996.
Willock, Roger. *Unaccustomed to Fear: A Biography of the Late General Roy S. Geiger, U.S.M.C.* Princeton, NJ: privately published, 1968.

General Subjects — Various Periods

U.S. Government Publications

Condit, Kenneth W., John H. Johnstone, and Ella W. Nargele. *A Brief History of Headquarters Marine Corps Staff Organization.* Washington, D.C.: Historical Division, Headquarters, U.S. Marine Corps, 1971.
Ellsworth, Harry A. *One Hundred Eighty Landings of United States Marines, 1800–1934.* Washington, D.C.: History and Museums Division, Headquarters, U.S. Marine Corps, 1974.
Fleming, Charles A. *Quantico: Crossroads of the Corps.* Washington, D.C.: Headquarters, U.S. Marine Corps, 1978.
Nalty, Bernard C., and Ralph F. Moody. *A Brief History of U.S. Marine Corps Officer Procurement, 1775–1969.* Washington, D.C.: Historical Division, Headquarters, U.S. Marine Corps, 1970.
Registers, United States Navy and Marine Corps Officers. Various dates from 1812 to the present.
Reports of the Commandant of the U.S. Marine Corps. Various dates from 1863 to the present.

Selected Books

Aldrich, M. Almy. *History of the United States Marine Corps.* Boston: Henry L. Shepard, 1875.
Blakeney, Jane. *Heroes, U.S. Marine Corps, 1861–1955; Armed Forces Awards, Flags.* Washington, D.C.: private printing, 1957.
Clark, George B. *Legendary Marines of the Old Corps.* Pike, NH: Brass Hat, 2002.
_____, ed. *United States Marine Corps Medal of Honor Recipients.* Jefferson, NC: McFarland, 2005.
Dupuy, R. Earnest, and Trevor Dupuy. *The Encyclopedia of Military History from 3500 B.C. to the Present.* New York: Harper & Row, 1977.
Heinl, Robert D. *Soldiers of the Sea, the U.S. Marine Corps, 1775–1962.* Annapolis, MD: United States Naval Institute, 1962.
Hogg, John W. *Compilation of Laws Relating to the Navy, Marine Corps, etc.* Washington, D.C.: Government Printing Office, 1883.
Kohn, George C. *Dictionary of Wars.* New York: Doubleday, 1986.
Mersky, Peter B. *U.S. Marine Corps Aviation, 1912 to the Present.* Annapolis, MD: Nautical and Aviation Publishing Company of America, 1983.
Metcalf, Clyde H. *A History of the United States Marine Corps.* New York: Putnam's, 1939.
Millett, Allan R. *Semper Fidelis: The History of the United States Marine Corps.* New York: Macmillan, 1980.
Robillard, Fred S. *As Robie Remembers.* Bridgeport, CT: Wright Investors Service, 1969.
Schmidt, Hans. *Maverick Marine: General Smedley D. Butler and the Contradictions of American Military History.* Lexington: University Press of Kentucky, 1987.
Schuon, Karl. *U.S. Marine Corps Biographical Dictionary.* New York: Franklin Watts, 1963.
U.S. Navy. *Medal of Honor 1861–1949.* Washington, D.C.: U.S. Navy, n.d. [1950?]

Index

Adams, John 26–28
Algeria 25, 32, 37, 134, 244
Argentina 45, 50

Baltimore 44
Barnett, Col. George 102–103, 120
Barney, Comm. Joshua 42–43
Barrett, Maj. Gen. Charles D. 170, 254, 255
Barrier Forts 74–77
Barron, Capt. Samuel 29, 36
Barry, Capt. John 20, 24–25
Bashaw of Tripoli 28, 29, 35–37; *see also* Tripoli
Bay of Tunis 37; *see also* Tunis
Bearss, Lt. Col. Hiram I. 99–100, 117–118, 136, 249, 250, 251
Belleau Wood 125–130; *see also* World War I
Biddle, Maj. William P. 83, 84, 93, 148, 249
Bladensburg 42–44, 46
Blanc Mont 137–142; *see also* World War I
Bougainville 170–174; *see also* World War II
Britain 8, 9, 12, 17–22, 24–32, 38–48, 56, 65, 67, 73, 74, 79–84, 89, 104, 111, 121–122, 137–38, 142, 153, 168, 243, 245, 247, 252, 253
Bull Run 66–67; *see also* Civil War
Burrows, William Ward 26, 29, 33
Butler, Capt. Smedley D. 82–84, 108–109, 112–114, 148–149, 249, 250

Caperton, Adm. William B. 112, 116, 119
Carlson, Col. Evans F. 164, 178

Carmick, Maj. Daniel 28–30, 38, 40, 44–45
Carter, Jimmy 92
Cates, Lt. Gen. Clifton B. 128, 160, 164, 196, 216
Catlin, Col. Albertus W. 101–102, 109–110, 126–127
Chaffee, Maj. Gen. Adna 83–85
Chapultepec 57, 59; *see also* Mexican War
China 8, 73–75, 77, 85–86; *see also* Chinese Expedition
Chinese Expedition: Peking Legation 79–86; Tientsin 79, 81–83, 85, 249; *see also* China
Cienfuegos 94, 102; *see also* Spanish-American-Cuban War
Civil War: Bull Run 66–67
Cochrane, Col. Henry C. 85
Cole, Maj. Eli K. 91–92, 112–113
Columbia (Panama) 85–92
Connor, Comm. David 57–58
Corregidor 156–158; *see also* World War II
Craney Island 41
Crowe, Col. Henry P. 175–178, 189
Cuba 8, 48–49, 67, 70, 89, 93–97, 101–107; *see also* Guantanamo
Cushman, Robert E., Jr. 170, 201, 204, 222, 225
Cuzco Wells 95–96; *see also* Spanish-American-Cuban War

Decatur, Comdr. Stephen 34, 37, 39, 45
Del Valle, Maj. Gen. Pedro A. 163, 209, 210, 230, 232

Dewey, Adm. George 93, 94, 97, 100, 249
Dominican Republic 114–116, 137, 251; Guayacanas 118; Las Trencheras 117–118
Doyen, Col. Charles 88–89, 122–124

Eaton, William 35–36
Edson, Maj. Gen. Merritt E. 160–163, 254
Elliott, Lt. Col. George F. 91, 95, 97, 98
Erskine, Maj. Gen. Graves B. 205, 216, 220

Farragut, Adm. David C. 69–70, 72
Feland, Col. Logan 98–99, 132–135, 139, 143, 150–151
Fletcher, Adm. Frank F. 108–110
Fletcher, Adm. Frank J. 161
Fort Dipitie 113; *see also* Haiti
Fort George 40
Fort Mackinac 42
Fort Riviere 113; *see also* Haiti
France 9, 17, 21, 23–32, 72, 73, 89, 105, 110–112, 114, 120–126, 128–142, 144, 146, 243, 244, 249, 251, 252, 253
Freeman, Lt. Co. William H. 51–52
Fuller, Capt. Ben H. 98
Funston, Brig Gen. Frederick 97, 110

Gale, Capt. Anthony 44, 48
Gamble, Capt. John M. 40–42, 243, 245
Garde d'Haiti 112, 114; *see also* Haiti
Gates, Gen. Horatio 18
Geiger, Maj. Gen. Roy S. 162,

253

164, 170, 199–201, 208, 230, 234–235, 240
Germany 9, 75, 80–81, 84, 86, 100, 105–106, 109–111, 116, 120–144, 146, 251, 252, 253, 262
Gillespie, Brevet Maj. Archibald H. 60–64, 247
Great Cypress Swamp 52
Guadalcanal 160–166; *see also* World War II
Guam 200–205; *see also* World War II
Guantanamo 91, 94–96, 103–107, 112; *see also* Cuba
Guayacanas 118; *see also* Dominican Republic

Haiti 27, 47–48, 50, 88, 106, 111–116, 137, 249; Fort Dipitie 113; Garde d'Haiti 112, 114; Fort Riviere 113
Hanneken, Maj. Gen. Herman H. 164, 206
Harding, Warren G. 114
Harris, Maj. John 52, 60, 69, 71, 246, 248
Hawaii 8, 153, 179, 216
Henderson, Lt. Col. Archibald 38, 48, 51, 56, 58
Heywood, Maj. Charles 69, 72, 89, 97
Holcomb, Thomas 85, 125, 127, 139, 253
Hopkins, Comm. Esek 19–20, 214
Hunt, Maj. Gen. LeRoy 132, 160, 254

Iwo Jima 216–230; *see also* World War II

Jackson, Gen. Andrew 44–45, 48, 51, 55, 245
Jefferson, Thomas 29, 30, 35
Jessup, Gen. Thomas S. 52
Jones, Capt. John Paul 20–23

Kane, Col. Theodore P. 88, 102, 112
Kearney, Maj. Gen. Stephen W. 63–64, 247
Korea 78–79

Larsen, Maj. Gen. Henry 132, 139, 140, 143
Las Trencheras 117–118; *see also* Dominican Republic
Lee, Col. Harry 85, 131, 134, 139

Lejeune, Maj. Gen. John A. 91, 96, 104, 109–110, 138–141, 146, 249, 250
Lincoln, Abraham 66, 72
Liversedge, Brig Gen. Harry J. 167–169, 217, 220
Lower California 65; *see also* Mexican War

Madison, James 30, 37, 38
Mahoney, Col. James E. 91–92, 104, 107
Manila Bay 8; *see also* Chinese Expedition
Marshalls 184–188; *see also* World War II
Mayo, Adm. Henry T. 108
McCalla, Capt. Bowman H. 78, 82, 89, 249
McCawley, Capt. Charles G. 59, 71, 90, 246
McDowell, Maj. Gen. Irvin 67
Meade, Col. Robert L. 82–83, 85
Meuse-Argonne 142–146; *see also* World War I
Mexican War: Chapultepec 57, 59; Lower California 65; Mexico City 57–60, 108, 246, 250; San Cosme Gate 59–60; San Gabriel 64; San Jose 65; San Pasqual 63; Vera Cruz 58, 108–110
Mexico 8, 9, 47, 57–65, 103, 108–110, 147, 150
Mexico City 57–60, 108, 246, 250; *see also* Mexican War
Midway Island 6, 11, 158–159; *see also* World War II
Miller, Lt. Col. Samuel 42–43, 47–48, 52
Monroe, James 9, 48
Monroe Doctrine: Corollary and Platt Amendment 8, 9, 101, 103, 107
Montgomery, Maj. Gen. Richard. 18
Moses, Lt. Col. Franklin J. 83, 102, 110, 147
Myers, Capt. John T. 79–80, 98, 249

Neville, Col. Wendell C. 94, 102, 109, 122, 126, 129, 131, 139, 141, 249
New Britain 180–184; *see also* World War II
New Georgia 168–169; *see also* World War II

New Orleans 29–31, 38, 44, 69, 116, 193
New Providence 19, 21
Nicaragua 9, 146–152, 249
Nicholas, Samuel 18
Noble, Maj. Gen. Alfred H. 134, 205
Novaleta 97; *see also* Chinese Expedition

O'Bannon, 1st Lt. Presley N. 29, 33, 35–37, 244
Okinawa 230–242; *see also* World War II

Peking Legation 79–86; *see also* Chinese Expedition
Peleliu 205–210; *see also* World War II
Pendleton, Col. Joseph 116–119, 148–149, 251
Penobscot Bay 21, 24
Perry, Capt. Matthew C. 57–58
Perry, Capt. Oliver H. 41
Pershing, Gen. John J. 120–121, 123–125, 137–138, 249, 252, 253
Philippine Insurrection: Manila Bay 8; Novaleta 97; Samar 97–100, 210, 213, 215; Sohotan 99–100; *see also* Philippines
Philippines 6, 85, 86, 93, 94, 97–100, 137, 153, 155–157, 169, 180, 201, 205, 210–216, 253; *see also* Philippine Insurrection
piracy 50
Pole, James K. 60
Pope, Col. Percival C. 87, 97
Porter, Capt. David 34, 40, 44, 49–50, 72, 99–100
Princeton 20
privateers 17, 18, 21–28, 30, 40, 50, 67
Puller, Col. Lewis B. 152, 163–164, 183, 206–210

Quallah Battoo 53–54
Quitman, Maj. Gen. John A. 59–60

Reynolds, Maj. John G 59, 66–68, 248
Rodgers, Comm. John 30, 33, 38, 67, 78
Roosevelt, Franklin D. 114, 249
Roosevelt, Theodore 9, 91, 101, 103

Rupertus, Maj. Gen. William H. 160, 180–182, 184, 206, 208, 210
Russell 166–168; *see also* World War II
Russell, John H., Jr. 250

Sackett's Harbor 39
St. Mihiel 135–137; *see also* World War I
Saipan 188–195; *see also* World War II
Samar 97–100, 210, 213, 215; *see also* Chinese Expedition
Samoa 8, 12, 5, 179
Sampson, Adm. William P. 94, 95
San Cosme Gate 59–60; *see also* Mexican War
San Gabriel 64; *see also* Mexican War
San Jose 65; *see also* Mexican War
San Pasqual 63; *see also* Mexican War
Santo Domingo *see* Dominican Republic
Schmidt, Lt. Gen. Harry 86, 184–185, 189, 196, 198–199, 216
Scott, Maj. Gen. Winfield 57–59
Shapley, Col. Alan 170, 172, 201, 231, 233, 238
Shepherd, Maj. Gen. Lemuel C. 126, 182–183, 200–201, 230–231, 233–234, 236
Shoup, Col. David M. 175, 177–179, 255
Smith, Lt. Gen. Holland McT. 117, 178, 189–191, 229
Smith, Maj. Gen. Julian 178–179
Sohotan 99–100; *see also* Chinese Expedition
Soissons 130–135; *see also* World War I
Spain 8, 9, 17, 22–23, 28, 40, 42, 47–49, 93–100
Spanish-American-Cuban War: Cienfuegos 94, 102; Cuzco Wells 95–96
Stockton, Comm. Robert 61–64

Tarawa 175–179; *see also* World War II
Taylor, Maj. Gen. Zachary 57
Tientsin 79, 81–83, 85, 249; *see also* Chinese Expedition

Tilton, Capt. McLane 78
Tinian 195–200; *see also* World War II
Trenton 20
Tripoli 25, 29, 32–37; *see also* Bashaw of Tripoli
Tunis 25, 32, 37; Bay of Tunis 37
Twiggs, Maj. Levi 45, 58–59, 246

United States Army (includes Continental Army) 6, 8, 38, 42, 50–51, 57–59, 66, 68–69, 79, 83, 85, 92, 94, 97–104, 108, 110, 123, 129, 136, 142, 153–157, 160, 165, 168, 182–183, 189–190, 195, 199–200, 210, 213–214, 229–230, 240–42, 245
United States Government: State Department 9, 48, 105, 108, 109, 116, 120, 148, 251
United States Marine Corps (USMC): Air Group (11) 209, (12) 213–215, (13) 188, (14) 165, 169, 214–215, 241, (15) 188, (21) 159, 169, 188, (22) 159, 188, 241, (23) 160, 165, 169, (24) 174, 214–215, (25) 165, 169, (31) 188, 241, (32) 214–215, (33) 241, (43) 241, Aviation 6, 150–151, 159, 184, 212, 216, 241; Battalions (1st Huntington's) 94–96, (6th Machine Gun) 123, 126, 127, 131; Brigades (1st) 85, 112, (1st Provisional) 102–104, 200–201, 204–205, (2nd) 149–150, (3rd) 105, 107, (3rd Provisional) 110, (4th) 105, 121–128, 130–131, 135–136, 138–143, 146, 251; Cactus Air Force 160; Commandants 8, 11, 130, 248, 249, 270; Division (1st) 6, 160–166, 180–183, 206–210, 230–241, 254, 255, (2nd) 160, 165–166, 175–176, 179, 189–199, 210, 235, 240–241, (3rd) 170–174, 189, 200–205, 216–217, 221–225, 228–229, 254, (4th) 184, 188–199, 217–219, 221–229, (5th) 216–218, 221, 224–229, (6th) 200, 205, 229–235, 238–241; Regiments (early) (1st) 83, 85, 102–107, (1st Provisional) 103–104, 148, (2nd) 99, 104, 108–109, 112, (2nd Provisional) 104; Regiments (later) (1st) 160, 180, 206–208, 238–239, (2nd) 110, 160, 164–165, 175, 189, 191, 193–195, 197, (3rd) 170, 173–174, 201–204, 229, (4th) 86, 100, 110, 116, 156–158, 201–203, 231–233, 238–240, 253, (5th) 121–124, 126–127, 129–135, 139–140, 142–144, 150, 160, 163–164, 181, 183, 206, 209, 236, 255, (6th) 122, 125, 127, 129–131, 134, 139–144, 146, 165–166, 178–179, 190–191, 193–194, 197, 199, 251, 254, 255, (7th) 105, 160, 162–164, 180, 183, 206–207, 231, 236, 238–239, (8th) 105, 110, 164–166, 178, 189, 191–194, 196–199, 240, (9th) 110, 170–174, 201–204, 221–222, 225–226, (10th) 165, 196, (11th) 65, 150, 181–182, 234, (12th) 171, 203, 225, (13th) 218, 226, (14th) 196, (15th) 233, 239, (18th) 178, (20th) 187, (21st) 171–174, 201–204, 217–222, 226, (22nd) 187–188, 202–205, 231–232, 235–239, (23rd) 184–186, 190, 192, 196–197, 219, 221, 223–234, (24th) 184–185, 190, 196–198, 217, 221–222, 224, (25th) 191–194, 196, 219, 223, 226, 228, (26th) 217–218, 221, 224–225, 229, (27th) 217, 219, 223–224, 227, (28th) 217, 219–220, 224, (29th) 205, 231–233, 238, 240; uniforms 20, 26, 29, 38, 55, 56, 121, 194

Vandegrift, Maj. Gen. Alexander A. 160–161, 164–165, 170
Vera Cruz 47, 58, 108–110; *see also* Mexican War
Verdun 120–124; *see also* World War I

Wainwright, Lt. Col. Robert D. 41, 49
Wake Island 11, 153–155, 253; *see also* World War II
Waller, Col. Littleton W. T. 80–85, 91, 96, 98–102, 110, 112
Washington, Gen. George 17–20, 24

Watson, Lt. Col. Samuel 58
Watson, Maj. Gen. Thomas 187–189, 196, 230
Wharton, Franklin 38, 244, 245
Wilson, Thomas Woodrow 9, 108, 253
Wise, Capt. Frederick M. 99, 117, 126, 128, 251
World War I: Belleau Wood 125–130; Blanc Mont 137–142; Meuse-Argonne 142–146; St. Mihiel 135–137; Soissons 130–135; Verdun 120–124
World War II: Bougainville 170–174; Corregidor 156–158; Guadalcanal 160–166; Guam 200–205; Iwo Jima 216–230; Marshalls 184–188; Midway Island 6, 11, 158–159; New Britain 180–184; New Georgia 168–169; Okinawa 230–242; Peleliu 205–210; Philippines 210–216; Russell 166–168; Saipan 188–195; Tarawa 175–179; Tinian 195–200; Wake Island 11, 153–155, 253

York 40–41, 46

Zeilen, Capt. Jacob 71, 246, 247, 248

www.ingramcontent.com/pod-product-compliance
Ingram Content Group UK Ltd.
Pitfield, Milton Keynes, MK11 3LW, UK
UKHW050536150426
5217IPUK00026B/1963